R. Gupta's®

POPULAR MASTER

Objective

HISTORY

A Collection of Highly Useful Questions for Competitive Exams

by

RPH Editorial Board

RAMESH PUBLISHING HOUSE, NEW DELHI

Published by
O.P. Gupta *for* Ramesh Publishing House

Admin. Office
12-H, New Daryaganj Road, Opp. Officers' Mess,
New Delhi-110002 ✆ 23275224, 23245124

E-mail: info@rameshpublishinghouse.com
For Online Shopping: www.rameshpublishinghouse.com

Showroom
• Balaji Market, Nai Sarak, Delhi-110006 ✆ 23282525 📱 9354373464
• 4457, Nai Sarak, Delhi-110006

Book Code: R-681

34th Edition: May 2026

ISBN: 978-81-7812-670-8

Price: ₹ 280

Printed at: Nidhi Printers, Delhi

CONTENTS

ANCIENT INDIA

MEDIEVAL INDIA

MODERN INDIA

OBJECTIVE HISTORY

SECTION–A

ANCIENT INDIA

INDUS -VALLEY CIVILISATION

1. Who were the first people to paint the pottery of Indus Valley Civilisation?
A. Chalcolithic B. Mesolithic
C. Iron Age men D. Neolithic

2. The races are arranged taking into account their arrival in India. Pick out the chronologically correct sequence:
A. Aryan, Dravidian, Proto Austroloid, Negrito
B. Negrito, Aryan, Proto Austroloid, Dravidian
C. Negrito, Proto Austroloid, Dravidian and Aryan
D. Dravidion, Aryan, Proto Austroloid, Negrito

3. Which one of the following may be regarded as a remote possibility for the origin of the Indus Culture?
A. Kulli Culture
B. Nal Culture
C. Sumerian Culture
D. Culture of the Village People of the Punjab

4. Who was the archaeologist who came upon a seal with pictographic writing while excavating a Buddhist establishment at Mohenjo-daro?
A. R.D. Banerjee
B. N.G. Majumdar
C. Alexander Cunningham
D. Daya Ram Sahni

5. What was the political structure of the Indus Valley.
A. Oligarchy B. Federalism
C. Autocracy D. Theocracy

6. Identify the one that is common between Indus and Mesopotamian civilisations among the following:
A. cylindrical seals
B. Bronze Age Culture
C. Planning towns with chess board system.
D. Knives with ribs in the middle.

7. Which of the following was not known to the Indus valley people.
A. Seasum B. Cotton
C. Potato D. Wheat

8. The humped Ox or Brahmani bull in the Indus valley was:
A. a monster
B. a beast of burden
C. a sacred animal
D. an unknown animal

9. What made the Harapans more away from urban settlements?
A. Foreign invasion
B. Demographic factors
C. Ecological changes
D. Hydrological changes

10. Which crop was the earliest to be cultivated by the people of Indus Valley?
A. Wheat B. Rice
C. Cotton D. Rye

11. The Harappan Civilisation was chiefly concentrated in:
A. Punjab, Rajasthan and Gujarat
B. Sindh, Punjab and Rajasthan
C. Haryana, Rajasthan and Tamil Nadu
D. Punjab, Rajasthan and Assam

12. The mature phase of the Harappan culture spanned aproximately:
A. 500 years B. 700 years
C. 300 years D. 1000 years

13. Indus valley skeletons reveal that the Harappans probably did not belong to one of the following races:
A. Mongoloid B. Alpine
C. Somite D. Proto-Austroloid

14. Which is controversial with regard to the granary in harappa?
A. The urban non-agricultural population was fed on it.
B. Suggest private ownership.
C. It indicated that there was surplus production.
D. The whole affair was looked after by an agency.

15. "They (the Indus valley people) were not on the whole an artistic people". It has been commented by:
A. Dr. Romila Thapar
B. Dr. A.D. Pusalkar
C. Dr. R.D. Mazumdar
D. Dr. A.L. Basham

16. "Sindon" was the name given by the Greeks to one of the following items. Which one was it?
A. Jute B. Wool
C. Cotton D. None of these

17. The Indus valley people were:
A. Vegetarian
B. Non-vegetarian
C. Both non-vegetarian and vegetarian
D. Were not beef eaters

18. The Indus valley people were worshippers of:
A. Shiva B. Mitra
C. Varuna D. Mother Goddess

19. Pre Harappan settlement was discovered in 1981 at the foot of the Bolan pass on the Bolan river at one of the following places. Identify it;
A. Mansa B. Manda
C. Mehergarh D. Alamgirpur

20. One thing is common among the following between the Indus and Mesopotamian civilisation. Identify:
A. Larger urban complex
B. Seals rolled on clay tablets
C. Ornamental architecture
D. Use of potter's wheel

21. Which among the following is not the distinctive pottery of the Indus people?
A. Black and Red ware
B. Glazed
C. Painted Grey ware
D. Poly chrome.

22. What is the approximate area which covered the Indus civilisation?
A. 1,300,000 square kilometres
B. 600,000 square kilometres
C. 600 square kilometres
D. 6000 square kilometres

23. The metal which perhaps not known to the Indus valley people was?
A. Copper B. Iron
C. Tin D. Gold and Silver

24. Which of the following reasons was not a purpose of the Great Bath at Mohenjodaro:
A. community bathing
B. water sports and exercises
C. to store water during draughts
D. used during Rituals and Sacrifices

25. Which one of the following items was not used by the Indus valley people as their staple diet?
A. Dairy Products B. Dates
C. Wheat D. Refined Sugar

26. How many of the known 250 Indus Valley sites can be classified as cities?
A. Eight B. Six
C. Hundred D. Seven

27. The first excavation in the Indus valley at Mohenjo-daro was carried out in the years:
A. 1909 A.D. B. 1920 A.D.
C. 1922 A.D. D. 1955 A.D.

28. Which of the following is not a characteristic feature of the Indus valley pottery?
A. Red and black polished ware
B. Painted black designs
C. Vegetal and geomatric patterns
D. None of the above

29. Well planned cities with all their common feature throughout Harappa suggest:
A. A single centralised state
B. Oligarchic commercial republic
C. Theoratic state
D. Free community

30. Kagzi refers to:
A. polychrome pottery
B. egg-shell pottery
C. perforated pottery
D. special paper for writing

31. Which of the following statement on the Harappan civilisation is controversial?
A. Harappan civilisation may be called peasant urban

B. It is not certain whether there was any closeness between the Indus urban areas and the country-side peasants.
C. Indus cities depended on their existence on food and raw material obtained from the country-side.
D. Indus cities provided marketing centres.

32. Which statement on the Harappan culture is incorrect?
A. The antiquities in all the seven layers at Mohenjo-daro are homogeneous.
B. There is no deterioration of masonary in the later occupation of the cities.
C. It is essentially a riverine culture.
D. Discovery of weapons in the later levels of Mohenjo-daro points to threat to life.

33. The jewellers of the Harappan civilisation primarily used two metals:
1. Bronze 2. Silver
3. Copper 4. Gold
Choose the correct answer from the codes given below:
A. 1 and 2 B. 2 and 3
C. 3 and 4 D. 2 and 4

34. The first concern of the Harappan town planners was:
A. to protect their cities from frequent floods
B. to make citadels to protect themselves from the enemies
C. to produce enough food surplus to feed towns
D. to develop sea-borne trade

35. Which of the the following statement on the men and women of the Indus valley is Not correct?
A. Men wore long hair.
B. Men wore robes but left one shoulder bare.
C. Women wore large necklaces but very light bangles.
D. The coiffeurs of women-were often elaborate.

36. Most unique feature of the Indus valley civilisation, the like of which has not yet been found in any other city of the same antiquity is:
A. weights and measures
B. drainage system
C. cultivation of land
D. double-story houses

37. Strike out which is not an important feature of Harappan culture.
A. Horse racing
B. Peace-loving community
C. Efficient civic organisation
D. Love for indoor hobbies, jewellery and cosmetics, dancing

38. The most intriguing thing about the Indus valley women is:
A. their jewellery
B. their foundness for handicrafts
C. their vanity
D. the care they bestowed on children

39. Which one of the following arts and crafts was not practised by the Harappans?
A. Masonry B. Seal cutting
C. Carpentry D. Iron-mongering

40. Paint out the incorrect statement:
A. Harappan probably did not practise canal irrigation
B. Whether or not the plough was used is controversial
C. Pesticides were invariably used
D. Enough surplus food was produced to feed the town dwellers

41. Which of the following was not an item of import for the Indus people?
A. Tin B. Copper
C. Textile D. Lapis Liazuli

42. The Harappan culture belongs to the Bronze Age. Which two metals are mixed to make this alloy?
1. Copper 2. Zinc
3. Brass 4. Tin
A. 1 and 2 only B. 1 and 3 only
C. 4 only D. None of these

43. Which of the following was not a feature of internal trade at the Harappans?
A. Trade was multifaceted.

B. It was opened on regional and inter-regional levels.
C. It was purely a barter-trade.
D. It was a guild system coupled with nomadic people.

44. No temples, or public places of worship, or monumental sculptures have been found at Harappan cities. This indicates that:
A. religion was a state or public affair.
B. the Harappans were atheists.
C. religion was more personal and private affair.
D. they were sceptical in disposition.

45. Which one of the following is false with regard to Harappan people?
A. The statues of Mother Goddess were crudely fashioned.
B. Tiny monkeys and squirrels were used as pinhead beds.
C. The statues of women were fully clothed with elaborate head-dresses.
D. For children they made monkeys sliding down a string, whistles and gods were made like birds etc.

46. Which West Asian site is associated with the discovery of a bale of cloth evidently an export from Harappan India?
A. Ur B. Umma
C. Susa D. Lagash

47. Evidence of the horse comes from which of the following Harappan sites?
A. Harappa, Lothal, Kalibangan
B. Lothal, Surkotada
C. Mohenjo-daro, Lothal, Banwali
D. Banwali, Ropar, Surkotada

48. The Indus valley people do not use one of the following weapons. What is that?
A. Swords B. Spears
C. Arrow-heads D. Axes

49. Which cults did the Harappan practise?
1. Fire 2. Female diety
3. Fertility 4. Fetism
A. Only 2 and 3 B. Only 1 and 2
C. 1, 2 and 3 D. All of these

50. The discovery, in the upper levels of a Harappan site, of human skeletons lying bell-mell, with a skull having injury mark, shows the invasion and massacre. What is that site?
A. Mohenjo-daro B. Harappa
C. Banawali D. Kalibangan

51. The main food crops of the Harappan were:
A. Wheat and Barley
B. Wheat and Bajra
C. Maize and Wheat
D. Wheat and Rice

52. Dwellers of Mohenjo-daro:
A. were utilitarians
B. were expert in carpenter's crafts
C. were aesthetes
D. loved ideas of luxury

53. Which expression does not apply to the Harappan culture?
A. Standardisation
B. Materialistic achievements
C. Homogeneity
D. Desire to emulate others

54. One feature of the Indus valley civilisation was not rivalled by any other civilisation till the time of the Romans. Indentify it.
A. The Great Bath
B. Sewage system
C. Use of cosmetics
D. Worship of some dieties

55. What is special about the Indus valley urban centres discovered in Saurashtra, Gujarat and Kathiawar?
A. horse known
B. discovery of wood-works
C. ship-building was known
D. cross influence between Harappan culture and local cultures of Chalcolithic nature.

56. Absence of windows in the Harappan houses implied that Harappan women were kept in strict seclusion is:
A. Proved fact B. Disproved
C. Controversial D. None of these

57. That the Indus women used rouge and

Lipstick is:
A. Proved B. Disproved
C. Debatable D. None of these

58. The Harappan cultivated the Land with:
A. hoe
B. plough share
C. hoe and plough share
D. either hoe or plough share or some other tool not known to us

59. Which was not a Harappan port?
A. Balakot B. Sutkagendor
C. Sotka Koh D. Kalibangan

60. The Indus valley belonged to:
A. Mediterranean race
B. Proto-Astraloid race
C. Tibetan Mongoloid race
D. Alpine race

61. The important public place discovered at Mohenjo-daro was:
A. the great bath
B. the great granary
C. the great cementery
D. the acropolis

62. Kalibanga is situated in:
A. Madhya Pradesh B. Rajasthan
C. Karnataka D. Baluchistan

63. Lothal in the Indus valley was famous as a/an:
A. port
B. administrative centre
C. place where graneries have been found
D. religious centre

64. The concept of decimal system as a measuring unit of length was:
A. Known to the Indus valley people due to their contacts with the Egyptians.
B. known to the Indus valley people, and was not borrowed.
C. not known to the Indus valley people
D. none of the above

65. The Indus valley people were not familiar with:
A. Cotton B. Barley
C. Tobacco D. Wheat

66. Where is Lothal situated?
A. Pakistan B. Gujarat
C. Rajasthan D. Haryana

67. Which of the following statement is incorrect?
A. The Indus valley people worshipped linga and yoni
B. The Indus valley people worshipped the pipal tree
C. The Indus valley people worshipped Mother Goddess
D. The Indus valley people performed horse sacrifices

68. Mohenjo-daro is situated in:
A. Sindh province of Pakistan
B. Gujarat State of India
C. Afghanistan
D. Punjab State of India

69. At one of the sites of the Indus valley civilisation a dockyard has been discovered. Which is that site?
A. Rangpur B. Kalibangan
C. Lothal D. Ropar

70. Which one of the following is not one of the Harappan sites related to the maritime activities of the Harappan people?
A. Sotka Koh B. Desalpur
C. Balakot D. Lothal

71. The social group in which the Indus valley people lived were:
A. Peasants, hunters, traders and labourers.
B. the learned ones, warriors, traders, artisans and manual workers.
C. Brahmans, Kshatriyas, Vaisyas and Sudras
D. None of these

72. At how many places have the Indus valley finds been discovered?
A. 250 sites B. 2 sites
C. 10 sites D. 50 sites

73. Which among the following is common design between Mohenjo-daro and Baluchistan pottery?
A. Animal designs
B. Geometrical design
C. Floral designs
D. Svastika

74. Which among the width of the widest streets of the Mohenjo-daro is correct? (Approximately).
A. 10 metres B. 20 metres
C. 15 metres D. 8 metres

75. Some of the streets of the Indus cities ran straight even upto:
A. 200 metres B. 800 metres
C. 400 metres D. 600 metres

76. Which kind of bricks is not be found among Indus cities?
A. Sawn bricks B. Rectangular
C. Wedge shaped D. Square

77. Where was the vanity case found?
A. Harappa B. Lothal
C. Kot Diji D. Mohenjo-daro

78. One of the following structures is not found in Harappa. Indenfity:
A. Granary B. Citadel
C. Storied houses D. Great bath

79. The local name of Mohenjo-daro is:
A. mound of the living
B. mound of the great
C. mound of the dead
D. mound of bones

80. Which statement on Kalibangan is Not Correct?
A. Pre-Harappan phase here shows that fields were ploughed in Rajasthan.
B. It is only here that fire-altars belonging to Harappan period have been discovered.
C. The lower Harappan town at Kalibangan is fortified.
D. Drying of the river Ghaggar caused its decline.

81. In 1958 a cursory digging extended Harappan frontiers in the east upto a place near to Meerut in UP. Identify the place:
A. Alamgirpur B. Banwali
C. Ropar D. Sutkagendor

82. The Harappans imported Lapis Lazuli, jade and turquoise from:
A. Khetri and Kolar
B. Mesopotamia
C. Badakshan, the Pamirs and Khorasan
D. Khorasan and Khetri

83. A terracotta model of ship with a stick impressed socket for the mast and eye-holes for fixing come from:
A. Lothal B. Surkotada
C. Harappa D. Mohenjo -daro

84. "The enemy of the Harappans was nature .... India and the barbarians hordes are exonerated". Whose view is this?
A. M. Wheeler's B. G.F. Dale's
C. Marshall's D. Mackey's

85. The birds worshipped by the Harappans were:
A. dove and pigeon
B. dove and peacock
C. pigeon and peacock
D. pigeon, dove and peacock

86. A scale has been found at which of the Harappan sites?
A. Harappa B. Lothal
C. Mohenjo-daro D. Surkotada

87. In which age were the Copper and Stone implements used?
A. Neolithic B. Chalcolithic
C. Microlithic D. Mesolithic

88. Who is considered as father of Indian Archaeology?
A. Alexander
B. Lord Curzon
C. Mortimer Wheeler
D. John Marshall

89. The Indus people were probably ruled by:
A. Kings
B. Priests
C. Merchants
D. An assemble of elected elders

90. Which of the following statement regarding the Indus valley people is very revealing?
A. Their script remain unchanged throughout their history.
B. They were in contact with Mesopotamia.
C. Their civilisation was possibly theocratic just like the Egyptains and Mesopotamians.

D. They learnt nothing from Mesopotamia.

91. The terracotta figures of men and women squatting with their arms folded round their knees and wearing round caps on their heads were probably those of:
A. Prisoners B. Slaves
C. Labourers D. Cultivators

92. 'Swastika' is symbol of:
A. Sangam origin
B. Indus valley origin
C. Aryan origin
D. None of the above

93. Which was the backbone of the Indus economy?
A. agriculture
B. trade
C. carpentry
D. wheel made pottery

94. Crude ochre colour pottery (though its origin is uncertain), discovered from the Yamuna-Gangetic Doab, has been associated with:
A. the migrant Harappans
B. the early Aryans
C. the later Aryans
D. the Mauryas

95. The most popular form of burial at Mohenjodaro was:
A. complete burial
B. fractional burial
C. post cremation burial
D. cremation

96. The disapearance of Indus valley civilisation was most probably because of:
A. diverse reasons
B. the floods of the Indus
C. Aryan invaders
D. unknown invaders

97. One possible factor you may not accept as responsible for the 'eclipse' of the Indus civilisation is:
A. over population
B. over cultivation hence decrease in fertility
C. fluctuations of salinity because of shift of the riverine situation
D. deforestation

98. According to Dr. S.R. Rao, the Indus script, originally a mixed writing of 62 signs including pictures was disciplind into an alphabetic script of:
A. 22 signs B. 26 signs
C. 30 signs D. 24 signs

99. Indus script is:
A. bonstrophedon B. indeographic
C. cuneiform D. logographic

100. Indus seals:
A. were purely secular in character
B. were used as means of exchange by Harappans
C. reveal their religions character
D. were exported in big numbers

101. Probably Slavery originated in the:
A. Rig-vedic period
B. Later vedic period
C. Buddhist period
D. Harappan period

102. What is the name of the Harappan settement discovered recently by archeaologists in an island within the Rann of Kutch?
A. Dholavira B. Nagada
C. Diamabad D. Desalpur

103. What material was used to make mirrors?
A. Copper B. Bronze
C. Silver D. Glass

104. What is the material that was used mostly for writing by the Indus valley people?
A. Steatite B. Pagyrus
C. Clay tablet D. Copper tablets

105. Which is the commonest of the zoomorphic signs that occur in the seals of the Indus valley?
A. fish B. deer
C. tiger D. bull

106. Which statement is false with regard to Harappan civilisation?
A. Each house had two to three windows
B. The Harappan cities had a fully developed scheme of town-planning
C. The streets of Harappa inter-sected at right angles
D. The doors of houses open in the backlanes

107. Which one of the following sites has furnished the proof of the sea faring activity of the Harappan people?

A. Lothal B. Sokta Koh
C. Kot Dizi D. Balakot

108. The historical importance of the Indus valley civilisation lies in the fact that:
A. It was an urban civilisation
B. It had an excellent municipal administration
C. It pushed back the history of India to pre-aryan times
D. All of the above

109. Where is the great granary discovered in the excavation of the Indus valley sites?
A. Lothal B. Harappa
C. Mohenjo-daro D. Kalibangan

110. Garments of Indus valley people were of:
A. Cotton only
B. Cotton and Silk
C. Cotton and Wool
D. Cotton, Wool and Silk

111. The Indus seals were made up of:
A. Steatite B. Copper
C. Plaster of Paris D. Terra Cotta

112. Evidence of furrowed fields comes from:
A. Ropar B. Manda
C. Rangpur D. Kalibangan

113. Evidence of cloth (cotton) from Indus valley comes from:
A. Harappa B. Lothal
C. Kalibangan D. Mohenjo-daro

114. Evidence of Indus valley civilisation can be obtained form.
A. Seals of Mesopotamia
B. Mesopotamian seals found in Harappa
C. Seals at both the places
D. None of these

115. The belief of Indus valley people in the concept of other world is proved by:
A. Seals
B. Inscriptions
C. Burial habits
D. They did not believe in life after death

116. Division of society of Indus valley civilisation was based on:
A. Class B. Caste
C. profession D. Colour

ANSWERS

1	2	3	4	5	6	7	8	9	10
A	C	C	A	D	B	C	C	D	C
11	**12**	**13**	**14**	**15**	**16**	**17**	**18**	**19**	**20**
A	C	C	A	A	C	C	D	C	D
21	**22**	**23**	**24**	**25**	**26**	**27**	**28**	**29**	**30**
C	A	B	C	D	B	C	D	A	B
31	**32**	**33**	**34**	**35**	**36**	**37**	**38**	**39**	**40**
B	B	B	A	C	B	A	C	D	C
41	**42**	**43**	**44**	**45**	**46**	**47**	**48**	**49**	**50**
C	B	C	C	C	B	B	A	D	A
51	**52**	**53**	**54**	**55**	**56**	**57**	**58**	**59**	**60**
A	A	D	B	D	C	A	C	D	A
61	**62**	**63**	**64**	**65**	**66**	**67**	**68**	**69**	**70**
A	B	A	B	C	B	D	A	C	B
71	**72**	**73**	**74**	**75**	**76**	**77**	**78**	**79**	**80**
A	A	D	A	B	D	A	D	C	B
81	**82**	**83**	**84**	**85**	**86**	**87**	**88**	**89**	**90**
A	C	A	B	A	B	B	A	C	D
91	**92**	**93**	**94**	**95**	**96**	**97**	**98**	**99**	**100**
B	B	A	A	A	A	A	B	D	B
101	**102**	**103**	**104**	**105**	**106**	**107**	**108**	**109**	**110**
D	A	B	A	A	A	A	D	B	C
111	**112**	**113**	**114**	**115**	**116**				
A	D	D	A	C	C				

THE VEDIC AGE

1. Who applied the name India to our country?
   A. Aryans B. Persians
   C. Greeks D. English
2. What is Avesta?
   A. It is a name of Vedic God
   B. It is a place in Iran
   C. It is the regligious book of the ancient Iranians
   D. It is a place in Central Asia
3. The main source of livelihood of the Rigvedic people was?
   A. Agriculture
   B. Cattle breeding
   C. Poultry
   D. Animal husbandry
4. The word "Aryan" derieved 'ari' in the vedic period meant:
   A. superior
   B. cultured
   C. foreigners of strangers
   D. noble
5. Who gave the Siva Cult to India?
   A. Mongoloids
   B. Proto-Australoids
   C. Dravidians
   D. Aryans
6. Who among the following was the first to suggest the similarity between Sanskrit language of Aryans, Greeks and Latin?
   A. Sir Williams Jones
   B. Monier Williams
   C. Max Muller
   D. None of the above
7. Which was not the cause of Aryans Victory over the Dasas or Dasyus?
   A. use of chariots in war
   B. use of horses in war
   C. use of metal armours and helmets
   D. use of elephant in war
8. Marriage by Purchase was called:
   A. Paisach B. Rakshasa
   C. Asura D. Gundharva
9. Initially the Aryans cleared the land by means of:
   A. fire B. bronze axe
   C. iron axe D. wooden plough
10. "The country that lies North of the ocean and south of the snowy mountains is called Bharata. From which text is this description taken?
    A. Rig-Ved B. Ramayana
    C. Mahabharata D. Vayu Purana
11. In which records do you find the use of the word Hindu for Sindhu?
    A. Greeks B. Persian
    C. Sumerian D. Egyptian
12. Probably slavery originated in:
    A. Rig vedic period
    B. Later vedic period
    C. Mauryan period
    D. Post-Mauryan period
13. The discovery of incriptions at Bogazkoi in Asia Minor is not about.
    A. The treaty between the kings of the Hitties and the Mitanis.
    B. The vedic gods Indra, Mitra, Varuna and the Asvins who are invoked to uphold the treaty.
    C. determining the age of Rig-veda.
    D. description of gods worshipped by later vedic age.
14. What is the importance of Avesta for vedic period?
    A. The words, phrases, stanzas, myths and legends in it suggest the similarity between Rig veda and Avesta and that the ancestors of the Hindus and the Persians had lived together for a long time.
    B. It has no importance to understand vedic culture.
    C. It shows the culture exchange between ancient Iranians and Rig-vedic people.
    D. It shows close similarity between the physical features of the Iranians-Aryan and the vedic-Aryan.
15. The Brahmis spoke a language similar to

the language spoken by:
A. Khasis B. Dravidians
C. Aryans D. Bhutiyas

16. Upanayana, the ceremony of initiation started during:
A. Later vedic-period
B. Rig-vedic period
C. The Maurya period
D. The Pallava period

17. The caste-system became rigid with the stringent laws on the Shudras which meant restrictions on—
A. the right to learn vedas
B. the sacred thread ceremony
C. the right to own property
D. the right to engage themselves in trade and commerce

18. The varna-based social division first appeared in:
A. 300 BC – 100 BC
B. Later vedic period
C. Rig-vedic period
D. Mauryan period

19. Which points regarding Rig-vedic woman is not correct?
A. She had to perform Symbolic self-immolation at the death of her husband.
B. She enjoyed an honourable position.
C. She had to burn herself on her husband's pyre.
D. She received education.
E. She participated in the deliberations of the Tribal Councils, the 'Sabha' and the 'Samiti'?

20. The Rig-vedic society was mainly:
A. a pastoral society
B. a food gathering society
C. a migrating society
D. a tribal society

21. The two epics, the Ramayana and the Mahabharata are concerned with events which took place between:
A. 300 and 100 B.C.
B. 700 and 300 B.C.
C. 1000 and 500 B.C.
D. 1000 and 700 B.C.

22. Which of the following was not one of the distinguished tribes of the later vedic-period?
A. Videhas B. Kurus
C. Bharatas D. Panchalas

23. The source of income of the Rig-vedic ruler was primarily:
A. Tributes
B. Spoils of war
C. Agriculture taxes
D. Pasturage tax

24. Chariot racing formed an important element of which one of the following sacrifices?
A. Rajasuya B. Vajapeya
C. Ashvamedha D. Agnihotra

25. The important characteristics of the vedic religion were:
1. Goddess like 'prithvi', 'Aditi' and 'Usha'
2. Goddess are co-equal to their male-partners
3. Predominance of male dieties.
4. Worship of nature.

Code:
A. only 3 and 4 B. only 2 and 4
C. only 1 and 4 D. only 1 and 3

26. Which of the following statement is not correct regarding Indra?
A. He was the god exclusively associated with sacrifices.
B. He was know as 'Purandara'
C. He killed the evil dragon 'Virata'
D. He was the god of Thunder.

27. Which of the following was not a factor responsible for the proliferation of castes in ancient India?
A. Guilds
B. Development of new crafts
C. Tribal affiliations
D. To maintain social purity

28. Which of the following are known as Brahmanas?
A. The original texts of the vedas
B. Explanatory prose manuals relating to prayer and sacrificial ceremony
C. Commentaries appended to the

Aryanas dealing with philosophic questions.

D. Books dealing with worship and contemplation meant for wood dwelling hermits.

29. Which one of the following abstract deities of the vedic religion has been admired most in the Rig-veda?
A. Sraddha (faith)
B. Apsaras (water-nymphs)
C. Gandharvas (aerial spirits)
D. Usha (goddes of dawn)

30. Which of the following statements about the vedic-king is correct?
A. The Mantri Parishad exercised check over the authority of the king.
B. Samiti and Sabha exercised check over the authority of the king.
C. There was no check on the authority of the king.
D. The people directly exercised control over the king.

31. In which veda do we find reference to locked waters and water wheels?
A. Rig-veda B. Yajur-veda
C. Sam-veda D. Atharva-veda

32. The wergeld fixed for the number of a Vaishya during the Rig-vedic period was:
A. 100 cows B. 200 cows
C. 150 cows D. 10 cows

33. Among amusements the Aryans gave first place to:
A. Dice B. Chariot-race
C. Music D. Dance

34. "In the utmost need cooked I the entrails of a dog among the gods I found no protection, I he held my wife in degradation" who said this int he Rig-vedic period?
A. a brahmin B. a kshartriya
C. a vaishya D. a non-Aryan

35. The charioteers or sutas are thought to have spring from the marriage of:
A. Shudras and Brahmin women
B. Kshatriyas and Brahmin women
C. Vaishyas and Kshatriyas women.
D. Vaishyas and Brahmin women.

36. Which of the following propounded the theory of a doubled invasion of India by Aryans at different periods of history?
A. Dr. Giles
B. Dr. Hoernle
C. Sir George Grierson
D. C.V. Vaidya

37. Which of the following is not correct about Aryan movement towards South?
A. Indo-Aryan conquest of northern India never affected peninsular portion of the country.
B. According to tradition, it was the vedic sage Agastya, who introduced Aryan ideas to the Dravidians.
C. Indo-Aryans made spiritual conquest of the south.
D. By peaceful penetration and not by sword, they succeeded in carrying their ideas and civilization to the forthest Corners of the south.

38. The vedic mountain "Mujavant" was the home of:
A. all gods
B. Indra
C. Soma
D. herbs and medicinal plants

39. Which of the following region was called "Arya varta"?
A. From Yamuna upto West Bengal
B. Punjab and Delhi Region
C. The whole of northern India
D. The region beyond Vindhya mountain

40. In India Varna law enjoyed:
A. Legal Sanction only
B. Religions Sanction only
C. Economic Sanction only
D. The Sanction of both the state and religion.

41. Which of the following god was borrowed by the Aryans from the Indus valley civilization?
A. Pashupti B. Hanuman
C. Ganesh D. Kartikeya

42. Which of the following is an Upanishad?
A. Dhammapada B. Mahabhashya
C. Svetasvatar D. Milindapandha

43. What was the common form of Govt.

during the Rigvedic period?
A. Parliamentary form of government
B. Presidential form of government
C. Military Dictatorship
D. Hereditary Monarchy

44. The Purusha-Sukta of the Rigveda contains:
A. Mantras in praise of Rudra
B. Mantras in praise of Usha
C. Rules of horse sacrifice
D. Mantras about the creation of the universe

45. Which of the following statements about the teaching of the Upanishad is incorrect?
A. They believe in the existence of a supreme all pervading universal soul.
B. They believe in rebirth.
C. They believe that moksha can be achieved by means of the knowledge of the ultimate reality.
D. They believe that moksha can be achieved by means of animal sacrifices.

46. Which of the following is correct?
A. The Upnishads denied the existence of an all pervading supreme universal soul.
B. The Upanishads believed in the transmigration of soul.
C. The Upanishads believed in animal sacrifices as means to attaining salvation.
D. The Upanishads did not believe in the theory of karma.

47. The vedic God in charge of right, truth and moral order (Rita) was:
A. Varuna B. Indra
C. Dyaus D. Prajapati

48. What was the centre of Aryan civilization during the later vedic-age?
A. Karnataka
B. Sindhu
C. Rajasthan
D. The territory between the Saraswati and Ganga

49. What was the name of the king to whom all the early Aryan dynasties traced their origin?
A. Parasuram
B. Sri Krishna
C. Sri Ram Chandra
D. Manu – Vaivaswata

50. The term Sudra is mentioned in the Rig-Veda only once. How many times does the term 'Vaisya appear in the Rig Veda?
A. 9 times B. 10 times
C. 3 times D. Only once

51. Which musical instrument was not known to the Aryans?
A. drum B. tabla
C. flute D. harp

52. The Caste System was prevalent in the vedic age. Which of the following shows the forfold division of the society?
A. Satpatha Brahmana
B. Arthrvaveda
C. Purush-Sukta of Rigveda
D. Yajurveda

53. The term "Jana" is used 275 times in the Rigveda. How many times the term "Janapada" is used in the Rigveda?
A. 275 times B. 300 times
C. only twice D. Not even once

54. Bali was the name of the voluntary offering during rigvedic period but when it became the compulsory tax?
A. Sangama Period
B. Buddhist Period
C. Later Vedic Period
D. Mauryan Period

55. The institution of "gotra" appear in:
A. Rigvedic period
B. Buddhist period
C. Mauryan period
D. Later vedic period

56. Which of the following vedas refers to the roat 'Kri' (to purchase) and 'Vanija' (to merchant) and also mentions haggling in the market?
A. Rig Veda B. Sam Veda
C. Yajur Veda D. Atharva Veda

57. Which Veda mentions the following terms: garments (dursa), coverlets (pavasta), barter (prapana), sale (Vikraya), exchange of merchandise (partipana)?

A. Rigveda B. Samveda
C. Yajurveda D. Atharvaveda

58. The change of "Aryanism" from the "Vedic" stage to Brahamanic stage, was marked by:

A. Incorporation of non-aryan features into Aryan society
B. Evolution of Caste hierarchy
C. Transformation from semi-nomadic pastoral economy to settle agrarian economy.
D. All of the above.

59. The bards or magadhas descended from:

A. Shudra fathers and brahman mothers
B. Kashtriya fathers and brahman mothers
C. Vaishya fathers and kashtriya mothers
D. Shudra fathers and kashtriya mothers

60. Which was not a primary duty of every Aryan?

A. Adhyayana B. Yajna
C. Dan D. Tapa

61. Which of the following had the most esteemed place in vedic village life and economy?

A. Carpenter B. Bronze Smith
C. Potter D. Weaver

62. Who was the second in importance during the later-vedic period?

A. Carpenter
B. metal-worker or iron-smith
C. Tanner
D. Weaver

63. The initiation of a brahman boy ordinarily took place in his:

A. 6th year B. 8th year
C. 10th year D. 12th year

64. The concept of Karma, in course of time, meant maintenance of the:

A. Dharma B. Natural laws
C. Social order D. Caste Laws

65. Which one of the feminine institutions was not rejected by the Aryans?

A. Matriarchy
B. Polyandry
C. Worship of goddesses
D. None of the above

66. Among the Hindus, marriage is:

A. a sacrament
B. a contract
C. a sacrament as well as a contract
D. violable

67. The 'Rajan' or king during early vedic period could NOT claim or receive.

A. regular taxes
B. portain of war booty
C. voluntary gifts
D. None of the above.

68. Who was Ganapati in the vedic period?

A. a god
B. priest
C. head of Aryan group
D. a demi-God

69. According to the vedic texts like the Rig-Veda and Atharveda the king was:

A. Elected
B. Chosen by lots
C. Heriditary
D. Victor in a great battle

70. In the Rig-Vedic Society, gopa or gopati was the epithet given to the:

A. king
B. head of the family
C. wealthy man
D. brahmana

71. Abhiseka ceremony replaced which one of the following rites in due course of time?

A. Asvamedha
B. Vajapeya
C. Rajasuya
D. None of the above

72. With whom did the people in later vedic period deposit the taxes?

A. Bhagadugha B. Gramani
C. Sangrihita D. Parjapati

73. The doctrine of royal divinity was explicity proclaimed for the first time in:

A. Epics B. Manu-Smriti
C. Vedas D. Six Darshana

74. During the later vedic period the eastern kings were known as:
A. Samrats B. Rajas
C. Bhojas D. Virats

75. The salient feature of the Rig-vedic civilization was the worship of:
A. Nature B. Mother Goddess
C. Trinity D. Pashupati

76. The chief impact of the vedic culture of Indian History was:
A. Progress of philosophy and religion
B. Rise of other wordly outlook
C. Rise of democratic theories
D. Growth of Sanskrit-literature

77. The metals which were used by the later vedic Aryans were:
A. Silver, gold-copper, iron and brass
B. Silver, gold and copper only
C. Silver and gold only
D. Silver and copper only

78. The Aryans came to India from outside and first settled in:
A. Punjab B. U.P.
C. Delhi D. Panchala

79. The original home of the Aryans, according to Lokmanya Balgangadhar Tilak was:
A. Central Asia B. Tibet
C. Arctic region D. Kashmir

80. Brihadaranyaka is:
A. A Smriti
B. An Upanishada
C. A treatise on Political Science
D. A Mahakavya

81. Which of the following are not included in the Vedic-literature?
A. Samhitas B. Aranyakas
C. Smritis D. Upanishadas

82. Which of the following is correct?
A. According to the vedic thinkers, monarch was the ultimate source of law
B. According to the vedic thinkers, people were the ultimate source of law
C. According to the vedic thinkers, the nature was the ultimate source of law
D. According to the vedic thinkers, Dharma, which sustained the world, was the ultimate source of law.

83. The concensus among historians that the vedic age began earliest in:
A. 1200 – 1000 BC B. 2500 – 800 BC
C. 2500 BC D. 1000 BC

84. Which of the following failed to develop into a city during later vedic age?
A. Indraprastha B. Mathura
C. Prayag D. Kashi

85. The most widely accepted dates of the composition of Rig-Veda is:
A. 1500 BC to 1000 BC
B. 1500 BC
C. About 45000 BC
D. 100 BC

86. According to Bhagavatism, there are .... incarnations of Vishnu:
A. six B. eight
C. ten D. twelve

87. The oldest Indian linguistic text is:
A. Mahabharat B. Ashtadhyayi
C. Ramayana D. Nirukta

88. "War begins in the minds of men." In which of the following books the above statement is stated?
A. Mundaka Upanishad
B. Atharvada (Atharvaveda)
C. Samaveda
D. Rigveda

89. The Caste System during the early vedic age:
A. Prohibited only interdining but not intermarriage
B. Prohibited interdining and intermarriages
C. Did not prohibit interdining and intermarriages
D. None of these

90. The philosophy of Upanishads emphasis on:
A. Bhakti B. Gyan
C. Karma D. Tapa

91. Who was the first poet of India?
A. Valmiki B. Vyasa
C. Kalidas D. Vashishta

92. The most common crime during the vedic period was:
A. theft, particularly cattle-stealing

B. murder
C. highway robbery
D. rakshasa marriage

93. The scared thread which the Brahman wore was made of
A. Silk B. Wool
C. Hemp D. Cotton

94. Which statement an asceticism is correct?
A. The Atharva Veda after refers to ascetics as Vratyas
B. By the time of the Upanishads, asceticism was widespread
C. Vratya was a priest of non-vedic fertility cult which involved ritual dancing and flagellation
D. All of the above.

95. The speculation of the upanishads centre around one word of the Rig veda which one is that?
A. Parjapati B. Varuna
C. Brahman D. Indra

96. Which statements on the status and bringing up of children in ancient India is correct?
A. Three personal ceremonies were performed before birth "garbhadhana" to promote conception, "Pumsavama" to procure a male child, and "Simantonnayana" to ensure the safety of the child in the womb.
B. The birth ceremony or the "Jatakarma" took place before the cutting of the unbilical cord.
C. Usually during the six months of the child the ceremony of (annaprasana) feeling of solid food was celebrated while the tonsure (culakarma) took place in the third year for only boys.
D. All of the above.

97. Which practices were not in existence during the Rig-vedic period?
A. Dowry B. Child-marriage
C. Divorce D. Widow-marriage

98. What is the name of that God, who is known by the name of 'Asura' and is possibly the same as Ahura Mazda in the Zoroastrian religion?
A. Agni B. Varuna
C. Prajapati D. Rudra

99. Gold, copper and bronze were found during the Rigvedic age. Which of the following was also known during that age?
A. Nishka B. Satmana
C. Suvarna D. Krishnala

100. A God who is described amoral, and object of fear archer God whose arrows caused disease, connected with the storm, and the guardian of healing herbs is known as:
A. Yama B. Varuna
C. Indra D. Rudra

101. "Gramani" was known as king-maker or Rajakartri. Which one of the following is the name for the head of Tribal-republic?
A. Purohita
B. Ganapati or Jyestha
C. Gramani
D. Mahishi

102. Match the following

(a) Akshavapa		1.	Superintendent of gambling
(b) Bhargadugha		2.	Chamberlain
(c) Kshattri		3.	Collector of taxes
(d) Samagrahitri		4.	Treasurer
(e) Adhikarita		5.	King companion in chase
(f) Govikartana		6.	Village official appointed by the king.

	(a)	*(b)*	*(c)*	*(d)*	*(e)*	*(f)*
A.	1	3	2	4	6	5
B.	3	1	4	2	5	6
C.	4	2	3	5	6	1
D.	2	3	1	4	5	6

103. The progenitor of the solar dynasty of Ayodhya was:
A. Mandhata B. Ikshavaku
C. Nahusa D. Bhartas

104. How did Kingship originate according to the Aitareya Brahmana?
A. By contract

B. By the will of God
C. The common consent of the people
D. By force

105. Which point relating to the transformation of Aryan economy of the post-vedic period shows the emergence of commerce?
A. The iron plough share came into existence.
B. Krishnala berry was a unit of weight and the nishka superseded the cow as a unit of value.
C. The astrologer became an important person in village-life.
D. The merchants made their house of kilnburnt bricks.

106. During the Rig-vedic period the people worshipped Gods:
A. for salvation
B. only for praja
C. for food, wealth, health and praja
D. for ending the miseries of existence

107. Which statement on Soma is NOT correct?
A. It was purely secular in nature
B. It was sanctified by religion
C. It was drunk at sacrifices
D. It was less intoxicating than "Sura".

108. According to Hindu mythology, the last Avatar Kalkin that is Vishnu appearing in the form of a man mounted on a white horse with a flaming sword in his hand, resembles one other belief. Which one is that?
A. Christian belief in the horseman of the Book of Revelation.
B. Buddhist belief in the coming of Maitreya Buddha.
C. Reincarnation of the souls in the vedas.
D. The general belief of the coming of the Messiah in almost all religions.

109. Which Goddess is not the fierce aspect of the Mother Goddess?
A. Durga B. Kali
C. Chandi D. Uma

110. In which century was the concept of Karma incorporated in Aryanism or Brahminism as an important feature of the way of life?
A. 400 BC B. 100 AD
C. 1000 BC D. 700 BC

111. Early Aryan worshipped:
A. 36 Gods B. 33 Gods
C. 22 Gods D. 11 Gods

112. The Brahmanas are books which deal with:
A. Yoga B. Philosophy
C. Rituals D. Meditation

113. The concept of Moksha is common to all of the following except:
A. Jainism B. Buddhism
C. Lokayatism D. Hinduism.

114. Which philosophical school evolved a system of Indian Syllogism?
A. The Nyaya School
B. The Yoga School
C. The Sankhya School
D. The Vaisesika School

115. Hindu mythology and folklore hold that the mother earth rests on the:
A. horns of a bull
B. horns of a cow
C. hood of a cobra
D. none of the above.

116. How many Gods has Hindu Pantheon:
A. 33 crores
B. as many as living people
C. 33 Gods
D. 1000 Gods

117. Match the philosophical system with their propounders?

(a) Nyaya	1. Jamini
(b) Sankhya	2. Badarayana
(c) Vaisesika	3. Kanda
(d) Yoga	4. Gautam
(e) Purva Mimansa	5. Kapila
(f) Uttra Mimansa	6. Patanjali

	(a)	*(b)*	*(c)*	*(d)*	*(e)*	*(f)*
A.	2	3	4	5	6	1
B.	4	5	3	6	1	2
C.	4	5	3	1	6	2
D.	4	5	3	6	2	1

118. Perhaps the oldest philosophical system was that of Sankhya whose legendry founder was the Sage Kapila. It talks of basic principles. Which statement on it is incorrect?

A. The first of the basic principle is Prakriti meaning matter.

B. Creation is not due to the operation of divinity but due to the inherent nature of Prakriti.

C. It is from Prakriti that the soul also develops.

D. The soul and Prakriti are different entities.

119. The fifth philosophical school was that of Mimansa. It emphasises that enternal value of the vedas and their finality. With which stream of vedic religion do you associate this philosophy?

A. Asceticism

B. Realization of the Brahman

C. Brahmanism

D. Heterodox Schools

120. The battle of ten kings is mentioned in which of the chapters of Rig-veda?

A. Book I B. Book III

C. Book VII D. Book X

121. Which Books or mandala of the Rig-veda are called family books?

A. All the ten

B. Book II to Book VII

C. Books II, III, IV, VII, IX

D. Only Books I and X

122. The characteristic feature of the Rig-Vedic Religion the deity supposed to preside over a particular aspect of nature was regarded at the time of its invocation as the greatest and the highest i.e. extolled above all the Gods is termed as:

A. Mono-theism B. Heno-theism

C. Poly-theism D. Pan-theism

123. Marine Archaeologists from the National Institute of Oceanography under the leadership of Dr. S.K. Rao have discovered a 3,500 year old 250 meters long fotwall off the estern coast of an Island about 2 km from Okha port, in the Gulf of Kutch which belonged to the now submerged city of ancient Dwarka. Identify the Island.

A. Bhaluka B. Dehot sarg

C. Dwarka D. Bet Dwarka

124. The word "aghanya" refers to:

A. horse B. cow

C. ox D. sheep

125. "Great flood" occured during the time of the:

A. 1st Manu B. 10th Manu

C. 11th Manu D. 2nd Manu

126. Which of the following is not to be called sruti?

A. Brahmans B. Samhitas

C. Aranyakas D. Epics

127. Which among the following is not to be called Smriti?

A. Grihya Sutra B. Dharma Sutra

C. Dharma Shastra D. Upanishads

128. Which among the following cannot be called Karmakanda?

A. Rig-veda B. Yajurveda

C. Brahmanas D. Upanishads

129. What is considered to be the fifth veda?

A. Brahmanas B. Aranyakas

C. Upanishads D. Mahabharata

130. Which among the following is not be called Vedanga?

A. Siksha B. Vyakarna

C. Jyotisha D. Manu Smriti

131. Identify the correct sequence among the following units of political organization.

A. kula, vis, grama, jana

B. jana, vis, grama, kula

C. vis, kula, jana, grama

D. grama, jana, kula, vis

132. One of the following does not go with the others:

A. Pana B. Pada

C. Vaha D. Patra

133. **Assertion (A):** Remarriage of a widow was allowed

Reason (R): Atharvaveda refers to it

Codes:

A. A and R are true and R is the correct explanation of A.

B. A and R are true but R is not the correct explanation of A.
C. A is true but R is false.
D. A is false but R is true.

134. Assertion (A): The Aryans are an indegenious people
Reason (R): There is no reference to the Aryan invasion of India in the Rig-Veda
Codes:
A. A and R are true and R is the correct explanation of A.
B. A and R are true but R is not the correct explanation of A.
C. A is true but R is false.
D. A is false but R is true.

135. Assertion (A): The vedic people know the sea.
Reason (R): The Sarasvati is stated to have reached the sea.
Codes:
A. A and R are true and R is the correct explanation of A.
B. A and R are true but R is not the correct explanation of A.
C. A is true but R is false.
D. A is false but R is true.

136. Which of the following theories of the origin of the state is not mentioned in the vedic-literature?
A. The contract theory.
B. The theory of devine origin.
C. The class theory.
D. The force theory.

137. Which of the following was one of the important and elaborate sacrifices of the vedic period.
A. Ashvamedha B. Rajasuya
C. Vajapeya D. All of the above

138. Which one of the following statements about the trade and commerce in the later vedic period is correct?
A. Trade and industry flourished and a class of heriditary merchants came into being.
B. Merchants were organised into guilds, as appears from reference to ganas or corporations and the "Shreshthins".
C. They used nishka, satamana and krishnala as the units of a value.
D. All of the above.

139. The earliest clear reference to four ashramas of the students house holder, forest-hermit, and recluse, is found in the:
A. Jabala Upanishad
B. Satpatha Brahmana
C. Chandogya Upanishad
D. Atharva Veda

140. The city of Hastinapur was washed away during the reign of:
A. Janamejaya B. Parikshita
C. Nickakshu D. Yudhisthira

141. The term Bharata after which the country Bharatvarsha was eventually named appears first in:
A. Rigveda B. Samaveda
C. Yajurveda D. Atharvaveda

142. Which one of the following was the centre of Aryan activity in the later vedic period?
A. The Punjab and Delhi region
B. Uttarapatha
C. From the Yamuna to the Western borders of Bengal
D. The north-west frontier

143. Which one of the following was the centre of Aryan activity in the Rig-vedic period?
A. Punjab and Delhi region
B. The region between Indus and Ghaggar
C. The land of the Indus and principal tributaries
D. The region from eastern Afganistan to the upper valley of Gangas.

144. Which of the following vedangas contains the 'Srauta' the 'Griha' and the 'Dharma Sutras'?
A. Nirukta B. Kalpa
C. Shiksha D. Chhandas

145. Which one of the following was the prevalent method of the disposal of the dead in the vedic period?
A. Only burial

B. Only cremation
C. Either cremation or burial
D. Post exposure burials

146. Which scriptures abound in the discussion and teachings of the early mystics?
A. Brahmanas B. Aryankas
C. Upnishads D. Dharmasutra

147. Which of the following are the Brahmans appended to the Rig veda?
A. Aitareya Brahmana and Kausitiki Brahmana
B. Gopatha Brahmana
C. Satapatha Brahmana
D. None of these

148. The term "Niyoga" means
A. Marriage of a childless widow with the brother or blood relation of her deceased husband for the sake of progeny.
B. To produce off spring by illegal means.
C. To remain unmarried through out the life.
D. None of the above.

149. The most ideal form of marriage among the eight forms of marriages prevalent in ancient India was:
A. Gandharva B. Arsa
C. Daiva D. Brahma

150. Which statement is true about the customs in the Epics and Smritis:
A. Condemned the eating of meal and the drinking of Liquor
B. Approved the eating of meat and the drinking of Liquor
C. Approved the murder of Brahmin
D. All of these

151. Who was the first consecrated king of the Earth?
A. Manu
B. Prithu
C. 10th Manu
D. None of the above

152. Aryan were basically:
A. Rural
B. Urban
C. Normal
D. None of the above

153. When Aryans first came to India they were divided into .... social classes.
A. Two B. three
C. four D. five

154. Rigveda has .... number of Mandals:
A. eight B. nine
C. ten D. twelve

155. The collections of the vedic hymns were known as:
A. Samhitas
B. Upnishads
C. Shrutis
D. None of the above

156. Which one of the vedas contains charms and spells?
A. Rigveda B. Samaveda
C. Yajurveda D. Atharvaveda

157. How many hymns are devoted to Indra?
A. 150 B. 200
C. 250 D. 300

158. How many hymns are devoted to Agni in Rigveda?
A. 100 B. 150
C. 200 D. 250

159. Who occupied the supreme position in the later vedic pantheon?
A. Indra B. Agni
C. Varuna D. Prajapati

160. Two dynasties, solar and Jaunar took birth from the son of the:
A. 10th Manu B. 1st Manu
C. 11th Manu D. 9th Manu

161. The word " Pathikrit" refers to:
A. Varuna B. Agni
C. Iron-Axe D. Bronze-Axe

162. "Rik" means:
A. Verse B. Sang
C. Prose passage D. Shortest rule

163. Who was defeated by Sudas, the king of the Bharatas on the bank of river Parushni?
A. Parukutsa B. Parikshit
C. Dhananganda D. Visvamitra

164. Which mandala of Rigveda is devoted wholly to soma drink?
A. 9th Mandala B. 10th Mandala

C. 1st Mandala D. 8th Mandala

165. Which region of the vedic period came to the known as Brahmavarta?
A. Ganges and Yamuna
B. Ravi and Sutlej
C. Sutlej and Yamuna
D. Saraswati and Yamuna

166. According to history, which two tribes disappeared after the Battle of Ten kings?
1. Kurus 2. Purus
3. Bharatas 4. Panchalas
Codes:
A. 2 and 3 B. 1 and 2
C. 3 and 4 D. 1 and 4

167. Atharva veda contains one of the following.
A. Science formula
B. Canons of music
C. Mathematical formula
D. Magical spells, incantations and something on music

168. The total number of Puranas is:
A. 18 B. 12
C. 16 D. 6

169. Puranas are written in:
A. Prophetic tone B. Sutra form
C. Poetry only D. Pali

170. Which veda is almost useless to historians?
A. Samaveda B. Rigveda
C. Yajurveda D. Atharvaveda

171. Which written constitute is the first specimens of prose in the world?
A. Vedas B. Brahmanas
C. Aranyakas D. Upanishads

172. The Pandvas belonged to the clan of:
A. Kurus B. Panchalas
C. Bharatas D. Alivas

173. At which city of the later vedic age, probably burnt brick was used for the first time?
A. Hastinapura B. Achicchatra
C. Kausambi D. Vaishali

174. During the early vedic period the chief product or crop was:
A. Barley B. Wheat
C. Rice D. Maize

175. Match the Sutra (List I) literature with the science or subject they deal with (List II).

List I	***List II***
(a) Kalpa	1. Etymology
(b) Siksha	2. Phonetic
(c) Nirkuta	3. Ritual
(d) Chhanda	4. Metre

Codes:

	(a)	*(b)*	*(c)*	*(d)*
A.	3	2	1	4
B.	1	2	3	4
C.	4	3	2	1
D.	2	3	4	1

176. The doctrine of transmigration is first noted in the:
A. Aitareya Brahmana
B. Panini's Asthadhyayi
C. Satapatha Brahmana
D. Rig vedic Samhita

177. Which book is at once a legal and religious treatise?
A. Ashtadhyayi
B. Manava Dharma Shastra
C. Mahabhashya
D. Arthashastra

178. Painted grey ware sites were probably those of:
A. Early Vedic Aryans
B. Later Vedic Aryans
C. Pains
D. Dasas

179. The painted grey ware sites are located in:
A. Eastern U.P., parts of Punjab, Haryana and Rajasthan
B. Western U.P., Adjoining areas of Punjab, Haryana and Rajasthan
C. The Doab region
D. Eastern U.P. and Magadha region

180. Which books shows that the medical men of the vedic times were familiar with the disease of the eyes, heart, stomach, lungs and skin?
A. Upvedas B. Brahmanas
C. Vedangas D. Upnishads

181. How many times did Sita live in exile?
A. one B. two
C. three D. four

182. The term 'adikavya' refers to:
A. Mahabharata B. Rig veda
C. Ramayana D. Sama veda

183. What is the total number of verses in the Mahabharata?
A. 100,000 B. 24,000
C. 50,000 D. 80,000

184. What are the total number of verses in the Ramayana?
A. 100,000 B. 24,000
C. 50,000 D. 80,000

185. In whose ashrama did Sita live during her second exile?
A. Valmiki B. Visvamitra
C. Vashishta D. Vyas

186. As a separate science which one of the following is the oldest work on Indian Geometry and Architecture?
A. Srautasutra B. Grihasutra
C. Dharmasutra D. Sulvasutra

187. Match the following according to the founder of the school of Indian Philosophy:

(a) Samkhya 1. Patanjali
(b) Nyaya 2. Kapila
(c) Vaisesika 3. Gotama
(d) Yoga 4. Kanada

Codes:

	(a)	*(b)*	*(c)*	*(d)*
A.	2	3	4	1
B.	3	1	2	4
C.	2	3	1	4
D.	3	2	1	4

188. Sama veda is an important source for one of the following, which one?
A. Painting B. Sculpture
C. Dance D. Music

189. What is the type of marriage in the vedic-period in which-in place of the dowry, them is token bride of a cow and a bull?
A. Arsa B. Brahma
C. Daiva D. Gandharva

190. Which of the following is not the correct pair:
A. Niyoga — Separation of a woman from her lover or husband
B. Anuloma — Marriage of a higher varna man with lower varna women
C. Pratiloma — Marriage of a lower varna man with higher varna women
D. Rajanya — Kshatriya

191. Which of the following reasons explains in a better manner the origin of asceticism?
A. The Sacrificial cult of the Brahmanas did not satisfy the spiritual langings of people in the eastern part of the Ganga basin.
B. Asceticism rose along with the rise of kingdoms and the mergence of material civilization.
C. Possibly the brahmanas themselves lost faith in the cosmic mystery of sacrifice.
D. Ascetics wanted to gain magical power just like the Brahmanas.

192. Which group of the Brahmans is a part of Rig veda?
A. Kena and Chhandogya
B. Isa and Brihadarnyaka
C. Aitareya and Kausitaki
D. Prasna and Mundaka

193. In ancient India, a boy was considered as animals before.
A. Budhakarma Sanskara
B. Jatakarma Sanskara
C. Upanayana Sanskara
D. Vidyarambha Sanskara

ANSWERS

1	2	3	4	5	6	7	8	9	10
C	C	C	D	C	A	D	C	A	D

11	12	13	14	15	16	17	18	19	20
B	A	D	A	B	A	B	B	C	B
21	**22**	**23**	**24**	**25**	**26**	**27**	**28**	**29**	**30**
D	C	B	B	A	A	D	B	D	B
31	**32**	**33**	**34**	**35**	**36**	**37**	**38**	**39**	**40**
A	A	B	A	B	B	A	C	B	D
41	**42**	**43**	**44**	**45**	**46**	**47**	**48**	**49**	**50**
A	C	D	D	D	B	A	B	D	D
51	**52**	**53**	**54**	**55**	**56**	**57**	**58**	**59**	**60**
B	C	D	C	D	A	D	D	C	D
61	**62**	**63**	**64**	**65**	**66**	**67**	**68**	**69**	**70**
A	B	B	D	C	A	A	C	A	A
71	**72**	**73**	**74**	**75**	**76**	**77**	**78**	**79**	**80**
C	A	A	A	A	A	A	A	C	B
81	**82**	**83**	**84**	**85**	**86**	**87**	**88**	**89**	**90**
C	D	D	A	A	C	D	B	C	B
91	**92**	**93**	**94**	**95**	**96**	**97**	**98**	**99**	**100**
A	A	D	D	C	D	B	B	A	D
101	**102**	**103**	**104**	**105**	**106**	**107**	**108**	**109**	**110**
B	A	B	C	B	C	A	B	D	D
111	**112**	**113**	**114**	**115**	**116**	**117**	**118**	**119**	**120**
B	C	C	A	C	A	B	D	C	C
121	**122**	**123**	**124**	**125**	**126**	**127**	**128**	**129**	**130**
B	B	D	B	B	D	D	D	D	D
131	**132**	**133**	**134**	**135**	**136**	**137**	**138**	**139**	**140**
B	D	A	D	A	C	D	D	A	C
141	**142**	**143**	**144**	**145**	**146**	**147**	**148**	**149**	**150**
A	A	A	B	B	B	A	A	D	A
151	**152**	**153**	**154**	**155**	**156**	**157**	**158**	**159**	**160**
B	A	B	C	A	D	C	C	D	A
161	**162**	**163**	**164**	**165**	**166**	**167**	**168**	**169**	**170**
B	A	A	A	C	A	D	A	A	A
171	**172**	**173**	**174**	**175**	**176**	**177**	**178**	**179**	**180**
B	A	C	A	A	C	B	B	B	A
181	**182**	**183**	**184**	**185**	**186**	**187**	**188**	**189**	**190**
B	C	A	B	A	D	A	D	A	A
191	**192**	**193**							
A	C	C							

THE RELIGIOUS MOVEMENTS

1. According to the Buddhist traditions the four great signs transformed the life of Gautama. Which one of the following is known as the "Four Great Signs"?
   A. The "four noble Truths".
   B. The sights of old age, disease, death and a medicant.
   C. The four heavenly signs which accompanied the birth of the Buddha.
   D. None of these.
2. Who said this: "The Buddha would have made a good general if he had not become a monk"?
   A. Charles Eliat B. Vincent Smith
   C. Rhyas Davids D. Romila Thaper
3. What was the name given to those who gave a demonstration of the incidents mentioned in the plays.
   A. Sobhanikas B. Ganikas
   C. Sthanikas D. Granthikas
4. What does the Stupa symbolise?
   A. Evanescence of this world
   B. Piety of the Budha
   C. Sanctity of the Budha
   D. Bhakti
5. Mahayana Buddhism originated in:
   A. Andhra Pradesh, 1st Century B.C.
   B. Bihar, 1st Century A.D.
   C. Kashmir, 3rd Century B.C.
   D. Bengal, 2nd Century A.D.
6. Where has the Rummindei Pillar been erected?
   A. The birth place of the Budha
   B. The place where he preached his eirmon first
   C. The place where the Budha died
   D. The place where he attained enlightenment
7. The third Buddhist council was held at Patliputra during the reign of Ashoka, 236 years after the death of Buddha to revise the Scriptures. Which of the following Pitaka was added to the existing two in this council?
   A. Sutta Pitakas
   B. Abhidhamma Pitakas
   C. Vinaya Pitakas
   D. None of these
8. Which of the following is not one of the "Four Noble Sentiments" that a person aspiring for 'nirvana' should cultivate?
   A. Karuna of Compassion
   B. Metta or Universal love
   C. Mudita or Sympathetic joy
   D. Upekkha or equanimity
9. Who said this—"Karma acts as a very pragmatic God".
   A. The Buddha B. Mahavira
   C. Parsva D. Upnishads
10. Which of the following has the bull capital?
    A. Rampurva B. Sarnath
    C. Lumbini D. Amaravati
11. Name the Greek ambassador at the court of Bindusara.
    A. Megasthenes B. Heliodorus
    C. Diamaehus D. Menander
12. Where is the Lomasa Rishi Cave?
    A. Barabar Area B. Ellora
    C. Bhaja D. Amaravati
13. Who said that the Indians did not drink (liquor) in the age of the Mauryas?
    A. Megasthenes B. Arrian
    C. Strabo D. Pliny
14. Where is the finest of the toranas found?
    A. Kerala B. Sanchi
    C. Bedsa D. Nagarjuni hills
15. Which one of the following has the quadripartite semi-lions on top?
    A. Rampurva
    B. Lauriya Nandangarh
    C. Sarnath
    D. Amaravati
16. Name the inscription in which the name of the contemporary rulers of the west are given.
    A. Rock Edict XIII B. Rock Edict IX
    C. Pillar Edict VII D. Bhabra Edict

17. Mahayanism has faith in:
A. Defication of the Buddha and icon worship.
B. Elaborate rituals
C. The Boddhisattavas and devotion to them
D. All of the above

18. Which one of the following councils made Sanskrit the vehicle of Buddhist scriptures?
A. first B. second
C. third D. fourth

19. Who is regarded as the founder of "Shunyavad"?
A. Vasumitra B. Nagarjuna
C. Ashvaghosha D. Upali

20. Which element of Mahayana Buddhism particularly distinguishes it from the Hinayana?
A. Liberal attitude
B. Bodhisattava ideal
C. Absolutist philosophy
D. Divinity of Buddha

21. The Buddhist doctrine of "Prititysamut Pada" or dependent origination contained in the second Noble Truth explains.
A. The path which leads to cessation of suffering.
B. The interconnection between desire, suffering and rebirth.
C. The momentariness of all worldly things.
D. The eight fold path very clearly.

22. Who has called Bindusara as Amitrachates?
A. Athenaeus B. Justin
C. Strabo D. Pliny

23. Match the following :
(a) Vijnanavada 1. Hinayana
(b) Shunyavada 2. Madhyanika School
(c) Syadvada 3. Yogachara
(d) Sthavirvada 4. Sapta-bhanginaya

	(a)	*(b)*	*(c)*	*(d)*
A.	3	2	4	1
B.	3	4	2	1
C.	1	2	3	4
D.	2	1	3	4

24. Who were described as the Pancharatrikas?
A. Bhagbatas B. Pasupatas
C. Digambaras D. Hinayanists

25. What word was used in the 6th century B.C. for a man who attained full holiness?
A. Svargi B. Nirvani
C. Arhant D. Buddha

26. Which one of the following was added to Buddhist canonical texts by the fourth council?
A. Jatakas
B. Vibhashas
C. Dhammapada
D. Kathavatthu, Prakarna

27. Early Schism in Buddhism divided the Buddhist order into:
A. Sthavirvadins and Mahasanghikas
B. Mahasanghikas Sunyavadins
C. Sunyavadins and Sarvastivadins
D. Sthavirvadins and Sarvastivadins

28. The Bhabru Edict records Ashoka's faith in:
A. Tisaranam
B. Toleration
C. Dharmaviiya
D. Solicitude for the Welfare of the people

29. The term 'Piyadassi' occurring in Mahavamsa is identified with Ashoka. It is also identified with another ruler. Identify.
A. Bindusara B. Samprati
C. Salisuka D. Chandragupta

30. Which of the Gods called Herakles by the Greeks?
A. Krishna B. Indra
C. Rudra D. Brahma

31. Which of the following Buddhist text declares the cattle to be of food, beauty and happiness (Annada, Vannada, Sukhada), and thus pleads for their protection?
A. Suttanipata B. Kathavathonu
C. Milindapanho D. Mahavamsa

32. Among which of the communities did

Jainism spread rapidly?
A. Trading Community
B. Agrarian tourists
C. Craftsmen
D. Warriors

33. Why are the majority of Buddhist caves in India to be found in Western Maharashtra?
A. The caves in this region provided a safesanctuary away from the marauding hordes of foreign-invoders.
B. There was a long-standing tradition in this region of royal patronage to rock-cut architecture.
C. The Sahayadri mountain in western Maharastra with its hard trap was best suited for rock-cut architecture.
D. None of these.

34. Name of the greatest Buddhist Commentator of the Buddhist Cononical literature who wrote Visuddhimagga, the first famous systematic and philosophical treatise on Buddhist doctrine.
A. Vasumitra B. Nagarjuna
C. Buddhaghosha D. Ashvaghosha

35. The Buddha had accepted the invitation to dinner from one of the following in preference to that of the lichchavis. Identify:
A. Ajatsatru B. Ambapali
C. Khema D. Visakha

36. Match the following:

(a) Kanda	1.	Sidhhartha's horse
(b) Channa	2.	Siddhartha's Charioteer
(c) Udraka	3.	Chief disciple of the Buddha
(d) Ananda	4.	Second teacher of Siddhartha
(e) Kauthaka	5.	The Smith who served the last meal to Buddha

	(a)	*(b)*	*(c)*	*(d)*	*(e)*
A.	5	2	4	3	1
B.	1	2	3	4	5
C.	2	3	5	1	4
D.	5	2	3	1	4

36. Match the following:

(a) Sutta Pitaka	1. A collection of religious discourses of the Buddha
(b) Vinaya Pitaka	2. Contains rules of Monastic discipline
(c) Abhidhamma Pitaka	3. Consists of meta physical disquisitions

	(a)	*(b)*	*(c)*
A.	2	3	1
B.	1	2	3
C.	3	1	2
D.	2	1	3

38. Mahavira gave up worldly life at the age of:
A. 30 B. 29
C. 40 D. 25

39. Who of the following wrote Madhyamika Karika?
A. Nagarjuna B. Vasubandhu
C. Buddhaghosa D. Adhvaghosa

40. How many years did the Buddha wonder before the enlightenment?
A. Seven B. Six
C. Twelve D. forty-five

41. Which one of the following is considered the most important vehicle of Buddhist ethical teachings?
A. Sutta Pitakas
B. Jatakastories
C. Vinaya Pitakas
D. Abhidhamma Pitakas

42. Who headed the Jaina exodus to the Mysore Country?
A. Chandragupta B. Bhadrabahu
C. Sthulabhadra D. Jamali

43. How many years did Mahavira spend as a religious teacher?
A. 30 B. 40
C. 35 D. 25

44. Which was the name of the son of the Buddha?
A. Rahula B. Mara
C. Jamali D. Sidhartha

45. Mahavira practised severe penance for:
A. 30 years B. 6 years
C. 10 years D. 12 years

46. Who was the first pontiff of Jainism after Mahavira?
A. Sudhaman B. Jamali
C. Sthulabhadra D. Bhadrababu

47. Which one of the following places can be regarded as the largest monastic establishment in western India (containing 130 caves)?
A. Kanheri
B. Junnair (Near Nasik)
C. Ajanta (Near Aurangabad)
D. Karle

48. Which one of the following statement correctly describe the difference between chaitya and a stupa?
A. Chaityas represented Mahayanism and stupas Hinayanism
B. Chaityas were constructed by the manasteries while stupas were constructed by the kings and the rich merchants.
C. Chaitya is a place of Prayers/Worship while stupa is a movement.
D. Chaitya is a religious term, while stupa is an architectural term for a mend containing a relic of the Buddha and later on of leading Buddhist saints.

49. Who of the following was the most renowned Buddhist scholar of Indian origin to propagate madhyamika Buddhism in China?
A. Fa-hiern B. Kumarjiva
C. I-tsing D. Hiven-Tsang

50. About 600 B.C. which one of the following was not a republic?
A. Sakyas B. Koliyar
C. Mallas D. Panchala

51. Who built the fort at Palaligram (Palimbothra) where the city of Pataliputra grew?
A. Ajatsatru
B. Bimbisara
C. Chandragupta Maurya
D. Dhanananda

52. One of the three Pitakas which deals with the Buddhist Curch discipline is known as:
A. Vinaya
B. Sutta
C. Abidhamma
D. None of the above

53. Which statement on Buddhists in the second half of the first millennium is not correct?
A. Buddhist monks took part in Hindu processions.
B. Buddhist families relied on the services of Brahmanas at births, marriages and deaths.
C. Buddhism denied the validity of the vedas.
D. Buddhism did not develop its own metaphysics and tratricism, as Hinduism.

54. Which feature of Buddhism gave it an edge over Aryanism?
A. Absence of Godhead
B. Acceptance of the cycle of birth and death
C. homely message
D. the jataka stories

55. Which country still possesses a branch of the original pipal tree, under which the Buddha had received enlightenment?
A. Indonnesia B. China
C. Ceylon D. Afghanistan

56. Which statement on the similarities between Buddhism and Jainism is not correct?
A. Both Buddhism and Jainism denied the authority of the vedas and opposed animal sacrifices and the performance of rituals and ceremonies.
B. Both the Buddha and Mahavira belonged to princely families and both taught in the language of the common people.
C. Both of them admitted diciplines from all castes and from both sexes.
D. Both spread in various parts of the world extensively.

57. True goal of Mahayana follower is the

achievement of:
A. Arhantship
B. Supreme Buddhahood
C. Perfection
D. Bodhisattvahood

58. Who was/were not a Zealous follower(s) of Buddhism?
A. Pala kings of Bengal
B. Sungas
C. Ashoka
D. Harsha

59. The charvakas, or Lokayat school of materialist philosophy did not believe in one of the following. Identify
A. Peraption (Pratyaksha) is the only means of valid knowledge. All interference is invalid.
B. Earth, Water, Finole and Air are the only elements.
C. There is other world.
D. Sensual pleasure is the summum bonum of life: enjoyment is the only end of human existence.

60. The angas literature is associated with:
A. Vaishnavism B. Saivism
C. Jainism D. Buddhism

61. The mother of Mahavira was:
A. Mahamaya B. Trishala
C. Yasoda D. Yasodhara

62. The event of the fight of Mohammed in 622 A.D. is known as Hijrat. What is Gautam's "Great going forth" (His leaving his father's palace) known as?
A. Mahabhiniskramana
B. Parinirvana
C. Mahaparinirvana
D. Nibbana-yatra

63. Who wrote Jaina Kalpasutra
A. Bhadrabahu B. Sthulbahu
C. Mahavira D. Parsvanath

64. Which one forms a bridge or rather a half way house between the old Buddhism and Hinduism?
A. the Hinayana School
B. the Mahayana School
C. the Vajrayana School
D. None of the above

65. Whose relation with the Buddha began with enmity and ended in complete dexotion?
A. Bimbisara's B. Ajatasatru's
C. Devadatta's D. Pradyota's

66. Which one of the following has been the richest source of the well known smooth images in black state and has also yielded an extensive series of Buddhist bronzes?
A. Amaravati B. Tanjore
C. Nalanda D. Kurkihar

67. At which one of the following places the earliest example of the Buddhist stupa architecture has been found?
A. Sarnath B. Sanchi
C. Lumbini D. Bodha-Gaya

68. To which one of the following school of art do the earliest images of Buddha in human form belong?
A. Mathura B. Gupta
C. Gandhara D. Amravati

69. The best images of Prajnaparamita, belongs to:
A. Sumatra B. Java
C. China D. India

70. Name the place where the Colossal figures of the Buddha modelled on an earlier Gandhara type, belonging to the 3rd and 4th centuries A.D. has been found.
A. Bamiyan, Afghanistan
B. Chinese Turkistan
C. Burma
D. Sri Lanka

71. Which statement regarding Buddha is true?
A. He was born on the day of full moon.
B. His birth and death took place on the day of full moon.
C. His birth, death and awaking — all the three took place on the day of full moon.
D. He became enlightened on the day of full moon.

72. Which of the following Buddhist philosophers is said to have visited Nepal in the

4th century in order to propagate his own doctrine?
A. Acharya Vasubandhu
B. Acharya Shantharakshita
C. Acharya Kamlashila
D. Acharya Aitsha

73. Who of the following monarchs of Tibet is credited with introduction of Buddhism in Tibet in the 7th century A.D.?
A. Dpal---hkhor---btsan
B. Khri---ide---sren---btas
C. Mu---ne---btsan---po
D. Sron---btsan---Sangam---po

74. The Shailendra kings of Indonesia were followers of Mahayana Buddhism. They establish monesteris at Nalanda and Nagapatinam and the Pala and the Chola emperors granted village for their maintenance. Which one of the following stupas built by them n Java is most renowned?
A. Singasari B. Borobudur
C. Mendut D. Kalasan

75. Which one of the following nurtured as individualistic traditions in Buddhism?
1. Shudras asseting their rights
2. Growing Urbanisation
3. Decaying Brahmanism
4. Republican background
A. only 2 and 4 B. only 1 and 3
C. only 1, 3 and 4 D. All the four

76. Which one of the following constitutes the chief significance of Korean Buddhism?
A. The role it played as an intermediary between China and Japan
B. The unique synthesis of the orthodox and the Tantric Schools of Buddhism.
C. The preservation of Mahayana Buddhism in its purest from.
D. None of the these.

77. When was Buddhism (Mahayana School) First introduced in Japan?
A. 1st Century A.D.
B. 3rd Century A.D.
C. 6th Century A.D.
D. 8th Century A.D.

78. Which factor disabled Buddhism from the very begining to emerge as the triumphant religion of India?
A. Lack of clarity regarding life after death.
B. Pride born out of Royal patronage.
C. Acceptance of some of the well known concepts of Aryanism.
D. Division of Buddhist ranks immediately after the death of Buddha.

79. In the field of religion every major religion of the world is represented in India with the exception of:
A. Confucianism
B. Zoroastrianism
C. Judaism
D. Latin Chriotianity

80. The 57-foot high status of Gomateshware at Srayana Belgola in Mysore was erected in about 981 A.D. by the Ganga minister.
A. Chamundraya B. Rachamal
C. Rishala D. Bharata

81. According to Buddhist tradition, who instigated Ajatsatru to kill his father Bimkisara?
A. Budha's cousin Devadatta
B. Bimbisara's wife Chellana
C. Bimbisara's wife Khena
D. Ajatasatru's wife Padmavati

82. One of the earliest references to Krishna as human hero is to be found in the:
A. Chhandogya Upanishad
B. Ghata Jataka
C. Jaina text Uttradyanana Sutra
D. Jaina Aupapatrika Sutra

83. To the classical i.e. Greek writers, Lord Krishna was known as:
A. Heracles B. Souraseni
C. Androkottas D. Sandro Kottas

84. "Para" means:
A. the highest aspect of Lord Vasudeva
B. the emanatory form of Vasudeva
C. the incarnatory form of Vasudeva
D. Vasudeva as the inner Controller of the actions of every individual

85. The fact that Jainas included Vasudeva and Baladeva among the 63 Solaka ----- Purushas or eminent Personalities, who influence the history of the world in various ways is:

A. true B. false

C. not likely D. disputed

86. Who was considered as the 9th Avatar of Vishnu?

A. Kapila B. Dattatreya

C. Vyasa D. the Buddha

87. The monolithic column at Besnogar in honour of Vasudeva was erected by Heliodorus in the:

A. 2nd Century B.C.

B. 1st Century B.C.

C. 1st Century A.D.

D. 2nd Century A.D.

88. Which statement on Vaishnavism is not correct?

A. Vasudeva — Krishna came to be gradually associated with the vedic deity Vishnu and this process was completed by the time the Bhagvat Gita was composed.

B. The Bhagvata religion is also known as Vaishnava Dharma.

C. Buddhist cannos of the first century B.C. mentioned the worshippers of Vasudeva.

D. The worship of Vishnu was certainly known to Megasthenes.

89. Which statement on Bhagavatism is not corrected?

A. It did not encourage image worship among the higher sections of the orthodox Indian people.

B. The Vishnu images of the early post. Christian era are mostly to be found in the Mathura regions.

C. The Bhagavata Shrines are mostly built by foreigners as the one referred to in the mora inscription.

D. A few fragments of the mora shrines are now to be found in the Mathura Museum.

90. Amongest the following who contributed most to the Bhagavat cult?

A. Indo-Greeks B. Seythians

C. Parthians D. Kushans

91. Theist religion means:

A. belief in one God

B. the God would reveal himself to the devotees

C. the opposite of montheism

D. the opposite of pontheism

92. The Gita steers a middle course between the two ideals of nivritti and pravritti:

A. correct B. incorrect

C. controversial D. Do not know

93. Which one is known as the layman's upnishad?

A. The Ramayana

B. The Gita

C. Mahabharata

D. The Jataka Stories

94. Which practice of early Buddhists largely enabled Buddhists to become a popular religion?

A. Preaching in Pali and the simplicity of the doctrine.

B. The personality of the Buddha

C. Acceptance of worship of trees and funerary practices.

D. The simplicity of the doctrine.

95. The system that must have become the basic doctrine of Buddhism is the:

A. Nyaya system B. Sankhya system

C. Uttar-Mimamsa D. None of these

96. Who listened to the first serman of the Buddha?

A. The five as ascetics or monks

B. Sujata

C. Angulimala

D. Upali

97. Symbol of Buddhism is:

A. four-spoked wheel

B. eight-spoked wheel

C. ten-spoked wheel

D. Not known

98. The future Buddha may be an incarnation in:

A. Human form

B. Semi-human form

C. Animal form

D. Acquastic animal form

99. Who was/were not a zealous follower(s) of Buddhism:
A. Harsha
B. Kanishka
C. Pala kings of Bengal
D. Sungas

100. "Buddhayana" refers to the:
A. First "Vehicle"
B. Second "Vehicle"
C. Third "Vehicle"
D. None of the above

101. Which sect is similar in thinking or indentical to that of the lokayatas?
A. Jains B. Charavakas
C. Brahmanas D. Sharamanas

102. Who said, "Don't ask the caste, ask the deeds whosoever does the right deals attains nirvana"?
A. Krishna B. Yajuavalkya
C. Mahavira D. Gautama

103. Which evidence does not reveal Ashoka's interest in Buddhism?
A. 6th major pillar inscription
B. Schism edicts
C. Nigalisagar pillar inscription
D. Rumindei's pillar inscription

104. One statement on charavaka philosophy is not correct. Identify that one.
A. Enjoyment is the only end of human life.
B. Gods do not exist.
C. Besides perception there are other means of valid knowledge, important among them being inference.
D. The Lokayat philosophy stated that everything, that exists, is experienced by sensory organs.

105. Which statement on the sect of the Ajivikas is wrong?
A. It attracted only men of humble origin.
B. It found fault with Bhramanas interpretation of Karma doctrine.
C. It criticised the caste-structure.
D. Gosala was its founder.

106. When did China received Buddhism?
A. Second century B.C.
B. First century B.C.
C. First century A.D.
D. Third century A.D.

107. Which one of the following works of Ashvaghosha is considered to be the oldest dramatic work extant in Sanskrit literature?
A. Shariputraprakarana
B. Buddhacharita
C. Samanta Pasadika
D. Saundarananda

108. Which one expression for describing the under-current of Indian History is more true than the others?
A. The story of Hinduism
B. Exploitation of the rural areas
C. Frequent invasions by foreigners
D. Elusive search for political unity

109. The only incarnation of Lord Siva as suggested in the Vayu and Linga Puranas is that of:
A. Kakulin
B. Basava
C. Gosala
D. Shankaracharya

110. Which was the earliest of the saiva seets?
A. Kalamukhas B. Kapalikas
C. Pasupata D. Lingayatas

111. The Garuda Pillar erected by the foreigner is at:
A. Besnagar B. Allahabad
C. Sanchi D. Ujjain

112. Who said: "When religion declines and evil-doers are to be destroyed, I shall be born, at different periods"?
A. Krishna B. The Buddha
C. Rama D. Mahavira

113. The first successful invador who annexed the Punjab territories to his empire was:
A. Cyrus I B. Darius I
C. Alexandar D. Darius III

114. Chandragupta Maurya liberated one of the following parts of India from Selukos. Which one was that:
A. North-Western B. South-Western

C. South-Eastern D. Western

115. Who said "Indians do not know the art of writing?

A. Kautilya B. Pliny
C. Megasthenes D. Plutarch

116. Who was referred to as "Vrishala" and "Kulahina":

A. Ashoka
B. Harsha
C. Chandragupta Maurya
D. Chandragupta

117. During the reign of Chandragupta Maurya the Sudarsan lake near Girnar was constructed by?

A. Suvisakha B. Pushyagupta
C. Tushapa D. Parnadatta

118. Tishyarakshita, who opposed the extraordinary generosity of Ashoka to the Buddhist, was:

A. the queen B. a sister
C. a daughter D. a grand-daughter

119. Who was welcomed by these word: "We neither oppose the prince, nor the king but the wicked ministers who oppress us"?

A. Bindusara B. Samprati
C. Kunala D. Jaluka

120. How many nights did Ashoka spend on his "dhammayatras" (Pilgrimage tours)?

A. 240 B. 256
C. 120 D. 280

121. Who saw Ashoka's statue dressed in a monk's robe?

A. Fahien B. Huen Tsang
C. I-tsing D. Alberuni

122. The essence of Law of Piety or Dhamma is:

A. Layman's version of Buddhism
B. Ashoka's version of religious consciousness
C. Porana Pakiti
D. An ideology to indotrinate people

123. Which points does Not show that Ashoka was against Bramhanism?

A. He looked down supon Sacrifice
B. He had something against the Devas
C. He equalted brahmanas with Ajivikas
D. He held that the goal for people was "Swarga"

124. Who was the only Mauran Successor whose name appears in an inscription as the donor of a cavein Barabar Hills bear Gaya?

A. Ḍasaratha B. Sampati
C. Kunala D. Jalauka

125. The "Vayu Purana" mentions the total number of kings after Ashoka as:

A. Six B. Ten
C. Seven D. Eight

126. Which of the following did for Buddhism in Japan, what Ashoka had done for it in India?

A. Heina B. Prince Shotoku
C. Emperor Suiko D. Kamakura

127. The stupa constructed at which one of the following places in southern India is not only earliest but also a Mahastupa enshrining the mortal remains of the Buddha?

A. Jaggayyapeta B. Amaravati
C. Nagarjunakonda D. Bhattiprolu

128. The serman of the Turning of the wheel of law was preached by the Buddha after his enlightment. Which statement on it is not correct?

A. It was preached in the Deer Park at Sarnath.
B. It is the basic teaching of all the Buddhist sects.
C. The five monks, Kondana, Vappa, Bhadiya, Mahanama and Assagi listened to it.
D. That was his first and last Serman.

129. The turning of the wheel of law was the centre of Buddhist teaching. Which of the following in not correct?

A. Four noble truths
B. Eight fold path
C. Belief in Bodhisattavas
D. The middle path

130. A Boddhisattva in Hinayana Buddhism is:

A. A being of immeasurable charity and compassion

B. The previous incarnation of Buddha
C. A dissident monk
D. The God on the earth in human form

131. Which among the following was absent from the organisation of Buddhist Sanghas?
A. Democratization
B. A central organisation of Sanghas
C. Separate Sanghas for Nuns (women)
D. Separate Sanghas for the followers of Hinayana and Mahayana sects

132. Which one of the following title was not used for Buddha?
A. Sakyamuni B. Tathagata
C. Jina D. Nayaputta

133. About whom Max Mullar called, "the greatest grammarian the world has ever known"?
A. Nagarjana B. Ashvaghosha
C. Panini D. Nayaputta

134. To which of the following countries Ashoka did not send his missionaries?
A. Egypt B. Sri Lanka
C. China D. Burma

135. By what name did the Greek writers call to the city commissioners?
A. Agronomoi B. Astynomoi
C. Sthanika D. Srenis

136. What is the ancient name for East Bengal?
A. Samatata B. Dhauli
C. Svarnagiri D. Gandhara

137. Which of the Greek writers refers to taking of image of Heracles in front of the Paurava army?
A. Curtius B. Jaustin
C. Strabo D. Measthenes

138. Who is described as the Indian Machiavelli?
A. Bimbisara B. Chanakya
C. Bana D. Kalidasa

139. Into how many books is Arthasastra divided?
A. 15 B. 20
C. 25 D. 150

140. Which one of the following statements about Yogachara (Founded by Maitreyanatha), the other branch of Mahayanism, is not correct?
A. It recognises three degrees of knowledge Parikalpila (illusory), Paratantra (empirical), and Parinishpanna (absolute).
B. The school is also known as Vijnanavada on account of the fact that it holds Vijnaptimatra (nothing but consciousness) to be the ultimate reality.
C. As against the qualified realism of Madhyamika School it advocates absolute realism.
D. It emphasises the practice of Yoga (Meditation) as the most effective method for the attainment of the highest truth (bodhi).

141. Who of the following Mahayanist Buddhist writers is regarded as the Kant of India by Dr. Stcharbatoky?
A. Dignaga B. Asanga
C. Dharmakirti D. Vasubandhu

142. Ashoka's Coronation took place in:
A. 261 BC B. 273 BC
C. 264 BC D. 250 BC

143. Tantrik-Sect first grew within:
A. Jainism B. Buddhism
C. Hinduism D. Bhagavatism

144. Which of the following was not one of the schools of Tantric-Buddhism?
A. Pratyeka-Buddhayana
B. Mantrayana
C. Vijrayana
D. Sahajayana

145. Which one of the following Buddhist scholars has been described as "Poet, Musician, Preacher, Moralist, Philosopher, Play-writer, tale-teller and inventor in all these arts .... he recalls Milton, Goethe, Kant and Voltaire"?
A. Vasubandhu
B. Asanga or Aryasanga
C. Ashvaghosha
D. Nagarjuna

146. Which one of the following Buddhist scholar enjoys great celebrity all over the

Buddhist world as grammarian, philosopher and poet?

A. Vasumitra B. Santideva
C. Chandragomin D. Panini

147. Assertion (A): The rise of Buddhism was protest movement against the Aryan-dominated Varna System.

Reason (R): The Buddha was a Khatriya.

Codes:

A. A and R are true and R is the correct explanation of A.
B. A and R are true but R is not the correct explanation of A.
C. A is true but R is false.
D. A is false but R is true.

148. Assertion (A): The rise of hetrodox religions in the 6th century B.C. was the outcome of a desire to have an intelligible easy, and less expensive way to salvation.

Reason (R): The Buddha and Mahavira introduced those changes in the old religious system as were necessary to satisfy this yearning.

Codes:

A. A and R are true and R is the correct explanation of A.
B. A and R are true but R is not the correct explanation of A.
C. A is true but R is false.
D. A is false but R is true.

149. Assertion (A): The rise of Buddhism was the result of the introduction of nees agricultural economy based in the use of the cattle.

Reason (R): The Buddha was opposed to sacrifice.

Codes:

A. A and R are true and R is the correct explanation of A.
B. A and R are true but R is not the correct explanation of A.
C. A is true but R is false.
D. A is false but R is true.

150. Assertion (A): Mahavira was only a reformer.

Reason (R): Jaina ideas were there even before his advent.

Codes:

A. A and R are true and R is the correct explanation of A.
B. A and R are true but R is not the correct explanation of A.
C. A is true but R is false.
D. A is false but R is true.

151. Assertion (A): Jainism failed to attract the masses.

Reason (R): Jainism did not very clearly mark itself from the Brahmanical religion.

Codes:

A. A and R are true and R is the correct explanation of A.
B. A and R are true but R is not the correct explanation of A.
C. A is true but R is false.
D. A is false but R is true.

152. Assertion (A): The ideas of the Buddha were not original.

Reason (R): He was indebted to the Upanishadic thought to some extent.

Codes:

A. A and R are true and R is the correct explanation of A.
B. A and R are true but R is not the correct explanation of A.
C. A is true but R is false.
D. A is false but R is true.

153. Assertion (A): The Buddha was a pessimist.

Reason (R): He said life is unhappy.

Codes:

A. A and R are true and R is the correct explanation of A.
B. A and R are true but R is not the correct explanation of A.
C. A is true but R is false.
D. A is false but R is true.

154. Assertion (A): The Buddha was not a democrat.

Reason (R): He did not make a frontal attack on the caste system.

Codes:

A. A and R are true and R is the correct explanation of A.
B. A and R are true but R is not the correct explanation of A.
C. A is true but R is false.
D. A is false but R is true.

155. **Assertion (A):** The Mauryan Empire collapsed on account of Brahmanical reaction.
Reason (R): The man who overthrew the last of the Mauryas was a Brahman.
Codes:
A. A and R are true and R is the correct explanation of A.
B. A and R are true but R is not the correct explanation of A.
C. A is true but R is false.
D. A is false but R is true.

156. **Assertion (A):** A Neglect of the North-West frontier was one of the causes of the decline of the Mauryan Empire.
Reason (R): It encouraged foreigners to invale India.
Codes:
A. A and R are true and R is the correct explanation of A.
B. A and R are true but R is not the correct explanation of A.
C. A is true but R is false.
D. A is false but R is true.

157. **Assertion (A):** A woman in the Mauryan period were held in honour.
Reason (R): We are told that Gods were pleased with those households where women were held in honour.
Codes:
A. A and R are true and R is the correct explanation of A.
B. A and R are true but R is not the correct explanation of A.
C. A is true but R is false.
D. A is false but R is true.

158. **Assertion (A):** Chandragupta Maurya became a Jaina.
Reason (R): He died by show starvation.
Codes:
A. A and R are true and R is the correct explanation of A.
B. A and R are true but R is not the correct explanation of A.
C. A is true but R is false.
D. A is false but R is true.

159. **Assertion (A):** The courtesans enjoyed a great social standing.
Reason (R): The prostitutes attended the royal court and were employed on a fat slavery.
Codes:
A. A and R are true and R is the correct explanation of A.
B. A and R are true but R is not the correct explanation of A.
C. A is true but R is false.
D. A is false but R is true.

160. Which one of the following about Bhagavatism is not correct?
A. Bhagavatism is a later development of Brahamism and is an integral part of Vaishnavism sect related to the worship of Narayana Vishnu and his incarnates.
B. Bhagavatism, unlike Vaishnavism, believes in the vedic rituals.
C. The term Bhagavatism is derived from the term "Bhavat" which was the title of the worshippers of Vasudeva Krishna.
D. The term Bhagavatism means the sect related to the worship of Vasudeva Krishna.

161. Which one of the following is the main Bhagavata texts?
A. The Puranas B. The Upanishadas
C. The Bhramanas D. The Smritis

162. Who among the following was the earliest known Greek followers of Bhagavatism?
A. Antialkidas B. Megasthenes
C. Heliodorus D. Dios

163. Besnagar Pillar inscription set up by Heliodorus belongs to the:
A. Sunga Period B. Mauryan Period

C. Gupta Period D. Kushan Period

164. In which of the following are the germs of the Bhagavata cult not to be found?
A. Upanishadas B. Vedic hymns
C. Pashupatas D. Jatakas

165. The Principal deity of the Bhagavatas is:
A. Shiva
B. Krishna
C. Vishnu-Narayana
D. Shakti

166. When did Bhagavatism first come into prominence and spread towards Western and Central India and the Deccan?
A. 1st Century A.D. B. 3rd Century A.D.
C. 6th Century B.C. D. 2nd Century B.C.

167. Which one of the following moral virtues is not a part of Bhagavatism?
A. Tapas (asceticim)
B. Dana (Charity)
C. Arjava (piety)
D. Samyaka Ajiva (rightful earning)

168. What is the significance of the first five incarnations of Lord Vishnu?
A. Victory of good over evil.
B. Story of evolution .
C. God has human attributes.
D. God punishes sin in various forms.

169. Which 'avatar' was almost fully equated with God Vishnu?
A. Rama B. Krishna
C. Vamana D. Parasurama

170. Who was considered as the 9th Avatar of Vishnu?
A. Kapila B. Dattatreya
C. Vyasa D. The Buddha

171. The Alvars were minstrels of the:
A. Shiva Cult B. Vishnu Cult
C. Yavna Cult D. Kali Cult

172. Which was the earliest of the Saiva Sect:
A. Kalamukhas B. Kapalikas
C. Pasupata D. Lingayats

173. Which statement on Bhagavatism is not correct?
A. It did not encourge image worship among the higher sections of the orthodox Indian people.
B. The Vishnu images of the early Post-Christian era are mostly to be found in Mathura region.
C. The Bhagavata Shrines are mostly built by foreigners as referred to in the Mora inscription.
D. A few fragments of the Mora Shrines are now to be found in Mathura Museum.

174. Which statement on the five-fold aspects of God Vasudeva is not correct?
A. Para is the highest aspect of the Lord
B. Vyuha is Lord's emanatory form
C. Vibhava is Lord's incarnatory form
D. Antaryamin characteristises him as the inner controller of the actions of every individual

175. To the classical Greek writers Lord Krishna was known as:
A. Heracles B. Sauraseni
C. Androkattas D. Sandrokattas

176. Which one of the following School of Philosophy was the main off shoot of Bhagavatism?
A. Sankhya B. Vaisheshika
C. Advaita D. Vishishtadvaita

177. The Garuda Pillar erected by a foreigner is at:
A. Besnagar B. Allahabad
C. Sanchi D. Ujjain

178. Brahmanism believes in:
A. the philosophy of equality of castes
B. spread of religion with force
C. the philosophy of transmigration of soul
D. national attitude to religion

179. Which of the following was the most important aspect of Brahmanism:
A. Sacrificial rituals
B. Practice of tapas
C. The concept of mantra
D. None of these

180. Brahmanism:
A. condemns idol worship
B. has no views about idol worship
C. discourage idol worship

D. believe in idol worship

181. Which one of the following is incorrect?
A. Brahmanism accepts Vamashrama System.
B. Brahmanism accepts idol worship.
C. Brahmanism does not accept the theory of avataras.
D. Bhramanism accepts Vasudeva-Krishna as an avatara of Vishnu.

182. Which one of the following concepts of Brahmanism is not accepted by Bhagavatism?
A. Doctrine of Samsara.
B. Doctrine of Karma.
C. Elaborate Sacrificial rituals as the only means of propitiating Gods.
D. Knowledge as a means of Salvation is not open at all.

183. The ritualistic part of Brahmanism, which had received a setback in the Mauryan period was revived by:
A. Bhumitra
B. Agnimitra
C. Pushyagupta
D. Pushyamitra Sunga

184. Idols according to Brahmanism are:
A. avoidable in worship
B. not needed in worship
C. essential for worship
D. just to be ignored in worship

185. Brahmanisms means:
A. dominance of Brahmanas
B. Aryan-Dravidan Synthesis
C. the metaphysics and the Parans
D. the social economic and religious life being integrated into one

186. Which one is known as the Layman's Upanishada?
A. Ramayana
B. The Mahabharta
C. The Gita
D. The Jataka Stories

187. The hub Brahmanism or Aryanism by the end of 1000 was:
A. Sacred Scriptures
B. the caste system
C. the Dharmashastras
D. the daily rituals, ceremonies and practices

188. Brahmanism did not believe in:
A. the sanctity of Caste divisions.
B. the ascendancy of Brahmans over other castes.
C. the Varnashrama System.
D. a inter-dining and inter-marriage.

189. Which statement on Brahmanism by the close of the ancient period is correct?
A. The primacy of Brahmanism was well established.
B. The number of new religious paths did appear including the extremists like Kapalikas, Kalamundhas and the followers of Tantricism.
C. Mimansa and Vedanta were the twin Pillars of Brahmanism.
D. Brahmanism continued to be youthful and vigorous.

190. Charvakas preached:
A. Total materialism
B. Bhakti
C. Gyan
D. God

191. Ajivikas were followers of a philosophy of:
A. Complete predetermination
B. Destiny
C. Asceticism
D. All the above

192. Bhagavatism revolved around the worship of:
A. Vishnu B. Indra
C. Krishna D. Rama

193. Who among the following Gods provided the concept of Siva in the Rigveda?
A. Indra B. Varuna
C. Rudra D. Surya

194. Bhagavatism started as a popular movement with the Bhakti of:
A. Vishnu B. Brahma
C. Krishna D. Rama

195. The most sacred text of Bhagavatism are/is:
A. The Upanishadas

B. The Puranas
C. The Ramayana
D. The Gita.

196. Mark the wrong one:
A. Gita believes in theory of incarnation.
B. Gita does not believe in the theory of incarnation.
C. Gita concentrates on theory of Karma.
D. Gita regards sacrifices of sense pleasures at the highest form of sacrifice.

197. Total number of incarnation of Vishnu according to Bhagavatism are:
A. Six B. Eight
C. Ten D. Twelve

198. Teaching of Vasudeva Krishna are to be found in:
A. Manduka Upanishada
B. The Ramayana
C. Samaveda
D. Gita

199. In which of the Upanishadas do we find reference to Saga Krishna?
A. Chhandogya B. Mundaka
C. Katha D. Mandukya

200. Fundamental Contribution of Bhagavatism to modern Hinduism is:
A. Its philosophy
B. Its texts
C. Image worship
D. None of the above

201. Which of the following are not to be found in Chhandogya Upanishada?
A. Dana B. Tapas
C. Animal Sacrifice D. None-Violence

202. According to the Chhandogya Upanishada, who was the teacher of Sri Krishna?
A. Gautham B. Ghora Angirasa
C. Panini D. Patanjali

203. Which of the following is incorrect:
A. Bhagavatism rejected the theory of avatara.
B. Bhagavatism rejected the idea of a Supreme God.
C. Bhagavatism rejected the theory of transmigration.
D. Bhagavatism rejected the conception of immortal souls.

204. Which of the following is incorrect:
A. Bhagavatism opposed to Saivism.
B. Brahmanism does not reject animal sacrifices.
C. Brahmanism accepts the Varna System.
D. Brahmanism believes in rebirth.

205. Tick the right one:
A. Bhagavatism rejected the theory of Karma.
B. Bhagavatism rejected devotion to God as a means of attaining Salvation.
C. Bhagavatism rejected the authority of vedas.
D. Bhagavatism believed in the existence of a Supreme God.

206. The unite of the Vedic Social System was the:
A. individual B. family
C. clan D. tribe

207. The Gayatri Mantra is associated with:
A. Savitri B. Agni
C. Vishnu D. Varuna

208. Who wrote "The Arctic Home in the vedas?
A. Vyas B. Gandhiji
C. Tilak D. Max Muellar

209. The conflict between Aryans and Dasyus Figures prominently in the:
A. Rig Veda B. Sama Veda
C. Epics D. Puranas

210. Probably slavery originated in:
A. Rig Vedic Period
B. Later Vedic Period
C. Mauryan Period
D. Post-Mauryan Period

211. Which was not known during Rig Vedic Period?
A. Prostitution B. Coinage
C. Loan or Rua D. Slavery

212. Marriage by Purchase was called:
A. Paisach B. Raksasa
C. Asura D. Gandharva

213. The wergild fixed for the murder of a Vaishya during the Rig Vedic Period was:
A. 100 Cows B. 200 Cows

C. 150 Cows D. 210 Cows

214. Who was not considered a 'dvija' during the vedic period?
A. a Shudra B. a Brahman
C. a Kshatriya D. a Vaishya

215. Regarding slaves, in which veda the earliest reference is to be found?
A. Rig-veda B. Yajur Veda
C. Sama Veda D. Atharva Veda

216. Who constituted the common people in vedic times?
A. Brahmanas B. Kshatriya
C. Vaishyas D. Shudras

217. The institutions of 'gotra' appeared in:
A. Rig Vedic Period
B. Later Vedic Period
C. Early Rig Vedic Period
D. Later Rig Vedic Period

218. The vedic term 'Kula' refers to:
A. family B. clan
C. country D. village

219. Who were the first to worship Vasudeva Krishna?
A. Bhagavatas B. Vedic Aryans
C. Tamilians D. Abhiras

220. The earliest reference to the deification of human hero Vasudeva, is found in:
A. The Chhandogya Upanishada
B. One of the Sutras of Panini's Ashtadhyayi
C. Patanjali's Mahabhasya
D. Manava Dharmasastra

221. The Jains considered Vasudeva to be a near relation of:
A. Rishabha, the first Tirthankara
B. Arishtanemi, the 22nd Tirthankara
C. Parsavanath, the 23rd Tirthankara
D. Mahavira, the last Tirthankara

222. Which statement on the Holy 'Gita' is incorrect?
A. The entire doctrine of the great Upanishada discussed and stated in the clearest terms.
B. The great Sankaracharya commented on it in the 8th century as an authoritative text to establish his doctrine of Advaita.
C. Muslim author, Alberuni, quotes its text when he discourses on the Hindu view of God.
D. It was a part of the 'Mahabharta" originally.

223. The Gita does not advocate:
1. renunciation of action
2. denunciation of dharma
3. Nishkama Karma
4. Synthesis of action, devotion and knowledge.

Codes:
A. 1 and 2 B. 1 and 3
C. 3 and 4 D. 1 and 4

224. Which statement may not be true on Bhagavatism?
A. It was opposed to Varnashrama System.
B. It helped reduce social tensions.
C. It aroused hope in lower orders — hence the hard work done by them.
D. It popularised the Cult of Vasudeva Krishna.

225. Bhagavatism does not believe in:
A. Even a 'Chandala' possessed of Sincere devotion is dearer to God than a Brahmana lacking true faith.
B. The central theme of Bhakti is transcendental love which is nectar like in its nature.
C. Renunciation of action.
D. Devotion to Vishnu.

226. Tracings of belief is Vishnu dated back to:
A. Atharva Veda B. Yajur Veda
C. Sama Veda D. Rig Veda

227. The later-day Krishna facet of the Bhagavata cult was probably derived:
A. Satavahanas
B. Abhiras
C. Ikshavakus
D. Thirkutakas

228. The hub of Brahamanism or Aryanism by the end of 1000 A.D. was:
A. the Sacred Scriptures

B. the Caste System
C. the Dharma Shastras
D. the daily ritual ceremonies and practices.

229. Who was the unique attribute of Brahmanism or Aryanism:
A. preserving the tradition.
B. incorporating the alien practices and concepts.
C. transforming itself by absorbing other concepts and practices.
D. retaining its dominance while adopting some concepts and practices of other communities.

230. What is known as Brahmanism or Aryanism is truely:
A. the Hindu religion
B. the caste system
C. the socio-religious system sanctified by Brahmanas.
D. a socio-religious system with an economic underpinning and the whole things sanctified in the name of religion.

231. Which statement on Brahmanism by the close of the ancient period is incorrect?
A. The primacy of Brahmanism was well-established.
B. A number of new religious path did appear including the extremists like Kapalikas, Kala mukhas and the followers of Tantricism.
C. Minansa and Vedanta were the twin pillars of Brahmanism.
D. Brahmanism continued to be youthful and vigorous.

232. Brahmanism did not believe in:
A. the sanctify of cast divisions.
B. the ascendency of Brahmans over other castes.
C. the Varnashrama System.
D. inter-dining and inter-marriages.

233. Brahmanism means:
A. Dominance of Brahmanas
B. Aryan Dravidian Synthesis
C. The metaphysics and the Puranas
D. The social, economic and religious life being integrated into one.

234. Vyuhavada is associated with:
A. military formations
B. an episode of the Mahabharta
C. Vaishnavism
D. Shaivism

235. The sacred thread which the Brahmanas wore was made of:
A. Silk B. Wool
C. Hemp D. Cotton

236. Pick out the correct match:
A. Brahmanical religion – Sacrifice
B. Bhagavatism – magical power
C. Jainism – devotion
D. Verjroyana – image workship

237. Which statement on Bhagavatism is incorrect?
A. There are reference to the worshippers of Vasudeva in the classical literature.
B. A "bhagavata" worshipped God Vasudeva in his 5-fold aspects – 'Para', 'Vyusha', 'Vibhava', 'Antaryamin', ard 'Arch'.
C. The author of the Gita says that Vasudeva was the same as Sankara the best of the Rudras – this shows definite attempts at a rapprochament between Saivism and Bhagavatism.
D. Christain religion, to a great extent influenced the growth of Bhagavatism.

238. Who said, "When religion declines and evidoers are to be destroyed, I shall be born at different periods"?
A. Buddha B. Mahavira
C. Rama D. Krishna

239. Which one of the following is the cause for reconciliation between Bhagavatism and Brahmanism?
A. Philosophy of Sankara.
B. Identification of Vishnu with Vasudeva Krishna.
C. Growth of image worship.
D. Believe in the devotional worship.

240. In which chronological order did the in-

carnations of lord Vishnu appear on the earth?
A. Fish, Tortoise, Varaha, Narasimha, Vamana
B. Fish, Tortoise, Narasimha, Varaha, Varmana
C. Tortoise, Fish, Varaha, Narasimha, Vamana
D. Fish, Tortoise, Varaha, Vamana, Narasimha.

241. Which one of the following kinds of devotion is primary devotion according to Bhagavatism?
A. Sattvika
B. Rajasa
C. Unmotivated and selfless devotion
D. Devotion of the distressed

242. Which of the following informed us that Bhagavatism first grew up around the Yamuna in Mathura district?
A. Strabo B. Megasthenes
C. Herodotus D. Pliny

243. Which statement on Brahmans is not correct?
A. Brahmans in corporated beliefs and teachings of others in order to strengthen their own position.
B. They recognised the popular heroes of other religions as incarnations of God.
C. Members of other cultures were given a social status without accepting them as Aryans.
D. Foreigners were not given any place in the caste structure.

244. Brahmanism came under criticism from Jainism on account of:
A. their practice of costly yajnas and rituals
B. laying stress that vedas were religious books.
C. their theory of Karma.
D. laying stress on fasts in religion.

245. Which of the following is incorrect?
A. Brahmanism believes in the theory of Karma.
B. Brahmanism does not reject animal sacrifices.
C. Brahmanism is opposed to Saivism.
D. Brahmanism believes in an universal God.

246. What is the central theme of the Upanishadas?
A. Karma
B. Nishkama Karma
C. Maya
D. Atman is Brahman and Brahman is Atman

247. The number of Vedangas is:
A. six B. five
C. four D. three

248. Which scriptures abound in the discussion and teaching of the early mystics?
A. Brahmans B. Upanishadas
C. Aranyakas D. Dharmasutras

249. The word 'Smhita' means:
A. Scripture
B. Oral tradition
C. Collection of hymns
D. Writing in Sanskrit

250. Two dynasties ..... Solar and Lunar ..... took birth from the soue of the:
A. 10th Manu B. 1st Manu
C. 11th Manu D. 9th Manu

251. The word 'Pathikrit' refers to:
A. Varuna B. Agni
C. Iron axe D. Bronze axe

252. The holy stream of Rig Vedic Period was:
A. Sarasavati B. Ganges
C. Indus D. Yamuna

253. The text of Brahmanical Hinduism is:
A. Rig veda B. Upanishadas
C. Manusmriti D. Samaveda

254. Which river is mentioned in the post-vedic literature?
A. Narmada B. Gomati
C. Vipasa D. Ganges

255. The Upnishadas are written in:
A. Verse
B. Prose
C. Verse, Prose and Verse Combined and Prose
D. Verse and Prose

256. The word 'Vedanta' is used for:
A. Upanishadas B. Vedangas

C. Brahmanas D. Aranyakas

257. The first 'Sutras' are:
A. Vedangas
B. Srauta, Grihya and Dharmasutras
C. Srauta
D. Dharmashastras

258. The Pandavas belonged to the clan of:
A. Kurus B. Panchalas
C. Bharatas D. Alinas

259. What is the total number of verses in the Mahabharta?
A. 100,000 B. 24,000
C. 50,000 D. 80,000

260. The term 'adikavya' refers to:
A. Mahabharta B. Rigveda
C. Ramayana D. Samaveda

261. The word 'Sutra' means:
A. thread B. shortest rule
C. formula D. All the three

262. Who was the Ist poet of India?
A. Valmiki B. Kalidas
C. Vyas D. Vasistha

263. What are the total numbers of verses in the Ramayana?
A. 100,000 B. 24,000
C. 50,000 D. 80,000

264. In whose ashrama did Sita live during her second exile?
A. Valmiki B. Visvamitra
C. Vashishta D. Vyas

265. The earliest extant book on the Dharmasastras is:
A. Narad Smiriti
B. Brihaspati Smiriti
C. Manusmiriti
D. None of the above

266. Who divided the vedas into four?
A. Vashishta B. Vyas
C. Visvamitra D. Valmiki

267. The word 'Puranas' means:
A. though ancient, yet new
B. old legend
C. old stories
D. none of the above

268. Which of the vedangas deals with Phonetics?
A. Siksha B. Vyakarana
C. Nirukta D. Chhandas

269. The scene that is depicted in the Ramayana in probability is:
A. Delhi-Meerut area
B. Western U.P.
C. Eastern U.P.
D. Western U.P.

270. How many times did Sita lives in exile?
A. one B. two
C. three D. four

271. Which book is at once a legal and religious treatise?
A. Ashtadhyayi
B. Manava Dharmashastra
C. Mahabhashya
D. Arthashastra

272. In which ancient literature was the flood legend first mentioned?
A. the Vedic Samhitas
B. the Brahmanas
C. the Aranyakas
D. the Upanishadas

273. In the field of Mathematics which one was known in the vedic period?
A. Pythagorean theorm
B. set rules for measurement
C. Zero
D. Algebra

274. Puranas are said to have been recited by the Suta lomahara Shana or his son known as:
A. Vyas
B. Ugrasravas
C. Virbhadra
D. Ugrasena

275. What are akin to real histories?
A. Puranas B. Vedas
C. Upanishadas D. Brahmanas

276. Puranas are written in:
A. Prophetic tone B. Sutra form
C. Poetry only D. Pali

277. Which writings constitute the first specimens of prose in the world?
A. Vedas B. Brahmanas
C. Aranyakas D. Upanishadas

ANSWERS

1	2	3	4	5	6	7	8	9	10
B	A	A	A	A	A	B	C	A	A
11	**12**	**13**	**14**	**15**	**16**	**17**	**18**	**19**	**20**
C	A	A	C	C	A	D	D	B	D
21	**22**	**23**	**24**	**25**	**26**	**27**	**28**	**29**	**30**
B	A	A	A	C	B	A	A	D	A
31	**32**	**33**	**34**	**35**	**36**	**37**	**38**	**39**	**40**
A	A	C	C	B	A	B	A	A	B
41	**42**	**43**	**44**	**45**	**46**	**47**	**48**	**49**	**50**
B	B	A	A	D	A	B	D	B	D
51	**52**	**53**	**54**	**55**	**56**	**57**	**58**	**59**	**60**
A	A	D	C	C	D	D	B	C	C
61	**62**	**63**	**64**	**65**	**66**	**67**	**68**	**69**	**70**
B	A	A	B	B	C	A	C	B	A
71	**72**	**73**	**74**	**75**	**76**	**77**	**78**	**79**	**80**
C	A	D	B	A	A	C	C	A	A
81	**82**	**83**	**84**	**85**	**86**	**87**	**88**	**89**	**90**
A	A	A	A	A	D	A	D	A	A
91	**92**	**93**	**94**	**95**	**96**	**97**	**98**	**99**	**100**
B	A	B	A	B	A	B	C	D	C
101	**102**	**103**	**104**	**105**	**106**	**107**	**108**	**109**	**110**
B	D	A	C	A	C	A	A	A	C
111	**112**	**113**	**114**	**115**	**116**	**117**	**118**	**119**	**120**
A	A	B	A	C	C	B	A	C	B
121	**122**	**123**	**124**	**125**	**126**	**127**	**128**	**129**	**130**
C	C	D	A	B	B	D	D	C	B
131	**132**	**133**	**134**	**135**	**136**	**137**	**138**	**139**	**140**
B	C	C	C	B	A	A	B	A	C
141	**142**	**143**	**144**	**145**	**146**	**147**	**148**	**149**	**150**
C	B	C	A	C	C	D	D	A	A
151	**152**	**153**	**154**	**155**	**156**	**157**	**158**	**159**	**160**
B	D	D	D	D	A	D	A	A	B
161	**162**	**163**	**164**	**165**	**166**	**167**	**168**	**169**	**170**
A	C	A	C	C	D	D	B	B	D
171	**172**	**173**	**174**	**175**	**176**	**177**	**178**	**179**	**180**
B	D	A	B	A	A	A	C	A	D
181	**182**	**183**	**184**	**185**	**186**	**187**	**188**	**189**	**190**
C	C	D	C	B	C	C	D	D	A
191	**192**	**193**	**194**	**195**	**196**	**197**	**198**	**199**	**200**
D	C	C	C	D	B	C	D	A	C
201	**202**	**203**	**204**	**205**	**206**	**207**	**208**	**209**	**210**
C	B	A	A	D	B	A	C	A	A

211	212	213	214	215	216	217	218	219	220
B	C	A	A	A	C	B	A	A	B
221	222	223	224	225	226	227	228	229	230
B	D	A	A	C	D	B	B	D	D
231	232	233	234	235	236	237	238	239	240
D	D	D	C	D	A	D	D	B	A
241	242	243	244	245	246	247	248	249	250
C	B	D	A	C	D	A	C	C	A
251	252	253	254	255	256	257	258	259	260
B	A	C	A	C	A	A	A	A	C
261	262	263	264	265	266	267	268	269	270
D	A	B	A	C	B	A	A	C	B
271	272	273	274	275	276	277			
B	A	B	B	A	A	B			

THE SANGAM AGE

1. Manimekalai is considered:
A. The idyllic of Tamil Poetry
B. The odyssey of Tamil Poetry
C. The Mahabharata of Tamil
D. The Ramayana of Tamil

2. The beginning of *civilized* communities in southern India was not because of one of the following. Identify.
A. The megalithic people moved from upland area into fertile river basins.
B. The coming of Jaina and Buddha missionaries made them aware of Northern material culture.
C. The history of early south India witnessed caste system of the northern type.
D. Roman contacts.

3. By how many Pandyan kings was the first Sangam patronised?
A. 89 B. 59
C. 49 D. 79

4. Which one of the following statements about the religious life of the Sangam age is not correct?
A. During the early Sangam age the Brahmanic vedic rituals had taken deep routs.
B. Chola kings patronised expensive sacrificial rituals.
C. The Samskaras, including the upnayan (Sacredthread ceremony) were not followed.
D. Amongst the higher classes (including merchants) marriages were solemnised according to the vedic rites.

5. There was an administrative unit under cholas name "Kuram". What did it mean?
A. A gram B. A tehsil
C. A district D. A group of village

6. The earliest Tamil literature is termed as Sangam literature because it was:
A. a joint creation of one school of scholars.
B. Patronized by the rulers of the Sangam dynasty.
C. Standralized by an academy (Sangam) of Scholars and poets maintained by Pandya rulers at Madurai.
D. Created at the Sangam of three South Indian rivers.

7. Contracts between northern Aryans and Tamils is conveyed in the tradition of:
A. Valmiki B. Agastya
C. Vishwamitra D. Vashishta

8. Sangam literature was written in:
A. Avadhi B. Tamil
C. Maithili D. Malayalam

9. The radiating point for civilization in the land south of Narmada was:
A. Godavari delta
B. Kaveri delta
C. Tungabhadra and Krisha region
D. Pannar river

10. Which one of the following is false with regard to the religious practices of the Sangam Age?
A. Banyan tree was considered to be the abode of God.
B. People worshipped the local God Murugan, who later came to be known as Subramaniam.
C. The kings performed vedic sacrifices.
D. The people had no faith in omens and astrology.

11. Where was the first Sangam held?
A. Madurai B. Kanchipuram
C. Mahabalipuram D. Kaveri Pattanam

12. The Sangam age dates back to:
A. 1200 BC – 1100 AD
B. 900 BC – 500 AD
C. 500 BC – 500 AD
D. 280 BC – 185 AD

13. Which Sangam work extols the virtuous wife?
A. Silapappadikaram
B. Manimekalai

C. Jivakachintamani
D. Kundala Kesi

14. The literature of the Sangam age was mostly in the form of :
A. Prose
B. Poetry
C. Drama
D. None of the above

15. Which one of the following statements on the Cheras is not correct?
A. The first Chera monarch Uidyanjeral was called Imayavaramban.
B. Their greatest ruler was San-u-Guttuven or Red Chera.
C. They used modified version of Tamil.
D. They were in alliance with the Pandyas.

16. Which one of the following statements regarding Sangam age is not correct?
A. Madurai is the Tamil word for Mathura.
B. Sangam literature is not logically connected.
C. Sangam literature refers to 2 or 3 Pandyan kings.
D. The chola kings patronized the Sangam poetry.

17. What is the acceptable date of the third Sangam?
A. 7th Century AD
B. 500 BC
C. 8th century AD
D. Ist three centuries of the Christian era.

18. Which among the following was not included as a seat of learning of the Sangams:
A. Kanchi B. Madurai
C. Mahabalipuram D. Kaveripattanam

19. What is the name of the Chola king who defeated the Pandya and Chera kings in the famous battle of Venni?
A. Karikala
B. Vijaya
C. Nendunjehyan
D. Tondaiaman Ilandiraiyan

20. Who was the king who formed the third Sangam?
A. Mudattiruraman
B. Ugrapperuvaludi
C. Nedunehelian
D. Kadungan

21. Which one of the following works belong to the third Sangam?
A. Pari Padal B. Kali
C. Gita Govinda D. Rajatarangini

22. Where did the second Sangam function from?
A. Madurai B. Puhar
C. Kapatapuram D. Kanchi

23. Which one of the following statement on the social life in the Sangam era is not correct?
A. The widows had to cut off their hair, discard all ornaments and eat only the plainest food.
B. Civil and military offices were held by the rich peasants called velalas.
C. Caste distinction existed.
D. Talkappiar calls the commercial community as vaisigas.

24. Which one of the following statement on Sangam literature is not correct?
A. It enables us to trace a connected political history of Tamil Kingdom
B. It sheds light on socio-religious aspects of Tamil-Kingdom.
C. It sheds light on trade relations with "Yavanas".
D. It sheds light on the pronounced fusion that had occurred between the Sanskrit and the Tamil culture.

25. Who wrote Talkappiyam?
A. Tolkappiyar B. Ravivarman
C. Kamban D. Deva Raya I

26. What find help us to determine the date of the third Sangam.
A. Arikkamedu B. Adichhanallur
C. Paiyampali D. Lothal

27. Pick-out the one which dose not go with the others:
A. Kuruntogai B. Ahananura
C. Paripadal D. Pattinappalai

28. Of the three Tamil monarchies of South India, the Pandyas occupied:
    A. the extreme south
    B. the Kaveri region
    C. western coastal strip
    D. undermarcated vast territories
29. The political and cultural centre of the Pandyas was:
    A. Vengi B. Madurai
    C. Kanchipuram D. Mahabalipuram
30. Which dynasty did not exist during the Sangam age?
    A. Chalukyas B. Chera
    C. Chola D. Pandya
31. For which line of rulers can we construct anything like a continuous geneology with the help of Sangam Literature?
    A. Cheras B. Pandyas
    C. Cholas D. Satyaputras
32. Which of the attributes does not refer the megalithic graves of Southern India?
    A. Graves were encircled by big pieces of stone.
    B. Alongwith the skeletons, objects of daily use were also buried.
    C. Arrowheads, spearheads, hoes and sickles were also found in the graves.
    D. The only iron implement found in the graves was the plough
33. Match three Sangams with the number of Pandyan Kings they were patronized:
    (a) First Sangam 1. 49
    (b) Second Sangam 2. 59
    (c) Third Sangam 3. 89

	(a)	*(b)*	*(c)*
A.	1	2	3
B.	3	2	1
C.	2	1	3
D.	3	1	2

34. Which statement on economic activity of ancient India projected the changing social life of the day?
    A. The Sangam poems often referred to Yavanas.
    B. The Greeks settle in large numbers at Kaveri-pattnam
    C. The foreigners, in course of time, were known as fallen Kashatriyas
    D. The presence of foreigners wielding political and economic power posed a threat to castesystem
35. Which one of the following statements on Sangam age is not corrected?
    A. Madurai, the capital city of Pandyas, was the centre of this literacy activity.
    B. The main function of the Sangam was to bring together the leading poets, scholars and thinkers for the creative and critical literary works.
    C. The term Sangam was popularised in the Tamilkam by the Jaina and Buddhist ascenities.
    D. The name of the North Indian Sage Agastya was not referred to in the Sangam Literature.
36. Which of the following works of the Sangam age is considered to be the greatest literary works of ancient Tamil Literature?
    A. Tolkappiyam
    B. Ettutogai (eight authologies)
    C. Perunga dai
    D. Muttollayiram
37. Which of the following statements about the maugram, the Sabha of this period, is not correct?
    A. It was the highest court of Justice.
    B. It was the comman meeting place in the village.
    C. According to rural, it was a general assembly dealing with all affairs.
    D. It served the purpose of political gathering.
38. Pick out the one which does not go with the others.
    A. Mullaippatu B. Nedunalvadai
    C. Paripadal D. Kurunjippattu
39. Match of the following works and groups to which they belong:
    (a) Narrinai 1. Epic
    (b) Maduraikanchi 2. Ettuthogoi
    (c) Thirukkural 3. Pathupattu
    (d) Silappadikaram 4. Padiven Kilkanakku Nool

	(a)	*(b)*	*(c)*	*(d)*
A.	2	3	4	1
B.	1	2	3	4
C.	3	2	1	4
D.	4	1	3	2

40. Match the following regions and the people who lived there:

(a) Marudam	1. Ayars
(b) Mullai	2. Kuravas
(c) Kurinji	3. Panadavars
(d) Neydal	4. Ulavars

Codes:

	(a)	*(b)*	*(c)*	*(d)*
A.	4	1	2	3
B.	1	2	3	4
C.	2	3	4	1
D.	3	4	1	2

41. Who was the president of the first Sangam?
A. Valmiki B. Vedavyas
C. Janaka D. Agastya

42. The last authology or group of Sangam literature known as, "Ten Idylls" is:
A. Kural B. Tolkappiyam
C. Pattupattu D. Manimekalai

43. In all, there were/was:
A. four Sangams B. three Sangams
C. two Sangams D. one Sangams

44. Among the following major epics of Tamil literature which one was produced during the age of the third Sangam?
A. Silappadikaram
B. Jinak Chintamani
C. Valayapti
D. Kundoolkeri

45. South Indians maintained a favourable trade with the Roman empire up to the:
A. 2nd Century A.D.
B. 3rd Century A.D.
C. 2nd Century A.D.
D. 3rd Century B.C.

46. The main items of export during Sangam was/were:
A. Medicinal herbs B. Pearls
C. Black peppar D. All the above

47. Primary items of import was/were:
A. Gold B. Wine
C. Horses D. All the above

48. What are the major epics of the Sangam age?
A. Silappadikaram, Manimekhalai, Jivakchintamani, Valayapati, Kundalakasi
B. Manimekhalai, Kavyam, Nalavenba
C. Naladiyar, Silappadikaram, Palamoli, Nilkasi
D. Pattinappalai, Nedunalvadai, Mullaiprathu

49. Which of the following was the great custom port and artificial harbour?
A. Paduca
B. Uraiyur
C. Puhar or Kaviripattinam
D. Tyndis

50. Which of the following was the important port of Eastern coast in the Sangam age?
A. Colchi B. Tyndis
C. Muziris D. Naura

51. What was the important port on the Western Coast in the Sangam, age?
A. Poduca B. Colchi
C. Balita D. Sopatma

52. Which of the following was a great centre of cotton trade?
A. Korkai B. Muziris
C. Balita D. Uraiyur

53. Which Roman wrote: "In no year does India draw our empire of less than five hundred and fifty millions of sesterces"?
A. Pliny B. Strabo
C. Justin D. Plutarch

54. On which of the following imports from India the Roman senate laid an embargo as it was a menace to the city's morals?
A. Saffron B. Wine
C. Pepper D. Muslin

55. The existence of the monsoon winds, blowing across the Indian ocean was discovered by:
A. Hippalus in 45 A.D.
B. Plutarch in 78 A.D.
C. Strabo in 56 B.C.
D. Pliny in 58 A.D.

56. The Tamil poetry in Sangam period was divided into two main groups, namely.
A. Palai and Mullani
B. Kurinji and Aham
C. Marudam and Puram
D. Agam and Puram

57. Match the following regions and their Gods:

(a) Marudam	1. Mayen		
(b) Mullai	2. Indran		
(c) Kurinji	3. Varuna		
(d) Neydal	4. Seyon		

Codes:

	(a)	*(b)*	*(c)*	*(d)*
A.	2	1	4	3
B.	1	2	3	4
C.	3	4	2	1
D.	4	3	1	2

58. Match the following regions and the occupation of the people who lived there.

(a) Marudam	1. Fishing
(b) Mullai	2. Cultivation
(c) Neydal	3. Hunting
(d) Kurinji	4. Rearing cattle and sheep

Codes:

	(a)	*(b)*	*(c)*	*(d)*
A.	2	4	1	3
B.	1	2	3	4
C.	3	4	2	1
D.	4	1	3	2

59. Who spoke of Pandya Kingdom being ruled by a woman in Sangam period?
A. Megasthenes B. Kautilya
C. Panini D. Patanjali

60. The greatest Pandya ruler was:
A. Nedunjeliyan B. Peruvaludi
C. Ilandiraiyan D. Mudikudumi

61. Which statement on the different ecotypes (tinai) refferred to in Sangam Literature is wrong:
A. The mountainous region (Kurinci) was the habitat of hunters and food gatherers like the tribes of the Kuruvars.
B. The tribes of herdsmen like the Ayar lived in the forest (mullai).
C. Robbers withdrew the barren land (Palai).
D. People made a living by fishing in the marutam area.

62. Karikala's greatest achivement was:
A. Victory over the Pandya and the Chera King at Venni
B. Conquest of Ceylon
C. Building of the city of Puhar at the mouth of Kaveri
D. Pioneering of the Grand Aricut at Srirangam.

63. Which of the statements on Sangam period is incorrect?
A. Monarchy was the prevalent form of Government.
B. The Tamil kings looked after their country like nurses tending children in their charge an ideal put before them by Ashoka the great.
C. "Chakravartin" ideal was dear to the Tamil Kings.
D. Brahmin advisers were not known to Tamil Kings.

64. What was the emblem of the Sangam-Cholas?
A. the tiger
B. the "Bow"
C. Eight-spoked wheel
D. Garuda

65. Two of the most recurring causes of warfare in Sangam period were:
1. Cattle lifting
2. refusal to give princesses in marriages
3. smuggling
4. family feuds

Codes:
A. 1 and 2 B. 1 and 3
C. 2 and 3 D. 4 and 1

66. Which one is supposed to be the fifth veda?
A. Trittondar Puranam
B. Akkatiyam
C. Jivak Chintamani
D. Tiru Kurul

67. Which of the statements regarding the art of warfare in Sangam period is incorrect.

A. Methods of fortification, and of assaulting and defending fortrsses appear to have been fairly well-developed

B. The traditional four-fold army-chariots, elephants, cavalry and infantry was in use.

C. Body armour made of tiger-skin was in use.

D. Women captured in war were-returned to their parents or husbands.

68. Match the following:

(a) Arikamedu	1. Broach
(b) Colchi	2. Korkai
(c) Tyndis	3. Panuai or Tondi
(d) Baryagaza	4. Cannanore
(e) Naura	5. Pondichery

Codes:

	(a)	*(b)*	*(c)*	*(d)*	*(e)*
A.	5	2	3	1	4
B.	5	3	2	4	1
C.	2	1	3	4	5
D.	5	3	4	2	1

69. Megasthenes refers to the rule of Heracles (Vasudeva Krishna's) daughter who was assigned villages to rule in Southern region, and who was probably the founder of Pandya kingdom. Identify her?

A. Pandia B. Panlavi
C. Maitri D. Pandara

70. Match the following:

(a) Puram	1. Pre-marital love
(b) Marudam	2. Post-marital love
(c) Kurinji	3. Marital heroism
(d) Mullai	4. The Lamentation of separated lovers
(e) Neydal	5. The wife's patient suffering during her lord's separation, longing for his returns

Codes:

	(a)	*(b)*	*(c)*	*(d)*	*(e)*
A.	4	3	2	1	5
B.	3	2	1	5	4
C.	2	3	1	4	5
D.	4	3	1	2	5

71. Say which is false among the following?

A. There were slave markets in Tamilkam in the Sangam age.

B. Kalingam was a famous variety of cotton cloth.

C. Bull fighting was a common pastime of the Sangam people.

D. Sangam people used tali as a symbol of marriage.

72. Pick out that which is false among the following:

A. Madalerudal was a practice connected with lovers

B. There was neither prohibition nor licensing of prostitution.

C. Pulippal tali was wrong as an ornament by boys and girls.

D. Sati was unknown to the Sangam people.

73. Pick out that which is correct.

A. Widows were permitted to remarry in the Sangam Age.

B. Sangam women had no right to choose their partners.

C. The wife was considered the luminary of the home.

D. Sangam women led a secluded life.

74. Match the following places and the cause of their fame:

(a) Kanchi	1. Cotton weaving
(b) Uraiyur	2. Silk weaving
(c) Korkai	3. Seat of Sangam
(d) Madurai	4. Port facilities

Codes:

	(a)	*(b)*	*(c)*	*(d)*
A.	2	1	4	3
B.	1	2	3	4
C.	3	4	2	1
D.	4	3	1	2

75. Match the following dynasties and the rulers to which they belong:

(a) Cholas	1. Gajabahu
(b) Cheras	2. Karikala
(c) Pandyas	3. Senguttuvan
(d) Ceylonese	4. Nedunchelian

Codes:

	(a)	(b)	(c)	(d)
A.	2	3	4	1
B.	1	2	3	4
C.	3	1	2	4
D.	4	2	1	3

76. Pick out that which is false:
A. Monarchy was the prevalent form of government among the Sangam people.
B. Succession was determined by the law of perimogeniture.
C. The king was assisted by ministers.
D. The Sangam works refer to the existence of Enberayan collective responsibility.

77. Match the following according to the author of the works:

(a) Nedunavadai	1. Kapilar
(b) Maduraikkanchi	2. Nathathanar
(c) Sirupanatruppadai	3. Maruthanas
(d) Kurinchippattu	4. Nakkirar

	(a)	(b)	(c)	(d)
A.	4	3	2	1
B.	4	3	1	2
C.	3	1	2	4
D.	1	2	3	4

78. Which one of the following Tamil Kings have sent the earliest embassy, (According to strabo) which was met by Augustus at Athens about 20 B.C.?
A. A Chola King B. A Chera King
C. A Pandya King D. A Pallave King

79. Which of the following kings made a grand anicut on the Kaveri, the water of which is now-a-days drawn off through a new channel called vennar?
A. Karikala B. Peruvaludi
C. Ilandiraiyan D. Nendunjeliyan

80. Which one of the following Chera king is the brother of Ilango, the author of the Sangam epic "Silappadikaram"?
A. Nedunjeral B. Karikala
C. Nedunjjelian D. Senuguttuvan

81. What are the "ma" and "vedi" in Sangam period?
A. The taxes of the period
B. The coinage of the time
C. The measures of land
D. The words for love and war.

82. The division of Sangam society was made according to the region of the Tamil land to which the poem referred. Match the Tamil words with the regions they are associated with:

(a) Palai	1. The jungle and wood land
(b) Mullai	2. The hills
(c) Kurinji	3. The dry lands
(d) Neydal	4. The Coast
(e) Marudam	5. The cultivated plains

	(a)	(b)	(c)	(d)	(e)
A.	3	1	2	5	4
B.	3	1	5	2	4
C.	2	3	1	4	5
D.	2	1	3	4	5

83. Which one the following is NOT the meaning of the word Karikala?
A. 'the man with the charred leg'
B. 'death to Kali'
C. 'death to the enemy (elephants)'
D. 'Incarnation of death (Jama)'

84. Who were the first to establish their ascendency in the south?
A. Cholas B. Pandyas
C. Cheras D. Satyaputras

85. Who had a mastery of the seven notes of Music?
A. Samudragupta B. Harsha
C. Karikala D. Chandragupta II

86. Basic objects of the conflict among the three Sangam kingdoms were:
1. Control over the fertile deltas.
2. access to the important trading stations along the coasts.
3. desire to become Chakravartin Kings i.e. digvijaya.
4. desire to increase the number of woman folk thus increase in population.

Codes:

A. only 1 and 2 B. only 2 and 3
C. only 3 and 4 D. only 2 and 4

87. What was the Capital of the Sangam Chera?
A. Vanji B. Madurai
C. Uraiyur D. Trichaurapolli

88. What was the Capital of the Chera King Nedunjeral Adam?
A. Marandai B. Saliyar
C. Kaveripattinam D. Ponnai

89. Indentify the ceylonese king who was a contemporary of the Chera king Senguttuvan and who was present in the Chera kingdom at the time of the establishment of the Pattini cult by the latter.
A. Gajabahu B. Paranar
C. Tissa D. Meghavarman

90. Who among the Chera monarchs is said to have fed sumptuonsly both the armies at Kurukshetra?
A. Udiyanjeral
B. Nedunjeral Adam
C. Senguttuvan
D. Anduvan

91. Who among the chera monarchs took the lead in organising the cult of Pattini, the Divine chaste wife, and was supported in his effort by the centemporary rulers of the Pandya and Chola countries and of Ceylon?
A. Senguttuvan
B. Udiyanjeral
C. Nedunjeral Adam
D. Anduvan

92. Which of the statements on the social life in the Sangam era is NOT correct?
A. Civilian and military offices were held by the rich peasants called vallalars.
B. Agriculture was carried out by lower class women.
C. There were several outcastes.
D. Caste distinctions existed.

93. Which of the statements on Sangam people is incorrect?
A. They used starch for stiffening clothes.
B. Their children wore necklaces of tiger teeth.
C. They enjoyed the eating of betel leaves with nuts.
D. Only women wore ornaments.

94. Which of the statements on "Sangam" woman is incorrect:
A. Women enjoyed much freedom of movement in Society.
B. 'Sati' system was much disliked.
C. The lot of widows was hard.
D. Widows preferred "Sati" to widowhood

95. The most important industry in Sangam period was:
A. raising of sugar cane
B. raising of pepper
C. production of cloth
D. arms manufacturing

96. Match the following:

(a) Baryagaze	1. Broach
(b) Naura	2. Cannanore or Mangalore
(c) Tyndis	3. Korkai
(d) Arikamedu	4. Pondicherry
(e) Colchi	5. Ponnani or Tondi

	(a)	*(b)*	*(c)*	*(d)*	*(e)*
A.	1	2	5	4	3
B.	1	2	3	4	5
C.	3	1	2	5	4
D.	4	3	1	2	5

97. Match the following:

(a) Camara	1. Pondicherry
(b) Poduca	2. Chaul
(c) Semylia	3. Cranganore
(d) Muziris	4. Kaveripatinam

	(a)	*(b)*	*(c)*	*(d)*
A.	4	1	2	3
B.	1	2	3	4
C.	3	4	1	2
D.	2	3	4	1

98. Match the names of the Sangam ports with their new or other names given in the second column.

(a) Balita	1. Verkalai
(b) Poduca	2. Pondicherry Arikamedu
(c) Sopatma	3. Markanam
(d) Camara	4. Kaveripattinam

	(a)	(b)	(c)	(d)
A.	1	2	3	4
B.	2	3	4	1
C.	3	4	1	2
D.	4	1	2	3

99. The Tamil name of the Vishnu is:
A. Tirumala B. Virkal
C. Subramaniam D. Skanda

100. Who was euraged widow who caused the destruction of the city of Madurai by plucking off her breast and hurling it over the town?
A. Kannagi B. Madhavi
C. Sita D. Savitri

101. "Pattni Cult" is associated with:
A. Kannagi B. Madhavi
C. Manimekalai D. None of them

102. The Golden Age in Tamil Literature is associated with:
A. Third Sangam era
B. Second Sangam era
C. First Sangam era
D. Second Century A.D.

103. Manime Kaloi, an epic in Tamil Literature, deals with:
A. the vicissitudes of a woman
B. a parable
C. a historical event
D. a contemporary king and Manimekalai

104. Match the following dynasties and their rulers and their seats of power.

(a) Cholas	1. Kodunkunram
(b) Pandyas	2. Uraiyur
(c) Pari	3. Vanji (Karuvur)
(d) Cheras	4. Madurai

	(a)	(b)	(c)	(d)
A.	2	4	1	3
B.	1	2	3	4
C.	3	1	2	4
D.	4	3	2	1

105. Match the following rulers and their achievements:

(a) Nedunchelian	1. Patran of Kapilar
(b) Karikala	2. Building a temple to Pattini Devi
(c) Senguttuvan	3. Victor of the battle of Talaiyalanganam
(d) Pari	4. Victor of the battle of venni

	(a)	(b)	(c)	(d)
A.	3	4	2	1
B.	2	1	3	4
C.	1	2	4	3
D.	4	3	1	2

106. Which among the following was a great centre of Jainism?
A. Kanchipuram B. Korkai
C. Puhar D. Muziri

107. Which among the following was a great centre of Buddhism in the Sangam period?
A. Vanji B. Tondi
C. Kaveripattanam D. Korkai

108. Which among the following is false?
A. Sangam people worshipped Nadukal
B. Sangam people worshipped Nature
C. Image worship was prevalent among the Sangam people
D. The Tamils did not perform Yagyas or great sacrifices.

109. Which two of the Rock Edicts of Ashoka mention the southern kingdoms Cholas, Pandyas, Satiyaputra, Keralaputra and Ceylon?
A. Third and Tenth
B. Second and Thirteenth
C. Six and Nineth
D. Fourth and fourteenth

110. The Romans, trading with Sangam kingdoms built a temple of Angustus at one of the following places. What is the name of the place?
A. Arikamedu B. Muziris
C. Nelcynda D. Naura

111. Which one of the following Sangam towns was famous for its pearls and muslins, the latter being as thin as the skin of the snake?
A. Uraiyur B. Muziris
C. Arikamedu D. Puhar

112. Identify the chera monarch who was called Imaya Varamban – "He who had the Himalaya for his boundary and who carved the chera emblem of the bow on the face of the great mountain."
A. Kuttuvan

B. Udaiyajeral
C. Nedunjeral Adan
D. Senguttuvan

113. The first historical reference to Tamils or Pandyas occurs in the work inscriptions of:
A. Megasthenes B. Periplus
C. Kautilya D. Ashoka

114. Which statement on Sangam history is incorrect?
A. Vishnu worship with Tulsi was popular among the Sangam people
B. The Sangam people did not worship Siva Balram and Krishna
C. Vedic religious of sacrifices was followed by the Sangam kings.
D. Buddhism and Jainism found a footing in the land of Sangam people.

115. Which statement of Karikala is incorrect?
A. He defeated the ceylonese and captured 12000 prisoners and put them to work at puhar, a seaport at the mouth of Kaveri.
B. He had the Grand Ancient Srirangam built, thus controlling the waters of the Kaveri at the head of the delta.
C. He patonized brahmanical religion and Tamil Literature.
D. He was defeated at the battle of venni.

116. Which one of the following was the correct Tamil designation of the ministers during the Sangam Age?
A. Surram B. Amaichehar
C. Mautri D. Amatya

117. After the death of which one of the following Roman Kings, the trade was conducted more by barter then by coins on account of the financial difficulties of the Roman Empire?
A. Pius B. Angustur
C. Nero D. Claudium

118. Identify the great poet who was contemporary of the Chola King Karikaral and the Chera King Senguttuvan.
A. Parnar B. Akkatiyar
C. Gajabahu D. Kalipar

119. Match the Tamil words with their meaning:

(a) Enadi	1. Captains of the army
(b) Malavar	2. Low class artisans
(c) Eyinar	3. Hunters
(d) Kalabhras	4. Evil rulers
(e) Pulaiyans	5. Robbers

Codes:

	(a)	*(b)*	*(c)*	*(d)*	*(e)*
A.	1	5	3	4	2
B.	1	2	3	4	5
C.	2	1	3	5	4
D.	1	5	4	3	2

120. What was the inland capital of the Sangam Cholas?
A. Tanjore B. Kaveripattanam
C. Trichaurapoli D. Uraiyur

121. "Ten Tens" deal mostly with the history of:
A. the Cheras B. the Cholas
C. the Satyaputras D. the Pandyas

122. The "Ten Tens" is the other name of:
A. Padidrupattu
B. Pattupattu
C. Ettuthokai
D. Padineukilkannku

123. Silapadikaram, the Tamil epic, written by Ilango literally means:
A. the jewelled anklet
B. the fair lady
C. the determined women
D. the chaste wife

124. One of the following is the most ancient language of India. Indentify?
A. Hindi B. Tamil
C. Malayalam D. Bengali

125. Who was the author of Tiruttondar-Puranam?
A. Sekkilar
B. Sittalai
C. Tiruthakkathevar
D. Agastya

126. Which one is supposed to be the fifth veda?
A. Trittondar-puranam
B. Tiru Kurul

C. Jivakchintamani
D. Akkatiyam

127. One statement on Cholas, Cheras and Pandyas of Sangam period is not correct. Identify:
A. The words for rice, ginger and cinnamon were borrowed from Tamil language
B. Puhar was the capital built by Karikala
C. They imported horses
D. The foot-soldiers went bare-footed

128. Tank was known in South India as:
A. eripatti B. talals
C. veli D. tinci

ANSWERS

1	**2**	**3**	**4**	**5**	**6**	**7**	**8**	**9**	**10**
B	C	A	B	D	C	B	B	B	D
11	**12**	**13**	**14**	**15**	**16**	**17**	**18**	**19**	**20**
A	C	A	B	D	D	D	D	A	A
21	**22**	**23**	**24**	**25**	**26**	**27**	**28**	**29**	**30**
A	C	D	A	A	A	D	A	B	A
31	**32**	**33**	**34**	**35**	**36**	**37**	**38**	**39**	**40**
A	D	A	D	D	B	D	C	D	A
41	**42**	**43**	**44**	**45**	**46**	**47**	**48**	**49**	**50**
D	C	B	A	A	D	D	A	C	A
51	**52**	**53**	**54**	**55**	**56**	**57**	**58**	**59**	**60**
C	D	A	D	A	D	A	A	A	A
61	**62**	**63**	**64**	**65**	**66**	**67**	**68**	**69**	**70**
C	D	D	A	A	D	D	A	A	B
71	**72**	**73**	**74**	**75**	**76**	**77**	**78**	**79**	**80**
D	D	C	A	A	D	A	C	A	D
81	**82**	**83**	**84**	**85**	**86**	**87**	**88**	**89**	**90**
C	A	D	A	C	A	A	A	A	A
91	**92**	**93**	**94**	**95**	**96**	**97**	**98**	**99**	**100**
A	D	D	B	C	A	A	A	A	A
101	**102**	**103**	**104**	**105**	**106**	**107**	**108**	**109**	**110**
A	D	D	A	A	A	C	D	B	B
111	**112**	**113**	**114**	**115**	**116**	**117**	**118**	**119**	**120**
A	C	A	B	D	B	C	A	A	A
121	**122**	**123**	**124**	**125**	**126**	**127**	**128**		
A	A	A	B	A	B	D	A		

MAURYAN EMPIRE

1. What is pranaya?
A. benevolences B. forced labour
C. marriage rites D. prayer

2. The officer-in-charge of survey and settlements under Ashoka were:
A. Dharma Mahamatya
B. Samahartas
C. Rajukas
D. Prati-Vedakas

3. Which statement on Arthasastra is not correct?
A. The Arthasastra devised the manufacture of liquor in government controlled breweries and gave several brief and cryptic recipes.
B. It suggests the appointment of a superintendent of liquor to control the scale of alcoholic drinks and also organise their manufacture.
C. Tavernkeepers should be instructed to make their establishment well furnished and comfortable.
D. It does not recognise drinking as an evil.

4. Who was Samaharta?
A. Collector General
B. Treasurer
C. Auditor General
D. Magistrate

5. The first to issue the coins in India were:
A. the Greeks
B. the Mauryas
C. the Janapadas
D. the Nandas

6. During whose time differences arose between the King and the Parishad in the Mauryan period?
A. Chandragupta Maurya
B. Samprati
C. Ashoka
D. Bindusara

7. What was the copper coin of Mauryan times?
A. Mashaka B. Nishka
C. Suvarna D. Pana

8. Among the virtues of royalty, Kautilya accords first place to:
A. danda-niti
B. practice of Dharma
C. self control
D. clan

9. Which one of the following group of people were not exempt from taxes in the Mauryan period?
A. Brahmins B. Hermits
C. Generals D. Priests

10. Which one is not a division of the provinces in the Mauryan period?
A. Janapadas B. Pradeshes
C. Ahars D. Vigitas

11. What was the standard of Mauryan times?
A. Pana B. Mashaka
C. Nishka D. Suvarna

12. What was the language of administration in Mauryan times?
A. Prakrit B. Sanskrit
C. Ardhamagadhi D. Kharoshti

13. What was the other name that used for the Parishad in the Mauryan period?
A. Sabha
B. Rajyasabha
C. Mantri Prishad
D. Pratinidhis

14. What is Vishti?
A. benevolences B. forced labour
C. marriage rites D. a district

15. What is Kara?
A. forced labour
B. a special harsh tax
C. benevolences
D. a bangle

16. During the Mauryan period committees were set up in administration which ones?
1. Military
2. Municipal Corporations
3. Provincial administration
4. Village administration

Codes:

A. 1 and 2 only B. 1, 2 and 3 only
C. 1, 2 and 4 only D. 2 and 3 only

17. The term 'ahara' as an administrative united appears in:
A. Arthasastra
B. Ashokan inscriptions
C. Rig Veda
D. Epics

18. Match the officers with their functions:

(a) Samaharta	1.	Chief Collector
(b) Sannidhata	2.	Chief Treasurer
(c) Sandhivigrahika	3.	Minister of Peace and war
(d) Pradvivaka	4.	Chief Judge
(e) Uparka	5.	Governor
(f) Rajjuka	6.	Land Surveyor or revenue officer

Codes:

	(a)	*(b)*	*(c)*	*(d)*	*(e)*	*(f)*
A.	1	2	3	4	6	5
B.	1	2	6	3	5	4
C.	1	3	2	4	5	6
D.	1	2	3	4	5	6

19. In which of the following do we find the rates of interest and regulations governing debt and mortgages for example the sliding scale of interest according to the caste of debtor.
A. Panini's Asthtadhayayi
B. Arthasastra
C. Indica
D. Epics

20. The Arthasastra for the first time gives enormous importance to:
A. Political state craft
B. Diplomacy
C. Origin of kingship
D. Regulation of economic activity

21. Which statement on Mauryan architecture is not correct?
A. Mauryan stone-building were modelled on wooden original.
B. Megasthenes mentions that the palace of Chandragupta Maurya was built of carved and gilded wood.
C. It was during Ashoka's reigon that stone in buildings was used on a greater scale.
D. Mauryan architectural traditions contained for long of India.

22. In the times of emergency, peasants in the Mauryan period were compelled to:
A. Raise more crops
B. Join the army
C. Pay more taxes
D. None of the above

23. Punishment was severe during the reign of the:
A. Mauryas B. Guptas
C. Sungas D. Chalukyas

24. Which edicts of Ashoka are sometimes called 'separate rock edicts'?
A. The two Kalinga Edicts
B. The Minor Rock Edicts
C. The Edicts at Shahbazgarhi and Mansehra
D. None of the above

25. Arthasastra, composed by Kautilya, is a treatise on:
A. Economics B. Polity
C. Commerce D. Numismatics

26. Which Ashokan Pillar bears the figure of a peacock, pointing to the association of Mauryan with it?
A. Nandangarh B. Sarnath
C. Allahabad D. Rummindei

27. To what primary cause would you assign the responsibility for the decline of Mauryan empire after Ashoka?
A. Pacifism of Ashoka
B. Over centralisation
C. Economic crisis
D. Brahmanical reaction after Ashoka's death

28. Which factor or forces strengthened and supported most the imperial system of the Mauryas?
1. a settled agrarian village economy
2. improvement in trade
3. trade with the Roman World
4. material advancement of the Vaisyas

Codes:

A. only 1 and 2 B. only 1, 2 and 3
C. all the four D. only 1, 2 and 4

29. "In the happiness of the subjects lay his happiness and in their troubles lay his troubles." In which book does the statement appears?
A. Indica B. Arthasastra
C. Mudra Rakshasa D. Mritcmakatika

30. Who is described as the Indian Machiavelli?
A. Bimbisara B. Chanakya
C. Bana D. Kalidasa

31. Which one of the following was not a function of the Parishad in the Mauryan period:
A. To keep a check on the whole of administrative system.
B. To implement the king's orders.
C. To keep a watch on the conduct of wars.
D. To decide matters in the absence of the kings.

32. Chandragupta Maurya was:
A. an autocrat
B. a statesman
C. a liberal
D. an enlightened despot

33. The most reliable source for fixing the date of Ashoka is:
A. Ceylonese Chronicles
B. Pali Canon
C. Indika
D. Rock Edicts

34. Who said this "All Indians were free and none of them was a slave". (In Mauryan age):
A. Strobo B. Pliny
C. Justin D. Arrian

35. Chandragupta belonged to the Moriya tribe of:
A. Brahmanas B. Kshatriyas
C. Vaishyas D. Shudra

36. Who said " Indians do not know the art of writing"?
A. Kautilya B. Pliny
C. Megasthenes D. Plutarch

37. Which one of the following is considered to be a controversial part of the treaty of 303 B.C. between Chandragupta and Seleucus?
A. Seleucus surrendered a large territory including, according to some historians' Paropanisadia (Kabul), Aria (Herat); Archosia (Quandhar) and Gedrosia (Baluchistan).
B. Chandragupta made a gift of 500 elephants to Seleucus.
C. Seleucus gave his daughter in marriage to Chandragupta
D. A Greek envoy (Megasthenes) was accredited to the Mauryan Court at Pataliputra.

38. Among the following, which one is false. Indentify?
A. Chandragupta Maurya concluded a favourable treaty with the Greeks.
B. Chandragupta became a Jain.
C. Chandragupta got the help of Alexander.
D. Chankya assisted Chandragupta in winning Magadha.

39. "All Indians are free and not one of them is a slave"? who said?
A. Itsing B. Fahien
C. Megasthenes D. Huein Tsang

40. Who conquered Deccan?
A. Ashoka B. Dasratha
C. Samprati D. Bindusara

41. Chandragupta Maurya liberated one of the following parts of India from Seleucus. Which one was that?
A. North-Western B. South-Western
C. South-Eastern D. Western

42. Where is the Lomasa Rishi Cave?
A. Barabar Area B. Ellora
C. Bhaja D. Amaravati

43. After abdication, Chandragupta Maurya probably left for:
A. Modern Andhra Pradesh
B. The white Jain tank
C. Chandragiri Hills
D. The modern City of Chikmagalur

44. Chandragupta Maurya defeated Seleucus

in 305 B.C. and presented him:
A. 500 war elephants
B. 50 war elephants
C. 100 war elephants
D. 200 war elephants

45. Which point on the imperial palace of Chandragupta Maurya is not correct?
A. It was close to the modern village of Kumaharahar.
B. It was designed in inmitation of the Persian palace at Persepolis.
C. The gilded pillars were adorned with golden vines and silver birds.
D. It has a natural cooling system.

46. Who said this? "The Buddha would have made a good general if he had not become a monk".
A. Charles Eliot B. Vincent Smith
C. Rhys Davids D. Romila Thapar

47. Who was Justin?
A. A Greek Poet
B. Greek Writer
C. Greek Philosopher
D. A Greek King

48. According to Kautilya, King:
A. Should be highly educated
B. Should be a person of integrity
C. Should save himself from hist, anger, greed etc.
D. All the above.

49. Who were described as the Pancharatrikas?
A. Bhagavatas B. Pasupatas
C. Digumbaras D. Hinayanists

50. Which among the following is the incorrect match?
A. Chandragupta — Vrishala
B. Bindusara — Amitraghata
C. The Nandas — Kulahinas
D. Mahavira — Arihant

51. Whom did Ashoka send to conduct missionary work in Ceylon?
A. Mahendra B. Aniruddha
C. Mahanaman D. Jamali

52. Who founded Mauryan dynasty?
A. Chanakya
B. Chandragupta Maurya
C. Ashoka
D. None of the above

53. According to Brahmanical tradition Chandragupta Maurya was born of:
A. Sudra Woman
B. Brahman Woman
C. Kshatriya Woman
D. Vaishya Woman

54. About the qualities of the ministers Kautilya lays down that they should be:
A. Men of high character
B. Loyal
C. Wise and brave
D. All the above

55. Which was not responsible for Chandragupta's success?
A. Kautilya's guidance
B. Brilliant generalship
C. Greek aid
D. Weakness of the Nanda ruler

56. Who was Sandrokottos?
A. Chandragupta B. Dasarath
C. Ashoka D. Amitraghata

57. What is the number of Vrishiniviras?
A. Five B. Three
C. Ten D. Four

58. Who said that the Indians did not drink (liquor) in the age of Mauryas?
A. Megasthenes B. Arrian
C. Strabo D. Pliny

59. Who was the author of Indica?
A. Kautilya B. Seleucus
C. Ashoka D. Megasthenes

60. Which God was called Herakles by the Greeks:
A. Krishna B. Indra
C. Rudra D. Brahma

61. One of the following occupations was not common between the Sudras and Vaishyas in the Mauryan period:
A. agriculture B. rearing cattle
C. trade D. teaching

62. "The evil of evils is the poverty of the people", who said this?
A. Mahavir B. Buddha
C. Megasthenes D. Kautilya

63. For how many years did Megasthenes stay in India?
A. Two B. Five

C. Ten D. Fourteen

64. Which of the following was not a part of Chandragupta's Empire?
A. Kashmir B. Kathiawar
C. Kalinga D. Afghanistan

65. Metals most frequently used during Chandragupta reign in minting the coins, were:
A. Gold and Silver
B. Silver and Copper
C. Copper and Bronze
D. Gold and Copper

66. Ashoka's coronation took place in:
A. 261 BC B. 273 BC
C. 264 BC D. 250 BC

67. When did Chandragupta Maurya ascend the Throne?
A. 321 BC B. 322 BC
C. 323 BC D. 324 BC

68. Punishment was severe during the reign of the:
A. Mauryas B. Guptas
C. Sungas D. Chalukyas

69. Who wrote "Mudrarakshasa"?
A. Kautilya B. Megasthenes
C. Vishakhadatta D. Vishnu Sharma

70. Which inscriptions mention the pilgrimages of the emperor to the holy places of Buddhism?
A. Major Rock Edicts
B. Bhabru Edicts
C. Cave inscriptions
D. Rummindei and Nigliva

71. Under the Mauryan administration:
A. Pataliputra was the capital
B. Administration was carried on by six committees
C. Each committee consisting of five members
D. All are correct

72. The espionage system was very extensive under:
A. Mauryas B. Cholas
C. Cheras D. Priest

73. Who was the first ruler of the world to issue a no war declaration?
A. Chandragupta Maurya
B. Alexander
C. Seleucus
D. Ashoka

74. Who was Chandragupta's successor?
A. Bindusara B. Ashoka
C. Dasratha D. Bimbisara

75. Where did Chandragupta Maurya met Alexander?
A. Greece
B. Magadha
C. Punjab
D. None of the above

76. The key note of Ashoka's policy of Dhamma was:
A. Charity B. Kindness
C. Self Control D. Moderation

77. Who is the first Indian king to speak directly to the people through his inscriptions:
A. Chandragupta Maurya
B. Bindusara
C. Ashoka
D. Dhana Nanda

78. Which was the most important city under Chandragupta Maurya?
A. Pataliputra B. Kausambi
C. Ujjain D. Taxila

79. The administrative system of Chandragupta consisted of:
A. Autonomous king
B. Decentralisation
C. Centralised bureaucracy
D. Mantri Prishad that had the right to over rule King's decision.

80. The palace of Chandragupta was constructed of:
A. Brick B. Stone
C. Wood D. Mud

81. Which religion did Chandragupta Maurya adopted during last year of his reign?
A. Hinduism B. Jainism
C. Buddhism D. Bhagavatism

82. When did Alexander die:
A. 320 BC B. 321 BC
C. 322 BC D. 323 BC

83. During whose reign did the Buddhist Church underwent recognisation?
A. Chandragupta Maurya
B. Bindusara

C. Ashoka
D. Dasratha

84. The Kalinga war was fought in:
A. 261 BC B. 273 BC
C. 218 AD D. 288 AD

85. Who was the last Mauryan King?
A. Bindusara B. Kanishka
C. Ashoka D. Dasratha

86. Who was the immediate heirs of what remained of the Mauryan empire?
A. Shungas B. Chalukyas
C. Huns D. Rashtrakutas

87. Image worship started during the Maurya Period among:
A. The Hindus
B. The Buddhist
C. The Jains
D. None of the above

88. Who has described the killer of Brihadratha as anarya?
A. Kalhana B. Bana
C. Kautilya D. Visakadatta

89. What was the strong hold of the Digambaras?
A. Gujarat B. Rajasthan
C. Karnataka D. Kathiawar

90. One of the following occupations was not common between the Sudras and Vaisyas in the Mauryan period:
A. agriculture B. rearing cattle
C. trade D. teaching

91. Match the coins with the dynasties which issued them:

(a) Mauryas	1. Silver, Karshapana, Gold, Suvrana
(b) Indo-Bactrian	2. Silver Pana, Ardha Pana, Pada
(c) Satavahnas	3. Gold Double dinara
(d) Kushans	4. Gold stalor, Silver tetradrachm and didrachm
(e) Guptas	5. Gold Suvarna

Codes:

	(a)	*(b)*	*(c)*	*(d)*	*(e)*
A.	2	4	1	3	5
B.	1	2	3	4	5
C.	2	4	1	5	3
D.	4	1	3	2	5

92. The earliest evidence of the practice of Sati dated 510 A.D. is from the:
A. Aihole Inscription
B. Airan Inscription
C. Nasik Inscription
D. Hathigumpha Inscription

93. Who was the author of Kalpasutra?
A. Bhadrabahu B. Panini
C. Subandhu D. Patanjali

94. To whom does Hathigumpha inscription of Orissa belong?
A. Ashoka B. Bindusara
C. Kanishka D. Kharavela

95. One of the following places was not noted for fine cotton fabrics in Mauryan times. Identify.
A. Varanasi B. Vanga
C. Madurai D. Karle

96. Which among the following was used in most of Ashoka's inscriptions?
A. Kharoshti B. Armaic
C. Brahmi D. Greek

97. Who was the first Shaka King in India?
A. Pushyamitra
B. Moga
C. Menander
D. None of the above

98. Who came to India in search of the great wealth of knowledge and literature in ancient times?
A. Sakas B. Greeks
C. Parthians D. Chinese

99. In which of the three Pitakas are the Jatakas included?
A. Sutta B. Vinaya
C. Abhidhamma D. None of these

100. Which among the following was not a seat of learning during the age of the Maurya?
A. Patliputra B. Taxila
C. Ujjain D. Varanasi

101. Which among the following was the coin of Silver used during the rule of the Mauryas?
A. Pana B. Masaki
C. Kakam D. None of the above

102. Who issued the gold coins first:
A. Mauryas B. Nandas
C. Indo-Bactrian D. Kushans

103. The author of the Mahabhasya was:
A. Bhassa B. Katyayana

C. Vakpati D. Patanjali

104. Jaina caves are found at:
A. Udayagiri B. Negarjuni hills
C. Barabar hills D. Elephanta

105. Which one of the following was paid in cash:
A. Bali B. Bhaga
C. Kara D. Hiranya

106. Which is the Birth place of the Buddha?
A. Kapilavastu B. Pava
C. Kusimagara D. Lumbini

107. Which of the Mauryan rulers had caused caves to be hewn in Barabar hills?
A. Ashoka B. Chandragupta
C. Brihadratha D. Jalanka

108. Which was not responsible for Chandragupta's success?
A. Kautilya's guidance
B. Brilliant generalship
C. Greek aid
D. Weakness of the Nanda rulers

109. Name which of the following rulers followed Mahayanism?
A. Ajatasatru B. Kanishka
C. Ashoka D. None of these

110. Which one of the Mauryan rulers was condemned by the Puranic writers?
A. Gunala B. Brihadratha
C. Dasratha D. Salisuka

111. At which council was the canon of the Sutta Pitaka settled?
A. Second Buddhist Council
B. First Buddhist Council
C. Third Buddhist Council
D. Fourth Buddhist Council

112. Which writer gives 600,000 as the number of foot soldiers in the Mauryan army?
A. Pliny B. Plutarch
C. Strabo D. Justin

113. Which of the following was not a part of Chandragupta's empire?
A. Kashmir B. Kathiawar
C. Kalinga D. Afghanistan

ANSWERS

1	**2**	**3**	**4**	**5**	**6**	**7**	**8**	**9**	**10**
A	C	C	A	C	A	A	C	C	D
11	**12**	**13**	**14**	**15**	**16**	**17**	**18**	**19**	**20**
A	A	C	B	B	A	B	D	B	D
21	**22**	**23**	**24**	**25**	**26**	**27**	**28**	**29**	**30**
D	A	A	A	B	A	B	A	B	B
31	**32**	**33**	**34**	**35**	**36**	**37**	**38**	**39**	**40**
C	D	D	D	B	C	C	C	C	D
41	**42**	**43**	**44**	**45**	**46**	**47**	**48**	**49**	**50**
A	A	C	A	D	A	B	D	A	C
51	**52**	**53**	**54**	**55**	**56**	**57**	**58**	**59**	**60**
A	B	A	D	C	A	A	A	D	A
61	**62**	**63**	**64**	**65**	**66**	**67**	**68**	**69**	**70**
D	D	B	C	B	B	D	A	C	D
71	**72**	**73**	**74**	**75**	**76**	**77**	**78**	**79**	**80**
D	A	D	A	C	D	C	A	C	C
81	**82**	**83**	**84**	**85**	**86**	**87**	**88**	**89**	**90**
B	D	C	A	D	A	D	B	C	D
91	**92**	**93**	**94**	**95**	**96**	**97**	**98**	**99**	**100**
A	B	A	D	D	C	B	D	A	A
101	**102**	**103**	**104**	**105**	**106**	**107**	**108**	**109**	**110**
A	D	D	A	D	D	A	C	B	D
111	**112**	**113**							
B	A	C							

PRE-GUPTA AND GUPTA PERIOD

1. During the pre-Gupta age, the foreign trade was most extensive with:
   A. China
   B. Roman Empire
   C. South-East Asian Countries
   D. Central Asia
2. What was the name of South Indian Money Lenders?
   A. Seths B. Banjaras
   C. Chettis D. Panis
3. What is not true about the functions of guilds?
   A. Organization of production.
   B. Guilds controlled the prices of manufactured articles.
   C. Guilds were politically amibitious and therefore played an important role in the Political arena.
   D. In several cities they seem to have issued coins.
4. What is not true of the guild system of the period:
   A. The vast majority of artisans joined the guilds, since it was difficult for them to complete as individuals against the guilds
   B. Guilds offered the artisans social status and a degree of general security.
   C. Guilds could change their location without the permission from the local authority.
   D. Some guilds began to employ hired labour and slaves to meet the growing demand of their products.
5. Which of the following is incorrect?
   A. There was no compound interest in pre-Gupta period.
   B. A debtor could sell his personal belonging for debt in pre-Gupta period.
   C. Loan were given on security of ornaments or debtor's personal property in pre-Gupta period.
   D. Money-lending was not in practice in pre-Gupta period.
6. The guilds during the Gupta age were under the control of:
   A. the king directly
   B. autonomous bodies
   C. provincial governors
   D. Vishayapati
7. What was the main reason for the expansion of internal trade during the Gupta period?
   A. Greater prosperity of the people
   B. Maintenance of law and order and strong Central rule
   C. Technological progress
   D. Better organisation guilds.
8. The most famous city for the production of cotton cloth during the period of the visit of Hiuen Tsang was:
   A. Banaras B. Pataliputra
   C. Surat D. Mathura
9. Among the previous stones, the most extensive foreign trade during the Gupta age was in that of:
   A. Ruby B. Diamonds
   C. Pearl D. Sapphire
10. Which of the following regions was most famous for pearl trade during the Gupta period?
    A. Gujarat B. Pandya Country
    C. Andhra Pradesh D. West Bengal
11. Imported coins were mostly used as:
    A. items of jewellery
    B. bullion
    C. foreign exchange
    D. currency of circulation
12. Which one of the following statements regarding the trade and commerce of the Gupta period is not correct?
    A. The Ganga valley was the principal trade area.
    B. The circulation of money expanded extensively.
    C. On account of development of roads, the

use of rivers as trade-routes declined.

D. Sale of certain commodities was subject to strict state control and there was royal monopoly in certain items of trade.

13. What was the caracteristic pottery of the period:

A. Northern black polished ware
B. Red ware with a brownship slip
C. Painted grey ware
D. Yellow and red

14. Which one of the following was not a feature of the industrial life of the Gupta period?

A. The artisans were held in high esteem.
B. There were also royal foundries.
C. Liquor was produced throughout the country.
D. Bonded labourers were also employed in the industries.

15. Who were Sarthavata?

A. They were caravan traders
B. They were grain merchants
C. They were money lenders
D. They were brokers.

16. Roman trade declined after 3rd century AD and with the Hun invasion of the Roman empire it came to an end. In which direction did the Indian Traders turn for business activities?

A. Africa B. China
C. Sri Lanka D. South-East Asia

17. Which of the following was not the commercial centre connected with Gupta rulers?

A. Calcutta B. Banaras
C. Kausambi D. Pataliputra

18. Which one of the following Indian commodities was not exported to Rome?

A. Pepper
B. Indian animals such as lions, tiger, apes
C. Ivory
D. Wine

19. Which of the following was not the port of east coast which handled South-East Asian Trade?

A. Chaul B. Tamralipti
C. Ghantashala D. Kadura

20. The merchant group of which one of the following towns did not issue coins?

A. Tripuri B. Kashi
C. Vidisa D. Magadha

21. In which metal, was Karshapana coins issued?

1. Gold 2. Silver
3. Copper 4. Lead

Codes:

A. 1 and 2 B. 1, 2 and 3
C. 3 and 4 D. All four

22. Which one of the following was the most commonly used coin?

A. Nishka (Gold)
B. Shatamana (Silver)
C. Kakini (Copper)
D. Karshapana

23. The trade and Industry during the pre-Gupta age were well organised into:

A. Srenis B. Eathavana
C. Jethaka D. Karshapana

24. The earliest reference to some sort of guild organisation in ancient India is found in:

A. Epics B. Smriti literature
C. Praśastis D. Vedic literature

25. Which empire opened the Red-Sea trade route of Greeks and Indians?

A. Greek B. Roman
C. Muslim D. None of these

26. The king who captured the famous silk route of Central Asia was:

A. Kanishka B. Harsha
C. Ashoka D. Menander

27. Which was not the cause of general stagnation and decline in trade and commerce between the seventh and tenth centuries in Northern India?

A. Collapse of the Roman empire in the West.
B. Rise of Islam and the Collapse of old

empires such as the Sassanid (Iranian) empire.

C. Political confrontation among different dynasties and lack of uniform administration in India.

D. Decline of the guilds.

28. The behaviour of the guild members was controlled through:

A. Council of senior member
B. The Elder
C. Specially appointed supervisors
D. Guild Court

29. Which of the following was not one of the leading guilds of the period?

A. Leather workers
B. Metal workers
C. Potters
D. Carpenters

30. Which one of the following rules were not fixed by the guilds?

A. Work B. Price
C. Distribution D. Social conduct

31. Which one of the following was the most advanced industry of the period?

A. Metal work B. Jewellery
C. Textile D. Minting of coins

32. Which of the following was not one of the varieties of textiles produced during the period?

A. Cotton B. Velvet
C. Wool D. Muslin

33. Which one of the following towns was not connected by land route from India?

A. Alexandrea
B. Susa
C. Persepolis
D. Seleucia

34. What became prominent in military tactics during Gupta period?

A. Chariots
B. Archery
C. Horse archery
D. None of the above

35. Main aim of Samudragupta in attacking the states of South India was:

A. Annexation
B. Plunder
C. Extension of his sphere of influence
D. Acceptance of his suzerainty by their rulers

36. The first Christian missionary entered India in the:

A. Ist Century BC B. Ist Century AD
C. 2nd Century AD D. 3rd Century AD

37. Who was the author of Natyashastra?

A. Vasumitra B. Nagarjuna
C. Asvagosha D. Bhasa

38. Who among the following was the author of Mrichhakatika?

A. Bhasa B. Sudraka
C. Nagarjuna D. Gargacharya

39. The earliest paintings of Ajanta caves date back to:

A. Ist Century BC B. Ist Century AD
C. 2nd Century AD D. 3rd Century AD

40. Choose the wrong one. During pre-Gupta and Gupta period:

A. Attitudes of the people in general were liberal
B. State and people enjoyed prosperity during the rules of Satavahanas
C. Agriculture and trade were the main professions of people
D. The king mostly encouraged Tamil language.

41. Choose the wrong one. During pre-Gupta and Gupta period:

A. The society was divided into four castes
B. It was divided on the basis of profession
C. Women commanded good respect in the society
D. Inter-Caste marriage were not permitted

42. Which of the following was called Yavanapriya in Sanskrit?

A. Ivory B. Indian pepper
C. Indian Cotton D. Pearls

43. Which was the most important item of export from India to the Roman Empire?

A. Spices B. Pearls
C. Muslin D. Precious stone

44. What was the major item of import from Roman Empire to India?
A. Metal B. Pottery
C. Wire D. Coins

45. Which one of the following were the main items of trade with the Roman Empire?
A. Industrial raw materials
B. Luxury goods
C. Agricultural commodities
D. Furniture goods

46. Which one of the following acted as intermediaries in East Roman Trade?
A. Iranian merchants
B. Arabs
C. Roman Merchants settled in India
D. Indian merchants

47. What is "periplus of the Erythrean Sea"?
A. The name of a book
B. The name of a Greek town
C. The name of a Central Asian Tribe
D. The name of a Greek God

48. Where was the port of Barbasicum situated?
A. At the mouth of Ganga
B. At the mouth of Cauvery
C. On the West Coast
D. On the Indus Delta

49. At which one of the following ports a sizable Roman settlement and a Roman factory have been discovered?
A. Tamralipti B. Barygaza
C. Kaveripattinam D. Arikamedu

50. When did Saka era begin?
A. 58 BC B. 78 BC
C. 58 AD D. 78 AD

51. One of the most noticeable feature of the religious life of the Gupta period was:
A. the growing importance of idols in Puja
B. listening to discourses on the Upanishadas
C. recitation of the Vedas
D. acceptance of the Ahimsa concept

52. One of the most flourishing marts during the Gupta times was:
A. Praithar B. Ujjain
C. Vaishali D. Tamralipti

53. Decentralisation of administrative authority in the Gupta period was caused by:
A. increased in grants of land and villages with fiscal and administrative immunities to priests and temples.
B. preponderant authority of provincial governors.
C. weak authority of general government.
D. the belief of the Guptas in provincial autonomy.

54. Out of the following which one was the most extensively practised industrial activity in the pre-Gupta period?
A. Pottery B. Carpentry
C. Cloth weaving D. Ivory work

55. In the pre-Gupta times the Ships heading for the Burma Coast and South India began their voyage at:
A. Tamralipti (Tamluk)
B. Bharukaccha
C. Barbaricum
D. Sopara

56. Which of the following is said to have introduced Indian Culture in Cambodia?
A. Kaundinya B. Kharavela
C. Fa-hsien D. Kshemeshvara

57. In the pre-Gupta period the ships heading for Burma Coast and South India began their voyage at:
A. Tamralipti (Tamluk)
B. Bharukachha
C. Patala
D. Sopara

58. Who designated Samudragupta as "Indian Nepoleon"?
A. R.C. Majumdar
B. Vincent Smith
C. Max Mueller
D. H.C. Raychaudhri

59. Who is depicted in the coins of Gupta dynasty as sitting cross legged on the couch playing the lute (vina)?
A. Srigupta B. Skandagupta
C. Ramagupta D. Samudragupta

60. Who is the author of Allahabad pillar inscription?

A. Sudaraka B. Bana

C. Harisena D. Patanjali

61. When was Gupta era started?

A. 319-20 AD B. 315-16 AD

C. 319-20 BC D. 335-36 AD

62. Arrange the following in an order:

1. Chandragupta I
2. Chandragupta Vikramaditya
3. Samudragupta
4. Kumaragupta

Codes:

A. 1, 2, 3, 4 B. 1, 3, 4, 2

C. 1, 4, 2, 3 D. 1, 3, 2, 4

63. Who was Prabhavati:

A. Samudragupta's daughter

B. Samudragupta's wife

C. Chandragupta's wife

D. Chandragupta's daughter

64. Which was the most important town during the pre-Gupta and Gupta period?

A. Pataliputra

B. Ujjain

C. Gandhar

D. None of the above

65. During Gupta period land tax collected varied from:

A. One third to one fourth

B. One fourth to one sixth

C. One third of the produce

D. One fourth of the produce

66. Who adopted the title of Vikramaditya amongst the Gupta Kings?

A. Chandragupta B. Samudragupta

C. Chandragupta II D. Skandgupta

67. Why did town prosper in the Kushana and Satavahana empires?

A. because there towns had gold reserves

B. good administration

C. they carried on thriving trade with the Roman empire

D. None of the above

68. Which statement on the guilds in the pre-Gupta period is not correct?

A. They controlled the equality of products as well as distribution.

B. They bought and sold as co-operative societies.

C. They trained apprentices.

D. They organised political opposition.

69. The writing of the Gupta period emphasise that the Brahmana should not have accepted food from the Sudra because:

A. it would reduce his spiritual strength

B. he would have lost his caste

C. he would have to perform prayaschitta

D. he would not attain Swarga

70. Why did the Vaishya cease to cultivate the land in ancient India?

A. They wanted a superior social status

B. They took to trade and commerce

C. They went over to Buddhism and Jainism

D. Sudras out numbered them as cultivators

71. Which inscription gives us a biographical sketch of the King Kharavela?

A. Besnagar B. Ayodhya

C. Hathigumpha D. Junagarh

72. Which one was the earliest Sanskrit Inscription?

A. Gimar Inscription

B. Mathura Inscription

C. Nasik Inscription

D. Hathigumpha Inscription

73. Which literature discouraged outright conquest by kings but encouraged lawful conquest, that is, conquered kingdoms being reduced to vassal status?

A. Early Vedic Literature

B. Later Vedic Literature

C. Epic and Smriti Literature

D. None of the above

74. The earliest reference to some sort of guild organisation in ancient India is found in:

A. Epics B. Smriti Literature

C. Prashastis D. Vedic Literature

75. What is the most important confirmation revealing that the guilds gave dominations to religious causes of all kinds:

A. Smriti Literature

B. Inscriptions
C. Cross references
D. Archaeological evidence

76. What is the most remarkable thing about the iron pillar of Mehrauli near Delhi:
A. its weight
B. its artistic value
C. it is chemically pure iron
D. the inscription on it

77. The Southern Trade route starting from Ujjain proceeded to the city of:
A. Kanchi B. Madurai
C. Pratisthana D. Malkhad

78. Which source does not speak anything about trade routes of ancient India?
A. Jataka stories
B. Milinda Panha
C. Periplus of the Erythrean Sea
D. Sangam Literature

79. Which fact relating to the post-Gupta period had no direct bearing on the changed agrarian system?
A. The revenue that was paid to the king was no longer partly used for maintaining public works.
B. The peasants were forced to pay more taxes in addition to the land tax.
C. Temples also collected additional ducs.
D. Decline of the guilds.

80. The land grants in the Gupta period led to:
A. Institutionalisation
B. Strong Central Government
C. Decline of the Guptas
D. Strengthening of the Guptas

81. One of the following was of marginal value in the emergence of guilds and trade in the pre-Gupta period. Which one was that?
A. The Cowri-Shells and the barter economy was replaced by system of coins.
B. The kings of the north-west issued coins superior to the punchmarked coins of the Mauryans.
C. Usury was accepted as a part of banking.
D. Interest was taken by financiers like Sreshthins according to one's caste.

82. Which statement on trade and commerce in the pre-Gupta period is not correct?
A. The trade with South East Asia was occasioned by the demand of Rome for more and more of spices.
B. Trade grew further when Indian traders settled in South-East Asia.
C. The trade with South East Asia was vigorously pursued by all the Coastal areas of India.
D. While the impact of Greco-Roman ideas was more evident in the North. The South witnessed the impact of Roman trade.

83. Which political event has no bearing on the growth of trade in the pre-Gupta period?
A. The construction of roads and a uniform system of administration by the Mauryas.
B. The occupation of North-Western India by non-Indian people.
C. The establishment of Indian kingdom in South East Asia.
D. Intercine warfare amongst the Indian kingdoms.

84. With regards to the number of trades referred to in a number of works which pair is wrong?
A. Disha Nikaya — two dozen
B. Mahavastu — thirty six
C. Milandapanho — seventy five
D. Divyavadana — one hundred and twenty five.

85. Which one triggered off external trade in the pre-Gupta period?
A. agricultural Surpluses
B. building of roads and protection by State
C. emergence of coins and precious metals for exchange.
D. demand for Indian goods in the West.

86. The king who controlled the famous silk route of Central Asia was:
A. Kanishka B. Harsha

C. Ashoka D. Menander

87. What is the meaning of the Chinese word 'yue-chi'?
A. Moon tribe B. Asian tribe
C. Sun tribe D. Young people

88. Who opened the great silk route to the Indians?
A. Kanishka B. Ashoka
C. Harsha D. Fa-hien

89. Which empire opened the Red-Sea trade route to Greeks and Indians?
A. Greek B. Roman
C. Muslim D. None of these

90. Who performed the Asvamedha Sacrifice for Pushyamitra Sunga?
A. Panini B. Patanjali
C. Badrayan D. Visvamitra

91. In which period was there more emphasis on the doctrine of avatars?
A. Maurya period
B. Sunga period
C. The period of Panini
D. Gupta period

92. Samudragupta adopted the policy of:
A. digvijaya
B. dharmavijaya
C. digvijaya as well as dharmvijaya
D. neither digvijaya nor dharmvijaya

93. Who issued the lion type of coins?
A. Chandragupta I B. Chandragupta II
C. Samudragupta D. Harsha

94. Which king made use of metonymics?
A. Mauryas B. Guptas
C. Satavahanas D. Pushyabhutis

95. Kushan coins show:
A. Economic isolation of Northern India
B. Growing economic relation between Northern and Southern India
C. Economic links with the Hellenistic and Roman world
D. Economic links with South-East Asia

96. Gupta inscriptions from Bengal show:
A. traders influence on local administration
B. government control on trade
C. decline in trade
D. weakening of trade guilds

97. Work on the Ajanta Caves began in the reigon of:
A. Maurya kings
B. Gupta kings
C. Satavahana kings
D. Chola kings

98. Tribal or Republican states in India disappeared because of:
A. Aryan invasion
B. Mauryan conquests
C. Inroads of Greeks, Sakas and Kushans
D. Gupta imperialism and Hun incursions.

99. Who were the first to adopt the title which conveyed king's divinity?
A. Greeks B. Sakas
C. Kushans D. Guptas

100. The earliest extant book on the Dharmasastra is:
A. Narad Smriti
B. Brihaspati Smriti
C. Manu Smriti
D. None of the above

101. During the second half of the first millennium changes occurred in the agrarian system of India, but one is debatable. Which one?
A. The beneficiaries of land undertook the task of cultivating the land themselves.
B. In all the old settled areas of North India, Sudras cultivated the land.
C. In the backward and mountainous areas such as Orissa and Deccan peasants were enjoined to stick to the land.
D. Religious sanctions were attributed to these changes.

102. Which facts relating to the agrarian system in the post-Gupta period caused misery both to the king and the peasant?
A. Although the feudatories were supposed to get revenue from land for life, they gradually appropriated proprietory rights.
B. The right of collecting revenue became proprietory and hereditary leading to

the feudatories disposing came into existence.

C. A large number of sub-feudatories came into existence.

D. Neither the king nor the feudatories invested money in crafts or trade.

103. One statement on culture in the post-Gupta period is not correct. Identify it.

A. Sub-nationalities having different customs and manners came into existence.

B. Sanskrit language became stylisted

C. Regional language with their own scripts had their beginning in the 7th century.

D. Sanskrit ceased to be used for official purposes.

104. Which fact relating to education around 1000 AD is not correct?

A. Formal education became mostly theological.

B. Schools and centres receiving royal patronage were open to the three upper castes.

C. Schools were attached to the local temples.

D. Buddhist monasteries included some nontheological education but they too changed over to the study of scriptures only.

105. Who uprooted the Bodhi tree at Bodh Gaya?

A. Pushyamitra Sunga

B. Rajendra Chola I

C. Sasanka

D. Samudragupta

106. Who is a nagarika?

A. an urban prostitute referred to in the kamasutra.

B. a comfortable well-off citizen as described in the kamasutra.

C. a nagar-seth living a life of comfort and gaiety as described in kamasutra.

D. a chaste-women.

107. Identify, out of the following features the one that provides clue to the understanding of decline of economic prosperity after the Guptas.

A. decay of towns as witnesses by Hiuen Tsang.

B. villages became self-sufficient.

C. rigid Varna System.

D. events that occurred beyond India like the rise of Islam, collapse of Roman Empire and Instrusion of China into Indo-China.

108. There are instances of women succeeding to the throne or acting as regent for their sons. Identify the woman who never ruled.

A. Prabhavati Gupta of the Vankataka family

B. Didda of Kashmir

C. Rudramma of the Kakatiyas

D. Rajashri of Kannauj

109. Who was the first king to adopt the title of Devaputra?

A. Ashoka

B. Chandragupta Maurya

C. Kanishka

D. Chandragupta I

110. The word agrarian means:

A. Agriculture

B. Agriculture and irrigation

C. Agriculture and allied sectors

D. Property right on land

111. In ancient India the conditions of the peasant was what it was because:

A. he was made a tenant or share-cropper

B. he cultivated land for the king or his chief

C. he cultivated land as though it was his own

D. he had the right of ownership

112. The practice of making land grants started with the:

A. Guptas B. Chalukyas

C. Mauryan D. Satavahanas

113. Which feature can you associate with the Indian feudalism?

A. Serfdom

B. Manorial system
C. Knight sernis
D. Zamindars exercised many of the royal powers and peasantry was dependent on them

114. What was the name of South Indian Money-lenders
A. Bania B. Banjaras
C. Chettis D. Panis

115. Who were the last pre-Muslim invaders of India?
A. Arabs B. Sakas
C. Huns D. Greeks

116. Who were the last foreign invaders of India to be socially and culturally absorbed by the Hindus?
A. Arbas B. Huns
C. Sakas D. Greeks

117. Which inscription refers to the defeat of Harsha by Pulukesin II?
A. Nasik Inscription
B. Aihole Inscription
C. Ayodhya Inscription
D. Junagarh Rock Inscription

118. Which title did Harsha adopt?
A. Siladitya B. Sakari
C. Devanampiya D. Daivaputra

119. Who was the "Lord of five Indies"?
A. Samundragupta B. Chandragupta II
C. Harsha D. Ashoka

ANSWERS

1	2	3	4	5	6	7	8	9	10
B	C	C	C	D	B	B	B	C	B
11	**12**	**13**	**14**	**15**	**16**	**17**	**18**	**19**	**20**
B	C	B	A	A	B	A	D	A	D
21	**22**	**23**	**24**	**25**	**26**	**27**	**28**	**29**	**30**
D	D	A	D	B	A	D	D	A	C
31	**32**	**33**	**34**	**35**	**36**	**37**	**38**	**39**	**40**
C	B	A	C	D	B	C	B	B	D
41	**42**	**43**	**44**	**45**	**46**	**47**	**48**	**49**	**50**
D	B	A	D	B	D	A	D	D	D
51	**52**	**53**	**54**	**55**	**56**	**57**	**58**	**59**	**60**
A	D	A	C	A	A	A	B	D	C
61	**62**	**63**	**64**	**65**	**66**	**67**	**68**	**69**	**70**
A	D	B	A	B	C	C	D	A	A
71	**72**	**73**	**74**	**75**	**76**	**77**	**78**	**79**	**80**
C	A	C	D	B	C	C	D	D	A
81	**82**	**83**	**84**	**85**	**86**	**87**	**88**	**89**	**90**
D	C	D	D	D	A	A	A	B	B
91	**92**	**93**	**94**	**95**	**96**	**97**	**98**	**99**	**100**
D	A	B	C	B	B	C	D	C	C
101	**102**	**103**	**104**	**105**	**106**	**107**	**108**	**109**	**110**
A	B	D	B	C	B	D	D	C	D
111	**112**	**113**	**114**	**115**	**116**	**117**	**118**	**119**	
C	D	D	C	C	B	B	A	C	

AGRARIAN AND SOCIAL STRUCTURE

1. What is the literal meaning of Pallava?
   A. Peasant
   B. Creeper
   C. Thief
   D. None of the above
2. Land grants became frequent in India from the:
   A. 2nd Century A.D.
   B. 3rd Century A.D.
   C. 4th Century A.D.
   D. 5th Century A.D.
3. Post-Gupta period saw more expansion of the agrarian economy. Why?
   A. Population increased
   B. Large number of foreigners came to India
   C. Large number of Land grants were made to the Brahmans
   D. None of the above
4. To which group of the people in the following list land grants were not made during the post-Gupta period?
   A. Members of the royal family
   B. The Brahmans
   C. The royal officials
   D. The temple priests
5. Which one of the following ruling dynasties made the largest grant of villages to temples and Brahmans:
   A. Palas B. Guptas
   C. Rashtrakutas D. Prathihars
6. The practice of land grants originated in the:
   A. Later Vedic Period
   B. Mauryan Period
   C. Satavahana Period
   D. Kushan Period
7. In the post-Gupta period when villages were granted in the tribal areas the agriculturists were placed under the Control of:
   A. Royal officials
   B. Villages headman
   C. The religious beneficiaries
   D. The tribal chief
8. Kalabhars patronised:
   A. Brahmans
   B. Jains
   C. Buddhist monasteries
   D. None of the above
9. Who were Kalabhars?
   A. Peasants B. Untouchables
   C. Run away slaves D. Evil rulers
10. Vakataka power was followed by:
    A. Rashtrakutas
    B. Guptas
    C. Harshavardhana
    D. Chalukyas of Badami
11. The world 'agrarian' means:
    A. Agriculture
    B. Agriculture and irrigation
    C. Agriculture and allied sectors
    D. Property rights on land
12. Which one was the most important consequence of the ancient Indian feudal system?
    A. Self-sufficiency of the village
    B. Development of rural economy
    C. Stability in the social system
    D. Extension of arable land
13. Who overthrew Chalukyas of Badami in 757 A.D.?
    A. Rashtrakutas B. Ikshavakus
    C. Vakatakas D. Pallavas
14. Who founded the Kadamba kingdom?
    A. Simueka
    B. Mayurasarman
    C. Krishna
    D. None of the above
15. In Northern Maharashtra and Vidarbha the Satavahanas were succeeded by the:
    A. Vakatakas
    B. Chalukyas
    C. Pandyas
    D. None of the above
16. Alvar Saints were great devotees of:
    A. Vishnu B. Siva

C. Tirthankars D. Other Goddess

17. The Ikshvakus were supplanted by the:
A. Chalukyas
B. Pallavas
C. Rashtrakutas
D. None of the above

18. Where did Pallava set up Capital?
A. Pataliputra B. Kannauj
C. Madurai D. Kanchi

19. Western Ganges made land grants to only:
A. Buddhists
B. Jains
C. Brahmans
D. None of the above

20. When did the land grants to the temples in South India become a common phenomenon?
A. After the 7th Century
B. After the 8th Century
C. After the 9th Century
D. After the 10th Century

21. The Dravidan language which got protection from the Rashtrakutas ruler was.
A. Kannada B. Tamil
C. Telugu D. Malayalam

22. In the field of fine arts, Chalukyas contributed most towards:
A. Painting B. Sculpture
C. Music D. Architecture

23. The empire of the chalukyas of Badami was destroyed by:
A. The Pallavas
B. The Cholas
C. The Pandyas
D. The Rashtrakutas

24. The Upanayana ceremony of children started:
A. During the later Vedic age
B. During the age of Buddha
C. During the age of Maurya
D. During the age of Pandyas

25. Who among the following started the practice of donating lands which finally resulted infeudal system?
A. The Mauryas
B. The Sungas
C. The Satavahanas
D. The Guptas

26. The Ankorvat Temple located in kaniby is that of:
A. Vishnu B. Brahma
C. Shiva D. Buddha

27. The Barabudur temple in Java is that of:
A. Shiva B. Vishnu
C. Brahma D. Buddha

28. The land revenue during post-Gupta age was:
A. 1/5 to 1/6 of the produce
B. 1/4 of the produce
C. 1/3 of the produce
D. 1/2 of the produce

29. In which of the following regions of India were the village councils most active?
A. East B. South
C. North D. West

30. During the post-Gupta period land revenue was relaised by:
A. The officers of the State.
B. The Zamindars
C. Village assembly
D. None of the above

31. Who distributed land among peasant during post-Gupta period?
A. The state
B. The fief holders
C. The village assemblies
D. The Zamindars

32. The natural resources which were donated by the king during the post-Gupta period were:
A. Forest land B. Mines
C. Water resources D. All the above

33. The land grants in which one of the following parts of India empowered the recipients to punish thieves and other criminals?
A. North
B. West
C. South
D. None of the above

34. The most important motive behind the grant of land to priests and officials was:
A. To weaken the power of big landlords

B. To ensure the regular flow of land revenue
C. To punish the recalcitrant peasants
D. To meet the deep social crisis that affected the ancient social order in the 3rd and 4th centuries A.D.

35. In the South Crown lands were rented out to:
A. Tenants in chief
B. Tenants-famous
C. Tenants-at-will
D. Permanent tenants

36. The Pallava rulers of South India were:
A. Shudras B. Vaishyas
C. Kshatriyas D. Brahmans

37. Which one of the following statement regarding the decline in the status of the agrarian classes is not correct?
A. The status of a free Vaishya peasant declined and he begun to be viewed as a Shudra.
B. The dependent peasants, whose number was much larger than that of the free peasants; were share-croppers.
C. The lowest stratum of dependent peasantry was represented by the plough-drivers and other field labourers who were mainly Shudras.
D. There were no restrictions on the practice of taking food from the Shudra share-croppers.

38. What was the range of land revenue in the South during the Pallava period as a proportion of the produce of land?
A. 1/3rd to 1/4th B. 1/4th to 1/6th
C. 1/6th to 1/10th D. 1/10th to 1/12th

39. The term " Vithi" refers to:
A. Dyer's street
B. Ivory worker's street
C. Weaver's locality
D. Metal-worker's street

40. Which of the following was the common medium of exchange according to Fa-hein?
A. Nishka B.Cowries
C. Karshapana D. Kakini

41. Which fact relating to society in the post-Gupta period has very little relevance to the changed agrarian system?
A. Many of the Brahman holders employed cultivators since cultivation was regarded as a low by occupation
B. Buddhist monasteries admitted women
C. Buddhist monasteries also employed tenants
D. Hereditary kingship was stressed which the divine origin of kingship was theorised.

42. 'Sulka' refers to:
A. a coin
B. a guild of weavers
C. tolls on the frontier collected from foreign merchants
D. None of these

43. The traditional view regarding the position of land in ancient India was that:
A. the king owned the land
B. the king was the custodian of land
C. the king was the protector of land and the people living on the land
D. the king had his own crown land while the people had property rights on the land possessed by them

44. Which was the most important means to extend the arable land:
A. Conquest
B. Land grants
C. Encouragement to peasants
D. Emergence of the towns

45. Which one of the following was the basic tax?
A. Bhaga B. Kara
C. Bali D. Hiranya

46. The labourers were paid wages in cash or as a share of the produce. What was their share of the produce if accompanied by food?
A. 1/3rd B. 1/4th
C. 1/5th D. 1/6th

47. What was malla-Karra and turshka-danda?
A. Taxation imposed on foreigners unauthorisedly settled in India.

B. Impost Ievied by the central government to deal with the menace from marauding tribes.
C. The fine imposed on those tax-payers who were found to have evaded payment of taxes.
D. Public collection for waging war against the Turks.

48. There was a special category of land in the South known as eripatti what was its revenue meant for?
A. Feeding of the poor
B. Maintenance of the village tank
C. Maintenance of village roads
D. Creation of permanent assets

49. Which of the following varieties of land available during the period, was generally donated by the way of salary?
A. Follow or waste land owned by the state and the land in newly-formed villages
B. Cultivated land owned by the state and treated as crown land
C. Privately owned land
D. Royall or Crown lands

50. 'Agrahara grants' were:
A. Those Lands which were donated to a temple for its upkeep
B. Lands granted to secular official in lieu of salary
C. Granted to Brahman and were tax-free
D. Made the intellectual class

51. Regarding the land attached to religious institution in Chola times:
A. It was from land tax
B. It was not free from land tax
C. We can say nothing specific about it
D. It was taxed arbitrarily

52. Which fact was the least responsible for the emergence of feudal or regional loyalities?
A. Minor kings sought impressive geneologies as found in Prithviraja Raso.
B. The king granted rent-free lands to his officers or select holders.
C. The Shudras who cultivated the land were made to hand over a fixed share of their produce to the land owners.
D. The feudatories could assign their lands to cultivators who paid them an agreed upon revenue.

53. In ancient India the condition of the peasants was what it was because:
A. he was made a tenant or share-cropper
B. he cultivated land for the king or his chief
C. he cultivated land as though it was his own
D. he had the right of ownership.

54. Which of the consequence of Brahmans being granted land in backward area was of crucial importance for India after the 5th and 6th centuries A.D.?
A. Brahmans took agriculture as well as Ayurveda to tribal area.
B. Writing of Prakrit and Sanskrit was disseminated.
C. The aboriginal peasants became the new Sudras.
D. The land grants in the development area down graded the importance of the Vaishya peasants.

55. Which of the following statements regarding the land grants during the period is not true?
A. The number of land grants considerably increased
B. All types of grants became hereditary and permanent in character.
C. Some of the grantees were also given transferred administrative functions
D. Land grants were also made to state officials thus ushering in the process of foundalisation.

56. Which one made the life of the peasants most miserable in the post-Gupta period?
A. The peasants paid various taxes like temple tax, and tax on goods produced besides land revenue.
B. On occasions the peasants were made to provide free labour.

C. The feaudatories even appropriated the common lands of the villages.
D. There was a proliferation of intermediaries between the king and the peasant.

57. Which feature can you associate with the Indian feudalism?
A. Serfdom
B. Manorial system
C. Knigh Service
D. Zamindars exercised many of the royal powers and peasantry was dependent on them

58. Which fact relating to the post-Gupta period had no direct bearing on the charged agrarain system?
A. The revenue that was paid to the king was no longer partly used for maintaining public works
B. The peasants were forced to pay more taxes in addition to the land tax.
C. Temples also collected additional dues.
D. Emergences of regional warfares.

59. How did the practice of land grants lead to the emergance of serfdom:
A. It aggravated their poverty forcing them to the position of slaves.
B. They were often required to work on the land even when it had been granted to others.
C. The exploitation of private landlords was greater than that of the king.
D. Due to obsentee Landlordism

60. Identify that of the following feature the one that provides a clue to the understanding of decline of economic prosperity after the Guptas:
A. Decay of towns as witnessed by Huien Tsang
B. Village became self-sufficient
C. Rigid varana system
D. Events that occurred beyond India like the rise of Islam, collapse of Roman Empire and intrusion of China into Indo-China.

61. The practice of land grants started with the:
A. Guptas B. Chalukyas
C. Mauryas D. Satavahanas

62. Which one was the most important consequence of the ancient Indian feudal system?
A. Self-sufficient of the village
B. Development of rural economy
C. Stability in the social system
D. Extension of the arable land

63. In which century did the donor not only transfer all sources of revenues to the grantee but also the rights to govern and punish the inhabitants of the villages?
A. 2nd Century A.D.
B. 3rd Century A.D.
C. 5th Century A.D.
D. 7th Century A.D.

64. In whose court did Asvogosha live!
A. Harsha B. Samudragupta
C. Kaniskha D. Ashoka

65. Who is the author of Rajatarangini?
A. Harsha B. Kalhana
C. Kalidasa D. Panini

66. Who wrote Ashtadhyayi?
A. Panini B. Hatyayna
C. Jayadeva D. Bharata

67. At whose hands did Harsha suffer a defeat?
A. Pulakesin II
B. Mahendravaraman I
C. Rajaraja Chola
D. Narasimharaman I

68. Which work recognises first the payment of fiscal officers by grants of land?
A. Kautilya's Arthasastra
B. Manusmriti
C. Megasthene's Indica
D. Harsha's three dramas

69. Which of the following were exempted from taxation according to the sacred law?
A. Student
B. Ascetics
C. Learned Brahmans
D. All the above

70. Which one of the following categories of

merchants appears to be most important according to this inscription?
A. Salt merchants B. Oil merchants
C. Grain merchants D. Cloth merchants

71. That the land grants were made to officers for their military and administrative services is directly evident from the epigraphics records of:
A. Maurya
B. Satavahanas
C. Guptas
D. post-Gupta period

72. Which one of the following places was famous for fragment rice?
A. Mathura B. Tanjore
C. Ujjain D. Magadha

73. What was the reason for the Indian visit of Hiuen Tsang:
A. to visit the holy places connected with Buddhism
B. to amass wealth
C. to know the geography of India
D. to establish political ties with India

74. Which among the following is true? Harsha held an assembly at Kannauj:
A. to distribute alms to the poor people
B. to commemorate his victories
C. to honour the visit of Hieun-Tsang
D. to settle the question of successors

75. The seven Pagodas at Mahabalipuram belong to one of the following. Identify:
A. Cholas
B. The Chalukyas
C. The Pallavas
D. The Rashtrakutas

76. The Aihole inscription records the achievements of one of the following. Identify?
A. Harsha B. Samudragupta
C. Pulakesin II D. Rajendra Chola

77. Who wrote Kadambani?
A. Bana B. Harsha
C. Kalidasa D. Kahana

78. The land grants of which one of the following parts of India empowered the recipients to punish thieves and other criminals?
A. West B. South
C. North D. Central India

79. Which one of the following term was used for the plough drivers who represented the section of field labourers?
A. Malavhaaka B. Karsakaka
C. Kinasa D. All the above

80. Which of the following was one of the services to be performed by the villagers, when royal troops and officials halted at the village?
A. Contributed provisions
B. Contributed money
C. Provide Cattle for transport
D. All the above

81. Which one of the following ruling dynasties made the largest grant of villages to temples and Brahmans?
A. Guptas B. Palas
C. Rastrakutas D. Pratiharas

82. What is said to be the original home of the Sungas?
A. Kalinga B. Vidisa
C. Berar D. Bharhut

83. For how many years did the Sungas rule?
A. 60 years B. 80 years
C. 95 years D. 112 years

84. Who was the leader of the Parthien revolt against Antiochus I?
A. Vonones B. Arsaces
C. Maues D. Euthydemus

85. Pick out the wrong match from the following?
A. Grahavarman — Pushyabhuti
B. Rudrasena — Vakataka
C. Nahapana — Kshaharata
D. Toramane — Huns

86. Who among the following has been described as the second Alexander?
A. Arsaces B. Antiochus
C. Demetrius D. Diodotus I

87. Whose general was Apallodotus?
A. Euthydemus B. Demetrius
C. Diodotus D. Antiochus

88. Permission was granted to a ceylonese king during Samudragupta's reign to

build a Buddhist monastery at one of the following places. Identify?
A. Pataliputra B. Bodh Gaya
C. Ujjain D. Vaisali

89. Who among the following could have started the Saka era:
A. Kanishka B. Kadphises II
C. Vasishka D. Chandragupta II

90. Who was the Kushana king? Who is stated to have taken the title 'Caesar'?
A. Kanishka II
B. Vasudeva
C. Wema Kadphises
D. Vasudeva I

91. Who wrote Buddha Charita?
A. Vasumitra B. Bana
C. Asvagosha D. Charaka

92. Who among the following was called Siloditya?
A. Kanishka
B. Harsha
C. Pulakesin II
D. Mahendra Verman I

93. Which school of Artists is said to have the "hand of a Greek but the heart of an Indian"?
A. Hellenistic B. Gandhara
C. Mathura D. Gupta

94. Pick out the wrong match from the following:
A. Agnimitra — Mauryas
B. Pushyamitra — Sungas
C. Kharavela — Kalinga
D. Demetrius — Greeks

95. Pick out the wrong match:
A. Vasudeva — Kanvas
B. Patanjali — Grammarian
C. Susarman — Mathematician
D. Devabhuti — Sunge

96. Pick out the wrong match:
A. Vidisa — Modern Besnagar in Eastern Malwa
B. Heliodorus — Greek Ambassador
C. Antiochus — Greek king of Syria
D. Patanjali — Gargi Samhita

97. The Sunga period saw the growth of one of the following religions. Identify?
A. Bhagavata religion
B. Saivism
C. Buddhism
D. Nature worship

98. The Kanvas were generally the followers of one of the religions given below. Identify:
A. Buddhism B. Jainism
C. Brahmanism D. Bhagavatism

99. Who among the Sunga rulers was the hero of Kalidas's work?
A. Agnimitra B. Pushyamitra
C. Vasumitra D. Bhagabhadra

100. Who was the last king of the Sunga dynasty?
A. Bhga B. Devabhuti
C. Agnimitra D. Vasumitra

101. Who was the foreign king who induced the Indian king, Subhagasena, to surrender a number of elephants?
A. Antiochus III B. Demetrius
C. Menander D. Maues

102. Who was the Sunga Prince who arrested the tide of Yaana (Greek) invasion?
A. Bhaga B. Pushyamitra
C. Agnimitra D. Vasumitra

103. Who is the author of 'Gathasaptasati'.
A. Apilaka
B. Hala
C. Satakarni II
D. Gautamiputra Satakarmi

104. Pick out the wrong combination:
A. Megasthenes — Indika
B. Patanjali — Mahabashya
C. Panini — Astadhyayi
D. Kalidasa — Mrichchhakatika

105. The relic tower of Peshawar was constructed by:
A. Huvishka B. Kanishka I
C. Vasudeva I D. Kadphises II

106. Who among the Kushans was called by the Chinese historians "yen-kao-ching"?
A. Kujula Kadphises
B. Kanishka II
C. Vasishka

D. Kadphises II

107. Who among the Kushans assumed the title 'Devaputra' (Son of Heaven)?
A. Hurishka B. Vasudeva I
C. Kanishka I D. Kadphises II

108. One of the following was an alumnus of the Nalanda University:
A. I-Ising B. Harsha
C. Bana D. Kautilya

109. Pick out the wrong match:
A. Harsha — Siladitya
B. Chandragputa II — Sakari
C. Yajnasri Satakarni — Trisamudradhipati
D. Samudragupta — Vikramaditya

110. Who among the following Satavahana kings was styled 'Lord of Pratishthana'?
A. Gautamiputra
B. Kuntala Satakarni
C. Hala
D. Sata Karni I

111. Who among the following is credited with treating mathematics as a distinct subject:
A. Varahamira B. Vagbhata
C. Aryabhatta D. Brahmagupta

112. Who was the Satavahana ruler who took the title 'Destroyer of Sakas, Yarvanas and Pallavas'?
A. Hala
B. Apilaka
C. Gautamiputra Satakari
D. Satkarni II

113. Who among the following is identified by some scholars with Vikramaditya of Indian tradition?
A. Vasishthiputra Pulumayi
B. Sivasri Satakarni
C. Kuntala Satakarni
D. Gautamiputra Satakarni

114. We get a short account of the Nalanda University from the writings of:
A. Huien Tsang B. Fa-Hien
C. Bana D. Harsha

115. Pick out the correct match:
A. Kalidasa — Malavikagnimitra
B. Asvagosha — Leading author on medicine
C. Nagarjuna — Grammarian
D. Panini — Dramatist

116. Pick out the correct match:
A. Nagarjuna — Madhyamika Sutras
B. Charak — Mahavibhasa Sastra
C. Patanjali — Ashtadhyayi
D. Panini — Mahabashya

117. Who was the Kushan king who assumed the title 'Satyadharmasthita'?
A. Kanishka B. Vasudeva I
C. Kadphises I D. Kadphises II

118. The Hathigumpha inscription is the source of information of one of the following rulers. Identify?
A. Pushyamitra B. Pulakesin II
C. Vasudeva D. Kharavela

119. Who was the founder of the Indo-Greek (Indo-Bactrian) dynasty in India?
A. Menander B. Antialcides
C. Demetrius D. Alexander

120. The caste system or the jathi system grew increasing rigid because of various factors but one of the most important was:
A. economic factor
B. foreign factor
C. the sanction of scriptures
D. the fear of God and divine punishment

121. The institution of matha was popular in the south but did not offer one of the facilities:
A. A rest – house
B. A temple
C. A feeding – centre
D. An education – centre

122. State in which one or the following fields the Varna distinctions were less rigid than those of the earlier period?
A. Commensality
B. Craft exclusiveness
C. Financial matters
D. Judicial matters

123. Identify one of the following which was not laid down by Manu, the law give regarding the Status of Sudras?
A. Sudras were meant for serving the

upper varnas.

B. In case of assault and similar crimes the punishments prescribed for them were very harsh.

C. Even when he had the opportunity of becoming wealthy, he might not do so.

D. The Dasi and Vrishali (Sudra women) were meant for satisfying the pleasures of the people of the upper classes.

124. Which of the following was not one of the factors responsible for proliferation of castes?

A. Tribal affiliations

B. Professional association (guilds)

C. Development of new crafts

D. The desire of the law givers to maintain social purity

125. Which of the following position was accorded by Manu to earlier Foreign immigrants?

A. Degraded Brahmanas

B. Kshtriyas

C. Fallen Kshatriyas

D. Sudras

126. Which statement on social classes in ancient India is not correct?

A. The priests and Kshatriyas were rulers.

B. It was not difficult for the castes to deviate from their rights and duties.

C. The Bhagawad Gita enjoined the people to abide by their own jathi dharma.

D. The lower classes worked hard hoping that they would go up in the caste hierarchy in their next birth.

127. Regarding the social structure in the second half of the first millennium, which of the statements is not correct?

A. There was a proliferation of the sub castes or jathi system as more and more areas were brought under effective cultivation, particularly those in remote areas like Orissa, Deccan and Eastern India.

B. The Dharmashastras prescribed economic rights of people according to the Varna to which one belonged.

C. Almost everything in society was graded according to the land possessed by a peasant.

D. Number of occupational castes was much less than the number of castes which had thier origin because of Varna-Sanskara.

128. Chinese scholars visited India primarily because:

A. They were interested in Buddhism

B. They were invited by Indian kings

C. They were sent by Chinese emperors to study Indian conditions.

D. They came to study India's political conditions.

129. Which one is not regarding the jathi system?

A. After the foreigners settled in India, the jathi system grew more complex.

B. When land in tribal regions was brought under cultivation more jathi's were in existence.

C. The jathi system enable Aryanism or Hinduism preserve its traditions

D. The Brahmanas primarily concentrated on religious practices and seeking salvation.

130. The social crisis between the 4th and 7th centuries was caused because of various factors except one. Which one was that?

A. According to the Puranic Texts. The Varnas disregarded the functions allotted to them.

B. Varna barries were a oppressive, with heavy taxes and impositions.

C. Sudras became cultivators in increasing number and mixed Vaishya cultivators.

D. To control the social situation, the king assumed greater powers.

131. The proliferation of the Sub-Caste in the last quarter of the first millennium AD was because of the following reasons; except one:

A. Expansion of Aryan culture into remote

parts of the century

B. The nature of economy under went a change

C. Although people pursued the same occupation; they belonged to different subcastes depending on the region they lived in

D. Number of Pratiloma marriage was much more than in any previous period.

132. What was the responsible for the emergence of jathi or sub-caste in Aryanism:

A. A large number of foreigners settled in the post towns and important urban areas

B. There was no system of individual conversion to Aryanism

C. A large number of people beyond the pole of Aryanism were brought into the fold

D. The law books written before 300 AD reiterate the superiority or the Brahmans.

133. What strengthened forces of orthodoxy in post-Gupta period:

1. Absence of the republics
2. Gradual decline of the merchantile community
3. Feudal organisation
4. Absence of an all India-kingdom

Codes:

A. only 2 and 3

B. only 1, 2 and 3

C. only 2, 3 and 4

D. All the four

134. Out of the services rendered by the jathi system or the so called caste system which one was the most important?

A. The jathi system enable the transmission of skills from generation to generation.

B. The occupation as enjoined by the jathi system promoted social interaction amongst the jathis in the village since each jathi pursued one occupation.

C. The jathi system enabled Aryanism to absorb foreigners as well as the indigenous people be they aboriginals or civilised communities.

D. The jathi system provided social security to its members.

135. Name one of the following with whom the later foreign immigrants who came after downfall of the Gupta are associated with?

A. Kshatriyas

B. Fallen Kshatriyas

C. Rajputs

D. Mlechhas

136. Which of the following type of marriage were not generally approved of, specially among the Brahmanas:

A. Brahma B. Gandharva

C. Daiva D. Arsa

137. To which one of the following traditional categories did the Svayamvara (Self choice) form of marriage, which later became popular among kshatriyas, belong?

A. Brahma B. Asura

C. Gandhara D. Arsa

138. Which one of the following allows a man to win over a girl by fair or foul means under special circumstances?

A. Manu B. Kautilya

C. Vatsyayana D. Baudhayana

139. Which of the following status was assigned to a person born of an anuloma marriage?

A. Same as that of the father

B. Same as that of the mother

C. Intermediate between that of the two parents

D. Lower than that of either parent

140. On a woman's death her personal property (Stridhana) passed on to her:

A. husband B. Sons

C. daughters D. daughter-in-law

141. Indicate one of the following which gave women an important place in their cult and instituted orders of female ascetics?

A. Jainas B. Buddhists

C. Ajivikas D. Tantric sects

142. In which of the following regions was prostitution in temples commonly found?

A. North B. South

C. East D. West

143. Identify one of the following which did not have a recognised judicial status:
A. Guild
B. Folk — assembly or council
C. Caste panchayat
D. The king

144. How were the illegitimate offsprings of a Brahman Couple counted?
A. Vaishyas B. Sudras
C. Untouchable D. Kshatriyas

145. To which one of the following traditional categories did the Svayamvara form of marriage belong?
A. Gandhara B. Asura
C. Prajapatya D. Daiva

146. Which of the following authorities lays down a list of priority in inheritance for women, which places the wife, followed by daughters, immediately after the sons?
A. Manu B. Yajnavalkya
C. Narada D. Brihaspati

147. Which of the following types of marriage was approved by the text books for the Brahmanas?
A. Daiva B. Arsa
C. Gandhara D. Brahma

148. What contributed most to the formation of administrative structure in the Gutpa period?
A. Economic activities and the needs of a vast empire
B. Land grants
C. Trade and Commerce
D. Belief in Divine Right of kingship

149. Which of the following disabilities was imposed on the Sudras for the Ist time during post-Gupta period?
A. It was laid down that the shadow of a Sudra could pollute the twice born
B. Inter-marriages between upper classes and the Sudras were forbidden
C. The Sudras were not permitted to read the vedic texts
D. The Sudras was not permitted to participate in Vedic Sacrifices.

150. Which one of the following is generally considered as the most important factor in the proliferation of castes in ancient India:
A. Turning of professional and occupational groups into castes
B. Turning of religious sects into castes
C. Increase in varnasamkara
D. Absorption of alien ethnic groups in Hindu society

151. In which of the following works does the hereditory caste system appear as chief determinant of social activity?
A. Bhagavad Gita
B. Manu Smiriti
C. Early Pali Literature
D. Kautilya's Arthasastra

152. Which of the following law givers of the post-Gupta period did not agree to the view that the shadow of a Chandala could pullute the members of the twice born castes?
A. Manu B. Medhatithi
C. Jimutavahana D. Vijnanesvara

153. Where did the first memorial of sati dated 510 A.D. is found?
A. North-West province
B. Rajasthan
C. Eran, Madhya Pradesh
D. Mysore

154. What was the status assigned to the earlier foreign immigrants by Manu?
A. Kshatriyas
B. Fallen Kshatriyas
C. Sudras
D. Degraded Brahmanas

155. What was the caste assigned to a cross between a Brahmana and a Sudra women?
A. Vaishya B. Kshatriya
C. Nishada D. Sudra

156. The division of society based on Varna appeared first in:
A. The Rig Vedic period
B. The Later Vedic period
C. The 6th Century B.C.
D. 500 B.C. — 500 A.D.

157. When did the Chandelas appear in Hindus Society?
A. 5th century B.C. B. Ist century B.C.
C. Ist century A.D. D. 4th Century B.C.

158. Historically speaking the four-fold division of society or caste system came into existence:
A. In the Vedic period
B. Around 600 B.C.
C. In the Maurya period
D. With the beginning of agriculture and trade

159. When did the concept of pollution emerge clearly?
A. In the Rig Vedic period
B. In the post-Vedic period
C. In the age of Dharma Shastra
D. In the post-Gupta age

ANSWERS

1	2	3	4	5	6	7	8	9	10
B	C	C	A	C	C	C	C	D	D
11	**12**	**13**	**14**	**15**	**16**	**17**	**18**	**19**	**20**
D	D	A	B	A	A	B	D	B	B
21	**22**	**23**	**24**	**25**	**26**	**27**	**28**	**29**	**30**
A	D	D	A	C	A	D	A	B	C
31	**32**	**33**	**34**	**35**	**36**	**37**	**38**	**39**	**40**
C	D	A	D	C	D	D	C	B	D
41	**42**	**43**	**44**	**45**	**46**	**47**	**48**	**49**	**50**
D	C	C	B	A	C	B	B	A	C
51	**52**	**53**	**54**	**55**	**56**	**57**	**58**	**59**	**60**
B	A	C	D	B	D	D	D	B	D
61	**62**	**63**	**64**	**65**	**66**	**67**	**68**	**69**	**70**
D	D	C	C	B	A	A	B	D	C
71	**72**	**73**	**74**	**75**	**76**	**77**	**78**	**79**	**80**
D	D	A	C	C	C	A	C	D	D
81	**82**	**83**	**84**	**85**	**86**	**87**	**88**	**89**	**90**
C	B	D	B	A	C	B	B	A	A
91	**92**	**93**	**94**	**95**	**96**	**97**	**98**	**99**	**100**
C	B	B	A	C	D	A	C	A	B
101	**102**	**103**	**104**	**105**	**106**	**107**	**108**	**109**	**110**
A	D	B	D	B	D	C	A	D	D
111	**112**	**113**	**114**	**115**	**116**	**117**	**118**	**119**	**120**
C	C	D	A	A	A	C	D	C	A
121	**122**	**123**	**124**	**125**	**126**	**127**	**128**	**129**	**130**
B	C	A	D	C	B	D	A	D	D
131	**132**	**133**	**134**	**135**	**136**	**137**	**138**	**139**	**140**
D	B	B	C	C	B	C	C	C	C
141	**142**	**143**	**144**	**145**	**146**	**147**	**148**	**149**	**150**
D	B	C	B	A	B	C	B	A	A
151	**152**	**153**	**154**	**155**	**156**	**157**	**158**	**159**	
B	D	C	B	C	B	A	D	C	

SOUTH INDIA AND THE CHOLAS

1. The first ruler of the Cholas, who maintained a strong navy, was:
   A. Rajendra I
   B. Karikala
   C. Parantaka
   D. Rajaraja the Great
2. The Chola administration was primarily based upon:
   A. Central Government
   B. Provincial administration
   C. Local self-Government
   D. Military power
3. The executive committee of which one of the following general assemblies was called Variyam?
   A. Ur B. Sabha
   C. Nagaram D. Mahasabha
4. During the time of Cholas "Valanadu" referred to a:
   A. Province
   B. Sub-division of a province
   C. Village
   D. Brahmana Village
5. What was the name of the Chola king who first conquered the whole of the island of Sri Lanka?
   A. Rajadhiraja I B. Vijayalaya
   C. Karilala D. Rajendra I
6. Identify the Chola king who sent to China in 1077 an embassy of 72 merchants:
   A. Kulottunga I B. Rajendra I
   C. Rajendra II D. Rajadhiraja I
7. Rajendra Chola attacked the Palas in the North probably in:
   A. 1018 A.D. B. 1020 A.D.
   C. 1021 A.D. D. 1023 A.D.
8. We know a great deal more about the Cholas than their predecessors because:
   A. they appointed court chroniclers
   B. many books were written during that period
   C. of long inscription on the walls of temples
   D. of the abundance of coins
9. Who adopted the title of Gangaikonda Chola?
   A. Karikala Chola B. Rajendra I
   C. Rajaraja I D. Rajadhiraja
10. Parantaka I established Chola power in:
    A. 897 A.D. B. 899 A.D.
    C. 905 A.D. D. 907 A.D.
11. The Cholas regained their power after the decline of the:
    A. Chalukyas B. Rashtrakutas
    C. Pallavas D. Kakatiyas
12. The founder of the Chola empire in the 10th century was:
    A. Vijayalaya
    B. Karikala
    C. Parantaka I
    D. Rajaraja the Great
13. What was the name of the Chola king who performed Asvamedha sacrifice?
    A. Rajendra I B. Karikala
    C. Parantaka D. Rajadhiraja I
14. Rajaraja Chola ascended the throne in:
    A. 1016 A.D. B. 1000 A.D.
    C. 985 A.D. D. 953 A.D.
15. Rajaraja and Rajendra I commemorated their victories by:
    A. erecting temples
    B. erecting pillars
    C. ordering inscriptions to be written
    D. issuing coins
16. By what other name is Kulattunga I known as?
    A. Vikrama Chola
    B. Gangaikonda Chola
    C. Pandit Chola
    D. Rajendra II Chalukya
17. To become a member of the Variyam, which one of the following was not necessary?
    A. Ownership of more than 1/4 of the tax-paying land
    B. Residence in a house built on one's own site.

C. Membership of the first three classes of society.
D. Age between 35 and 70 years.

18. Rajendra Chola ascended the throne in:
A. 1044 A.D. B. 1012 A.D.
C. 985 A.D. D. 1000 A.D.

19. Vishti denoted forced labour in Mauryan times. What is the second word meaning forced labour?
A. Vetti B. Sulka
C. Sondhar D. Kara

20. The primary cause of the prosperity of the Chola empire was:
A. agricultural progress
B. trade with foreign countries
C. industries
D. war-booty

21. One of the following did not from an item of export to China and the The West:
A. Jewellery B. Elephants
C. Perfumes D. Spices

22. What was the most important port of the Chola period (10th Century A.D.)?
A. Sopatma B. Camara
C. Kaveripattinam D. Colchi

23. The meetings of the general assembly were held:
A. under a tree
B. on the bank of a tank
C. in a building specially constructed for the purpose
D. at the village temple

24. Devadasi system had become very popular during the period of the:
A. Pandyas B. Cholas
C. Chera D. Chalukyas

25. What was the name of local merchant guilds in Chola times?
A. Ur B. Sabha
C. Nagaram D. Mahasabha

26. Who was the Chola king who bore the name "Arulmolivarman"?
A. Rajendra I B. Parantaka I
C. Rajaraja I D. Kulottunga I

27. Who build the Brihadesvara temple?
A. Parantaka I B. Rajaraja I
C. Rajendra I D. Rajaraja II

28. Who is the author of Kalingattupparani?
A. Kambar B. Ottakuttar
C. Jayangondar D. Pugalendi

29. Who was the founder of Virasaivism?
A. Appar B. Bijjala
C. Basava D. Sundarar

30. Among the places mentioned below no college existed in the Chola period. Identify.
A. Eunayiram B. Tribhuvanam
C. Tiruvaduthurai D. Tiruchi

31. Who patronised the Kannada poet, Rauna?
A. Satyasraya B. Taila II
C. Vikramaditya VI D. Jayasimha II

32. To which of the following did Kannada literature owe much?
A. Brahmanism B. Jainism
C. Buddhism D. Virasaivism

33. The Cholas charged land-tax at the rate of:
A. 1/2 of the produce
B. 1/3 of the produce
C. 1/4 of the produce
D. 1/6 of the produce

34. The main source of income to the Cholas was:
A. toll tax
B. land tax
C. taxes an occupations, wines and forests
D. annexation of neighbouring territories

35. Possibly the South Indian Vimanas were copies from the:
A. Mandapas B. Rathas
C. Gopurams D. Viharas

36. Which one is an open Pavilion?
A. Mandapas B. Gopurams
C. Ratha D. Viharas

37. The continued incursions of who among the following people weakened the Cholas?
A. Hoysalas B. Western Gangas
C. Yadavas D. Kakatiyas

38. Which among the followng did not contribute significantly for the final disinte-

gration of the Cholas?
A. Hoysalas B. Pandyas
C. Kakatiyas D. Yadavas

39. Who was the first Chalukya-Chola ruler?
A. Virarjendra B. Kulottunga I
C. Vijayalaya D. Vimaladitya

40. Name the most eminent images constructed under Chola?
A. Images of Vishnu
B. Images of Kuladevta
C. Images of Natraja
D. Images of King's ancestors

41. Which one was the most important item of import?
A. Horses B. Metal-ware
C. Pottery D. Salt

42. The Chola kings primarily were the worshippers of:
A. Shiva B. Ganesha
C. Vishnu D. Kartikeya

43. What was the basic feature of Chola temple architecture:
A. Garbhagriha B. Mandaps
C. Gopurams D. Vimanas

44. The land revenue under the rule of the Chola was:
A. 1/2 of the produce
B. 1/4 of the produce
C. 1/3 of the produce
D. 1/5 of the produce

45. The Pallava-Chola style of architecture is commonly known as:
A. Pallava B. Chola
C. Nagar D. Dravida

46. Temple architecture in the South attained its climax under:
A. Cheras B. Pandyas
C. Cholas D. Chalukyas

47. The chief features of the temple constructed by the Cholas was their:
A. Gopurams B. Pillars
C. Assembly halls D. Vimanas

48. Which language is patronised by Chola rulers?
A. Sanskrit B. Tamil
C. Telugu D. Kannada

49. Which among the following did not constitute a part of Chola army?
A. Navy B. War elephants
C. Chariots D. Infantry

50. Who amongst the Chola ruler adopted the title Gangaikonda?
A. Rajaraja B. Rajaraja II
C. Rajendra Chola D. Virarajendra

51. Who destroyed the Cheras navy at Trivandrum?
A. Rajaraja B. Rajendra I
C. Sri Vijaya D. Vijayalaya

52. The primary reason of Rajendra Chola in attacking North India was:
A. to establish his supremacy in entire India
B. to capture territories of the North India
C. to perform Aswamedha Yajna
D. to demonstrate his strength

53. The Cholas ruler mostly patronised:
A. Hinduism B. Buddhism
C. Jainism D. Bhagavatism

54. Vijayalaya, the founder of the Chola dynasty, was a feudatory of:
A. The Pallavas
B. The Pandyas
C. The Rashtrakutas
D. None of the above

55. What was the name of the Chola King who made conquest in Sumatra and Malay peninsula?
A. Rajendra I B. Rajaraja I
C. Rajadhiraja I D. Virarajendra

56. There was an administrative unit under the Cholas Kurran. What did it signify?
A. A village
B. A province
C. A district
D. A group of villages

57. What was the most serious set-back to the Chola empire in the 9th century?
A. Cholas were completely uprooted their position against Rashtrakutas
B. Cholas were hard out to defend their position

C. Cholas did not have a strong army
D. None of the above

58. Which one of the following terms stands for the regular royal troops of the Cholas?
A. Kadagams B. Nattupaddi
C. Kaikkolar D. Bhrtaka

59. Under Cholas the local merchant guilds were called:
A. Nagaram
B. Manigramam
C. Valanjiyar
D. None of the above

60. During the reign of Chola rulers Indian foreign trade flourished most with:
A. Persia B. Arabia
C. South-East Asia D. China

61. The social life of the Cholas was characterised by:
A. An extreme sense of exclusiveness
B. An inter mixture of castes
C. Priestly dominance
D. Social harmony

62. Which one of the Rashtrakuta Kings defeated Parantaka I and caused a temporary eclipse of the Cholas?
A. Amonghvarsha I B. Govinda III
C. Indra III D. Krishna III

63. Chola empire was established on the ruins of:
A. Pandyas B. Pallavas
C. Chalukyas D. Rashtrakutas

64. Which style of architecture came into vogue during this period?
A. Nagara
B. Dravida
C. Mandapa
D. None of the above

65. What was Mandap in temple?
A. A pillard hall
B. Monastery
C. Deity Room
D. None of the above

66. Name the Chinese Pilgrim who commented that Chola country was deserted and wild succession of marshes and jungles.
A. I-Tsing
B. Hiuen Tsang
C. Fa-hien
D. None of the above

67. During the whose reign was Raja-rajesvara temple constructed?
A. Vijayalaya B. Rajendra
C. Rajaraja II D. Rajaraja III

68. Who founded the Capital Gangaikondacholapuram?
A. Parantaka I B. Rajendra Chola
C. Rajadhiraja I D. Rajaraja I

69. What is a "Garbhagriha" in the Dravida style of architecture:
A. A pillard hall
B. Monastery
C. Corridor
D. Chief deity's room

70. Where is the Gomateswar temple in the South India situated?
A. Madurai B. Tanjore
C. Halebed D. Sravana belgola

71. Nayanars were devotees of:
A. Shiva B. Vishnu
C. Durga D. Tirthankaras

72. Which among the following represented the local mercantile interests:
A. Ur B. Nagaram
C. Mahasabha D. Sabha

73. Navibe Audar Nambi the famous scholar who arranged the Saiva Canons was a contemporary of:
A. Virarajendra B. Rajendra I
C. Rajaraja I D. Rajendra II

74. Chola style of temple architecture is called:
A. Mandap B. Dravida
C. Mandham D. Gopuram

75. Who wrote Ramayana in Tamil language?
A. Kamban B. Kuttan
C. Rugulendi D. Kalladanar

76. Which among the following was not conquerred by Rajendra Chola I?
A. Pandya and Chera territories
B. Sri Lanka
C. Sailendra Empire

D. Southern provinces of the Chalukyas of Kalyani

77. Sudras or slaves or prisoners of war were employed as a scale to reclaim waste land and clear forests for the first time under the:

A. Mauryas B. Satavahanas
C. Cholas D. Guptas

78. Chau-Ju-Khan, a Chinese author of early thirteenth century left an important account on one of the following dynasty. Identify.

A. Chola dynasty B. Slave dynasty
C. Khilji dynasty D. Yadava dynasty

79. The conquest of Sri Lanka was completed during the reign of:

A. Rajaraja B. Rajendra I
C. Parantaka I D. Aditya I

80. The chief social obligation of the Chola state was:

A. to protect the brahmans
B. to protect the women
C. to maintain peace and security in the society
D. to protect temples

81. In which style were the temples at Bhuvaneshwar, Puri and Khajuraho built?

A. Nagara Style
B. Vasara Style
C. Dravida Style
D. None of the above

82. Kamban is believed to have lived at the Court of:

A. Pandya king B. Chola king
C. Pallava king D. Chalukya king

83. Devotees of Vishnu were called:

A. Brahmanas
B. Nayanars
C. Alvars
D. None of the above

84. Capitals, like Tanjore, Gangaikonda-cholapuram; Kanchi were constructed by:

A. Pratiharas B. Cheras
C. Cholas D. Chalukyas

85. When did the Venetian traveller Marco Polo came to Kerala?

A. 10th Century B. 11th Century
C. 12th Century D. 13th Century

86. The South-Indian King who invaded the overseas kingdom of Shrivijaya in South-east Asia was:

A. Rajadhiraja B. Rajaraja I
C. Rajendra I D. Parantaka I

87. Parantaka I established Chola power in:

A. Century 897 A.D.
B. Century 899 A.D.
C. Century 905 A.D.
D. Century 907 A.D.

88. We know a great deal more about the Cholas than their predecessors because:

A. they appointed Court Chroniclers
B. many books were written during that period
C. of long inscriptions on the walls of temples
D. of the abundance of coins

89. Rajaraja and Rajendra I commemorated their victories by:

A. erecting temples
B. erecting pillars
C. ordering inscriptions to be written
D. issuing coins

90. Regarding religion during the Chola period are point 'is' incorrect. Which is?

A. Cholas were Brahmanical Hindus, and most of them worshipped Vishnu
B. Rajaraja built a temple dedicated to Shiva
C. Royal gifts were normally monopolised by Brahmans
D. Chola kings rarely performed Vedic Sacrifices

91. Who built the world famous temples at Khajuraho?

A. Pratiharas B. Pushyabhnis
C. Chandolas D. Tomars

92. Which style of architecture as mentioned by Silpsastra was popular in the Deccan:

A. Nagara
B. Vesara
C. Dravida

D. None of the above

93. Ghatika is a sattlement of:
A. Merchants B. Brahmans
C. Buddhist monks D. Jain monks

94. Who was the south Indian Kings, whose troops reached the banks of the Ganges, but did not hold the northern region for long, and whose position was similar to that of Samudraguptas campaign in the south?
A. Rajaraja I B. Rajendra I
C. Rajadhiraja D. Vijayalaya

95. Lokamahadevi, the chief queen of a Chola king performed the "Hiranyagrabha" ceremony. Whose wife was she?
A. Rajaraja I B. Rajendra Chola
C. Rajadhiraja D. Kulotunga Chola

96. The founder of the Chola empire in the 10th century was:
A. Vijayalaya B. Karikala
C. Parantaka D. Rajaraja

97. Which of the facts of the administration of the Cholas is incorrect?
A. The kings adopted high sounding title
B. The statues of the dead rulers were worshipped
C. The rajaguru was both the confident and confessor of the royal family
D. The royal household was maintained in a very austere manner typyfing the southern tradition.

98. Who is the author of Kural which is regarded as the Tamil Veda?
A. Tiruthakathevar B. Ilango
C. Tiruvalluvar D. Sittali Sattana

99. Which one is an open pavillion?
A. Mandapam B. Gopuram
C. Ratha D. Vihar

100. The Chola empire decline in:
A. early 13th century
B. early 12th century
C. later 11th century
D. middle 12th century

101. Who was the Chola king who was defeated by the Rashtrakuta king Krishna III, in about 949 A.D. in the battle of Takkolam?
A. Rajaditya
B. Uttamchola Madurantheka
C. Rajaraja I
D. Parantaka I

102. What was the most important part of Chola period (10th Century A.D.)?
A. Sopatma B. Camara
C. Kaveripattinam D. Colchi

103. Possibly South Indian Vimanas were copied from the:
A. Mandapams B. Gopuram
C. Ratha D. Vihar

104. Rajendra Chola attacked the Palas in the North probably in:
A. 1018 A.D. B. 1020 A.D.
C. 1021 A.D. D. 1023 A.D.

105. The general assembly consists of the tax paying residents of an ordinary Chola Village was known as:
A. Ur B. Sabha
C. Nagaram D. Kurram

106. Which of the statement about the Chola villages might not be true?
A. They enjoyed autonomy
B. The officials participated in villages affairs more as advisers and observers than as administrators
C. Each village had an assembly of villagers, authority being vested in it
D. Larger villages had a variety of assemblies but a villager could be a member of only one.

107. Which statement regarding Chola social structure is incorrect?
A. The Brahmans continued to represent an alien culture
B. Very little known about Kshatriya Vaishyas and Shudras
C. The concept of pollution was known
D. Both men and women were sold as slaves and some of them to the temple.

108. Which is not the Bhakti literature of Saivas?
A. Prabandham
B. Tevaram
C. Tiruvadhakam

D. None of the above

109. Who adopted the title of Gangaikonda Chola?
A. Karikal Chola B. Rajendra I
C. Rajaraja I D. Rajadhiraja

110. Which one of the following is the most lasting contribution of the Rashtrakutas?
A. Kailasa Temple
B. Pampa, Panna, Ranna: three writers of Kannada Poetry and Kailasa temple
C. Patronage of Jainism
D. Checkmating the Pratiharas

111. Name the Chola king who is said to have brought back 12000 Ceylonese prisoners after his successful campaign in Ceylon and employed them as labourers for the Kaveri irrigation project.
A. Elara B. Karikala Chola
C. Nedimudikilli D. Kupperum Chola

112. Vishti denoted forced labour in Mauryan times. What is the second word meaning forced labour?
A. Vetti B. Sulka
C. Sondhar D. Kara

113. Devadasi system had become very popular during the period of:
A. Pandaya B. Cholas
C. Chera D. Chalukyas

114. Which fact regarding Rajendra Chola I is not correct?
A. Chola power received a setback
B. He annexed the whole of Ceylon
C. He waged war the Chalukya king Jayasimha II
D. He conquered territories north of the Tungabhadra

115. Which statement as Rajaraja I is not correct?
A. With him began the history of the great Cholas.
B. He defeated the Chera naval power and occupied a part of Ceylon.
C. He defeated Vimaladitya, the Chalukya king of Vengi, and probably conquered Kalinga.
D. In the end he was killed by his own son.

116. Who were not associated with the development of Dravidian style of architecture of far South?
A. Pandyas B. Pallavas
C. Chalukyas D. Cholas

117. The Uttaramerur inscription gives details of how the local Sabha functioned refers to the autonomy enjoyed by the village of the:
A. Pandyas B. Cheras
C. Cholas D. Chalukyas

118. Chola Kingdom in the 11th Century was divided into provinces known as:
A. Nandalam B. Valanadus
C. Nadu D. Muiyar

119. The Uttaramerur inscription gives details of the functioning of which village assembly?
A. Ur B. Sabha
C. Ur and Sabha D. Nagaram

120. The object of South India King invading the South East Asian Kingdom of Shrivijaya was:
A. colonisation
B. an attempt to conquer more of the hinterland
C. the protection of Indian commercial interests from interference
D. to enhance his prestige at home

ANSWERS

1	2	3	4	5	6	7	8	9	10
D	C	B	B	D	A	C	A	B	D
11	**12**	**13**	**14**	**15**	**16**	**17**	**18**	**19**	**20**
C	C	D	C	A	D	C	B	A	B

21	**22**	**23**	**24**	**25**	**26**	**27**	**28**	**29**	**30**
C	C	D	D	C	C	B	C	C	D
31	**32**	**33**	**34**	**35**	**36**	**37**	**38**	**39**	**40**
B	D	B	C	B	A	A	D	B	C
41	**42**	**43**	**44**	**45**	**46**	**47**	**48**	**49**	**50**
A	A	D	B	D	C	D	B	C	C
51	**52**	**53**	**54**	**55**	**56**	**57**	**58**	**59**	**60**
A	D	A	A	A	D	B	C	A	D
61	**62**	**63**	**64**	**65**	**66**	**67**	**68**	**69**	**70**
D	D	B	B	A	B	B	B	D	D
71	**72**	**73**	**74**	**75**	**76**	**77**	**78**	**79**	**80**
A	B	B	B	A	C	A	A	B	C
81	**82**	**83**	**84**	**85**	**86**	**87**	**88**	**89**	**90**
A	B	C	C	D	C	D	C	A	A
91	**92**	**93**	**94**	**95**	**96**	**97**	**98**	**99**	**100**
C	B	A	B	A	C	D	C	A	A
101	**102**	**103**	**104**	**105**	**106**	**107**	**108**	**109**	**110**
D	C	B	C	A	D	A	A	B	B
111	**112**	**113**	**114**	**115**	**116**	**117**	**118**	**119**	**120**
B	A	B	A	D	C	C	A	B	C

PRE-MEDIEVAL INDIA

1. In the Rashtrakuta Kingdom, the directly administered areas were divided into:
   A. Rashtra B. Vaisya
   C. Bhukti D. All the above
2. The Vaisya was like:
   A. Village B. Province
   C. A Taluk D. Modern district
3. What was the basic unit of administration under Rashtrakuta:
   A. Province B. Family
   C. District D. Village
4. In Northern India the period 500-1200 A.D. is considered as a:
   A. Period of cultural uplift
   B. Period of social uplift
   C. Period of stagnation and decline
   D. Continuation of Golden age
5. Who among the following Pratihara rulers, was defeated by the Rashtrakuta ruler Govinda III?
   A. Vatsraja B. Nagabhatta II
   C. Mihirbhoja D. Mahipala
6. The Rashtrakutas were successors of the:
   A. Pallavas of Kanchi
   B. Chalukyas of Kalyani
   C. Chalukyas of Badami
   D. None of these
7. Chalukyas established their empire in:
   A. Gujarat B. Malwa
   C. Deccan D. Far South India
8. The Palas of Bengal patronised:
   A. Hinduism
   B. Jainism
   C. Hinayana Buddhism
   D. Tantrika Buddhism
9. Rashtrakutas rulers patronised:
   A. Shaivism B. Vaishnavism
   C. Jainism D. All the three
10. Who was the contemporary of Palas in the Deccan?
    A. Pratiharas
    B. Chalukyas
    C. Rashtrakutas
    D. None of the above
11. Who checkmated Bhoja's away on the east?
    A. Gopala
    B. Dharmapala
    C. Devpala
    D. None of the above
12. How did Pratiharas gain prominence?
    A. Because they were local officials
    B. They were big Zamindars
    C. On account of their resistance to Arab incursions
    D. None of the above
13. Rulers of Sailendra dynasty were:
    A. Buddhist in faith
    B. Jains
    C. Brahmans
    D. None of the above
14. Which amongst the Pala kings tried to extend their power to Assam?
    A. Gopala
    B. Dharmapala
    C. Mahendrapala
    D. None of the above
15. The Pala empire was founded by:
    A. Dharmapala
    B. Gopala
    C. Dhruva
    D. None of the above
16. Amonghavarsha was a:
    A. Parthihara king
    B. Chalukya king
    C. Rashtrakuta king
    D. Pala king
17. The system of administration in Rashtrakuta empires was based on the ideas and practices of the:
    A. Gupta empire
    B. Harshas kingdom
    C. Chalukyas in the Deccan
    D. All the above
18. The author of Gita-Govinda was:
    A. Jayadeva
    B. Bana

C. Dandi
D. None of the above

19. The University of Vikramasila was established under the patronage of:
A. The palas
B. The senas
C. The pratiharas
D. Yosovarman of Kannauj

20. Which one of the following aspects of feudal relationship gradually gained importance during this period?
A. Attendance at court
B. Paying of tribute
C. Hierarchy among the feudatories
D. Military service

21. Where did the Pala king have his seat of authority?
A. Kannauj B. Pataliputra
C. Tamralipti D. Monghyr

22. Name the Pala king who founded the Vikramasila University:
A. Dharmapala B. Devapala
C. Ramapala D. Gopala

23. The Pratihara army was considered to be the best of its kind mainly because of the efficiency of its:
A. Infantry B. Cavalry
C. Chariots D. Elephants

24. The Pratiharas first settled at:
A. Ujjain B. Mandor
C. Kannauj D. Chedi

25. Nagabhatta II established Pratihara Supremacy at:
A. Kannauj B. Ajmer
C. Tripuri D. Anhilwada

26. The main basis of social organisation in India during the early medieval period was:
A. Clan B. Religion
C. Caste D. Kingship

27. Which of the following empires lasted the longest?
A. Chalukya empire
B. Pala empire
C. Pratihara empire
D. Rashtrakuta empire

28. The Pala empire was founded by Gopala, probably in:
A. 600 A.D. B. 650 A.D.
C. 750 A.D. D. 800 A.D.

29. Who was the founder of Chalukya dynasty of Kalyani?
A. Taila
B. Gopala
C. Aditya
D. None of the above

30. The history of the Pallavas becomes more-definite from the time of:
A. Vishnugopa
B. Mahendravarman I
C. Simhavishnu
D. Narsimhavarman

31. Which one of the following engaged in a three pronged struggle, was the strongest and lasted out the longest:
A. Palas B. Pratiharas
C. Rashtrakutas D. Chalukyas

32. The contest for the mastery of Kannauj started during the reign of the Pala king:
A. Gopala B. Dharmapala
C. Devapala D. Vigrahapala

33. Which one of the following is the most lasting contribution of the Rashtrakutas?
A. Kailasa temple
B. Pampa, Ponna, Ranna; three writers of Kannada poetry and Kailasa temple
C. Patronage of Jainism
D. Checkmating the Prathiharas

34. From among the following name the greatest Pala king that ever ruled in Bengal:
A. Gopala B. Dharmapala
C. Devapala D. Mahipala

35. Who, among the following Pratihara rulers, was defeated by the Rashtrakuta ruler Govinda III?
A. Vatsaraja B. Nagabhatta II
C. Mihir Bhoja D. Mahipala

36. Who built the first great empire south of the Penner and the Tungabhadra?
A. The early Chalukyas
B. The Palas

C. Later Chalukyas
D. The Pallavas

37. Who amongst the Pallava Kings bore the epithet of Vichitrachitta?
A. Narsimhavarman I
B. Vikramaditya I
C. Mahendravarman I
D. Rajsimha

38. Where did Chalukyas have their first Capital?
A. Madurai B. Kanchi
C. Vatapi D. Kannauj

39. Who executed the Kailas temple at Ellora?
A. Dantidurga B. Krishna I
C. Amoghvarsha D. Govinda III

40. Where was the second Capital of Rashtrakutas?
A. Vatapi B. Tanjore
C. Madura D. Manyakheta

41. Name the Rashtrakuta King who defeated the Pratihara ruler, Nagabhatta:
A. Amoghavarsha I B. Govinda III
C. Indra III D. Krishna III

42. The founder of the Rashtrakutas dynasty was:
A. Govinda
B. Dhruva
C. Dhantivarman
D. Kannara or Krishna I

43. Identify the region where the first invasion of Muhammad of Ghaur was launched.
A. Punjab B. Multan
C. Sindh D. Gujarat

44. Which was the capital of the Hindu Shahiya Kingdom when it was attacked by Mahmud?
A. Kabul
B. Peshawar
C. Attock
D. Udabhanda or Und

45. Which of the following set up a Kingdom for the Hoyasala dynasty?
A. Vishnuvardhana (Sala)
B. Ballalala
C. Bhillama
D. Harihara

46. Which one of the following were the bitterest enemies of the Chauhans?
A. Chandellas
B. Solankis
C. Tomaras
D. Gahadavalas of Kannauj

47. In which of the following empires did the Pandyas finally merge?
A. Bahmani B. Chera
C. Vijayanagar D. Delhi Sultanate

48. Dhillika (Delhi) was founded in 736 A.D. by the:
A. Gahadavalas B. Tomaras
C. Paramaras D. Chauhans

49. To which Rajput clan did Jai Chand belong?
A. Chauhans
B. Rathors or Gaharwars
C. Kalachuris
D. Chandallas

50. Which of Mahmud Gazni's invasions of temple towns was the most famous?
A. Somnath B. Mathura
C. Thaneswar D. Kannauj

51. Which one of the following came to India at the instance of Sultan Mahmud?
A. Al-Masudi B. Sulaiman
C. Al-Beruni D. Ibn Hauqual

52. Which of the following looked after Muhammad Ghuri's affairs in India when he was engaged with the Turks in Central Asia?
A. Bakhtiyar Khalji
B. Ikhtiyar-ud-din Muhammad
C. Qutb-ud-din Aibak
D. Muiz-ud-din Muhammad bin sam

53. Which one of the following defeated the Chalukyas of Vatapi (Badami) and founded the Rashtrakuta empire?
A. Dhruva B. Govinda III
C. Dantidurga D. Amoghavarsha

54. Which of the following were the most important rivals of the Rashtrakutas?
A. Palas B. Chalukyas
C. Pallavas D. Pratiharas

55. Where was the capital of the Rashtrakutas

located?

A. Badami B. Kalyani
C. Vengi D. Malkhed

56. Who among the Rashtrakuta rulers, constructed the famous Kailasha temple at Ellora?

A. Krishna I B. Govinda II
C. Dhruva D. Govinda III

57. The Paramara dynasty was founded by:

A. Upendra B. Bhoja
C. Vakpati-Munja D. Sindhuraja

58. Dhara, the Capital of the Paramara dynasty, was raised to a position of a eminence by:

A. Sindhuraja B. Bhoja
C. Upendra D. Vakpati-Munja

59. The dynasty of the Chalukyas of Anhilwada was founded by:

A. Mularaja B. Raji
C. Bhima I D. Karna

60. Jainism was patronised by the:

A. Chalukyas B. Chandellas
C. Rathores D. Kalachuris

61. Who overthrew the last ruler of the western Chalukyas of Badami?

A. Dantidurga B. Taila
C. Gopala D. Bhoja

62. Which two Kings defeated the Arabs of Sind?

1. Dhruva 2. Nagabhatta II
3. Mihira Bhoja 4. Krishna III

Codes:

A. 1 and 2 B. 2 and 3
C. 1 and 3 D. 3 and 4

63. Who founded the Brahmana Shahi Dynasty?

A. Kallar B. Samanta
C. Bhima D. Didda

64. Who was the Ghaznavid ruler who fought against Jayapala at Ghuzak?

A. Alptigin B. Ismail
C. Sabuktigin D. Mahmud

65. Who among the Brahmana Shahu got converted to Islam and later abjured it?

A. Anandapala B. Jayapala
C. Trilochanapala D. Sukhapala

66. Who introduced Kulinism among the Brahmanas?

A. Vijaya Sena B. Hemanta Sena
C. Samanta Sena D. Vallala Sena

67. To which race did Mahmud belong?

A. Arabs B. Afghans
C. Mongols D. Turks

68. Who were the Yaminis?

A. Khaljis B. Ghurida
C. Ghaznavids D. Tughluqs

69. Who said that the Rashtrakutas were the most feared rulers of India?

A. Utbi B. Al-Beruni
C. Al-Kazwini D. Sulaiman

70. The continued incursious of which, among the following people weakened the Cholas?

A. Hoysalas B. Western Gangas
C. Yadavas D. Kakatiyas

71. Who was the Chola King who bore the name "Arulmolivarman"?

A. Rajendra I B. Parantake I
C. Rajaraja I D. Kulottunga I

72. Who built the Brihadisvara temple?

A. Parantaka I B. Rajaraja I
C. Rajendra I D. Rajaraja II

73. Who is the author of Kalingattupparani?

A. Kambar B. Ottakuttar
C. Jayangondar D. Pugalendi

74. Which inscription gives details of the election to village assembly?

A. Tiruvalangadu Plates
B. Uttaramerur inscription
C. Velvikkudi grant
D. Anbil grant

75. Who used the Traikutaka era?

A. Chandellas B. Kalachuris
C. Paramaras D. Chahamanas

76. Name the Kalachuri who issued coins with his name and figure of Lakshmi:

A. Lakshmi–Karna B. Gangeyadeva
C. Kokalla II D. Yasah-Karna

77. Who established a college for Sanskrit studies at Dhar?

A. Sindhuraja B. Bhoja I
C. Vakpatiraja II D. Arjunavarman

78. In which language was the dictionary "Paiyalachchhi" compiled?

A. Prakrit B. Pali

C. Sanskrit D. Telugu

79. Who among the following assumed the title "Navasahasanka".

A. Bhoja B. Sindhuraja
C. Harsha Siyaka II D. Krishnaraja

80. What is the meaning of Paramara?

A. Conqueror of the enemy
B. Slayer of the enemy
C. A virtuous man
D. An immortal

81. Who founded the Simha era?

A. Mularaja
B. Bhimadeva I
C. Karnadeva
D. Jayasimha Siddharaja

82. In whose reign were the Gurjara Pratiharas deprived of highly prized Vishnu image?

A. Mahipala B. Mahendapala
C. Devapala D. Vijayapala

83. To which of the original clan did the Chandellas Bundelkhand are said to be related?

A. Gonds B. Santhals
C. Kols D. Mundas

84. Name the Pala who made the Pala dynasty a force in North India Politics:

A. Dharmapala B. Mahipala
C. Gopala D. Vigrahapala

85. In which language was "Karpuramanjari" written?

A. Sanskrit B. Prakrit
C. Pali D. Telugu

86. Who founded the Chandella dynasty of Bundelkhand?

A. Jayasakti B. Yasovarman
C. Dhanga D. Nannuka

87. Who was the founder of Virasaivism?

A. Appar B. Bijjala
C. Basava D. Sundaran

88. To which of the following did Kannada literature much:

A. Brahmanism B. Jainism
C. Buddhism D. Virasaivism

89. Who among the following Kings abdicated?

1. Chandragupta Maurya
2. Chandragupta I
3. Samudragupta
4. Rajyavadhan

Codes:

A. only 1 B. only 2
C. only 1 and 2 D. only 1, 2 and 4

90. The Chola period constitutes the most creative phase of South Indian History and is one during which Tamil culture reached a peak in the field of:

A. Literature
B. Literature, temple building
C. Literature, temple building and bronze-casting
D. Literature, temple-building, bronze-casting and self-government

91. The earliest to be Brahmanished in the Deccan were the:

A. Satavahanas B. Pallavas
C. Cholas D. Pandyas

92. Which point on trade and commerce during 800 and 1200 A.D. is incorrect?

A. Malwa and Gujarat benefited the most
B. The North Indian trade languished
C. Some shrenis emerged as sub-caste
D. No ban on sea travel by the Dharmasastras

93. Which one was the chief factor for the successful establishment of Jainism in Western India?

A. Patronage extended by Rashtrakutas, Chalukyas of Kalyani and Parmaras of Malwa.
B. Prosperity because of trade and commerce
C. Hindu influence was weak in the region
D. None of these

94. The founder of the Rashtrakutas dynasty was:

A. Govinda B. Dhruva
C. Dantidurga D. Krishna

95. Which city was the base of contention between the Rashtrakutas, the Pratiharas and the Palas?

A. Kannauj B. Ujjain

C. Pataliputra D. Paithan

96. Who issued the gold coins first?
A. Mauryas B. Nandas
C. Indo-Bactrians D. Kushans

97. Who is known as the South Indian Manu?
A. Bhadrabahu B. Apasthamba
C. Akkatiyar D. Tiruvalluvar

98. Who among the following Sultans did not take the royal title?
A. Kuhsrav Khan
B. Jalal-ud-din Khilji
C. Khizr Khan
D. Bahlol Khan Lodi

99. Who patronised the Kannada Poet, Ranna?
A. Satyasraya B. Taila II
C. Vikramaditya VI D. Jayasimha II

100. Where did the Yadavas establish their power?
A. Sevuna B. Godawari delta
C. Dvarasamudra D. Orissa

101. Who founded Devagiri?
A. Jaitugi B. Bhillama
C. Sennchandra D. Singhana

102. Where were the "Sevunas"?
A. Pallavas
B. Western Gangas
C. Yadavas of Devagiri
D. Eastern Chalukyas of Vengi

103. Who was the ruler when Changez Khan reached Indian borders for the first time in 1221 A.D.?
A. Balban
B. Qutb-ud-din Aibak
C. Iltutmish
D. Raziyya

104. Who built the Quwwat-ut-Islam?
A. Qutb-ud-din B. Iltutmish
C. Balban D. Raziyya

105. Who was called the Lakh Baksha?
A. Iltutmish
B. Qutb-ud-din Aibak
C. Jalal-ud-din Khalji
D. Aram Shah

106. Which of the following cities was renamed Khizrabad:
A. Ranthambhor B. Chittor
C. Jalore D. Jhain

107. The most popular medium of exchange in gold during the early Gupta period was known as:
A. Dinara B. Dramma
C. Karshapana D. Suvanna

108. The kings of which one of the dynasties adopted the policy of nominating successors?
A. Maurya B. Gupta
C. Sunga D. Kanva

109. Rasthrakutas continual struggle with the Pratiharas and the Palas was fostered by the fact that:
A. the possession of Kannauj would enhance their prestige
B. they attached great importance to the control of Malwa and Gujarat
C. they wanted to guard the trade routes
D. they wanted to safeguard their outer flank

110. Which fact relating to the Rashtrakutas is of significance?
A. Patronage extended to Jainism
B. Acquiescence of Muslim rule in Sind and the preaching of Islam
C. Patronage of Sanskrit Scholars such as Rajashekhara
D. Earliest work on poetics in Kannada by Amoghavarsha

111. They were great builders and are still remembered for thier magnificent rock-cut temples and pagodas at Mahabali-puram near Madras. Identify them.
A. Guptas B. Chalukyas
C. Cholas D. Pallavas

112. The great Nayanaras and Alvars were the contemporaries of:
A. Sangam Cholas B. Pallavas
C. Satavahanas D. Sangam Cheras

113. What is the Chola's contribution to art and architecture?
A. Bronze Natarajas and Gopuram
B. Rock-cut caves and frescoes

C. Bronze Natarajas and rock-cut caves
D. None of the above

114. What was the name of local merchant guilds in Chola times?
A. Ur B. Sabha
C. Nagaram D. Mahasabha

115. The Cholas regained their power after the declines of the:
A. Chalukyas B. Rashtrakutas
C. Pallavas D. Kakatiyas

116. Identify the Chola king who sent to China in 1077 an embassry of 72 merchants.
A. Kulottunga I B. Rajendra I
C. Rajendra II D. Rajaraja II

117. During the time of Chola "Valanadu" referred to:
A. a province
B. a sub-division of province
C. a village
D. a Brahman village

118. The best remembered Chola king were:
A. Rajaraja I and Rajendra
B. Vijayalaya and Parantaka
C. Rajaraja I and Parantaka
D. Rajaraja I and Rajaraja II

119. The battle of Takkolaur in 949 A.D. led to:
A. a temporary eclipse of the Cholas
B. the totals eclipse of the Pallavas
C. the end of the Rashtrakutas
D. the death of the Parantaka I

120. Which one was the most significant achievement of Cholas?
A. Periodic survey of land
B. Variety of village institutions
C. Perfection of the Dravidian style of architecture that was pioneered by the pallavas.
D. Overseas conquest

ANSWERS

1	2	3	4	5	6	7	8	9	10
D	D	D	C	B	C	C	D	D	C
11	**12**	**13**	**14**	**15**	**16**	**17**	**18**	**19**	**20**
C	C	A	B	B	C	D	A	A	D
21	**22**	**23**	**24**	**25**	**26**	**27**	**28**	**29**	**30**
D	A	B	B	A	C	D	C	A	C
31	**32**	**33**	**34**	**35**	**36**	**37**	**38**	**39**	**40**
C	B	B	B	B	D	C	C	B	D
41	**42**	**43**	**44**	**45**	**46**	**47**	**48**	**49**	**50**
B	C	B	D	A	D	C	B	B	A
51	**52**	**53**	**54**	**55**	**56**	**57**	**58**	**59**	**60**
C	C	C	D	D	A	A	B	A	A
61	**62**	**63**	**64**	**65**	**66**	**67**	**68**	**69**	**70**
A	A	A	C	D	D	D	C	D	A
71	**72**	**73**	**74**	**75**	**76**	**77**	**78**	**79**	**80**
C	B	C	B	B	B	B	A	B	B
81	**82**	**83**	**84**	**85**	**86**	**87**	**88**	**89**	**90**
D	C	A	A	B	D	C	D	C	D
91	**92**	**93**	**94**	**95**	**96**	**97**	**98**	**99**	**100**
A	D	B	C	A	D	B	C	B	A
101	**102**	**103**	**104**	**105**	**106**	**107**	**108**	**109**	**110**
B	C	C	A	B	B	A	B	B	B
111	**112**	**113**	**114**	**115**	**116**	**117**	**118**	**119**	**120**
D	B	A	C	C	A	B	A	A	B

SECTION –B

MEDIEVAL INDIA

THE DELHI SULTANATE

1. The immediate successor of Qutub-ud-din Aibak was:
A. Iltutmish
B. Aram Shah
C. Ruku-ud-din Firoz Shah
D. Bahram Shah

2. The cause of the Qutub-ud-din's death was:
A. Fall from a horse while playing polo
B. Assassination
C. Serious illness
D. Due to some unknown reason

3. Who was known as "Lakh Baksh"?
A. Aibak B. Babur
C. Iltutmish D. Raziya

4. Name one of the following who was not a source of information as the history of the Delhi Sultanate:
A. Abbas Khan Sharwani
B. Amir Khusrau
C. Isami
D. Shams-i-Siraj-Afif

5. Who was the first Sultan of Delhi who strove to make monarchy hereditary?
A. Iltutmish B. Aibak
C. Balban D. Alau'd-din Khalji

6. Who was the first Sultan of Delhi to emphasise the divinity of the king?
A. Aibak B. Iltutmish
C. Balban D. Alau'd-din Khalji

7. Who was the first to adopt the title of Sultan:
A. Mahmud of Ghazni
B. Aibak
C. Iltutmish
D. Balban

8. In spite of her virtues "Raziya" was not successful because:
A. she married Altuniya
B. she behaved like a man
C. of her Orthodox religious belief
D. the nobles did not like the rule of a woman.

9. Raziya was assassinated at:
A. Kaithal B. Delhi
C. Lahore D. Bhatinda

10. Cite one of the following who was not a traveller and therefore not a source of information about events of the period–
A. Ibn Batutah
B. Marco Polo
C. Abdur Razzaq
D. Athanasisus Nikitian

11. Qutb-ud-din's greatest achievement was:
A. the construction of Qutub Minar
B. establishment of Muslim Power in India
C. ending India's connections with Ghazni
D. his generosity towards his generals

12. The Mongols appeared on the border of India for the first time during the region of:
A. Iltutmish B. Balban
C. Ala-ud-din D. Ghauri

13. Who was the immediate successor of Iltutmish?
A. Ruknuddin Firoz
B. Raziya
C. Bahram
D. Nasiruddin Mahmud

14. Name the Sultan who refused to speak to conmmon people:
A. Balban
B. Alau'd-din-Khalji
C. Mohd-bin-Tughlaq
D. Iltutmish

15. Who was extremely social with the nobles and officials?
A. Balban
B. Alau'd-din-Khalji
C. Ghiyas-ud-din-Tughlaq
D. Mohammad Tughlaq

16. "New Muslims" were the followers of:
A. Changez Khan B. Hulagu
C. Ulugh D. Shah Turkan

17. Name the Sultan who thought of

becoming a prophet:
A. Alau'd-din Khalji
B. Balban
C. Mohd-bin-Tughluq
D. Firuz Tughluq

18. Which of the following cities was not founded by Firoz Shah Tughlaq?
A. Firozabad B. Hissar
C. Jaunpur D. Meerut

19. To which city did Sikandar Lodi Shift his capital?
A. Dholpur B. Agra
C. Gwalior D. Jaunpur

20. Who were "Munhiyas" during the reign of Ala-ud-din Khalji?
A. They were revenue officers
B. They were body-guards of the kings
C. They were head of the market control organisation.
D. They were secret police services who used to give reports about the rates and working of markets.

21. Who among the following rulers ordered a huge bell to be hung at the gate of his palace so that an aggrieved person could ring it at any time of right?
A. Aibak B. Iltutmish
C. Jahandar D. Shah Jahan

22. Which dynasty during the Sultanate period had minimum numbers of Sultans?
A. Slave B. Khilji
C. Tughluq D. Syed

23. Which one of the following was not one of the agrarian measures of Firoz Tughluq:
A. He abolished many taxes and unjust cesses.
B. He undertook revaluation of land to ascertain its assessment
C. He allowed the imposition of only four kinds of taxes.
D. He was generous in granting land to civil and military officers and in favouring out land.

24. Alau'd-din Khalji's greatest contribution to the agrarian condition was that:
A. he brought the peasant in direct relation with the state
B. he tried to curb and check the intermediaries
C. the records of the village accountant were audited
D. he was the first to introduce the system of measurement of land for the assessment of revenue.

25. Amongst the draconian measures taken by Alaud-din-Khalji to stabilise his authority, which one had most bearing on the agrarian system of the day?
A. Mostly Hindus were made to pay half of their gross produced to the state and even the pasturage taxes were enhanced.
B. The Sultan abolished the privileges which the Hindus, Muquddams and Khuls enjoyed.
C. Hindus were made to pay jizya
D. He compelled the peasants to sell their produce to the grain dealers at fixed rates.

26. Who among the following had a Hindu Kotwal, named Biruathan?
A. Alau'd-din-Khalji
B. Firoz Tughlaq
C. Mohammad Tughlaq
D. Balban

27. Which one of the following Sultans had the largest standing army?
A. Alau'd-din-Khalji
B. Mohammad-bin-Tughlaq
C. Firoz Tughlaq
D. Ibrahim Lodi

28. Iqta was the name given to small plots, whose owners were known as Iqtadar. What was the name given to the holders of very large plots?
A. Amil B. Muqta
C. Wajhdars D. Nadim

29. The most serious sectarian conflict between the Sunnis and the Shias occurred during the reign of:
A. Raziya
B. Balban

C. Alau'd-din Khalji
D. Muhd-bin-Tughlaq

30. "Zakat" was:
A. a religious tax levied as muslims only
B. a land tax paid by Hindus only
C. a land tax paid by Muslims only
D. the state's share of 1/5th of the spoils of war

31. "Ushrah" means:
A. Land tax paid by Muslims
B. Land tax paid by Hindus
C. Religious tax levied upon Muslims only
D. Religious tax levied upon Hindus only

32. Who levied irrigation tax as the cultivators?
A. Firoz Tughlaq
B. Alau'd-din-Khalji
C. Muhd-bin-Tughlaq
D. Balban

33. "Ratan" a Hindu was appointed as a revenue officer during the reign of:
A. Muhammad-bin-Tughlaq
B. Firoz Tughlaq
C. Sher Shah
D. Akbar

34. "Kham" means:
A. tax levied on Muslims only
B. land tax paid by Hindus
C. land-tax paid by Muslims
D. State's share of 1/5th of the spoils of war.

35. Who is the founder of Muslim rule in India?
A. Muhammad Ghori
B. Babur
C. Timur
D. Qutub-ud-din Aibak

36. Who declared himself independent ruler of Multan when Iltutmish came to power?
A. Ali Mardan
B. Razia
C. Qubacha
D. None of the above

37. Who is regarded as the real founder of Turkish conquests in North-India?
A. Aibak
B. Mahmud of Ghazni
C. Muhammad Ghori
D. Iltutmish

38. The rulers of Lodi dynasty were:
A. Pure Afghans B. Pure Turks
C. Timurid Turks D. None of these

39. Which historian has highlighted the fact that Muhammad invaded India seventeen times?
A. R.C. Majumdar
B. K. Dutta
C. Sir Henery Elliot
D. Iswari Prasad

40. "Kharaj" was:
A. tax levied as muslims only
B. land tax paid by Hindus
C. land tax paid by Muslims
D. state's share of 1/5th of the spoils of war

41. Alberuni came to India in:
A. 9th Century A.D.
B. 10th Century A.D.
C. 11th Century A.D.
D. 12th Century A.D.

42. Who was responsible for the destruction of the power of Chandelas?
A. Prithviraj Chauhan
B. Jayachandra
C. Qutubuddin
D. Balban

43. Who was succeeded by Aibak?
A. Balban B. Alauddin
C. Razia D. Iltutmish

44. Who succeeded Muhammad Ghori in 1206 A.D. in India?
A. Iltutmish
B. Babur
C. Qutabuddin Aibak
D. Qubacha

45. Who is the author of Shahnama?
A. Faizi B. Badauni
C. Afif D. Firdausi

46. "The interest of Muhammad Ghori were not confined to India." Who said the above line?
A. V.A. Smith B. Tara Chand
C. Ishwari Prasad D. Moreland

47. Alaud-din-Khilji believed in:
A. Benevolent despotism
B. Absolute despotism
C. Despotism by consent
D. Rule with the help of nobility

48. When did Mohammad Ghazni carried out his last expedition to India?
A. 1025 A.D. B. 1020 A.D.
C. 1017 A.D. D. 1027 A.D.

49. Which language was patronised by Delhi Sultanate?
A. Arabic B. Turki
C. Persian D. Urdu

50. Who was the first Turk to attack India?
A. Mahmud Ghazni
B. Alaptgin
C. Subuktgin
D. None of above

51. The famous attack of Sarnath temple by Mohammad Ghori was in _____ century.
A. Seventeenth B. Eleventh
C. Fifteenth D. Fourteenth

52. Balban belonged to the:
A. Ilbari tribe
B. Moorish race
C. Khilji dynasty
D. None of the above

53. The Sultanate period lasted from:
A. 1091 – 1526 B. 1026 – 1526
C. 1092 – 1530 D. 1398 – 1530

54. Muhammad Ghori's forces defeated Jai Chand in the year:
A. 1192 A.D. B. 1194 A.D.
C. 1195 A.D. D. 1193 A.D.

55. What was the cause of Aibaks death?
A. He fell from his library
B. He fell from his horse
C. He was poisoned by the nobles
D. None of the above

56. When was the raid against Sarnath in Gujarat undertaken?
A. 1017 B. 1018
C. 1025 D. 1030

57. Against whom were the initial raids of Muhammad of Ghazni directed?
A. Tanashani dynasty
B. South Indian Rulers
C. Rulers of Gujarat
D. Hindustani dynasty

58. Who accompanied Mahmud Ghazni during invasions of India?
A. Muhammad-bin-Qasim
B. Al be runi
C. Utbi
D. Euiot

59. Who was the ruler of Delhi at the time of Timur's invasion?
A. Firoz Shah B. Mahmud Shah
C. Khizr Shah D. Nusrat Shah

60. Who founded the Chandala dynasty?
A. Dhanga B. Nannuka
C. Kokalla D. Upendra

61. The generals who were able to carve out a separate spheres of authority later on assumed the title of:
A. Ghazi B. Amir-ul-Umara
C. Sultan D. Amir

62. "The Indian believe that there is no country but theirs, no nationa like theirs, no king like theirs, no relegion, like theirs no science like theirs." Who said this?
A. Al-beruni B. Sulaiman
C. Al-Qaqashaudi D. Al-Kazwini

63. Who is the author of Shahnama?
A. Al-beruni B. Firdausi
C. Utbi D. Unsuri

64. Who amongst the Sultans earned the title of "Butshikan".
A. Muhmud Ghazni
B. Muhammad Ghori
C. Alauddin Khilji
D. None of the above.

65. Attachment to the land family and honour was the chief characteristic of:
A. Chlolas B. Chalukyas
C. Pandoyas D. Rajputs

66. Where did the Chauhans establish themselves?
A. Ajmer B. Kannauj
C. Jabalpur D. Malwa

67. Who among the following sacked Delhi in 1398?

A. Targhi B. Timur
C. Changez Khan D. Hulaqu Khan

68. The first Pathan State in Delhi was established by:
A. Ala-ud-din Alam Shah
B. Bahlul Lodi
C. Balban
D. Khizr Khan

69. Who amongst the following Sultans did not take the royal title.
A. Khusrau Khan
B. Jalal-ud-din Khalji
C. Khizr Khan
D. Bahlul Khan Lodi

70. Which one of the following was not the work of Amir Khusrau.
A. Tarikhi-i-Alai
B. Tarikhi-i-Firozshahi
C. Tughlaq Nama
D. Ashiqa

71. Who founded Agra?
A. Sikandar Lodi B. Khizr Khan
C. Ala-ud-din D. Ibrahim Lodi

72. What is Ve Sara?
A. an art Style B. a literary piece
C. a painting D. a work as music

73. Among the places given below one was not touched by Timur. Identify:
A. Meerut B. Jammu
C. Hardwar D. Kannauj

74. Who had been appointed in charge of some areas beyond Banaras?
A. Aibak
B. Muizzudin
C. Bakhtiyar Khaliji
D. None of the above

75. Name the ruler who stayed away and did not help Prithviraja during the second battle of Tarain:
A. Hemchandra B. Jaichandra
C. Anandpala D. Jaipala

76. Who were the two ambitious contenders in the first battle of Tarain?
A. Mahmud of Ghazni and Alauddin
B. Muhammad Ghori and Alaudin
C. Prithviraja and Mahmud of Ghazni
D. Prithviraja and Muhammad Ghori

77. Who ordered the judicial functionaries to compile census registered for the various quarters of Delhi?
A. Muhd.-bin-Tughlak
B. Firoz-Tughlaq
C. Sher Shah
D. Ala-ud-din Khilji

78. Who among the following Sultans of Delhi was not the son of Hindu mother?
A. Ghiyasuddin Tughlaq
B. Firoz Tughlaq
C. Buhlul Lodi
D. Shihabuddin Umar

79. What was the nature of the Sultanate?
A. Police state B. Benevolent state
C. Welfare state D. Culture state

80. Who founded Devagiri?
A. Jaitugi B. Bhillama
C. Senuchandra D. Singhana

81. Who were the "Sevunas"?
A. Pallavas
B. Western Gangas
C. Yadavas of Devagiri
D. Eastern Chalukyas of Vengi

82. Who is the author of Zafer Namah?
A. Firdausi
B. Alberuni
C. Al-Qalqashandi
D. Sharaf-ud-din Ali Yazdi

83. Who was the first Sultan of Delhi born of a Hindu Mother?
A. Shahbuddin Khilji
B. Ghiyasuddin Tughlaq
C. Firoz Tughluq
D. Nasiruddin Khasrau

84. Who was the only Sultan to ascend the throne of Delhi in spite of the great fact that his father was alive?
A. Ala-ud-din Khilji B. Kaiqubad
C. Firoz Tughluq D. Sikandar Lodi

85. One of the following saw the reigns of eight Sultans of Delhi, Identify him.
A. Zia Barani B. Shams-i-Siraj Afif
C. Amir Khusrau D. Ibn Batuta

86. What was the original name of

Muhammad-bin-Tughlaq?
A. Ghiyas-ud-din B. Yanna
C. Firoz Shah D. Tughlaq Shah

87. Who among the following made Agra his capital?
A. Sikandar Lodi B. Ibrahim Lodi
C. Bahlul Lodi D. Khizr Khan

88. Who was the victor at Sripurambiyan?
A. Aparajita B. Aditya
C. Varaguna II D. Govinda III

89. Who was called the Lakh Baksha?
A. Iltutmish
B. Qutb-ud-din Aibak
C. Jalal-ud-din Khalji
D. Aram Shah

90. Who built Quwwat-ul-Islam?
A. Qutb-ud-din B. Iltutmish
C. Balban D. Raziya

91. Which of the following was the capital of Eastern Gangas?
A. Konarak B. Mukhalingam
C. Bhuvaneswar D. Puri

92. Which one was the built by Ala-ud-din Khalji?
A. Alai Darwaza B. Buland Darwaza
C. Lal Quila D. Qutub Minar

93. Which Sultan's power stretched from Delhi to Palam as per the opinion of the people?
A. Shah Alam
B. Muhammad Shah
C. Mubarak Shah
D. Khizr Khan Sayyid

94. What was the original name of Ala-ud-din Khalji?
A. Ali Gurshasp B. Jafer Khan
C. Alp Khan D. Chajju

95. One of the following cannot be attributed to Ala-ud-din:
A. Siri Fort B. Hazar Sutun
C. Hauz-i-Khas D. Purana Quila

96. Who were called the New Muslim?
A. Hindu converts to Islam
B. Mongol converts to Islam
C. Turkish converts to Islam
D. Persian converts to Islam

97. Which was the most powerful cause for Ibrahim's defeat?
A. Use of artilley
B. Incompetence of Ibrahim Lodi
C. Babur's generalship
D. Dissensions among the Afghan nobles

98. Harihara and Bukka were originally the notives of:
A. Bellary
B. Dwara Samudra
C. Kampili
D. None of the above

99. Krishnadeva Raya patronished:
A. one language B. two language
C. three language D. four language

100. Which poet who adorned the court of Krishnadeva Raya is known all over South India for his wit & humour?
A. Purandradasa B. Vediraja
C. Haridass D. Tenali Rama

101. What was the mainstay of the income under the Delhi Sultanate?
A. Jaziya
B. Zakat
C. Land Revenue
D. Mines and treasure troue

102. Who declared himself independent ruler of Multan when Iltutmish came to power?
A. Ali Mardan
B. Razia
C. Qubacha
D. None of the above

103. What game was being played by Aibak when he fell from the horse?
A. Changan (Polo)
B. Horse riding
C. Hunting
D. None of the above

104. Who among the Delhi Sultans was called "Mixture of opposites"?
A. Ala-ud-din Khilji
B. Balban
C. Muhammad-bin-Tughlaq
D. Firoz Tughlaq

105. What was the basis of Rajput society?
A. Clan B. Family

C. Village D. Individual

106. Name the ruler who stayed away and did not help Prithviraja during the second battle of Tarain:

A. Hemchandra B. Jaichandra

C. Anandpala D. Jaipala

107. The fortress of Vijayanagar was located on the bank of river:

A. Krishna B. Tungabhadra

C. Godavari D. Pennar

108. Who died screaming that Mahmud Gawan was tearing him to pieces:

A. Muhammmad Shah III

B. Firoz Shah

C. Hasan Bahmani

D. Ahmed Shah

109. The first Bahmani ruler had his capital on:

A. Daultabad B. Warangal

C. Berar D. Gulburga

110. Romantically called "The war of the Goldsmith's daughter", took place between.

A. Firoz Shah and Deva Raya

B. Firuz Shah and Harihara II

C. Ala-ud-din Khilji and Karnadeva

D. Ala-ud-din Khilji and Hamir Deva

111. Who among the following Sultans did not follow the policy of conquering new territories?

A. Aibak

B. Firuz Tughlaq

C. Balban

D. Ghiyasuddin Tughlaq

112. Which was the second capital of Vijayanagar empire?

A. Vijayanagar B. Penugonda

C. Kampali D. Harihar

113. Babur defeated the Delhi Sultan Ibrahim Lodi in the first battle of Panipat when one of the following South Indian empires was flourishing:

A. Bahwani empire

B. Chola empire

C. Pandaya empire

D. Vijayanagar empire

114. The most vivid account about the destruction of the city of Vijayanagar was given by:

A. Sewell B. Father Heras

C. Nicolo Canti D. Abdur – Razzaq

115. Krishnadeva Raya was commonly known by the title of:

A. Vikramaditya B. Andhra Kesari

C. Andhra Bhoja D. Telugu Bhoja

116. Krishnadeva Raya was a follower of:

A. Vaishnavism B. Shaivism

C. Buddhism D. Jainism

117. Against whom were the initial raids of Mahmud of Ghazni directed?

A. Tanashahi dynasty

B. South Indian rulers

C. Rulers of Gujarat

D. Hindustani dynasty

118. Where did Chauhans establish themselves?

A. Ajmer B. Kannauj

C. Jabalpur D. Malwa

119. Balban was a deputy of:

A. Iltutmish

B. Aibak

C. Razia

D. Nasiruddin Muhammad

120. Diwan-Ariz dealt with:

A. Religious affairs

B. Military affairs

C. Law affairs

D. None of the above

121. The name of the Khalifa was retained in the Kutbha because of one of the following reasons. Identify.

A. The Khalifa had a right to interfere in the affairs of the Sultan.

B. The Khalifa received regular tribute from the Sultan.

C. The Khalifa appointed the Sultan.

D. Opposition to the Sultan who called himself a deputy of the Khalifa was regarded as contrary to the Holy Law.

122. Pick out the correct sequence from among the groups of officers arranged in descending orders.

A. Sultan, Naib, Wazir, Quzi
B. Sultan, Wazir, Naib, Quzi
C. Sultan, Quzi, Naib, Wazir
D. Sultan, Quzi, Wazir, Naib

123. One of the following was not an officer of the royal household.
A. Vahil-i-dar B. Barbak
C. Amir-i-Shikar D. Sadar-us-Sudur

124. What was the real source of authority of the Delhi Sultan?
A. Population Support
B. Support of the Ulemas
C. Support of Khalifa
D. Army

125. One among the following factors may be regarded as the most decisive one in the choice of the Sultan. Identify.
A. Priority of birth
B. Efficiency
C. Nomination by the dead king
D. Nobility

126. What can be the most appropriate way of describing the form of the government of the Delhi Sultan?
A. Constitutional Monarchy
B. Elective Monarchy
C. Oligarchy
D. Despotism

127. Pick-out the correct sequence of the ranks in the army in descending order.
A. Malik, Amir, Siphasalar and Sar-i-Khail
B. Amir, Malik, Sipahasalar and Sar-i-Khail
C. Sar-i-Khail, Malik, Amir and Sipahasalar
D. Sipahasalar, Amir, Malik and Sar-i-Khail

128. What was the salary of a well-equipped trooper with one horse in the time of Ala-ud-din Khalji?
A. 500 tankas B. 234 tankas
C. 434 tankas D. 300 tankas

129. Pick out the wrong match–
A. Ariz-in-mamalik-Army
B. Diwan-in-insha-royal correspondence
C. Diwan-in-risarat-foreign affairs
D. Sadr-us-Sudur-justice

130. One of the following army divisions was not important in the Delhi Sultanate period. Identify.
A. Cavalry B. Archers
C. Artillery D. Elephants

131. At times, Ala-ud-din defied the Quranic law which among the following reasons can be considered the most important?
A. He was not a pious Musalman
B. Quranic law clashed with his personal interests.
C. He had the support of a powerful army
D. He wanted to establish a secular state

132. Who among the following Sultans of Delhi called himself the Khalifa?
A. Balban
B. Muhammad bin Tuglaq
C. Muharat Khalji
D. Iltutmish

133. One among the following did not receive a letter of investiture from the Khalifa. Identify.
A. Iltutmish
B. Muhammad bin Tughlaq
C. Firoz Tughlaq
D. Ala-ud-din Khalji

134. What was the religious tax collected from the Muslims?
A. Ushr B. Khams
C. Jizya D. Zakat

135. Who among the following interpreted law?
A. Mufti B. Muqti
C. Quazi D. Sadr

136. Who had laid out 1200 orchards in the vicinity of Delhi?
A. Muhammad Tughlaq
B. Firoz-Tughlaq
C. Ibrahim Lodi
D. Babur

137. When could sericulture have been introduced into India?
A. 12th Century B. 13th Century
C. 14th Century D. 16th Century

138. The Indian peasant during the period of

the Sultanate did not bother about one of the following. Identify.

A. Claim of superior classes over his crops

B. Claim of superior class over his persons

C. Property rights over land he killed

D. Jizya

139. What is Charai?

A. Land Revenue B. House Tax

C. Poll Tax D. Cattle Tax

140. Where was ginger of the best quality produced during the period of the Sultanate?

A. Malabar B. Kankan

C. Cernatic D. Gujarat

141. What is a farman?

A. Paper document by which lands made over to the grantees.

B. Sultan's judicial pronouncement.

C. Descriptive roll

D. An important

142. Pick out the wrong match—

A. Khutas – Large Landholder (Headmen)

B. Balahars – Petty Landholders (Village Menials)

C. Ranas – Rural Aristocracy

D. Rawats – Royal official in the villages

143. What was the main source of wealth of India during the Sultanate period?

A. Industry B. Trade

C. Agriculture D. Colonies

144. One of the following was not the three cause of increased agricultural output during the role of Delhi Sultans. Identify.

A. Natural fertility of the Soil

B. Copious rainfall

C. Irrigational facilities

D. Agrarian policy of the Government

145. In whose time was the department of agriculture created?

A. Muhammad-bin-Tughlaq

B. Balban

C. Ghiyas-ud-din Tughlaq

D. Firoz-Tughlaq

146. Pick out the correct match–

A. Diwan-in-Amir Kohi–Agriculture

B. Diwan-i-Mustakhraj–Charity

C. Diwan-i-Khailat–Pensions.

D. Diwan-i-Istihqah–Intelligence

147. According to Nizami, the Indian peasant did not suffer from lack of one of the following. Identify:

A. Seeds B. Pair of Oxen

C. Implement D. Land

148. What does the term Chaudhri indicate?

A. Village Headman

B. Knights of the Rais

C. Governor

D. Local magnate held answerable for collection of revenue in each Pargana.

149. What is biswa?

A. a unit of area B. a tax

C. a tax collector D. measuring rod

150. Pick out the wrong match:

A. Alwab – Additional cesses

B. Sondbar – Loans to ryots

C. Haqq-i-Shurb – Water tax

D. Waqf – Transfer of agrarian surplus to the ruling class and its soldiers

151. Who was the first ruler of India who dug canals for promoting agriculture?

A. Ghiyas-ud-din – Tughlaq

B. Firoz – Tughlaq

C. Muhammad-bin-Tughlaq

D. Bahlol Lodi

152. Who among the following has created the biggest network of Canals known in India until Kth 19th century?

A. Balban B. Ala-ud-din Khalji

C. Firoz Tughlaq D. Sikander Lodi

153. By what name was the main instrument of transfering agrarian surplus called?

A. Milk B. Inam

C. Waqf D. Iqta

154. Who was the first Muslim Sultan of Kashmir?

A. Shamsh ud-din Shah

B. Shiha-ud-din-Shah

C. Haider Shah

D. Jamshid Shah

155. Identify the name Dalucha?

A. An Arab Mercenary

B. A Mangol Leader

C. A Mughal Governor
D. A Muslim Minister in the Court of the Hindu ruler of Kashmir

156. Who among the following rulers earned the title of:
A. Shamsuddin Shah
B. Qutbuddin Shah
C. Zainul-Abidin
D. Sikandar Shah

157. Who built the Bara Sona Masjid?
A. Nusrat Shah
B. Hussain Shah
C. Jalal-ud-din-Muhammad
D. Barbak Shah

158. What was the percentage of the State demand during the region of Ala-ud-din Khalji?
A. 33 ⅓ % B. 25%
C. 16 ⅔ % D. 50%

159. Who has said that along the coastal road of Malbar there was not a span of land left uncultivated?
A. Ibn Batutah B. Abdur Razzaq
C. Barbosa D. Paes

160. Under whose orders a Bengali version of the Mahabharata was written?
A. Hussain Shah
B. Jalal-ud-din Muhammad
C. Nusrat Shah
D. Haji Iliyas

161. Firoz Tughlaq founded the city of Jaunpur to perpetuate the memory of:
A. Ghiyasuddin Tughluq
B. Ala-ud-din Khalji
C. Muhammad bin Tughlaq
D. Giyas-ud-din Balban

162. Who was the greatest ruler of Sharqi dynasty?
A. Mallu Iqbal
B. Malik Garwar
C. Shamsuddin Ibrahim
D. Muhammad Shah

163. Which among the following causes may not be regarded as a cause of vital importane for the rise of Independent Bengal?
A. Its distance from Delhi
B. Its profuse wealth
C. Weakness of the Delhi Sultans
D. Timur's invasion

164. Who built a magnificent mosque at Adine?
A. Haji Iliyas
B. Sikandar Shah
C. Ghiyas-ud-din Azam
D. Ala-ud-din Firus Shah

165. Sharqui Kingdom of Jaunpur was defeated by:
A. Bahlol Lodi
B. Ibrahim Lodi
C. Sikandar Lodi
D. Rama Sangram Singh

166. Which city of North India was known as 'Shiraz of India?
A. Agra B. Jaunpur
C. Kannoj D. Lahore

167. Which of the Sultans of Bengal sent Embassies to China?
A. Haji Iliyas
B. Sikandar Shah
C. Ghiyas-ud-din Azam
D. Ala-ud-din Firoz Shah

168. What was the original name of Jalal-ud-din of Bengal?
A. Jadusen B. Shiva Sinha
C. Devi Sinha D. Ganesh

169. Kashmir had the reputation of being the centre of one of the following before the arrival of the Muslim ruler?
A. Buddism B. Jainism
C. Vaishnavism D. Shaivism

170. Who did Rana Kumbha succeed?
A. Mokala B. Kshetra Singh
C. Rana Hamir D. Chunda

171. What does the title, Danujamarolama Deva mean?
A. Devoted to the feet of Godness Chandi
B. Devoted to the feet of Vishnu
C. Devoted to the feet of Brahma
D. Devoted to the feet of Siva

172. Who took the title Damujamardana Deva?
A. Raja Ganesh B. Jadusen
C. Shiva Sinha D. Devi Sinha

173. How did the Persian manuscripts refer Raja Ganesh?
A. Jalal-ud-din B. Hamza Shah
C. Kans D. Jadusen

174. The brilliant face in the history of Orissa in the medieval period is marked by the rule of:
A. Ganga dynasty
B. The Gajapati dynasty
C. The Bhoi dynasty
D. The Chandravanshi dynasty

175. What is Bhoi?
A. Name of Tribe
B. The Northern Region of Orissa
C. Writer Caste of Orissa
D. One of the ruling dynasties

176. During the rule of which dynasty of Orissa were the temple of Jagannath at Puri and Sun-temple at Konark constructed?
A. Chandravanshi dynasty
B. Gajapati dynasty
C. Bhoi dynasty
D. Choda Ganga dynasty

177. Which of the following statement are correct with regard to Rana Sanga?
1. He had remarkable military ability and was described as 'the fragment of a Soldier?
2. He defeated and captured Mahmud II of Malwa.
3. He was defeated by Babur at Khanna in 1527.
4. The Rajputs of the period recognised his supremacy codes.

A. 1 and 2 only B. 1, 2 and 3 only
C. 3 only D. 1, 2, 3 and 4 only

178. Under whose leadership did Marwar which was under the occupation of Mewar become independent?
A. Rawal B. Rao Jodha
C. Lakha D. Mokala

179. Who founded the City of Bikaner in 1464?
A. Rao Jodha B. Bika
C. Chunda D. Maldeva

180. Who got the Mahabharta translated into Bengali?
A. Ala-ud-din Hussain Shah
B. Nasir-ud-din-Nusrat Shah
C. Nasir-ud-din Mahmud Shah II
D. Ghiyas-ud-din-Mahmud Shah

181. From which one of the following tribes did the Ahams from which the name of Assam is derived form a section?
A. Bado B. Shana
C. Bhuiyas D. Kacharis

182. Which ruler of Assam adopted the title of Syarga Narayan?
A. Suhungmung B. Vishasimha
C. Darlabha D. Sukhangpha

183. Which was not the reason why Bengal was frequently independent of the Central of Delhi?
A. The distance from Delhi
B. Its climate
C. The composition of its population
D. The fact that much of its communications depended upon water ways with which the Turkish rulers were unfamiliar

184. Who became the king of Bengal under the title of Saifud-din-Firoz?
A. Raja Ganesh B. Indil Khan
C. Nasib Khan D. Barbak Shah

185. Which king of the Hussain Shahi dynasty was ruling when Sikander Lodi attacked Bengal?
A. Ala-ud-din Hussain Shah
B. Nasir-ud-din Nusrat Shah
C. Ala-ud-din Firuz Shah
D. Ghiyas-ud-din Mahmud Shah

186. Who gave the title of Dilwar Khan to Husain Ghuri?
A. Sikander Lodi
B. Firoz Shah Tughlaq
C. Bahlol Lodi
D. Muhammad-bin-Tughlaq

187. Which pair is not correct:
A. Alp Khan – Hushang Shah
B. Muhammad Shah – Mohmud Khalji
C. Mallu Khan – Qudir Shah
D. Ghiyas Shah – Abdul Qadir Nasir Shah

188. By what name to the State of Amber

known as:

A. Jaipur B. Jodhpur
C. Udaipur D. Bikaner

189. During whose reign did the kingdom of Gujarat reach its extreme limit?

A. Ahmad Shah
B. Muhammad Shah
C. Qutub-ud-din Ahmad
D. Abdul Fateh Khan

190. Which Malwa ruler collected about 1600 slave girls during his various campaigns?

A. Ghiyas Shah B. Mahmud II
C. Nasir Shah D. Qudir Shah

191. In which year Khandesh was annexed by Akbar?

A. 1600 B. 1601
C. 1603 D. 1604

192. Who founded the Langah dynasty of Multan?

A. Rai Sahrah
B. Shaikh Yusuf Zakaria
C. Shah Beg
D. Langar Khan

193. Which of the following dynasty ruled over Sind?

1. Sumar dynasty
2. Summa dynasty
3. Arghun dynasty

Codes:

A. 1 and 2 only B. 2 and 3 only
C. 1 and 3 only D. All the above

194. The last ruler of the Bahamani Kingdom was:

A. Kalimullah Shah
B. Qasim
C. Amir Ali Bario
D. Mahmud Shah

195. What was the name of the Russian traveller who visited the Bahamani Kingdom in 1417 AD.

A. Nicola Conti
B. Marco Polo
C. Abdul Razaq
D. Athanasius Nikitin

196. The Muslim kingdom of Golkunda grew upon the ruins of the old kingdom of:

A. Deogiri B. Dulara Samudra
C. Warangal D. Kanchi

197. Which Bahamani king invited the famous Persian poet Itafis?

A. Muhammad Shah II
B. Muhammad Shah I
C. Mujahid Shah
D. Duad Khan

198. Which one of the following statements about the cause of Strife between the Dakhinis (domiciled immigrants and local converts) and the Pardesis or Afaqis (recently arrived foreigners) nobles of the Bahamani kingdom is not correct?

A. Paradesis were more energetic and enterprising than the Dakhinis
B. A majority of the Pardesis were Shias whereas most of the Dakhinis were Sunnis
C. From the very beginning the Pardesis wielded considerable influence in the politics of the country which wear resented by the Dakhinis
D. The Paradesis were in favour of persecution of the Hindi population where as Dakhinis were opposed to such a policy.

199. Match the following kingdom with their respective dynasties:

a. Bijapur	1. Qutb Shai
b. Ahmadnagar	2. Barid Shahi
c. Golkunda	3. Imad Shahi
d. Bidar	4. Ahmad Shai
e. Berar	5. Adil Shahi

Codes—

	a	*b*	*c*	*d*	*e*
A.	1	3	2	5	4
B.	5	4	1	2	3
C.	5	4	1	3	2
D.	3	4	2	1	5

200. Chand Bibi the famous queen who fought valiently against Akbar belonged to which kingdom?

A. Bijapur B. Golkunda
C. Ahmadnagar D. Berar

201. Which Bahamani king is said to have taken interest in developing the points of

Chaul and Dabnel?
A. Muhammad Shah
B. Taj-ud-din Firua Shah
C. Ahmad Shah
D. Ala-ud-din II

202. Match the following dynasties with their founders:

a.	Bijapur	1.	Qutb Shah
b.	Ahmadnagar	2.	Amir Ali Bario
c.	Golkunda	3.	Yusuf Adil Shah
d.	Bidar	4.	Malik Ahmad
e.	Berar	5.	Fatech Ullah Imad Shah

Codes—

	a	*b*	*c*	*d*	*e*
A.	3	4	1	2	5
B.	3	1	4	5	2
C.	2	5	1	3	4
D.	5	3	2	1	4

203. Who was the founder of the Bahamani kingdom?
A. Ala-ud-din Hasan
B. Gangoo
C. Ismail Mukh
D. Muhammad Shah II

204. Which one of the following is false with regard to the region of Ahmad Shah?
A. He transferred his capital from Gulbarga to Bidar (1425).
B. The rivalry between the Dakhin party and foreign party became accentuated during his period.
C. He conquered Warangal in 1424-25.
D. He annexed the kingdom of Gujarat to his empire.

205. Hasan divided his kingdom into 4 provinces (tarafs). Identify the introcider.
A. Gulbarga B. Daula Taboo
C. Golkunda D. Bidar

206. The title Malik-us-Sharq (Lord of the East) was confered by Mahmud Tughlaq on:
A. Mahmud Gawan B. Malik Darwar
C. Hussain D. Barbak

207. During the reign of which one of the following kings did Sikander Lodi attack Bengal?
A. Susrat Shah B. Firuz Shah
C. Mahmud Shah D. Husain Shah

208. Name of the ruler who founded the city of Jaunpur to perpetuate the memory of Prince Jauna.
A. Feruz Tughlaq
B. Khizr Khan
C. Ghyas-ud-din Tughlaq
D. Rajah Tughlaq

209. Which one of the following places was known as the "Shiraz-i-Hind"?
A. Malwa B. Pandua
C. Sonargaon D. Jaunpur

210. The new towns of Muhammadabad and Mustafabad was founded by Mahmud Begarha after his victory over.
A. The fort of champaner
B. The fort of Girnar
C. The fort of Chittor
D. The fort of Delhi

211. What was the name of the Muslim adventurer, who having entered the Service of the Hindu prince of Kashmir, seized the throne and forcibly married queen Kota Devi upon latter's death?
A. Mir Jumla B. Shah Mirza
C. Mirza Haidu D. Sikander Shah

212. Marwar became independent under the leadership of:
A. Rao Jodha B. Mokala
C. Lakha D. Rawal

213. Which one of the following ruler of Malwa is said to have received a letter of investitur from caliph of Egypt for his military exploits:
A. Nasir-ud-din
B. Mahmud Khalji I
C. Mahmud Khalji II
D. Ghiyas-ud-din

214. The Capital of Malwa was the ancient Hindu City Dhar. Which one of the following rulers shifted it to Mandu?
A. Hoshang
B. Baz Bahadur
C. Mahmud Khan Khalji
D. Ghiyas-ud-din

215. Rana Kumbha constructed the 'Tower of Victory' at Chittor. What was the occasion for that?
A. His victory against the Rao Jodha of Marwar
B. His victory against Mahmud Khilji of Malwa
C. His victory against Ahmad Shah of Gujarat
D. None of these

216. During whose reign Malwa was absorbed in Gujarat in 1951 AD?
A. Baz Bahadur B. Mahmud II
C. Nasir-ud-din D. None of these

217. What was Amir-i-Jumla?
A. He was the minister of finance
B. He was the minister of foreign affairs
C. He supervised the work of all the minister
D. None of these

218. Which of the following kings faced a devastating famine which reged over a decade in the Deccan?
A. Firoz Shah
B. Mujahid Shah
C. Ala-ud-din Bahmani Shah
D. Shams-ud-din

219. Match the following:

a.	Waxir-i-Ashraf	1.	Minister of Foreign Affairs.
b.	Wazir-i-Kull	2.	Supervised the work of all the ministers.
c.	Vakil-i-Sultan	3.	Lieutenant of the kingdom.
d.	Wazir	4.	Assistant Minister of Finance.

Codes—

	a	*b*	*c*	*d*
A.	1	2	3	4
B.	2	3	1	4
C.	3	1	2	4
D.	4	1	2	3

220. During the reign of which one of the following dynasties of Orissa were the temple of Jaganath Puri and the Sun temple at Konark constructed?
A. Chandravanshi dynasty
B. Gajapati dynasty
C. Bhoi dynasty
D. Chola-Ganga dynasty

ANSWERS

1	2	3	4	5	6	7	8	9	10
B	A	A	A	A	C	A	D	A	C
11	**12**	**13**	**14**	**15**	**16**	**17**	**18**	**19**	**20**
B	A	A	A	C	C	A	D	B	D
21	**22**	**23**	**24**	**25**	**26**	**27**	**28**	**29**	**30**
B	D	C	D	B	B	A	B	A	A
31	**32**	**33**	**34**	**35**	**36**	**37**	**38**	**39**	**40**
A	A	A	D	A	C	D	A	C	B
41	**42**	**43**	**44**	**45**	**46**	**47**	**48**	**49**	**50**
C	C	D	C	D	A	B	D	C	A
51	**52**	**53**	**54**	**55**	**56**	**57**	**58**	**59**	**60**
B	A	B	B	B	C	D	B	B	B
61	**62**	**63**	**64**	**65**	**66**	**67**	**68**	**69**	**70**
C	A	B	A	D	A	B	B	C	B
71	**72**	**73**	**74**	**75**	**76**	**77**	**78**	**79**	**80**
A	A	D	C	B	D	A	C	A	B

81	82	83	84	85	86	87	88	89	90
C	D	A	B	C	B	A	A	B	A
91	**92**	**93**	**94**	**95**	**96**	**97**	**98**	**99**	**100**
B	A	A	A	D	B	A	D	D	D
101	**102**	**103**	**104**	**105**	**106**	**107**	**108**	**109**	**110**
C	C	A	C	A	B	B	A	D	A
111	**112**	**113**	**114**	**115**	**116**	**117**	**118**	**119**	**120**
C	B	D	A	C	A	D	A	C	B
121	**122**	**123**	**124**	**125**	**126**	**127**	**128**	**129**	**130**
D	A	D	D	D	D	A	B	D	C
131	**132**	**133**	**134**	**135**	**136**	**137**	**138**	**139**	**140**
C	C	D	D	A	B	C	C	D	A
141	**142**	**143**	**144**	**145**	**146**	**147**	**148**	**149**	**150**
A	D	C	D	A	A	D	D	A	D
151	**152**	**153**	**154**	**155**	**156**	**157**	**158**	**159**	**160**
A	C	D	A	B	D	A	D	A	C
161	**162**	**163**	**164**	**165**	**166**	**167**	**168**	**169**	**170**
C	C	D	B	B	B	C	A	D	A
171	**172**	**173**	**174**	**175**	**176**	**177**	**178**	**179**	**180**
A	A	A	B	C	D	D	B	B	B
181	**182**	**183**	**184**	**185**	**186**	**187**	**188**	**189**	**190**
B	A	C	B	A	B	D	A	D	A
191	**192**	**193**	**194**	**195**	**196**	**197**	**198**	**199**	**200**
B	B	D	A	D	C	A	D	B	C
201	**202**	**203**	**204**	**205**	**206**	**207**	**208**	**209**	**210**
B	A	A	D	C	B	D	A	D	C
211	**212**	**213**	**214**	**215**	**216**	**217**	**218**	**219**	**220**
B	A	B	A	B	B	A	A	A	D

THE INDO-ISLAMIC CULTURE

1. Match the dynastics of Sultanates with the cities they built:

a.	Slaves	1.	Siri
b.	Khiljis	2.	Tughlaqabad, Jahanpanah, Feroz Kotla
c.	Tughlak	3.	Khizrabad and Mubarakbad
d.	Saiyyads	4.	Oila-i-Rai Pithura

Codes—

	a	*b*	*c*	*d*
A.	4	1	2	3
B.	1	2	3	4
C.	2	3	1	4
D.	4	2	1	3

2. Who among the following was an exponent of Sudhadavaita?
   A. Ramanuja B. Vallabhacharya
   C. Chaitanya D. Sankar
3. Match the dynastics or kings with the coins they issued:

a. Iltutmish	1. Silver tanka
b. Muhammad-bin-Tughlaq	2. Gold dinar and Silver Adils
c. Sher Shah	3. Silver Rupvah
d. Vijayanagar king	4. Gold Pagoda, Varaha, Kopeki, Fanam and Copper Digital

Codes—

	a	*b*	*c*	*d*
A.	2	1	3	4
B.	1	3	2	4
C.	1	2	3	4
D.	2	4	1	3

4. What led to the growth of a composite or Indo-Islamic Culture?
   A. The important effects of the Arab invasion in India
   B. The adaptability of the Turkish rulers of the Delhi Sultanate to the prevailing conditions in India.
   C. The fusion of the cultural traditions of the Hinduism and Islam
   D. None of these
5. Which statements is/are correct?
   1. The ceremonies connected with the worship of Muslim saints are more Indian than Islamic in details
   2. Casteism began appearing in Muslim Society
   3. Some aristocratic Muslim families adopted the Hindus Customs of Sati and Jauhar

   Codes:
   A. 1 only
   B. 1 and 2 only
   C. 2 only
   D. 1, 2, 3
6. Horse shoe arch is distinctive feature of one of the following building. Identify it:
   A. Sultan Gachi
   B. Tomb of Iltutmish
   C. Tomb of Balban
   D. Alai Darwaza
7. Many temples were converted into mosques. One such was a Jain temple and it is the earliest known mosque in India. Identify it.
   A. Arhai Din Ka Jhonpra at Ajmer
   B. Badshahi Mosque at Badaun
   C. Quwwat-ul-Islam Mosque at Delhi
   D. None of these
8. The Qutub Minar was completed by Iltutmish. It was dedicated to:
   A. Muhammad Ghori
   B. Qutb-ud-din Ailbak
   C. Qutb-ud-din Bakhtiyar
   D. None of these
9. What exposed some of the evils of Hinduism?
   A. The islamic concept of Jehad or holy war
   B. The Islamic tenets of brotherhood and equality
   C. The Islamic practice of Secluding women
   D. Both (a) and (b).

10. Which of the following customs was followed by both Hindus and Muslims?
A. Celebrating marriages with pump and show
B. The Pardah system
C. The 'arti' ceremony
D. All the above

11. Match the building with their location:

a.	Adina Mosqe	1.	Pandua
b.	Mahud Gawan's Madarsa	2.	Bidar
c.	Jahaz Mahal	3.	Mandu
d.	Kalam Masjid	4.	Delhi

Codes—

	a	*b*	*c*	*d*
A.	2	1	3	4
B.	1	3	2	4
C.	1	2	3	4
D.	2	4	1	3

12. Match the following provincial architectural structures with teh rulers who built them:

a.	Jami Masjid at Gujarat	1.	Mahmud Begarha
b.	The mosque at Champner	2.	Ahmed Shah
c.	Jami Masjid at Mandu	3.	Hoshung Shah
d.	Mosque of Sidi Sayyed	4.	Mahmud Khilji

Codes—

	a	*b*	*c*	*d*
A.	2	1	4	3
B.	2	1	3	4
C.	1	3	4	2
D.	3	1	4	1

13. Where is Arhai Din Ka Jhonpra situated?
A. Delhi B. Jaunpur
C. Agra D. Ajmer

14. Arabs freely borrowed Hindu motifs. Which were they?
A. Bell motif B. Swastika
C. Lotus D. All the above

15. Which was the most magnificient building constructed by the Turks in 13th century?
A. Quwat-ul-Islam Mosque
B. Hauz Khas
C. Qutab Minar
D. Siri

16. Who built the Capital at Siri?
A. Alauddin Khilji
B. Balban
C. Aibak
D. Muhammad Tughlaq

17. In about AD 1300, a number of works on the Mimamsa were written by:
A. Rupa Goswami
B. Parthasarathi Mishra
C. Hemachandra Suri
D. Madhawa

18. Who translated the Bhagvat Gita into Bengali?
A. Krithivas B. Kavindra
C. Maladhar Vasu D. Srikar Nandi

19. During the Sultanate period who was the ruling class?
A. Turkish noble B. Muslims
C. Arabs D. Hindus

20. The first contact of Indians with Islam began with the:
A. Arab traders B. Roman traders
C. Turkish Traders D. Turkish invaders

21. Which of the following provinces was a sent of Hindu Craftsmanship?
A. Bengal B. Jaunpur
C. Gujarat D. None of these

22. The tall curved spiral roof and the mandapam (ante room) were features of which style of architecture?
A. Nagara B. Shikara
C. Sharqi D. Bengal

23. Which language was patronised by the rulers of Delhi Sultanate?
A. Hindi B. Urdu
C. Persian D. Turki

24. Which social evil gained impetus with the coming of the Muslims?
A. Purdah System B. Polygamy
C. Polyandry D. Child marriage

25. Ibn-i-Batutah came in the court of:
A. Iltutmish
B. Balban
C. Muhammad-bin-Tughlaq
D. Sikandar Lodi

26. Where is Atala Devi Masjid situated?
A. Lahore B. Padua
C. Jaunpur D. Delhi

27. Firoz Tughlaq was the author of:
A. Tarik--i-Firoz Shahi
B. Fatwah-i-Jahandari
C. Futuhat-i-Firoz Shahi
D. Sirat-i-Firoz Shahi

28. Octagonal-Shaped tombs are associated with:
A. the Khiljis B. The Tughlaqs
C. The Sayyids D. The Lodis

29. Alai Darwaza was added by:
A. Iltutmish
B. Balban
C. Alaudin Khilji
D. Muhammad Tughlaq

30. Match the words with their authors:
(a) Tarika-i-Yamini 1. Muhammad-al-utbi
(b) Tarika-i-Feroz Shahi 2. Shams-i-Siraj Afif
(c) Tarika-i-Hind 3. Alberuni
(d) Taj-ul-Hassan Masir 4. Hasan Nizami

Codes:

	(a)	*(b)*	*(c)*	*(d)*
A.	1	2	3	4
B.	2	1	3	4
C.	4	1	3	2
D.	1	4	3	2

31. Match the following works with their authors who wrote in Sanskrit:
(a) Gita Govinda 1. Vallabha
(b) Hammira 2. Jimuta Vahana
(c) Anubhashya 3. Jayasingh Suri
(d) Dharmaratna 4. Jayadev

Codes:

	(a)	*(b)*	*(c)*	*(d)*
A.	4	3	1	2
B.	3	2	4	1
C.	2	4	3	1
D.	2	1	3	4

32. Match the following Literary figures with the language in which they wrote.
(a) Timmana 1. Gujarati
(b) Chandidas 2. Bengali
(c) Bhattadeva 3. Kannada
(d) Narsimha Mehta 4. Assamese

Codes:

	(a)	*(b)*	*(c)*	*(d)*
A.	1	2	3	4
B.	4	2	1	3
C.	4	2	3	1
D.	3	2	4	1

33. Match the following books with their respective authors:
(a) Prithviraj Raso 1. Malik Muhd. Jaisi
(b) Hamir Raso 2. Chand Bardai
(c) Sri Krishna Vijaya 3. Maladhar basu
(d) Padmavat 4. Sarangdhar

Codes:

	(a)	*(b)*	*(c)*	*(d)*
A.	2	4	3	1
B.	2	3	4	1
C.	3	2	1	4
D.	1	2	3	4

34. Who wrote Fatawa-i-Jahandari?
A. Amir Khusrau B. Ziauddin Barani
C. Afif D. None of these

35. The vocabulary of Urdu has been drawn from:
A. Persian and Hindi
B. Hindi, Tamil, Persian, Oriya
C. Arabic, Persian, Hindi
D. Hindi, Arabic, Persian, Turkish

36. Who got Rajtarangani and Mahabharata translated into Persian?
A. Feroz Shah Tughlaq
B. Sikander Lodi
C. Zain-ul-Abidin
D. None of these

37. Lakshmidhara wrote Smritikalpataru. Its subject matter is:
A. Philosophy B. Music
C. Law D. Medicine

38. Who was given the title of Nayak or master of both the theory and practice of music?
A. Amir Khusrau

B. Sadi
C. Malik Muhammad Jaisi
D. None of these

39. Where was Amir Khusrau born?
A. Badaun B. Delhi
C. Paliali D. Lahore

40. Who was the author of 'Khazain-ul-Futuh'?
A. Hasan Nizami
B. Amir Khusrau
C. Yahya Bin Ahmad
D. Abdul Fazal

41. Smriti Literature flourished in Mithila and Bengal. Two of its outstanding authors were:
A. Jai Singh Suri and Gangadhar
B. Jayadeva and Madhava Vidyaratna
C. Vachspati Misra and Raghunandan
D. Kabir and Surdas

42. Who among the following authors translated the Bhagavat Gita into Bengali?
A. Krithivas B. Kavindra
C. Malandhar D. Sirkar Nandi

43. Sanskrit Books on medicine and music were translated into Persian during the reigns of:
A. Muhammad-bin-Tughlaq and Zain-ul-Abidin
B. Muhammad-bin-Tughlaq and Nusrat Shah
C. Feroz Shah Tughlaq and Zain-ul-Abidin
D. Muhammad-bin-Tughlaq and Feroz Shah Tughlaq

44. Which among the following was the most important of the causes for struggle between Begarha and the Portuguese?
A. cutting off the trade of the Muslims
B. establishment of Portuguese settlement on the western coast
C. ill-treatment of the Muslims
D. refusal to pay tributes

45. Who said that with the execution of Mahmud Gawan, all the cohesion and power of the Bahmani Kingdom departed?
A. Firishta
B. Sayyid Ali Tabataba
C. Meadows Taylor
D. Stanley Lane-Poole

46. Pick out the wrong match:
A. Allasani Peddana – Manucharita
B. Vyasaraya – Nyayamrita
C. Lolla Lakshmidhare – Sarasvathivilasa
D. Krishnadeva Raya – Parvatiparinaya

47. Who is called the Akbar of Kashmire?
A. Shah Mirza B. Jamshid
C. Ali shah D. Zain-ul-Abidin

48. In which respect did Zain-ul-Abidin differ from Akbar?
A. Universal toleration
B. Patronage to art and literature
C. Abstention from eating flesh
D. Contingence

49. Who had put an end to the independance of Sind in about 1514?
A. Babur
B. Shah Beg Arghun
C. Mahmud Begarha
D. Mohmud of Ghazni

50. Who among the following witnessed the Mahanavami festival?
A. Athanasius Nikitin
B. Nieolo Conti
C. Caesar Frederick
D. Abdul Razzaq

51. Which of the flesh of the following animals was not consumed by the people in the Vijayanagar period?
A. Oxen B. Sheep
C. Lizard D. Rats

52. Which among the following is not applicable to Vijaynagar period.
A. Sati was prevalent
B. Polygamy was known
C. Dowry system was prevalent
D. Child marriage was unknown

53. Pick out the wrong match
A. Mirat-i-Sikandar-Lodis
B. Burhan-i-Ma'qsir-Bahman
C. Riyaz-us-Salatin-Bengal
D. Rajatarangini-Kashmir

54. Who has been described as the pattern of excellence?
A. Ahmad Shah

B. Muhammad Shah
C. Bahadur Shah
D. Mahmud Begarha

55. Identify the foreign traveller who speaks about Mahmud Begarha
A. Ludovico di Varthema
B. Nicolo Conti
C. Nuniz D. Poes

56. Who among the following has described himself as the Second Alexander on his coins?
A. Ala-ud-din-Khalji
B. Ahmad Shah
C. Muhammad Shah I
D. Firoz Shah

57. Who made Bidar the capital of the Bahman kingdom?
A. Ala-ud-din Bahman shah
B. Firuz Shah
C. Ahmad Shah
D. Muhammad Shah I

58. Which among the following was the most important achievement of Muhmud Gawan?
A. Education of the king
B. Capture of Goa
C. Getting the support of Gujarat against Malwa
D. Annexation of Bankapur

59. Were did Mahmud Begarha register a naval victory over the Portuguese?
A. Diu B. Daman
C. Goa D. Chaul

60. From whom did the Portuguese obtain permission to build a factor at Diu?
A. Mahmud Begarha
B. Ahmad Shah
C. Hushang Shah
D. Muhammad Shah

61. What provided the background for the rise of sufi Movement?
A. Jain philosophy
B. Buddhist philosophy
C. Indian and Greek ideas
D. None of the above

62. The Qutab Minar was dedicated to
A. Qutab-ud-din-Aibak
B. The Sufi Saint, Qutab-ud-din Bakhtiyar Kaki
C. Khawaja Moin-ud-din chisti
D. The Chishti Saint, Nizam ud-din Auliya

63. Match the following.
(a) Timmana 1. Gujarati
(b) Chandidas 2. Bengali
(c) Bhattadeva 3. Kannada
(d) Narsimha Mehta 4. Assamese

Codes:

	(a)	*(b)*	*(c)*	*(d)*
A.	1	2	3	4
B.	4	2	1	3
C.	4	2	3	1
D.	3	2	4	1

64. What was sq. inch?
A. An architectural form
B. A musical instrument
C. A style of writing
D. None of these

65. One of the administrative language of Bahmani Kingdom was
A. Gujarati B. Bengali
C. Marathi D. Sanskrit

66. Prithuviraja Raso was written by
A. Chandra Bardai B. Jayadeva
C. Bana D. Amir Khusrau

67. Which decorative device is generally found in the building of Firoz Shah Tughlaq?
A. Shankh B. Bell
C. Lotus D. Swastika

68. Lodis borrowed enamelled tiles from
A. Persia B. Rome
C. Egypt D. South India

69. Which one of the following is best known for the Persian form of Masnavi?
A. Zai Nakashabi
B. Amir Khusrau
C. Malik Mohammad Jaisi
D. None of these

70. Which ruler of Bengali had the Mahabharata and Ramayana translated into Bengali?
A. Hussian Shah B. Nusrat Shah
C. Bahman Shah D. None of these

71. The decorative device found in all the buildings of Feroz Tughlaq is
A. Swastik B. The lotus
C. The Shankh D. The bell

72. Which one of the following language profited most from the religious reformation movement of the 15-16th Centuries?
A. Urdu B. Hindi
C. Sanskrit D. Persian

73. Which one of the following was not borrowed by Hindu astronomers from the Muslims.
A. Cosmology
B. Calculations of altitude and longitude
C. Technical terms
D. Some item of the Calendar (Zich)

74. Who was given the title of nayak
A. Amir Khusrau
B. Sodi
C. Malik Muhammad Jaisi
D. None

75. Aiman-Ghora and Sanam are Perso-Arabic
A. Tals B. Ragas
C. Both (a) and (b) D. None of these

76. Which one of the following was not borrowed by Hindu astronomers from the Muslims
A. Cosmology
B. Calculation of altitude and longitude
C. Technical terms
D. Some items of the Calendar (Zich)

77. Which of the following instruments was not brought by the Turks to India?
A. Veena B. Rabab
C. Sarangi D. None of these

78. What was the basic reason for the growth of a beautiful style of Indo-Islamic architecture in Gujarat?
A. Import of foreign architects from Persia
B. Availability of almost an infinite variety of material
C. Presence of a splendid indigenous style before the coming of the Muslims
D. The special interest taken by the rulers of Gujarat

79. The Bhagavata was translated into Bengali by
A. Rupa Goswami B. Chemdidas
C. Maladhar Basu D. None of these

80. The Tabla is believed to have been invented by
A. Malik Mohammad Jaisi
B. Amir Khusrau
C. Zain-ul-Abidin
D. None of these

81. Which one of the following was not borrowed by Hindu astronomers from the Muslims?
A. Cosmology
B. Calculation of altitude and longitude
C. Technical terms
D. Some items of the Calendar

82. Which one of the following Indian musical instrument is the finest example of Indo-Islamic Synthesis?
A. Tabla B. Sitar
C. Sarangi D. Shehanai

83. Which one of the following Hindu motifs was not borrowed by the Turkish Sultans of Delhi in the sphere of decoration of buildings?
A. The Lotus B. The bell motif
C. Swastika D. The fish motif

84. Who translated the Bhagvat Gita into Bengali?
A. Krithivas B. Kavindra
C. Maladhar Vasu D. Srikar Nandi

85. Under the patronage of the Vijayanagar rulers, the literature of which language developed in South India?
A. Tamil B. Malayalam
C. Kannada D. Telugu

86. Who among the following was the exponent of the Tauhid-i-Wajudi?
A. Ibn-i-Wajudi
B. Khwaja Moin-ud-din Chisti
C. Nasir-ud-din Chiragh-i-Delhi
D. Nizam-ud-din Auliya

87. Which one of the following ragas was not

introduced by Amir Khusrau?
A. Aiman B. Ghora
C. Sanam D. Dhrupad

88. Match the following.

(a) Ghazals 1. Panegyrics
(b) Qaatas Brothe 2. Fragments
(c) Qasidas 3. Odes

Codes:

	(a)	*(b)*	*(c)*
A.	1	3	2
B.	3	2	1
C.	1	2	3
D.	2	1	3

89. What was the basic reason for the growth of a beautiful style of Indo-Islamic architecture in Gujarat?
A. Import of foreign architects from Persia
B. Availability of almost an infinite variety of material
C. Presence of a splendid indigenous style before the coming of the Muslims
D. The special interest taken by the rulers of Gujarat

90. In South India the architecture of the Bahmanis was a composite mixture of several elements. Which of the following was not one of them?
A. Turkish B. Indian
C. Monogoloid D. Egyptian

91. The Ist Sultan of Delhi who initiated the policy of associating Indian Muslims with administration was
A. Balban B. Feroz Tughlaq
C. Iltutmish D. Alauddin Khilji

92. Who was the author of 'Khazain-ul-Futuh'?
A. Masan Nizami
B. Amir Khusrau
C. Yahya Bin Ahmad
D. Abdul Fazal

93. Which of the following was not one of the distinguishing features of Indian architecture?
A. Topping of the arch with a lintel
B. Flat roof
C. Corbelling of the towers of the temples
D. The decorative motifs

94. The author of the Tabaqat-i-Nasir was
A. Zaiuddin Barni B. Amir Khusran
C. Minha-jud-din D. Shams-i-Siraj

95. Which of the following was the peculiar feature of Jaunpur mosques?
A. Absence of minarets
B. Slopping walls
C. Absence of correct turrets
D. Square pillars

96. The Qutab Minar was dedicated to
A. Qutab-ud-din Aibak
B. Sufi Saint, Qutab-ud-din Bakhtiyar Kaki
C. Khwaja Moin-ud din Chisti
D. The Chishti Saint, Nizam-ud-din Auliya

97. From where did the Lodis borrow a new type of decoration enamelled ties?
A. Egypt
B. Persia
C. Central Asia
D. South-Western Europe

98. The decorative device found in all the buildings of Feroz Tughlaq is
A. Swastika B. Lotus
C. Shankh D. Bell

99. Who among the following was an exponent of Sudhadavaita?
A. Ramanuja B. Vallabhacharya
C. Chaitanya D. Sankar

100. The tall curved Spiral roof and the mandapam were feature of which style of architecture
A. Nagara B. Shikara
C. Sharqi D. Bengal

ANSWERS

1	2	3	4	5	6	7	8	9	10
A	B	B	C	D	D	C	C	B	D

11	12	13	14	15	16	17	18	19	20
C	B	D	D	C	A	B	C	B	A
21	**22**	**23**	**24**	**25**	**26**	**27**	**28**	**29**	**30**
C	A	C	A	C	C	C	D	C	A
31	**32**	**33**	**34**	**35**	**36**	**37**	**38**	**39**	**40**
A	D	A	B	D	C	C	A	C	B
41	**42**	**43**	**44**	**45**	**46**	**47**	**48**	**49**	**50**
C	C	C	A	C	D	D	D	B	D
51	**52**	**53**	**54**	**55**	**56**	**57**	**58**	**59**	**60**
A	D	A	D	A	A	C	B	D	A
61	**62**	**63**	**64**	**65**	**66**	**67**	**68**	**69**	**70**
C	B	C	A	C	A	C	A	B	B
71	**72**	**73**	**74**	**75**	**76**	**77**	**78**	**79**	**80**
B	C	D	A	B	A	A	C	C	B
81	**82**	**83**	**84**	**85**	**86**	**87**	**88**	**89**	**90**
A	C	D	C	D	B	D	B	C	C
91	**92**	**93**	**94**	**95**	**96**	**97**	**98**	**99**	**100**
B	B	D	C	A	B	B	B	B	A

VIJAYANAGAR EMPIRE

1. Which one of the following statements regarding the imperial council is not true?
   A. The Prime Minister used to be the President of the Council
   B. The king presided over the council when grave matters had to be discussed and decided
   C. The members of the council had complete control over the policy of the state
   D. The council was extremely powerful and the king was a puppet in its hands
2. Who was the pradhani or Sirah pradhani?
   A. Commander-in-chief of the forces
   B. The judge at the imperial headquarters
   C. An administrative officer incharge of the general administration of the empire
   D. Head priests
3. Identify the wrong statement with regard to the Ayagar System
   A. The Ayagars could sell or mortgage their offices
   B. They were granted tax-free lands (Manyams)
   C. These 'Ayagars' had no hereditary rights over their offices
   D. The Reddi Karnam, and Karnika were some of the important Ayagar officials.
4. The number of the provinces of the Vijaynagar empire was:
   A. Four B. Six
   C. Five D. Three
5. Which statement on Vijayanagar village is not correct?
   A. The village was the unit of administration
   B. The village moot, corresponding to the Panchayat of Northern India, managed its own affairs.
   C. The hereditary officer of the village moot was known as "Mahanayakacharya.
   D. The hereditary officer of the village moot was known as Ayagar?
6. The ruler of Vijayanagar empire was called
   A. Raya
   B. Raja
   C. Mandalesvras
   D. Mahammandalesvaras
7. Which of the following statement is false with regard to the policy of Vijayanagar empire?
   A. The Vijayanagar kings claimed divine origin for their power
   B. The selection of the ruler appears to have been made generally with the common consensus of the ministers and nobles
   C. There are instances of kings like Krishnadeva Raya abdicating in favour of their sons.
   D. The Vijayanagar kings used to sometimes appoint their sons as Yuvaraja to obviate the disputes regarding succession
8. Which of the following was not one of the important officers of the state?
   A. Custom of the Jewels
   B. Chief Treasurer
   C. Chief Master of Horses
   D. Provider of the Harem
9. Which one of the following was the largest administrative division in the Vijayanagar empire?
   A. Rajya B. Mandalam
   C. Kottam D. Nadu
10. Which one of the following was not the expressions used for provinces.
    A. Rajya B. Mandala
    C. Rashtra D. Chavadi
11. Locate which one of the following was not one of the provinces of the empire of Vijayanagar?
    A. Udayagiri B. Penugonda

C. Padaividu D. Raichur

12. Which one of the following was not provinces of the Vijayanagar empire?
    A. Grama
    B. Naduka, Valitas or Vanitas
    C. Sthala, Sammat or Kampana
    D. Sima
13. What was the function of the Mahanayakacharya, one of the king's officer?
    A. To supervise the work of the nayaks
    B. To exercise general supervision over the village administration.
    C. To supervise the observance of dharma
    D. None of the above
14. What was Kuttagai?
    A. Lease system of cultivation
    B. Beneficiary tenures like brahmadeya, devadeya and mathapura
    C. Service tenure for military or civil service
    D. Grant of land to certain categories of craftsmen such as potters, goldsmith etc.
15. 'Amaram' stands for
    A. It was a tax levied on the Muslims
    B. Territory with a fixed revenue to military chiefs
    C. Head of the village community
    D. Areas which were under the control of subordinate rulers
16. Cite one of the following statements about the position of women in Vijayanagar empire which is not correct?
    A. Women in general occupied a high position in society
    B. They look active part in the political, social and literary life of the country
    C. Some of them were trained in wrestling and handling swords and Shields
    D. They were generally married after attaining the age of puberty.
17. Which statement on Vijayanagar society is incorrect.
    A. Duelling was recognised method of settling disputes
    B. Only non-Brahmans consumed all kinds of meat
    C. Even Brahmans ate all kinds of meat
    D. The flesh of Cattle was strictly prohibited
18. Which one of the following types of marriage was the most popular?
    A. Brahma B. Daiva
    C. Arsa D. Prajapatya
19. Which of the following taxes was not impractice in the time of the rulers of Vijayanagar empire?
    A. Grazing tax B. Tax on Pilgrims
    C. Land tax D. Marriage tax
20. What was known as Varam?
    A. The best quality of land
    B. The system of sharing of agriculture income between landlord and the tenant
    C. A special method of cultivation which was kept as a closely guarded secret among certain classes of cultivators
    D. The dowry given to the bridegroom in terms of land.
21. Which of the statement is justified regarding the high position of the women in the society of Vijayanagar empire?
    A. Polygamy was not in practice
    B. There was no Sati System
    C. There was no child marriage
    D. Women were engaged in all types of professions.
22. Amongst the things that were built during the days of Krishnadeva Rays, the outstanding one was.
    A. the modern city of Hospet
    B. embellishment of the Vittalaswamy temple
    C. the statue of Narasimha which was carved out of a single piece of granite
    D. the Harzara temple
23. Mention one of the following statements outlining the role played by the temple in the economic life of the people which

is incorrect.

A. It was the largest employer in the village

B. It was often the biggest single landowner and consumer in an area

C. It largely controlled rural credit

D. It however did very little to encourage rural development

24. At which place were ships in use for coasting and overseas trade built?

A. Eli B. Quilon

C. Calicut D. Maldiva Islands

25. Krishadeva Raya patronised

A. One language B. Two language

C. Three language D. Four language

26. What was the main source of Income of Vijayanagar Kingdom?

A. Trade B. Industries

C. Land revenue D. War booty

27. Define Kaikkolas?

A. Temple priests

B. A community of acrobats

C. An influential community of weavers living around temple precints

D. An anti-religious group which entertained the people by caricaturing various God heads.

28. Nikitin, a Russian traveller, who visited the Bahamani Kingdom describes

(a) That the country was overpopulated

(b) Misery of the people

(c) Life of Luscury of the nobles

(d) Overgrowth of military establishment

(e) Armies being maintained by nobles

Codes:

A. *a*, *b* and *c*

B. *a*, *b* and *d*

C. *a*, *b*, *c* and *e*

D. All the above

29. Match the foreign travellers and their nationalities?

(a) Nicolo Conti 1. Russian

(b) Athanasius Nikitin 2. Italian (Venetian)

(c) Abdur Razzaq 3. Portuguese

(d) Domingos Poes 4. Arab

Codes:

	(a)	(b)	(c)	(d)
A.	1	2	4	3
B.	2	1	4	3
C.	3	2	4	1
D.	1	4	2	3

30. Which factors kept the Vijayanagar state survive for 200 years?

(a) Fire of Hindu patriotism

(b) Threat of Bahamani empire

(c) Ability and Courage of the kings

(d) Foreign help

Codes:

A. *a*, *b* and *c*

B. *a*, *b* and *d*

C. *b*, *c* and *d*

D. *a*, *c* and *d*

31. Sewell writes 'Goa rose and fell simultaneously with the rise and fall of the Tuluva dynasty' why?

A. Goa was a part of the Vijayanagar empire

B. The City enjoyed protection and trade concession

C. The Tuluva kings always had Goa as the last refuge after losing war

D. None of the above

32. Krishnadeva Raya was a followers of

A. Vaishnavism B. Shaivism

C. Buddism D. Jainism

33. Virupaksha was a

A. Shaivite deity

B. Vaishnavite deity

C. A representation of Vallabha

D. A deity popularised by Smartas

34. Which language benefited the most from the patronage of letters by Krishnadeva Raya

A. Telugu B. Kannada

C. Sanskrit D. Tamil

35. Who was the author of Madhura Vijayam?

A. Tirumalamba B. Tukkadevi

C. Chinnadevi D. Gangadevi

36. "The Forgotten Empire" is a book written by

A. Domingos Poes

B. Sewell

C. Nicoli Conti

D. Meadows Taylor

37. Who wrote "What I saw (Vijayanagar) was same what as large as Rome and very beautiful to sight. This is the best provided city in the world"?

A. Poes B. Muniz
C. Abdur Razzaq D. Nikitin

38. Who was the author of Panduranga Mahatyam?

A. Tenali Ramakrishna
B. Suranna
C. Peddana
D. Tirumalamba

39. Athavana tantram is a

A. Document on the revenue system of the Vijayanagar empire
B. A book on Music
C. A book on Tantricism
D. A book on concerning Polity

40. Whose words are these "with great care and according to your power you should attend to the work of protecting the good and the punishing the wicked without neglecting anything that you see or hear"?

A. Tirumala
B. Vir Narasimha
C. Krishnadeva Raya
D. Harihara II

41. "A crowned king should always rule with an eye towards dharma" who authored these lines?

A. Krishnadeva Raya
B. Tirumala
C. Achyuta Raya
D. Deva Raya II

42. Name the language that Krishnadeva Raya used to write his major work 'Amuktamalyada'?

A. Sanskrit B. Tamil
C. Kannada D. Telgu

43. Name the King during whose rule lord Venkateshwara of Tirupati replaced Virupaksha?

A. Tirumala
B. Venkatadri or Venkata I
C. Krishnadeva Raya
D. Venkata II

44. Who was the real founder of the independent Sultanate of Gujarat?

A. Zafar Khan B. Tatar Khan
C. Shams Khan D. Ahmad Shah

45. Who built the city of Ahmedabad?

A. Zafar Khan
B. Ahmed Shah
C. Mahmud Bengarha
D. Muzaffar II

46. Which of the following is described as the Shiraz of India?

A. Gaur B. Agra
C. Jaunpur D. Ikdala

47. Pick out the wrong match.

A. Atala-Masjid – Jaunpur
B. Bara Sona Masjid – Gaur
C. Adina Masjid – Pandua
D. Gol Gumbaz – Ajmer

48. What was the name of the old town near which Ahmedabad was built?

A. Janugarh B. Siri
C. Asawal D. Mandu

49. One of the following factors contributed most to the development of Bengali literature. Identify.

A. Patronage of Muhammadan Emperors and Chiefs.
B. The support given by the Hindu Rayas
C. Religious activity
D. Economic properity

50. Jaunpur was hailed as the "Shiraz of India". What could be the most important reason for such a description?

A. Some of the Sharqi rulers were themselves of culture
B. the Sharqi rule was marked by prosperity
C. It was not involved in any war with its neighbour
D. It was nearer to Delhi

51. Pick out the wrong match.

A. Khaljis — Malwa
B. Sharqis — Jaunpur
C. Husain Shahi — Bengal
D. Iliyas Shahi — Gujarat

52. Pick out the correct match.
A. Tower of Victory — Chitor
B. Shiraz of India — Delhi
C. Gol Gumbaz — Bijapur
D. Vittalasvami Temple — Belur

53. Who is the founder of the cult of Satyapir?
A. Husain Shah B. Sikandar II
C. Nasir-ud-din D. Haji Iliyas

54. Pick out the wrong match.
A. Bengal — Haji Iliyas
B. Jaunpur — Khwaja Jahan
C. Malwa — Dilawar Khan Ghuri
D. Gujarat — Tatar Khan

55. One of the following may not be regarded as the cause of external invasions of Gujarat. Identify
A. fertility
B. wealth due to active commerce
C. natural resources
D. strategic importance

56. Pick out the wrong match—
A. Nusrat Shah — Qadam Rasul
B. Raya Ganesh — Danujamardana Deva
C. Ala-ud-din Hussain Shah — Ikdala
D. Indil Khan — Bengali version of the Mahabharata

57. Which is not a correct pair—
A. Nicolo Conti — Deva Raya I
B. Abdur Razzaq— Deva Raya II
C. Barbosa — Krishnadeva Raya
D. Idn Datula — Ghiyasuddin Tughluq

58. Whom do you regard the ablest of the Muslim ruler of Malwa?
A. Hushang Shah B. Mahmud I
C. Mahmud II D. Nasiruddin

59. Name the ruler who assisted Mahmud II to oust Medini Raj
A. Rana Sanga B. Ratan Singh
C. Muzaffar Shah D. Chand Khan

60. Who built the Bara Masjid
A. Nusrat Shah
B. Hussain Shah
C. Jalal-ud-din Muhammad
D. Barbak Shah

61. Urdu whose orders a Bengali version of the Mahabharata was written?
A. Hussain Shah
B. Jalal-ud-din Muhammad
C. Nusrat Shah
D. Haji Iliyas

62. Pick out the correct sequence
A. Sangama, Aravidu, Tuluva and Saluva
B. Sangama, Tuluva, Saluva and Aravidu
C. Sangama, Saluva, Tuluva and Aravidu
D. Sangama, Aravidu, Saluva and Tuluva

63. One of the following did not visit the city of Vijayanagar. Identify
A. Nicolo Conti
B. Abdur Razzaq
C. Fernao
D. Athanarius Nikitin

64. One of the following did not join the Deccani Sultans against Vijayanagar in the battle of Rakshasa-Tangadi. Identify
A. Bijapur B. Golkunde
C. Ahmadnagar D. Berar

65. This is the best provided city in the world. Who has said this about — Vijayanagar
A. Domingos Poes B. Nuniz
C. Nicolo Conti D. Edoardo Borbosa

66. Pick out the correct sequence
A. Sangama, Bukka I, Virupaksha II and Devaraya I
B. Sangama, Virupaksha II, Devaraya I and Bukka I
C. Sangama, Bukka I, Devaraya I and Virupaksha II
D. Sangama, Devaraya I, Bukka I and Virupaksha II

67. One of the following was not regarded as one of the four Indians of the state :
A. Diwan-i-Wizarut
B. Diwan-i-Insha
C. Diwan-i-Arz
D. Diwan-i-Kharisat

68. From whom did the Turks know the association of divinity with kingship?
A. The Hindus B. The Chinese
C. The Sassanians D. The Arbas

69. Which one of the following defects of Vijayanagar empire may be regarded as the most serious one?

A. Independence enjoyed by the Provincial governors

B. Failure to develop a sustained commercial activity in spite of the facilities available

C. Permission given to the portuguese to settle on the west coast

D. Failure to develop a desciplined army

70. The authorship of one of the following is not ascribed to Krishnadeva Raya. Identify

A. Amuktamalyada

B. Ushaparivaya

C. Jambuvati – Kalyana

D. Narayana – Vilasa

71. We have reference to the following local divisions in the Karnataka portion under the Vijayanagar rulers. Pick out the correct sequence in descending order

A. Nadu, Sima, Ventha, Village

B. Ventha, Nadu, Sima, Village

C. Sima, Ventha, Nadu, Village

D. Ventha, Sima, Nadu, Village

72. Who was the founder of the city of Zainabad?

A. Malik Nasir B. Adi Khan

C. Malik Raja D. Muzaffar Shah

73. What was the original name of Ahsanabad?

A. Gulbanga B. Badami

C. Kalyan D. Malkhed

74. What was the charge levelled against Mahmud Gawan?

A. Gawan was blind to the interests of the state

B. Gawan was organising a baronial chique against the Sultan

C. Gawan was in treasonable correspondence with the Raya of Vijayanagar.

D. Gawan indulged in tyrannical acts.

75. Which among the following not applicable to Vijayanagar period?

A. bloody sacrifices on festive occasions

B. a ban on prostitutes

C. use of flowers by women

D. sale of animals for food alive

76. Pick out the wrong match.

A. History of Kashmir — Jonaraja

B. History of Bahmani Kingdom — Bushan-i-Massir

C. History of Gujarat — Mirat-i-Sikandar

D. History of Bengal — Chanchnama

77. Pick out the wrong one among the attributes ascribed to Ahmad Shah of Gujarat?

A. Warlike B. Lover of justice

C. Munificent D. Tolerant

78. Who was called the Zar Bakhsha?

A. Ahmad Shah

B. Qutab-ud-din Ahmad

C. Muhammad Sha II

D. Mahmud Begarbha

79. What was the original name of Muhammadabad?

A. Dwaraka B. Junagarh

C. Champanir D. Surat

80. The nature of the rule of the kings of Vijayanagar was

A. Benevolent despotism

B. Rule by the Council of Minister

C. Oligrachical rule

D. On the principles of democracy

81. When point on Krishnadeva Raya is not correct

A. He belonged to Tuluga dynasty

B. He ruled from 1509 to 1530

C. He was defeated by the Bijapur Sultan

D. He recaptured Raichur Doob

82. Romantically called "The war of the Goldsmith's Daughter" took place between

A. Firoz Shah and Deva Raya

B. Firoz Shah and Hari Hara II

C. Ala-ud-din Khalji and Karnadeva

D. Ala-ud-din Khalji and Hamir Deva

83. Which two dynastics came to the throne after the 'First Usurpation' and 'Second Usurpation' respectively

A. Sangama and Saluva dynastics

B. Saluva and Aravidu dynastics

C. Saluva and Tuluva dynastics
D. Sangama and Aravidu dynastics

84. What was the second capital of Vijaynagar.
A. Chandrajiri B. Pernugoda
C. Kampali D. Mysore

85. Who among the following rulers of Vijayanagar entered into a treaty with the Portuguese Governor, Almedia for purchasing all the horses imported by him?
A. Achyuta Raya
B. Vir Narsimha
C. Saluva Narsimha
D. Krishnadeva Raya

86. Who was the ruler who participated in war with the Bahamani confederacy?
A. Narsimha Saluva
B. Vira Narasimha
C. Krishnadeva Raya
D. Rama Raya

87. Which fact regarding the battle of Talikota or Rakshasa-Tangadi is of significance in the history of India?
A. Hussain Nizam Shah personally killed Rama Raya
B. The Aravidu Dynasty continued the traditions of the Vijaynagar empire
C. Bijapur and Ahmadnagar attacked Goa in 1569
D. Shivaji claimed descent from Vijayanagar rulers?

88. Which region constituted the bone of contention between the Vijayanagar and Bahamani rulers?
A. Raichur Doab
B. Cauvery Doab
C. Tungabhadra Doab
D. Kolar Doab

89. Where from did South India get its ships during the Vijayanagar period?
A. Ceylon B. Portugal
C. Maldives D. Persia

90. During the reign of which Sultan of Delhi did the Vijayanagar Empire come into existence
A. Ghiyas-ud-din Tughlaq
B. Muhammad-bin Tughlaq
C. Firoz Shah Tughlaq
D. Khizr Khan

91. Match the following dynastics with their founders.
(a) Sangama dynasty 1. Narasimha
(b) Saluva dynasty 2. Harihara
(c) Tuluva dynasty 3. Tirumala
(d) Aravidu dynasty 4. Vir Narasimha

Codes:

	(a)	*(b)*	*(c)*	*(d)*
A.	1	2	3	4
B.	2	1	3	4
C.	2	1	4	3
D.	4	3	2	1

92. Who succeeded Krishnadeva Raya after his death?
A. Deva Raya II B. Rama Raya
C. Sadasiva Raya D. Achyuta Raya

93. Who gave permission to the Portuguese Governor Albuquerque to build a fort at Bhatkal
A. Deva Raya I
B. Deva Raya II
C. Krishnadeva Raya
D. Rama Raya

94. Who built the Vitthalasvami temple?
A. Bukka I
B. Devaraya II
C. Tirumala
D. Krishnadeva Raya

95. One of the following was not an important industry during the Vijayanagar period. Identify
A. Textiles B. Mining
C. Metallurgy D. Perfumery

96. Which of the following is not one of the theories propounded by scholars regarding the origin of Valangai (right hand) and Idangai (left hand) castes?
A. Those who stood on the right hand side of the king were called valangais and other who stood on the left side were called Idangais
B. Valangais were agriculturists and

Idangais were traders, the distinction arising on account of foreign trade and contact

C. On account of great animosity between the two classes of people, they got there tables.

D. It had its origin in the method of work i.e. those working with right hand came to be known as Valangais and left handers as Idangis

97. Which one of the following statement about the practice of becoming a Sati or Sahagamana is not correct?

A. The Sati's sacrifice was comm-emorated by erection of Sati Kals

B. There was no compulsion and it was done voluntarily

C. It was very popular and widespread

D. There was no social disabilities attached to widows who did not choose to become Satis

98. The City of Vijayanagar had seven fortified walls one within the other. The palace of the king was located at the centre in the seventh fortress, which one of the following occupied pride of place between the third and the seventh fortress?

A. Gardens

B. Shops and Bazaars

C. Houses of Nobles

D. Quarters of Courtesans

99. Arrange the foreign travellers in choronological order :

(a) Nikitin

(b) Ibn Batuta

(c) Marco Polo

(d) Nicolo Conti

(e) Abdur Razzaq

(f) Barbosa

Codes:

A.	*(c)*	*(b)*	*(e)*	*(d)*	*(a)*	*(f)*
B.	*(a)*	*(b)*	*(c)*	*(d)*	*(e)*	*(f)*
C.	*(b)*	*(c)*	*(d)*	*(e)*	*(a)*	*(f)*
D.	*(c)*	*(b)*	*(d)*	*(e)*	*(a)*	*(f)*

100. The fortress of Vijayanagar was located on the bank of the river—

A. Godavari B. Krishna

C. Tungabhadra D. Kaveri

101. Arrange the rulers of Vijayanagar in chronological order

(a) Virupaksha I

(b) Devaraya I

(c) Vir Narasimha

(d) Krishnadeva Raya

(e) Tirumalla

Codes:

A.	*a*	*b*	*c*	*d*	*e*
B.	*a*	*c*	*d*	*b*	*e*
C.	*b*	*c*	*a*	*d*	*e*
D.	*c*	*b*	*a*	*e*	*d*

102. Who died (aged 29) screaming that Mahmud Gawan was tearing him to pieces?

A. Ahmad Shah

B. Hasan Bahmani

C. Firoz Shah (1397-1422)

D. Muhammed Shah III (1463-82)

103. Proficiency in which of the following was rewarded and recognised by the state?

A. Chess B. Shadow plays

C. Wrestling D. Gambling

104. According to Abdur Razzaq, the pay of the Policemen of Vijayanagar was paid from the proceeds of—

A. Brothels B. Taxes on goods

C. Land revenue D. Wine shops

105. Match the name of the founders with Vijayanagar dynastics.

(a) Vir Narasimha	1. Saluva dynasty in 1486
(b) Harihara and Bukka	2. Sangam dynasty in 1336
(c) Tirumal	3. Aravidu dynasty in 1570
(d) Immadi Nara Simha	4. Taluva dynasty in 1506

Codes:

	(a)	*(b)*	*(c)*	*(d)*
A.	1	2	3	4
B.	2	1	4	3
C.	3	2	1	4
D.	1	2	4	3

106. Who says "The land is over stocked with people, but those in the country are very miserable while the nobles are extremely affluent and delight in luxury?

A. Nuniz B. Marçopola
C. Nikitin D. Abdur Razzaq

107. Under the Vijayanagar empire, the Central Government maintained contact with the village through an officer called

A. Pattanasvami
B. Mahanayakacharya
C. Yukta
D. Nayak

108. Which of the following festivals was most important and celebrated with great enthusiasm in Vijayanagar

A. Mahanavami B. Holi
C. Deepawali D. Pongal

109. Which of the following was one of the categories into which land was classified for the purpose of assessment

A. orchard B. wet
C. dry D. all of the above

110. Generally the land tax was one-third of the produce. Besides the land tax, which of the following was one of the sources from which the income of state was derived?

(a) Property tax
(b) Tax on sale of produce
(c) Tax on marriage
(d) Profession taxes
(e) Military contribution
(f) All of the above

Codes:

A. *a, c* and *e*
B. *b, d* and *f*
C. *a, c, e* and *f*
D. All of the above

111. Which of the following points regarding Vijayanagar empire is correct?

A. The Vijayanagar empire was founded by Harihara and Bukka
B. The empire was the outcome of conscious attempt of Hindus to checkmate the ambitions of Islam
C. Its rules pursued the traditional principles of administration relating to taxation, patronage of culture and art, and religious toleration
D. All of the above

112. Match the following

(a) Kaivinaikuddi 1. Hired Labour
(b) Varam 2. The system of sharing of agricultural income between the landlord and the tenant
(c) Kaikkolas 3. An influential community of weavers living around temple precinets
(d) Sthanikas 4. Those changed with the management of the temple

Codes:

	(a)	(b)	(c)	(d)
A.	1	2	3	4
B.	2	1	4	3
C.	3	2	1	4
D.	1	2	4	3

113. In the medieval times, the kingdom of Viayanagar was known by several names. Which one of the following names does not refer to Vijayanagar?

A. Hastinavati–Vidyanagar
B. Vidyanagara
C. Vijayagiri
D. Hampe Hastinavati

114. Athavana – tantram is a

A. Document on the revenue system of the empire of Vijayanagar
B. A book on Music
C. A book on Tantricism
D. None of these

115. Which one of the following statements about Krishnadeva Raya is correct?

A. He belonged to Taluva dynasty
B. He ruled from 1509 to 1530
C. He recaptured Raichur Doab
D. All of the above

116. Which one of the following rulers was

known by the title of Andhra Bhoja?
A. Deva Raya II
B. Krishnadeva Raya
C. Harihara
D. Rama Raya

117. The foreign travellers named one of the famous coins of Vijayanagar as Pagoda. What is that?
A. Pon B. The Gold Varaha
C. Hun D. Fanam

118. What was the second capital of Vijayanagar empire?
A. Kampali B. Penugonda
C. Udayagiri D. Padaividu

119. The Vijayanagar empire was finally extinguished by
A. Golkonda B. Bijapur
C. Shivaji D. The Mughals

120. The special feature of the financial system of Vijayanagar was
A. Surplus revenue of the state
B. Its currency system
C. The land tax
D. The private mints

121. The four-runner of the Maratha-astapradhana in the Vijayanagar administration was
A. Pradhani B. Rayasam
C. Mantriparisad D. None of the above

ANSWERS

1	2	3	4	5	6	7	8	9	10
D	C	C	B	D	A	C	D	B	C
11	**12**	**13**	**14**	**15**	**16**	**17**	**18**	**19**	**20**
D	A	B	A	B	D	C	A	B	B
21	**22**	**23**	**24**	**25**	**26**	**27**	**28**	**29**	**30**
D	C	D	D	D	C	C	D	B	D
31	**32**	**33**	**34**	**35**	**36**	**37**	**38**	**39**	**40**
B	A	B	A	B	B	A	A	A	C
41	**42**	**43**	**44**	**45**	**46**	**47**	**48**	**49**	**50**
A	D	D	D	B	C	D	C	A	A
51	**52**	**53**	**54**	**55**	**56**	**57**	**58**	**59**	**60**
D	A	A	D	D	D	D	B	C	A
61	**62**	**63**	**64**	**65**	**66**	**67**	**68**	**69**	**70**
C	C	D	D	A	C	D	C	B	D
71	**72**	**73**	**74**	**75**	**76**	**77**	**78**	**79**	**80**
B	A	A	C	B	D	D	C	C	A
81	**82**	**83**	**84**	**85**	**86**	**87**	**88**	**89**	**90**
C	A	C	B	B	D	D	A	C	B
91	**92**	**93**	**94**	**95**	**96**	**97**	**98**	**99**	**100**
C	D	C	D	D	D	D	B	D	C
101	**102**	**103**	**104**	**105**	**106**	**107**	**108**	**109**	**110**
A	D	A	A	A	C	B	A	D	D
111	**112**	**113**	**114**	**115**	**116**	**117**	**118**	**119**	**120**
D	A	C	A	D	B	B	B	C	B
121									
C									

RELIGIOUS MOVEMENTS OF THE 15th & 16th CENTURIES

1. Who was Sayana?
   A. a commentator of Vedas
   B. a governor of the Vijayanagar empire
   C. father of Krishnadeva Raya
   D. the founder of the Aravidu dynasty
2. Who has described the Brahmanas as honest men given to merchandise–but little fit for hard work?
   A. Nicolo Conti B. Nuniz
   C. Paes D. Barbosa
3. Who has said that the Vijayanagar empire possessed 300 sea ports?
   A. Abdul Razzaq B. Nuniz
   C. Paes D. Caesar Frederick
4. Pick out the wrong match :
   A. Amuktamalyada–Telugu
   B. Prabhulingabile–Kannada
   C. Kalaviyal–Tamil
   D. Madhura Vijayam–Malayalam
5. By what name is Vishnu Cithya known?
   A. Markandeya Purana
   B. Amuktamalayada
   C. Jambavati Kalyana
   D. Parvati Parinaya
6. The assimilation of Muslims into Indian Society was rendered easier by many factors. One of the following may not be correct. Identify
   A. Absence of large scale immigration from Afghanistan and Western Asia
   B. Muslim were in a minority
   C. Advantages to be gained by conversion were not great
   D. Persecution
7. Why did Mahmud attack Multan?
   A. The ruler followed the heterodox doctrine of the Qarmatrori Seat
   B. The ruler was weak
   C. Wealth of Multan
   D. Desire to bring it under his control
8. Who was Gangu?
   A. founder of Bahmani Kingdom
   B. astrologer of Delhi
   C. descendant of the Persian hero Bahman
   D. Governor of Daulatabad
9. Pick out the wrong match.
   A. Nizam Shahi — Ahmadnagar
   B. Qutub Shahi — Golkunda
   C. Barid Shahi — Berar
   D. Adil Shahi — Bijapur
10. By what name is the tomb of Muhammad Adil Shah called?
    A. Gol Gumbaz B. Bara Gumbaz
    C. Shib Gumbaz D. Dadi Ka Gumbaz
11. Which among the following may be regarded on the most significant achievements of Vijayanagar empire.
    A. Building up a vast empire
    B. Efficient administration
    C. Economic prosperity
    D. Saving the Hindu religion and culture from being engulfed by the rush of new forces.
12. In what language was Basavapurana written.
    A. Sanskrit B. Tamil
    C. Telgu D. Prakrit
13. When was the battle of Talikota fought.
    A. 1565 AD B. 1526 AD
    C. 1556 AD D. 1509 AD
14. Who among the Bahmani Sultans was called the Zalim?
    A. Ala-ud-din II B. Humayun
    C. Muhammad III D. Ahmad
15. "With him departed all the cohesion and power of the Bahmani kingdom"—about whom was this said?
    A. Mahmud Gawan
    B. Ahmad Shah
    C. Muhammad Shah III
    D. Humayun
16. One of the five Deccani Sultanates was annexed by Ahmadnagar. Identify
    A. Bijapur B. Berar

C. Golkunda D. Bidar

17. Pick out the wrong match.
A. Chaitanya – Bengali
B. Sankara Deva – Assamese
C. Mira Bai – Rajasthani
D. Kabir – Gujarati

18. One of the following was not a Maratha Saint. Identify
A. Jnanesvar B. Ramdas
C. Namadeva D. Vallabha

19. Who composed 'Sursagar'.
A. Jayadeva
B. Surdas
C. Bana
D. None of the above

20. Where is Quwat-ul-Islam mosque situated?
A. Ajmer B. Agra
C. Fatehpur Sikri D. Delhi

21. One of the following composed verses in praise of God Siva. Identify
A. Mira Bai B. Surdas
C. Chaitanya D. Lalla

22. Who among the following spoke about achieving union with God through love of God?
A. Shiahs B. Sunnis
C. Sufis D. Ulemas

23. By what name is the philosophy of Ramanuja known?
A. Dvaita B. Advaita
C. Visista Dvaita D. Sankhya

24. Kabir Panthis were the followers of:
A. Meera Bai B. Namdev
C. Kabir D. Nanak

25. Where was Guru Nanak born:
A. Hissar B. Amritsar
C. Talwandi D. None of these

26. Namdeva, a Marathi Saint flourished in:
A. 10th century B. 11th century
C. 13th centure D. 14th century

27. Seeds of Bhakti can be found in
A. Upanishads B. Shrutis
C. Upredas D. Vedas

28. Who said that the Hindu and the Turks were pots of the same clay?
A. Kabir B. Nanak
C. Lalla D. Vallabha

29. One of the following belonged to the chisti order. Identify?
A. Barani B. Mahmud Gawan
C. Firishta D. Lalla

30. Where was the order of Firdausi popular
A. Ghazi B. Bihar
C. Delhi D. Sind

31. "Dohas" are—
A. The religious teaching of Sufis
B. The Muslim devotees who emphasised the personal devotion of man to God through love
C. A group of merchants who sent large caravans
D. Couples which Kabir composed and by which he taught his followers.

32. The language of Bhakti movement was
A. The language of the reformers
B. Sanskrit/Prakrit
C. Hindi/Perisan
D. Perisan and Urdu

33. The Bhakti teachers delivered their message mainly through:
A. Homely Sermars B. Simple Parables
C. Bhajans D. Public Prayer

34. In one of the following the Bhakti saints differed from the Sufis. Identify?
A. Needs for Union with God
B. Stress on love on the basis of relationship with
C. Acceptance of a Guru or Pir
D. Encouraging mysticism

35. One of the following did not help the rise of the Urdu language. Identify?
A. Arabic B. Sanskrit
C. Persian D. Bengali

36. Pick out the wrong match:
A. Chand Minar — Daulatabad
B. Madarasa of Mahmud Gawan — Bidar
C. Mihtar Mahal — Golkunda
D. Shah Bazar Maszid — Gulbarga

37. Who wrote "I am neither in Kaaba nor in Kailash?
A. Kabir B. Nanak

C. Eknath D. Chaitanya

38. Who said "God is the breath of all Breath"?
A. Kabir B. Nanak
C. Mira Bai D. Chaitanya

39. Pick out the correct match:
A. Ramdas — Amritanubhava
B. Jnanesvar — Dasabodha
C. Ramanuja — Sri Bashya
D. Krithivasa — Bengali translation of Mahabharata

40. Which saint was a contemporary of Shivaji and Samartha Guru?
A. Tukaram B. Raskhan
C. Narasimha D. Surdas

41. One of the following poets was not a contemporary of the rest of four, Identify.
A. Tulsidas B. Surdas
C. Raskhan D. Mira Bai

42. Rahim composed popular poetry in—
A. Braj Bhasa B. Persian
C. Urdu D. Hindi

43. Nirguna school believes in
A. Absolute God free from human attributes
B. God who is richly endowed with human virtues
C. God who is omnipresent
D. God who is within each human being

44. Guru Nanak was born in
A. 1469 AD B. 1470 AD
C. 1450 AD D. 1445 AD

45. The poet Amir Khusrau was a follower of
A. Chisti order
B. Suhrawardi order
C. Qadiria order
D. Was not a follower of any order of Sufis

46. In which field did the Arabs gain from India?
A. Metaphysics, medicine and mathematics
B. System of administration
C. Art of military organisation
D. Literature and arts

47. Kabir was born in
A. 1440 AD B. 1430 AD
C. 1450 AD D. 1445 AD

48. Who wrote the Telugu version of Mahabharata—
A. Nannaya
B. Akkatiyar
C. Tiruvaliuvar
D. None of the above

49. Who was the great Acharya, who counselled Surdas teaching of Lord's creative play (Bhagavat Lila)
A. Vallabhacharya B. Ramananda
C. Ramanuja D. Shankaracharya

50. Which one is not the work of Surdas?
A. Sahitya Lehari B. Sur-Sagar
C. Sur-Saravalli D. Sur-Darshan

51. Ramananda was a philosopher of
A. Vaishanavism B. Shaivism
C. Jainism D. Buddhism

52. Shankaracharya had explicit — faith in
A. Vaishnavism B. Shaivism
C. Jainism D. Hinduism

53. According to the legand, Sikandhar Lodi, the Sultan of Delhi tried various means to kill
A. Kabir B. Nanak
C. Mira D. Chaitanya

54. The script of Sikhs is
A. Guruvani B. Devanagari
C. Gurutipi D. Gurumukhi

55. The word Sikh means
A. Simple B. devotee
C. disciple D. fighter

56. The name of the last Sikh Guru is
A. Guru Amardas
B. Guru Tegh Bahadur
C. Guru Govind Singh
D. Guru Har Govind

57. Kabir didn't write in one of the following language. Which are:
A. Bhojpuri B. Brajabhasa
C. Awadhi D. Rajasthani

58. Who did not allow his followers to have any kind of social intercourse with women?
A. Chaitanya B. Nanak
C. Ramananda D. Shankaracharya

59. Namadeva and Eknath wrote in
A. Hindi B. Marathi
C. Tamil D. Gujarati

60. The name of the Guru who compiled the 'Adi Granth' is
A. Guru Govind Singh
B. Guru Tegh Bahadur
C. Guru Arjun Dev
D. Guru Nanak

61. Who did not write in Gujarati Language?
A. Mira Bai B. Narasimha
C. Kesavadas D. Kabir

62. Mira did not see one of the following. Identify.
A. Tulsidas B. Akbar
C. Tansen D. Surdas

63. Match the works with their authors:

(a)	Tarikh-i Hind	1.	Muhammad-ul-Utbi
(b)	Tarikh-i-Yamini	2.	Shams-i-Siraj Ali
(c)	Taj-ul-Ma'asir	3.	Alberuni
(d)	Tarikh-i-Firoz Shahi	4.	Hasan Nizami

Codes:

	(a)	*(b)*	*(c)*	*(d)*
A.	3	1	4	2
B.	1	2	3	4
C.	2	3	4	1
D.	4	1	3	2

64. Match the works with their authors:

(a)	Tarikh-i-Firoz Shahi	1.	Firoz Shah Tughluq
(b)	Fatuhat-i-Firoz Shahi	2.	Yahaya-bin-Sirhindi
(c)	Tarikh-a-Alai	3.	Zia-ud-din-Barani
(d)	Tarikh-i-Mubarak Shah	4.	Khusrau

Codes:

	(a)	*(b)*	*(c)*	*(d)*
A.	3	1	4	2
B.	3	4	1	2
C.	2	1	4	3
D.	4	1	3	2

65. A no. of Sanskrit works were rendered into persian for the first time during the reign of
A. Balban
B. Muhammad-bin-Tughluq
C. Firu Tughluq
D. Sher Shah

66. Which one of the following was not the saint poet of Maharashtra?
A. Jnaneswar B. Namdev
C. Tukaram D. Mira Bai

67. Name the Sufi Saint whose philosophy greatly influenced Aurangzeb?
A. Shaikh Ahmad Sirhindi
B. Khwaja Bagi Billagh
C. Shau Pir of Meerut
D. Shaikh Qadiri

68. Which Sufi order of saints tried to live like ascetics?
A. Subhrawardi B. Qadiri
C. Chisthi D. Naqsh bandi

69. Though Sufi and Bhakti thoughts converged on several points, one of following was not one of them?
A. Belief in the need to unite with God
B. Stress on love as the basis of relationship with God
C. Belief in mysticism
D. The need for the help of a religious preceptor, at least in the initial stages.

70. Which beliefs were not common to Sufi and Bhakti thoughts?
(a) The need to unite with God
(b) Stress on love as the basis of the relactionship with God
(c) Need of the Guru or a Pir in initial stages
(d) Mysticism
Codes:
A. only *(a)* and *(d)* B. only *(a)* and *(c)*
C. only *(d)* and *(c)* D. all four

71. The first Muslim building erected in India was the
A. Qutb Minar
B. Adhai-din-ka-Jhonpra
C. Quwwat-ul-Islam Mosque
D. Alai-Darwaza

72. Who claimed their decent from the prophet?
A. Shaikhs B. Sayyids
C. Mughals D. Qarunah Turks

73. School attached to mosque were known as
A. Madarasa B. Maktab
C. Talimghan D. Persia

74. Balban's monarchial ideals were those of the ancient kings of
A. Mesopotamia B. Saudi Arabia
C. Turkestan D. Persia

75. Who have been termed as "The Brahmana of Islam"?
A. Sayyids B. Shaikhs
C. Pirs D. Ulema

76. Which are of Sufi orders was at first the most orthodox?
A. Suhrawardi B. Qadiri
C. Naqshbandi D. Chishti

77. Who introduced Qadiri Silsila in India?
A. Shaikh Abdul Quadirisi
B. Sayyid Makhdum Muhammad Gilani
C. Abdul Qadir
D. Shaikh Mir Muhammad

78. Which Sufi Silsila tried to counteract the liberal religious policies of Akbar
A. Quadiri B. Firdausi
C. Suhrawardi D. Naqshbandi

79. The Theory of Islamic Mysticism (Sufism) was profound by
A. Muin-ud-din Chisti
B. Hamid-ud-din Nagar
C. Sheikh Muhi-ud-din Ibnual Arabi
D. Nizam-ud-din Auliya

80. Which of the following principles was not preached by the saints of Bhakti movement
A. Unity of God
B. Opposed Casteism
C. Idol Worship
D. No need of particular language to worship

81. Shankaracharya had explicit faith in
A. Vaishnavism B. Shaivism
C. Jainism D. Hinduism

82. Which one of the the Sufi order was at frist the most orthodox?
A. Subhrawardi B. Qadiri
C. Naqshbandi D. Chisti

83. Ramananda was philosopher of
A. Vaishnavism B. Shaivism
C. Jainism D. Bhuddism

84. Arrange the following sufi saints of the Chisti Silsila Chronologically.
1. Shaikh Farid
2. Shaikh Nizamuddin Auliya
3. Shaikh Bhaktiyar Kaki
4. Shaikh Muinuddin Chisthi

Codes:
A. 1, 2, 3, 4 B. 1, 3, 2, 4
C. 1, 3, 4, 2 D. 4, 3, 1, 2

85. Who was the bridge between the Bhakshi movement of the south and the North?
A. Chaitanya B. Namadeva
C. Ramananda D. Nanak

86. Name one of the Bhakti saints who had twelve disciples belonging to the poorest classes?
A. Vallabhacharya B. Ramananda
C. Kabir D. Surdas

87. Identify one order of the Bhakti Cult who was influenced by Islam?
A. Ramanuja B. Namadeva
C. Chaitanya D. Ramananda

88. Who among the following was not a Chisti Saint?
A. Bakhtiyar Kaki
B. Hamid-ud-din
C. Farid-ud-din Ganj-i-Shallar
D. Baha-ud-din Zakaria

89. Name one of the following who established the Chisti order in India?
A. Shaikh Muniuddin Chishti
B. Khawaja Muinuddin Chishti
C. Nizamuddin Auliya
D. Farid-ud-din Ganj-i-Shakar

90. Match the following Bhakti saints with the theories they preached.

(a) Ramanuja	1. Unqualified Monism
(b) Nimvark	2. Qualified Monism
(c) Chaitanya	3. Dualism & Non dualism
(d) Vallabha-charya	4. Pure non-dualism
(e) Shankara-charya	5. Dualistic non-dualism

Codes:

	(a)	*(b)*	*(c)*	*(d)*	*(e)*
A.	2	5	3	4	1
B.	5	4	3	2	1
C.	1	3	4	2	5
D.	4	1	5	3	2

91. Bakhtiyar Kaki, a chishti saint, refused

the post of Shaikh-ul-Islam offered to him by
A. Iltutmish
B. Balban
C. Ala-ud-din Khalji
D. Muhammad-bin-Tughluq

92. Name the Sufi saint whose philosophy greatly influenced Aurangzeb.
A. Shaikh Ahmad Sirhindi
B. Khwaja Bagi Billagh
C. Shah Pir of Meerut
D. Shaikh Qadari

93. In which of the following territories was the Firdausi order popular
A. In & Around Delhi
B. Sind
C. Bihar
D. Deccan

94. Who was the Bhakti saint regarded by his followers as an incarnation of Vishnu
A. Ramananda B. Ramanuja
C. Namadeva D. Chaitanya

95. With which religion do we associate the five k's?
A. Jainism B. Buddism
C. Sikhism D. Islam

96. Who was born at Kalady (Malabar) in 783 AD?
A. Shankaracharya B. Ramanuja
C. Ramananda D. Madhavacharya

97. Which sufi saint remarked 'Haur Dilli Dur Ast" (Delhi is still far away)
A. Nizamuddin Auliya
B. Shaikh Salim Chisthi
C. Nasiruddin Chiragh-i-Delhwi
D. Shaikh Farid

98. Which one of the following was the earliest teacher of Bhakti Cult in Maharashtra.
A. Tuka Ram B. Namadeva
C. Dadu D. Ram Das

99. Who was the most famous disciple of Ramananda?
A. Tuka Ram B. Tulsi Das
C. Kabir D. Dadu

100. Who was the author of Ramacharitamanas?
A. Ramananda B. Mira Bai
C. Kabir D. Tulsi Das

101. Mira Bai was married to a prince of which princely state
A. Chittor B. Mewar
C. Amber D. Marwar

102. Vallabhacharya visited for discussion the court of
A. Krishnadeva Raya
B. Firoz ShahTughlaq
C. Muhammad Shah Bahamani
D. Zain-ul-Abidin

103. Vallabhacharya was the worshipper of
A. Rama B. Vishnu
C. Mahavira D. Krishna

104. Chaitanya popularised as a mode of worship
A. Silent prayer
B. Recital of Vedic mantras
C. Kirtana
D. Penance

105. The one major achievement of the Bhakti movement towards Indian society was
A. Unity among the Hindus and the Muslims
B. Reforms in religion
C. Growth of Vernacular literatures
D. Religious tolerance

106. Which one of the following did not use the vernacular to write about Hindu life and tradition
A. Amir Khusro
B. Malik Muhammad Jayasi
C. Amir Hasan Dehlvi
D. Ras Khan

107. The Bhakti saints came from a diversity of back ground, by and large their adherents were
A. Artisans B. Merchants
C. Middle classes D. Lower classes

108. Adi Granth, the bible of Sikhism was compiled by
A. Guru Nanak
B. Guru Amar Das
C. Guru Arjun Dev
D. Guru Govind Singh

109. The script of Sikhs is
A. Kharoshthi B. Devanagari
C. Persian D. Gurumukhi

110. Guru Nanak was born in
A. 1469 A.D. B. 1470 A.D.
C. 1450 A.D. D. 1445 A.D.

111. Chaitanya was the worshipper of
A. Rama B. Krishna
C. Vishnu D. Siva

112. Chaitanya was born in
A. 1485 A.D. B. 1469 A.D.
C. 1450 A.D. D. 1533 A.D.

113. In which part of the country was Ramanuja born?
A. Assam B. Bengal
C. Andhra Pradesh D. Gujarat

114. Where did the Bhakti cult grow and develop when it was launched?
A. North India B. South India
C. Eastern India D. Western India

115. Namadeva was a disciple of
A. Visoba Khecar B. Ramananda
C. Vitthal D. Sarvananda

116. Namadeva and Eknath wrote in
A. Hindi B. Marathi
C. Kannada D. Gujarati

117. Kabir did not write in one of the following language.
A. Bhojpuri B. Brajabhasa
C. Awadhi D. Khariboli

118. Ramananda preached worship of
A. Vishnu B. Sita & Ram
C. Shiva D. Radha & Krishna

ANSWERS

1	2	3	4	5	6	7	8	9	10
A	B	A	D	B	D	A	B	C	A
11	**12**	**13**	**14**	**15**	**16**	**17**	**18**	**19**	**20**
D	C	A	B	A	B	D	D	B	D
21	**22**	**23**	**24**	**25**	**26**	**27**	**28**	**29**	**30**
D	C	C	C	C	D	A	A	A	B
31	**32**	**33**	**34**	**35**	**36**	**37**	**38**	**39**	**40**
D	A	A	D	D	C	A	A	C	A
41	**42**	**43**	**44**	**45**	**46**	**47**	**48**	**49**	**50**
C	A	A	A	A	A	A	A	A	D
51	**52**	**53**	**54**	**55**	**56**	**57**	**58**	**59**	**60**
A	D	A	D	C	C	D	A	B	C
61	**62**	**63**	**64**	**65**	**66**	**67**	**68**	**69**	**70**
D	D	A	A	C	D	A	C	C	D
71	**72**	**73**	**74**	**75**	**76**	**77**	**78**	**79**	**80**
C	B	B	D	B	C	B	D	C	C
81	**82**	**83**	**84**	**85**	**86**	**87**	**88**	**89**	**90**
D	C	A	C	C	B	B	D	B	A
91	**92**	**93**	**94**	**95**	**96**	**97**	**98**	**99**	**100**
A	A	A	D	C	A	A	C	C	D
101	**102**	**103**	**104**	**105**	**106**	**107**	**108**	**109**	**110**
A	A	D	C	C	C	D	C	D	A
111	**112**	**113**	**114**	**115**	**116**	**117**	**118**		
B	A	C	B	A	B	C	B		

THE MUGHAL EMPIRE

1. Once Sher Shah exclaimed that he had lost the empire of Hindustan for a handful of bajra. What does this means.
   A. Once he got stranded in the desert of Rajasthan with getting food for 17 days and he would have been killed but for timely supply of bajra rotis by the Rajput kings, Maldev
   B. Sher Shah never gave such an exclamination.
   C. The troops of Jaila & Kumpa, two famous generals of Maldev, the Rajput king of Jodhpur (Marwar) cut their way to the very heart of Sher Shah's Camp and he would have been killed but for timely help.
   D. One of the Rajput kings served him with bajra rotis containing position and he would have been killed but for timely medical help.
2. What made Bairam Khan rebel against Akbar?
   A. He was the man of masterful personality.
   B. He was increased by the outrageous conduct of Pir Muhammad, his old servant now in Akbar's favour, who wanted to hustle him out the country.
   C. He was stung by the outrageous conduct of Akbar, who dismissed him & asked him to go to Mecca.
   D. He was tempted by the youth of Akbar and wanted the throne for himself.
3. During which period Bairam Khan worked as regent of Akbar?
   A. 1556 A.D. — 1558 A.D.
   B. 1556 A.D. — 1564 A.D.
   C. 1556 A.D. — 1560 A.D.
   D. 1556 A.D. — 1605 A.D.
4. Which of the following was not a result of the Rajput policy of Akbar?
   A. The Rajputs gave cooperation to the administrative machinery of Akbar
   B. The Rajputs gave help to the military achievements of Akbar
   C. It developed the Indo-Islamic culture
   D. The cooperation of the Rajputs changed the minds of the orthodox Muslim Ulemas and they became liberal.
5. Which chronological order of Babur's battles in Hindustan is correct?
   A. Panipat, Ghaghara, Chanderi, Khanua
   B. Panipat, Chanderi, Khanua, Ghaghara
   C. Panipat, Khanua, Chanderi, Ghaghara
   D. Panipat, Khanua, Ghaghara, Chanderi
6. The first Rajput Chief who entered into matrimonial alliance with Akbar was
   A. The ruler of Ranthambor
   B. The ruler of Marwar
   C. The ruler of Jaipur
   D. The ruler of Kalinjar
7. The only state in Northern India which Akbar failed to annex was—
   A. Kashmir B. Malwa
   C. Mewar D. Gondwana
8. The second battle of Panipat was fought in 1556 A.D. between—
   A. Akbar & Uday Singh
   B. Akbar & Rana Pratap
   C. Akbar & Hemmu
   D. Akbar & Raja Surjan Rai
9. Which of the following states of Southern India was completely annexed by Akbar
   A. Ahmedanagar B. Bijapur
   C. Khandesh D. Golkunda
10. The Mughals were—
    A. Turks B. Mongols
    C. Arabs D. Chaghtais
11. Which Battle did Babur fight against the Afghans?
    A. Panipat B. Ghaghara
    C. Khanua D. Chanderi
12. Why was Akbar interested in extending his sway to the south of Narmada and which are of the following factors did not

shape his Deccan policy in this regard?

A. His desire to bring the whole of India under his sway and to repeat the experiments of the Sultans of Delhi in the Deccan

B. For the expulsion of the Europeans, particularly the Portuguese, the annexation of the Deccan was essential.

C. The Deccan had become the centre of bitter religious controversies, which would have disturbed the religious peace he was trying to restore in the North.

D. As in the case of Ala-ud-din Khalji, the Wealth of the South was one of the biggest inducements to him

13. Humayun fought his decisive battle against Sher Shah at:

A. Chausa B. Chunargah
C. Bilgram D. Panipat

14. The task of initiating the disciple into the new faith (i.e. Din-i-Ilahi) was done on

A. Monday B. Tuesday
C. Saturday D. Sunday

15. Match the following.

(a) Abolition of Jaziya	1. A.D.1563
(b) Abolition of Pilgrims Tax	2. A.D. 1564
(c) Abolition of enslaving war prisoner	3. A.D. 1562
(d) Fall of Bairam Khan	4. A.D. 1560

Codes:

	(a)	*(b)*	*(c)*	*(d)*
A.	2	1	3	4
B.	4	1	3	2
C.	1	2	3	4
D.	3	4	2	1

16. The infallibility Decree assured to Akbar so far as any written instrument called have such effect, the atmost power that any man could claim to exercise, within the limits of Islam, which of the following historians express the above view about the infallibility decree?

A. Stanley Lane Poole
B. V.A. Smith
C. Edwards and Garret
D. S.R. Sharma

17. Arrange chronologically.

1. Construction of Ibadat Khana
2. Promulgation of Din-i-Ilahi
3. Insuring of Mazharuama

Codes:

A. 1, 2, 3 B. 3, 1, 2
C. 1, 3, 2 D. 2, 3, 1

18. The first step that Akbar took to make him free from the influence of the Ulemas (religious Jurists of Islam) was to read the Khutaba in his own name from the mosque at Fatehpur Sikri on the

A. 22nd October, 1573
B. 22nd June, 1579
C. 3rd March, 1574
D. 3rd March, 1580

19. It is generally held that Jahangir as a prince was in love with Mehr-un-nisa when she was a maiden and the emperor arranged the murder of her husband Sher Afghans to marry her. Dr. Beni Prasad attempts to exonerate Jahangir of this charge which of the following reason have not been advanced by Dr. Beni Prasad in support of this thesis?

A. No contemporary chronicler has made the charge against the emperor

B. Contemporary European writers who are otherwise critical of Jahangir do not impute the crime to Jahangir

C. if Jahangir as a prince took Sher Afgan as his rival in love, he would have got him killed when Sher Afghan was placed under Prince Salim

D. The chroniclers of Shah Jahan's reign also make no mention of the affair.

20. Which of the following historians has supported the view that Jahangir was a strange "compound of opposites"?

A. V.A. Smith
B. Ishwari Prasad
C. Beni Prasad
D. I.H. Quereshi

21. The reading of the Khutba by the emperor caused resentment among the Ulemas to silence them, Akar issued the "Infallibility Decree" (Mahzar) on the
A. 26th June, 1579
B. 2nd September, 1579
C. 3rd March, 1580
D. 10th December, 1580

22. Which of the following historian described "Din-i-Ilahi" as a movement of Akbar's folly, not of his wisdom"?
A. V.A. Smith
B. Stanley-Lave-Poole
C. Beni Prasad
D. Eduards and Garret

23. The reconciliation between Akbar and Prince Salim was achieved with the effects of
A. Salima Sultan Begam
B. Khan Azam
C. Man Singh
D. Hamida Banu Begam

24. Jahangir ascended the throne in the year.
A. 1600 A.D. B. 1605 A.D.
C. 1590 A.D. D. 1627 A.D.

25. Akbar promulgated Din-i-Ilahi in 1582. It was
A. Islamic doctrine
B. Code of conduct
C. Hindu law influenced by Islam
D. None of the above

26. Which of the following is correct?
A. Shah Jahan conquered Quandhar but lost to the Uzbegs at Balkh
B. Shah Jahan did not conquer Quandhar but defeated the Uzbegs at Balkh
C. Shah Jahan both conquered Quandhar and defeated the Uzbegs at Balkh
D. Shah Jahan failed both in conquering Quandhar and in fighting the Uzbegs at Balkh

27. Todarmal classified the land into from they are:
1. Polaj 2. Parauti
3. Krori 4. Chachar
5. Potadar 6. Banjar

Codes:
A. 1, 2, 4, 6 B. 1, 2, 3, 4
C. 1, 3, 5, 6 D. 2, 3, 4, 5

28. Match the following categories of land with the respective names assigned to them

(a) Polja	(1) Land which was cultivated almost every year.
(b) Paraufi	(2) Land which had been fol low for one or two year
(c) Chachar	(3) Fallow hand
(d) Banjar	(4) Land which had been fal low for three or four year

Codes:

	(a)	*(b)*	*(c)*	*(d)*
A.	1	2	4	3
B.	3	1	4	2
C.	1	3	4	2
D.	2	1	4	3

29. Who was the first Mughal ruler to introduce prohibition?
A. Babur B. Akbar
C. Humayun D. Jahangir

30. The "Chain of Justice" is associated with
A. Akbar B. Jahangir
C. Nur Jahan D. Shah Jahan

31. Name one of the following who acted as check on Subahdar?
A. Diwan B. Bakhshi
C. Faujdar D. Waqa-i-Navis

32. A faujdar was incharge of
A. A Pargana B. A Province
C. A Sarkar D. A Village

33. Who was the first to rebel against Jahangir after his accession to the throne?
A. Prince Khusrow B. Rana Raj Singh
C. Prince Shahryar D. Prince Khurram

34. The Mugal empire reached its territorial climax under
A. Akbar B. Jahangir
C. Shah Jahan D. Aurangzeb

35. Who among the following, was the revenue officer of a Sarkar?
A. Amal Guzar B. Amil
C. Bitikchi D. Khazandar

36. The Yusufzair rose in revolt against

Aurangzeb in the year—

A. 1658 A.D. B. 1667 A.D.

C. 1678 A.D. D. 1687 A.D.

37. Aurangzeb reimposed Jaziya in

A. 1675 A.D. B. 1679 A.D.

C. 1681 A.D. D. 1682 A.D.

38. Among the following who was an illiterate?

A. Babar B. Akbar

C. Jahangir D. Aurangzeb

39. What was the name of the Sikh Guru who was executed by Aurangzeb?

A. Guru Hargovind

B. Guru Har Rai

C. Guru Arjun Dev

D. Guru Teg Bahadur

40. During the Mughal rule, the chief of the city was

A. Shiqdar B. Munsif

C. Kotwal D. Muqaddam

41. Match the following government officials with their respective functions:

(a) Khan-i-Saman	1. Household department and karkhanas
(b) Sadra-Us-Sudur	2. Chief adviser to the emperor on ecclesiastical affairs and chief justice of the empire
(c) Wazir	3. Prime Minister and the intermediary between the ruler and the rest of the officials
(d) Vakil	4. Finance Minister

Codes:

	(a)	*(b)*	*(c)*	*(d)*
A.	1	2	3	4
B.	2	3	1	4
C.	4	3	2	1
D.	1	2	4	3

42. Which one of the following was the auditor general?

A. Mir Alish B. Mustafi

C. Mushriff D. Mir Barr

43. What was Nur Jahan's real name?

A. Arjumand Banu Begam

B. Mehr-un-nisa

C. Hamida Banu Begam

D. Ruqaiya Begam

44. Shalimar garden at Labore was raised by:

A. Akbar B. Shah Jahan

C. Jahangir D. Aurangzeb

45. The mansab was only—

A. An office B. A post

C. A rank D. Grade of pay

46. The range of the Mansabs as organised by Akbar was:

A. 100 to 5000 B. 10 to 5000

C. 10 to 7000 D. 10 to 10000

47. In what language was Padmavat written?

A. Hindi B. Urdu

C. Sanskrit D. Persian

48. Who wrote Padmavat?

A. Amir Khusrau B. Muhammad Jaisi

C. Narahari D. Tulsi Das

49. The most important industry during the Mughal period was

A. Silk B. Sculpture

C. Cotton D. Handicrafts

50. Who was the designer of Taj Mahal?

A. Ustad Ahmed Lahori

B. Ali Mardan

C. Abdus Samad

D. Sanwal Das

51. Pick out the wrong match

A. Khaljis — Malwa

B. Sharqis — Jaunpur

C. Hussain Shahi — Bengal

D. Iliyas Shahi — Gujarat

52. Pick out the correct match.

A. Tower of Victory — Chittor

B. Shiraz of India — Delhi

C. Gol Gumbaz — Bijapur

D. Vittalasvami Temple — Belur

53. Who is the founder of the cult of Satyapir?

A. Hussain Shah B. Sikandar II

C. Nasir-ud-din D. Haji Iliyas

54. Pick out the wrong match.

A. Bengal — Haji Iliyas

B. Jaunpur — Khwaja Jahan
C. Malwa — Dilawar Khan Ghuri
D. Gujarat — Tatar Khan

55. One of the following may not be regarded as the cause of External invasions of Gujarat. Identify.
A. fertility
B. wealth due to active commerce
C. natural resources
D. strategic importance

56. Pick out the wrong match.
A. Nusrat Shah — Qadam Rasul
B. Raya Ganesh — Danujamardana Deva
C. Ala-ud-din Hussain Shah — Ikadala
D. Indil Khan — Bengali version of the Mahabharata

57. Which is not a correct pair
A. Nicolo Conti — Deva Raya I
B. Abdur Razzaq — Deva Raya II
C. Barbosa — Krishnadeva Raya
D. Idn Datula — Ghiyasuddin Tughluq

58. Whom do you regard the ablest of the Muslim ruler of Malwa?
A. Hushang Shah B. Mahmud I
C. Mahmud II D. Nasiruddin

59. Name the ruler who assisted Mahmud II to oust Medini Raj
A. Rana Sanga B. Ratan Singh
C. Muzaffar Shah D. Chand Khan

60. Who built the Bara Masjid
A. Nusrat Shah
B. Hussain Shah
C. Jalal-ud-din Muhammad
D. Barbak Shah

61. Which among the following was completed during the reign of Sher Shah?
A. Padmavat B. Tughlaq-nama
C. Padshah-nama D. Razm-nama

62. The Jama Masjid at Delhi was constructed by
A. Akbar B. Jahangir
C. Aurangzeb D. Shah Jahan

63. Match the following.
(a) Battle of Bahadurpur — 1. Fought between Dara and Shuja
(b) Battle of Dharmat — 2. Fought between Dara and Aurangzeb
(c) Battle of Samugarh — 3. Fought between Dara and Combined armies of Aurangzeb and Murad

Codes:

	(a)	*(b)*	*(c)*
A.	1	3	2
B.	2	3	1
C.	1	2	3
D.	3	1	2

64. The Shalimar garden at Srinagar was raised by
A. Akbar B. Shah Jahan
C. Aurangzeb D. Jahangir

65. Pick out the wrong match
A. Jama — Assessed revenue
B. Mal — State's share of the actual crop
C. Desturu' lamal — Schedule of Cash revenue rates
D. Zabti — Simple sharing of the harvested grain?

66. Which kind of Revenue system prevailed in Bengal?
A. Muqtai B. Zabti
C. Dausala D. Batai

67. Pick out the wrong match
A. Batai — Sharing of harvested grain
B. Kaukut — Fixing land revenue on the basis of average produce and average prices.
C. Zabti — Assessment based on measurement
D. Muqtai — Fixed demand

68. Pick out the correct match
A. Ramdas — Paintings
B. Abdul Samad — Calligraphy

C. Maulana Beqir — Musician
D. Nitam-ud-din — Historian

69. One of the following was not translated into persian during the reign of Akbar. Identify.
A. Quran,
B. The Bible
C. The Mahabharata
D. The Rig Veda

70. Many movements were organised against Aurangzeb, but the causes were different. Identify the wrong match.
A. Rajputs — Successions
B. Marathas — Local independence
C. Jats — Agrarian background
D. Sikhs — Economic factor

71. The leader of various movements against Aurangzeb are given below. Pick out the wrong match.
A. Gokla — Jats
B. Churaman — Satnámis
C. Akmalkhan — Afridis
D. Govind Singh — Sikhs

72. One of the following Mughal emperors did not dream of the conquest of central Asia. Identify.
A. Babur B. Shah Jahan
C. Aurangzeb D. Akbar

73. Who introduced tobacco cultivation in India?
A. Arabs B. Persians
C. The Portuguese D. The Dutch

74. Who built the I'timad-ud-daulah's tomb?
A. Akbar B. Mumtaz Mahal
C. Nur Jahan D. Shah Jahan

75. At what cost was Taj Mahal built?
A. fifty lacs of rupees
B. one hundred lacs of rupees
C. seventy-five lacs of rupees
D. forty lacs of rupees

76. Which among the following was opened by Akbar by keys of gold?
A. Ahmadnagar B. Chittor
C. Surat D. Asirgarh

77. What was the last conquest of Akbar?
A. Ahmadnagar B. Berar
C. Orissa D. Khandesh

78. What was the religion of Tansen?
A. Jainism B. Vaishnavism
C. Islam D. Saivism

79. Pick out the wrong match.
A. Tuka Ram — Marathi
B. Mira Bai — Hindi
C. Madhusudana — Telgu
D. Paranjoti — Tamil

80. The names of the wives of the Mughal rulers are given below, Pick out the wrong match.
A. Akbar — Jodha Bai
B. Jahangir — Mehr-un-nisa
C. Shah Jahan — Arjumand Banu Begam
D. Humayun — Asmat Begam

81. Pick out the correct match?
A. Bajar — Land that was left fallow for a year or two
B. Polaj — Land that was continuously cultivated
C. Banjar — Land that was left fallow for three years
D. Parauti — Land that was left fallow for five years and more

82. The new capital of Akbar was
A. Lahore B. Delhi
C. Fatehpur Sikri D. Asirgarh

83. Who among the following took the title of Alamgir?
A. Akbar B. Jahangir
C. Shah Jahan D. Aurangzeb

84. Humayun recaptured Qandhar & Kabul in:
A. 1540 A.D. B. 1542 A.D.
C. 1543 A.D. D. 1555 A.D.

85. When was Humayun able to recover Delhi—
A. 1545 A.D. B. 1546 A.D.
C. 1550 A.D. D. 1555 A.D.

86. The fortress belonging to the Mores was
A. Singarh B. Raigarh
C. Satora D. Javli

87. The headquarters of Shivaji's fleet was at:
A. Daman B. Kolaba

C. Kolhapur D. Cochin

88. Who succeeded Sher Shah after his death?
A. Humayun
B. Islam Shah
C. Abbas
D. None of the above

89. Who was the founder of Pondicherry?
A. Duplex B. Martin
C. Dumas D. Law

90. The first English "factory" in India was set up in
A. Cambay B. Bombay
C. Surat D. Cochin

91. Parganas were under the charge of
A. Shiqdar B. Munsif
C. Amil D. None of these

92. Who built Purana Qila?
A. Akbar B. Humayun
C. Sher Shah D. Babur

93. Vasco-da-Gama reached Calicut in
A. 1453 A.D. B. 1458 A.D.
C. 1498 A.D. D. 1508 A.D.

94. When Vasco-da-Gama come to India, he was helped by
A. the ruler of Cochin
B. the Zamorin of Kozhikode
C. the king of Vijayanagar
D. the Sultan of Bijapur

95. Who invited Babur to invade India?
A. Ibrahim Lodi
B. Daulat Khan
C. Rana Sanga
D. None of the above

96. When was the first battle of Panipat fought?
A. Ist Feb 1526 B. 3rd March 1527
C. Ist May 1526 D. 21st April 1526

97. The Waggouers of the sea were the
A. English B. French
C. Portuguese D. Dutch

98. Who was defeated and killed in the first battle of Panipat?
A. Sikandar Lodi B. Ibrahim Lodi
C. Rana Sanga D. Rana Kumbha

99. When did Babur die?
A. 1529 B. 1530
C. 1531 D. 1540

100. Shahu was in the imperial palace of the Mughals for
A. 17 years B. 19 years
C. 21 years D. 7 years

101. The Headquarters of the Sidis were at:
A. Bassein B. Goa
C. Salsette D. Janjira

102. When did Humayun die?
A. 1550 A.D. B. 1556 A.D.
C. 1557 A.D. D. 1560 A.D.

103. When was Akbar born?
A. 1540 A.D. B. 1541 A.D.
C. 1542 A.D. D. 1543 A.D.

104. The adventurous European Soldier employed by Mahadaji Sindhia was
A. Count de Lally B. Perron
C. Benoit-de-Boigue D. Francis-Marrtin

105. Babur was descended on his father's side from
A. Timur B. Chingiz Khan
C. Lodis D. Afghans

106. Who was Akbars mother?
A. Hamida Banu
B. Maham Anga
C. Jodha Bai
D. None of the above

107. Ahalya Bai was the ruler of
A. Gwalior B. Indore
C. Baroda D. Nagpur

108. When did second battle of Panipat take place?
A. 1526 A.D. B. 1530 A.D.
C. 1556 A.D. D. 1561 A.D.

109. Babur in the beginning inherited the principality of
A. Kashmir
B. Lahore
C. Farghana
D. None of the above

110. When was the famous battle of Haldighati fought?
A. 1556 A.D. B. 1566 A.D.
C. 1576 A.D. D. 1586 A.D.

111. Contribution of Mughal empire to India has been
A. Unified ruler B. Secular Policy

C. Horticulture D. All the above

112. Which statements are correct?

(a) The Delhi Sultans tried to transform India into Dar-ul-Islam

(b) The overwhelming majority of the raiyyats of the Sultans of Delhi happened to be non-muslims

(c) The so-called millat constituted but a part of the Subjects of the Sultans of Delhi

(d) With the exceptions of Ala-ud-din Khilji and Mubarak Khilji, all other Sultans styled themselves as deputies of the Caliph.

Codes:

A. All the four B. only *a, b* and *c*

C. only *b, c* and *d* D. only *c* and *d*

113. What styled himself as the "Khalifa of age"?

A. Sher Shah B. Akbar

C. Ala-ud-din Khilji D. Mohamed bin Tughlaq

114. Noor Jehan was the wife of

A. Akbar B. Jahangir

C. Shah Jahan D. Aurangzeb

115. Who amongst the Mughal rulers was famous for his love for Justice?

A. Babur B. Humayun

C. Jahangir D. Aurangzeb

116. The Amalguzar was incharge of

A. Pargana B. Sarkar

C. Subbah D. Village

117. Bairam Khan was Akbar's—

A. Amalguzar B. Bakshi

C. Wazir D. Qazi

118. What is Jama?

A. Income B. Assessed income

C. Dams D. Jagirs

119. The Maratha Council of Minister consisted of

A. 4 members B. 6 members

C. 8 members D. 10 members

120. Who persuaded Shivaji to visit the Mughal Court?

A. Raj Singh B. Ram Singh

C. Jai Singh D. Jaswant Singh

121. Bairam Khan was regent of Akbar during

A. 1555 – 1556 A.D.

B. 1556 – 1558 A.D.

C. 1555 – 1558 A.D.

D. 1556 – 1560 A.D.

122. Mughal bureaucracy lived lavishly on

A. Large Jagirs B. Good Payscales

C. Kharkhanas D. Military Plunder

123. Which one of the following is not a cultural contribution of the Great Mughals?

A. calligraphy

B. rag dhrupad and rag darbari

C. kathak

D. decorative work

124. Which factor helped Ala-ud-din Khilji most in maintaining his state system?

a. Standing Army

b. South India riches

c. Market regulation

d. Cutting the nobility to size

Codes:

A. *a* and *b* B. *c* and *d*

C. *a, b* and *c* D. *a, b* and *d*

125. Which of the following was responsible for expounding Muslim law?

A. Qazi B. Mir Adil

C. Mufti D. None of these

126. Under the Mughal mansabdari the mansab of a person donated.

a Numerically expressed rank

b his position in official hierarchy

c his office as well as the functions of the Mughal officials

d. his salary and certain expectations

Codes:

A. only *a, b, d* B. only *a, b, c*

C. only *b, c, d* D. all the four

127. Which one of the following was not a cause of the fall of the Mughal Empire?

A. decline strength of their army

B. outdated weapons

C. lack of a powerful navy

D. mutual rivalry of their officers

128. The Maratha Government under the Peshawa was—

A. highly centralised

B. democratic in nature
C. highly despotic
D. a loose confederacy

129. What was the standard of living of Peasants under Mughals?
A. Very High B. High
C. Average D. Low

130. Match the battles with the participants

(a) Karnal	1. Mughal emperors & Muhammad Shah
(b) Panipat	2. The Nawab of carnatic and the three allies–the french, chanda Sahib and Muzaffar Jung
(c) Mailapur	3. Ahmad Shah Durrani and the Marathas
(d) Amber	4. The Nawab of Carnatic and the French
(e) Bedara	5. The English and the Dutch

Codes:

	(a)	*(b)*	*(c)*	*(d)*	*(e)*
A.	1	3	4	2	5
B.	3	1	2	5	4
C.	2	3	1	5	4
D.	4	3	1	2	5

131. The industry affected most adversely the Indian economy was
A. Silk cloth B. cotton cloth
C. Glass ware D. Ivory

132. In the field of painting and architecture the Mughal cultural torch was taken by
A. Oudh B. Hyderabad
C. Bengal D. Rajasthan

133. What do the names of Mir Sayyied Ali and Khawaja Abdur Samad stand for in Mughal history?
A. Persian literature
B. Calligraphy
C. Architecture
D. Painting

134. To which Mughal party or group did the king makers, Sayyed brothers belong?
A. Irani Party B. Hindustani Party
C. Turki Party D. Turani Party

135. What was the main cause for the decline of the Mughal Empire?
A. the fratricide
B. rebellions governors
C. factionalists in amongst nobility
D. The quality of the Mughal emperor after Aurangzeb.

136. Who were the ladies to fight heroically against the Mughals?
(a) Jodha Bai
(b) Chand Bibi
(c) Tara Bai
(d) Mira Bai
Codes:
A. only *a*, *b* B. only *b*, *c*
C. only *c*, *d* D. *b*, *c* and *d*

137. The Mughal policy of the conquest and annexation of the Deccan states to the Mughal empire was started by
A. Akbar B. Jahangir
C. Shah Jahan D. Aurangzeb

138. What was the singular weakness of the Mughal nobility?
A. over-ambitiousness
B. love of luxury
C. parasitical tendency
D. effeminate

139. The decline of the Mughal empire began with;
A. Jahangir B. Akbar
C. Shah Jahan D. Aurangzeb

140. From which time onwards finances proved to be the bane of the Mughal Empire?
A. Babur B. Humayun
C. Akbar D. Shah Jahan

141. The stress that was laid on the building of Mausoleums by the Mughals goes back to the
A. Afghans B. Persians
C. Turks D. Arabs

142. Which of the following towns was never conquered by a Mughal emperor as an

Indian ruler?
A. Samarqand B. Qandhar
C. Balkh D. Badakhshah

143. What was the architectural feature that was new in the building of Shah Jahan?
A. Makrana Marble
B. Bulbansdome
C. Large structures
D. tapering pillars

144. Where is the poem written by Abdul Fazl inscribed?
A. Fatehpur Sikri
B. on a temple in Kashmir
C. on the tomb of Salim chishti
D. on the Ibadat-Khana

145. Who among the Mughal Emperors achieved the throne with the help of the two Sayyed Brothers, Abdullah Khan and Hussain Ali Khan?
(a) Bahadur Shah I
(b) Jahandar Shah
(c) Farrukhsiyar
(d) Rafi-ud-Du rajat
(e) Rafi-ud-Daulat
(f) Mohammad Shah
Codes:
A. all the above
B. only *a*, *b*, *c* and *d*
C. only *b*, *c*, *d* and *e*
D. only *c*, *d*, *e* and *f*

146. Match the term with their meaning.

(a) Jama-i-dami	1. accessed income from a Jagir
(b) Hasil	2. actual income from a Jagir
(c) Ijara	3. the system of giving contract for revenue collection for an agreed amount of money.
(d) Mustajir	4. Revenue-farmer

Codes:

	(a)	*(b)*	*(c)*	*(d)*
A.	1	2	4	3
B.	2	1	3	4
C.	2	1	4	3
D.	1	2	3	4

147. Which factors contributed to the stability of the Mughal Empire?
(a) The personalities of the emperor
(b) The rajput alliance or understanding
(c) The policy of toleration
(d) The balance of power
Codes:
A. only *a*, *b*
B. only *a*, *b*, *c*
C. all four
D. only *b*, *c* and *d*

148. Pair names of the Mughal emperors with the location of their mausoleums

(a) Babur	1. Agra
(b) Humayun	2. Lahore
(c) Akbar	3. Sikandra
(d) Jahangir	4. Delhi
(e) Shah Jahan	5. Kabul

Codes:

	(a)	*(b)*	*(c)*	*(d)*	*(e)*
A.	1	2	3	4	5
B.	2	5	1	3	4
C.	2	4	3	5	1
D.	5	4	3	2	1

149. Which one is considered as the beginning of Mughal architecture in India?
A. Kabuli Bagh Mosque
B. Humayun's tomb
C. Diwan-i-Am
D. Diwan-i-Khas

150. Aurangzeb was a scholar of—
A. Poetry
B. Muslim theology and Jurisprudence
C. Persian Literature
D. Persian Warfare

151. Match the Mughal officers with their functions:

(a) Mir Saman	1. kept accounts of the department of royal kharkhanas
(b) Diwan-i-Bayutat	2. incharge of Cash Salaries
(c) Diwan-i-Tan	3. head accountant
(d) Mushrif	4. incharge of royal kharkhans and stores
(e) Zawabit	5. Secular decrees

Codes:

	(a)	(b)	(c)	(d)	(e)
A.	1	2	3	4	5
B.	4	1	2	3	5
C.	4	3	2	1	5
D.	4	2	1	3	5

152. Which book is regarded as the greatest digest of Muslim law made in India?
A. Masir-i-Alamgiri
B. Muntakhab-ul-Lubab
C. Khulasat-ut-Tawarik
D. Fatwa-i-Alamgiri

153. Which was farmed out in the revenue system of the Mughals?
A. Land revenue only
B. Land revenue and customs
C. Transit tolls and mint
D. Mint and land revenue

154. Todarmal classified the land into four they are—
(a) Paloj *(b)* Parauti
(c) Krori *(d)* Chachar
(e) Potdar *(f)* Banjar
Codes:
A. *(a), (b), (d), (f)* B. *(a), (b), (c), (d)*
C. *(a), (c), (d), (f)* D. *(b), (c), (d), (f)*

155. What was the most acceptable law of royal succession under the Mughals?
A. Birth and Royal nomination
B. Birth and system of Primogeniture
C. Royal nomination and force
D. Birth and force

156. Mughals issued Gold coins known as
A. Rupaya B. Ashrafi
C. Dinar D. Riyal

157. The term "Karori" becomes synonymous under the Mughal with
A. khalsa land
B. a revenue collector
C. ijaradar
D. revenue-free lands

158. A Deshmukh during the Mughal period was
A. a chief in the southern parts of India
B. equivalent to the North India Chaudhari
C. equivalent to a Zamindar in South India
D. equivalent to the Talukdar in North India

159. Who was conferred with the honourable title of "Khan" by Jahangir?
A. Drake B. Sir Thomas Roe
C. Hawking D. Terry

160. Akbar divided his empire into well defined provinces. In 1602 A.D. they numbered
A. 12 B. 15
C. 10 D. 14

161. The land through out the who empire is considered the property of the sovereign", who wrote this?
A. Thamas Roe B. Hawkins
C. Drake D. Bernier

162. The last movement in the series of octagonal tombs is
A. Humayun's tomb at Delhi
B. The tomb of Usa Khan, Delhi
C. The tomb of Adham Khan, Delhi
D. The tomb of Muhammad Ghaus, Gwalior

163. The land which was never allowed to lie fallow in the Mughal period was called—
A. Poloj B. Parauti
C. Chachar D. Banjar

164. In spirit and in structure, Humayun's tomb stands as an example of the synthesis of two of the great building traditions of Asia.
A. The Hindu and the Muslim
B. The Arab and the Indian
C. The Persian and the Indian
D. The Central Asian and the Rajput

165. The most important industry during the Mughal period was
A. Silk B. Sculpture
C. Cotton D. Handicrafts

166. Who was the author of "Ganga Lahri"?
A. Tulsidas
B. Surdas
C. Panditraj Jaganath
D. Mira Bai

167. Which of the following Mughal Emperor is credited with the composition of many

Hindi songs?
A. Humayun B. Babur
C. Akbar D. Jahangir

168. Which one of the following painters at Jahangir's court was not a foreigner?
A. Ustad Mansur
B. Abdul Hasan
C. Aga Reza
D. Muhammad Nadir

169. Which one of the following system of land revenue amendment was not followed under Akbar?
A. Dahsala System B. Zabti System
C. Batai System D. Patta System

170. Which was the most crucial stage in the evolution of Akbar's religions?
A. Mother's and teacher's influences
B. Influences of Sheikh Mubarak
C. his mixing with people in cognito
D. failure of discussion in Ibadat Khana

171. Match the works with their authors.
(a) Tarikh-i-Rashidi 1. Mirza Haider Dughlat
(b) Tuzuk-i-Babari 2. Babur
(c) Tarikh-i-Waqiat 3. Jauhar Aftabchi
(d) Humayun Namah 4. Gulbadan Began

Codes:

	(a)	(b)	(c)	(d)
A.	1	2	3	4
B.	1	3	4	2
C.	2	3	1	4
D.	3	2	1	4

172. The french traveller Francois Bernier served as physician to
A. Akbar B. Jahangir
C. Shahjahan D. Aurangzeb

173. Who got the Gita translated into Persian?
A. Shahjahan B. Akbar
C. Dara D. Murad

174. Which of the following was not of the Chief components of the school of painting imported by the Mughal into India?
A. Chinese B. Persian
C. Indian D. Bectrian

175. The Structures of Shahjahan are superior to those of Akbar in
A. Originally
B. Grandeur
C. Lavis in display
D. Blending of Persian and Indian styles

176. The battle of Haldi Ghati was fought between
A. Akbar and Rana Udai Singh
B. Akbar and Bharmal
C. Sher Shah and Humayun
D. The Mughal General Man Singh and Rana Pratap Singh

177. The Nishat and Shalimar gardens near Srinagar were laid out by
A. Babur B. Akbar
C. Jahangir D. None of these

178. Match the following:
(a) The fort at Attock 1. Akbar
(b) Shahjahanabad 2. Shahjahan
(c) The Jama Masjid at Sambhal 3. Sher Shah Suri
(d) The Purana Quila at Delhi 4. Babur

Codes:

	(a)	(b)	(c)	(d)
A.	1	2	4	3
B.	2	1	3	4
C.	1	3	4	2
D.	1	2	3	4

179. Match the following:
(a) Dastur-ul-amal 1. Document sharing the different land revenue system.
(b) Arsatha 2. Document sharing income and expenditure of a particular pargana
3. Document sharing all the revenue rates.

Codes:

	(a)	(b)
A.	2	3
B.	1	2
C.	3	2
D.	3	1

180. Babur's Memories were translated from Turki to Persian during Akbar's reign by
A. Abdur Rahim khan-i-khana
B. Abul Fazal
C. Mir-a-Aziz koka
D. None of these

181. The leading poet of Akbar's age was
A. Murad B. Faizi
C. Dilkash Khan D. None of these

182. Jodha Bai's palace is in
A. Delhi B. Fatehpur Sikri
C. Agra D. None of these

183. Dinpanah was built by
A. Sher Shah B. Babur
C. Humayun D. Akbar

184. Medieval Hindi was called
A. Hindavi B. Avaadhi
C. Brij D. None of these

185. Sculpture was encouraged by
A. Babur B. Humayun
C. Akbar D. None of these

186. During Akbar's reign what were Akharas?
A. Wrestling bouts
B. Musical contests
C. Literary competitions
D. Schools for painters

187. The main theme of Rajasthani painting is
A. The love of Radha and Krishna
B. The Ramayana
C. Nature
D. None of these

188. Villages with no Zamindari rights were called
A. Raiyati B. Milkiyat
C. Peshkash D. Bisvi

189. The author of "Storio Dor Mogor" is
A. Manucci B. Berneir
C. Monserrate D. Travernier

190. The main theme of Mughal painting was
A. Religious
B. Court life and nature
C. Both (a) and (b)
D. None of these

191. The art of Mosque-building reached its climax under
A. Akbar B. Jahangir
C. Shahjahan D. Aurangzeb

192. The crop rate (Rai) method was introduced by:
A. Sher Shah Suri B. Shahjahan
C. Akbar D. None of these

193. The master of Portrait painting was
A. Mansur B. Saunad Beg
C. Mir Hussain D. Murad

194. The subject matter of Hamta Nama is
A. Architecture B. Painting
C. Music D. Philosophy

195. The credit founding the Mughal School of painting goes to:
A. Humayun B. Akbar
C. Jahangir D. Aurangzeb

196. Of the building built during the time of Shah Jahan, which one had the peacock throne?
A. Rang Mahal B. Diwan-i-khas
C. Diwan-i-Am D. Jama Masjid

197. The City of Fatehpur Sikri was the new capital of
A. Akbar B. Jahangir
C. Shahjahan D. Aurangzeb

198. The Mughal ruler proficient in playing the Veena was
A. Akbar B. Jahangir
C. Shahjahan D. Aurangzeb

199. What was Dam?
A. A cash levy of one copper coin
B. Total revenue in terms of cash
C. An agricultural cess
D. None of these

200. Jagirs were
A. Royal lands
B. Assignments of revenue
C. Revenue paying villages
D. None of these

201. Land not assigned in Jagirs was called
A. Kharaj B. Mal
C. Khalisa D. Talab

202. During the later Mughal period the Sayyed brothers played a vital role in the appointment of at least?
A. two rulers B. three rulers

C. four rulers D. five rulers

203. Bahadur Shah tried to conciliate the rebellious sikhs by making peace with a Sikh leader and giving him a high mansab. Identify him:
A. Fateh Singh
B. Kapur Singh
C. Banda Bahadur
D. Guru Govind Singh

204. Ahmad Shah Abdali defeated the Marathas in the third Battle of Panipat in 1761. This happened in the reign of:
A. Alamgir II B. Muhammad Shah
C. Shah Alam II D. Jahandar Shah

205. Name the person Ahmed Shah Abdali proclaimed emperor of India before leaving India after the third battle of Panipat?
A. Alamgir II B. Shah Jahan III
C. Shah Alam II D. Akbar II

206. Who among the following sons of Aurangzeb, won the war of succession after his death?
A. Prince Muazzam
B. Prince Kambaksh
C. Prince Azam
D. Akbar II

207. Identify one of the following which was not the outcome of Nadir Shah's invasion?
A. It caused an irreparable loss to the prestige of the empire
B. It exposed the hidden weakness of the empire to the Maratha sardars and the foreign trading companies
C. It ruined imperial finances and adversely affected the economic-life of the country.
D. It destroyed all the initiative of the impoverished most of whom retired from active court life.

208. The most important consequence of the decline of the Mughal empire was:
A. Emergence of the British challenge
B. Invasions of Nadir Shah and Ahmad Shah Abdali
C. Rise of the Maratha Power in India
D. Growth of independent autonomous states.

209. "His departure was symbolic of the flight of loyalty and virtue from the empire". This statement is about:
A. Nizam-ul-Mulk
B. Muhammad Amir Khan
C. Adulla Beg
D. Zulfiquar Khan

210. Rafi-ud-darajat and Rafi-ud-dualah whom the king makers raised to the throne in quick succession were the sons of
A. Jahandar Shah B. Azim-us-Shan
C. Rafi-us-Shan D. Jahan Shah

211. Nadir Shah looted Delhi in 1739 A.D. Who was the Mughal ruler at the time?
A. Jahandar Shah B. Muhammad Shah
C. Alamgir II D. Faruk Siyar

212. Though Ahmad Shah Abdali or Durrani was one of Nadir Shah's ablest generals, he was defeated once and put to flight during one of his invasions of India. Which one was it?
A. First B. Third
C. Fifty D. Seventh

213. Identify the person, Ahmad Shah Abdali appointed the chief administrator and regent in India?
A. Ahmad Khan Bangash
B. Munir-ud-Bangash
C. Najb-ud-dulah
D. Qamar-ud-din Khan

214. Which of the following later Mughal rulers ruled for the longest period?
A. Muhammad Shah
B. Alamgir II
C. Shah Alam II
D. Bahadur Shah II

215. Nizam-ul-mulk played a leading role in the overthrow of the Sayyid brothers. He was suitably rewarded with the viceroyality of Deccan by:
A. Muhammad Shah
B. Ahmad Shah
C. Alamgir II
D. Shah Alam II

216. Assertion (A): The first machine-based industries that were started in India in the middle of the 19th Century were Iron and steel works.

Reason (R): The 19th century India also witnessed the growth of several plantation industries such as indigo, tea and coffee.

Codes:

A. A and R are true and R is the correct explanation of A.
B. A and R are true but R is not the correct explanation of A.
C. A is true but R is false.
D. A is false but R is true.

217. Assertion (A): Under the late Mughals, the practice of 'Ijara' came into existence for the first time.

Reason (R): The ijaradars caused a great amount of damage to agriculture in general and to agriculturists in particular.

Codes:

A. A and R are true and R is the correct explanation of A.
B. A and R are true but R is not the correct explanation of A.
C. A is true but R is false.
D. A is false but R is true.

218. Assertion (A): Dalip Singh, the last ruler of independent Punjab, was despossessed and pensioned off by Lord Dalhousie.

Reason (R): Dalip Singh was later implicated in a conspiracy case and executed by the British.

Codes:

A. A and R are true and R is the correct explanation of A.
B. A and R are true but R is not the correct explanation of A.
C. A is true but R is false.
D. A is false but R is true.

219. Assertion (A): From 1748, onwards the Nawabs of Oudh came to be called the "Nawab Wazirs".

Reason (R): Since 1748, the Nawabs of Awadh held both in the Nawabship of Awadh and the Wazirship of Mughal empire simultaneously.

Codes:

A. A and R are true and R is the correct explanation of A.
B. A and R are true but R is not the correct explanation of A.
C. A is true but R is false.
D. A is false but R is true.

220. Assertion (A): Tipu Sultan was one of the few Indian rulers to have realised the importance of modern navy.

Reason (R): He established two dockyards in 1796, and models of the ships were supplied by himself.

Codes:

A. A and R are true and R is the correct explanation of A.
B. A and R are true but R is not the correct explanation of A.
C. A is true but R is false.
D. A is false but R is true.

ANSWERS

1	2	3	4	5	6	7	8	9	10
C	B	C	D	C	C	C	C	C	D
11	**12**	**13**	**14**	**15**	**16**	**17**	**18**	**19**	**20**
B	D	C	D	A	B	C	C	C	A
21	**22**	**23**	**24**	**25**	**26**	**27**	**28**	**29**	**30**
B	A	A	D	B	C	A	A	D	B
31	**32**	**33**	**34**	**35**	**36**	**37**	**38**	**39**	**40**
A	C	A	D	A	B	B	B	D	C

41	42	43	44	45	46	47	48	49	50
D	B	B	B	C	D	A	B	C	A
51	52	53	54	55	56	57	58	59	60
D	A	A	D	D	D	D	B	C	A
61	62	63	64	65	66	67	68	69	70
A	D	A	D	D	A	B	D	D	D
71	72	73	74	75	76	77	78	79	80
B	C	C	C	A	D	D	B	C	D
81	82	83	84	85	86	87	88	89	90
B	C	D	C	D	D	B	B	B	C
91	92	93	94	95	96	97	98	99	100
A	C	C	B	B	D	D	B	B	B
101	102	103	104	105	106	107	108	109	110
D	B	C	C	A	A	B	C	C	C
111	112	113	114	115	116	117	118	119	120
D	C	A	B	C	B	C	B	C	C
121	122	123	124	125	126	127	128	129	130
D	A	D	A	C	A	C	D	D	A
131	132	133	134	135	136	137	138	139	140
B	D	D	B	D	B	A	C	C	D
141	142	143	144	145	146	147	148	149	150
C	B	B	C	D	D	C	D	B	B
151	152	153	154	155	156	157	158	159	160
B	D	B	A	D	B	C	A	C	B
161	162	163	164	165	166	167	168	169	170
D	C	A	C	C	C	D	A	D	D
171	172	173	174	175	176	177	178	179	180
A	D	C	D	C	D	C	A	C	A
181	182	183	184	185	186	187	188	189	190
B	B	C	C	C	B	A	A	A	B
191	192	193	194	195	196	197	198	199	200
C	A	A	B	B	C	A	D	A	B
201	202	203	204	205	206	207	208	209	210
C	C	D	C	C	A	D	A	A	C
211	212	213	214	215	216	217	218	219	220
B	A	A	C	A	D	D	C	A	A

SECTION–C

MODERN INDIA

THE DECLINE OF THE MUGHAL EMPIRE

1. Match the following.

List I	List II
(a) First Anglo-Mysore War	1. Sir Eyre Coot
(b) Second Anglo-Mysore War	2. General Stuart
(c) Third Anglo-Mysore War	3. General Smith
(d) Fourth Anglo-Mysore War	4. Major General Medows

Codes:

	(a)	(b)	(c)	(d)
A.	3	1	4	2
B.	2	3	4	1
C.	3	2	1	4
D.	1	4	3	2

2. Match the following.

List I	List II
(a) Death of Haider	1. 1782
(b) Death of Tipu	2. 1784
(c) Treaty of Srirangapatnam	3. 1792
(d) Treaty of Mangalore	4. 1799

Codes:

	(a)	(b)	(c)	(d)
A.	2	3	1	4
B.	1	3	4	2
C.	2	4	3	1
D.	1	4	3	2

3. Who was the Governor General during Second Anglo-Mysore War?

A. Warren Hastings
B. Lord Cornwallis
C. Sir John Shore
D. Lord Wellesly

4. Which of the following statements about the First and the Second Anglo-Mysore War are incorrect?

1. The First Anglo-Mysore War began in 1746 and ended in 1750.
2. The Second Anglo-Mysore War began in 1780 and ended in 1784.
3. The first defensive treaty between the British and Mysore was concluded in 1784.
4. One of the causes for the outbreak of the second war was the British capture of Mahe, a French settlement within Haider's Jurisdiction.

Codes:

A. 1 and 2 B. 1 and 3
C. 2 and 3 D. 3 and 4

5. The treaty of Srirangapatnam signed by Tipu and Cornawallis, contained

1. Surrender of almost Tipu's half of the territories which were to be shared among the English the Nizam and the Marathas
2. Payment of a war indemnity of about Rs. 3 crores by Tipu
3. Stationing of a British resident at Srirangapatnam
4. Sending two of his sons by Tipu as hostages to the British Camp.

Codes:

A. 1 and 2 B. 3 and 1
C. 1, 2 and 4 D. 1, 3 and 4

6. From which of the following countries did Tipu seek help to expel the British from India?

1. France 2. Arabia
3. Afghanism 4. Russia

Codes:

A. 1, 2 and 4 B. 2, 3 and 5
C. 1, 2, 3 and 4 D. 1, 2, 3 and 5

7. Which of the following statements are correct about the Fourth Anglo-Mysore War?

1. The immediate cause of this war was the landing of a small French force at Mangalore in April 1798.
2. Lord Wellesly was the Governor-General during the war.
3. Tipu Sultan was successively defeated at Seda Seer and Malvelley by the British

4. Tipu was captured and executed by the British after this war.
5. Arthur Wellesly, the future duke of Wellington and the person who later defeated Napolean in the water battle of waterloo, participated in this war.

Codes:

A. 1, 2, 3 and 4 B. 2, 3, 4 and 5
C. 1, 2, 3 and 5 D. 1, 3, 4 and 5

8. Which of the following statements about the state of Mysore are not true?

1. After the Fourth Anglo-Mysore War, a major part of Mysore was annexed by the British.
2. A small portion of it was destored to a minor son of Tipu Sultan.
3. A subsidiary treaty was signed by the British with the new ruler of Mysore
4. In 1849, Lord Dallousie took over the administration of Mysore because of misgovernment by its ruler
5. In 1881 Lord Ripon restored it to its ruler.

Codes:

A. 1 and 2 B. 2 and 4
C. 2 and 3 D. 3 and 5

9. Which of the following statement about Ranjit Singh are true?

1. Before his rise into prominence, Punjab was ruled by 12 Sikh 'Misls'.
2. He was born to the chief of Kanhiya Misl.
3. He succeeded to the chieftainship of his 'Misl' as a minor with his mother as the Regant.
4. He assumed full charge.

Codes:

A. 1 and 2 B. 3 and 4
C. 1, 3 and 4 D. 2, 3 and 4

10. Arrange the following conquests of Ranjit Singh in the chronological order

1. Ludhiana 2. Amritsar
2. Kangra 4. Lahore

Codes:

A. 4, 2, 1 and 3 B. 2, 1, 3 and 4
C. 2, 4, 3 and 1 D. 1, 3, 4 and 2

11. Arrange the following events in the reign of Ranjit Singh in the chronological sequence.

1. Aquisition of the Kohinoor by Ranjit Singh from Shah Suja of Afghanistan.
2. Assumption of the title of Maharaja of Lahore by Ranjit Singh
3. Meeting between Ranjit Singh and Bentinck
4. Mission of Metcalf to Ranjit Singh
5. Occupation of Kashmir by Ranjit Singh

Codes:

A. 3, 1, 4, 5 and 2 B. 1, 3, 4, 2 and 5
C. 4, 2, 1, 5 and 3 D. 2, 5, 4 and 3

12. Ranjit Singh did

1. organise his army on western lines with the help of Europeans
2. cooperate with Zaman Shah of Afghanistan when the latter invaded Punjab in 1799
3. recruit only Sikhs as soldiers
4. establish modern foundaries to manufacture Canon

Codes:

A. 1, 2 and 3 B. 1, 2 and 4
C. 2 and 4 D. 3, 4

13. Which of the following were the signatories to the Tripartiate treaty?

1. Zaman Shah
2. Ranjit Singh
3. William Bentinck
4. Shah Siya
5. Lord Auckland

14. Arrange the following successors of Ranjit Singh in the chronological order

1. Sher Singh 2. Kharak Singh
3. Dalip Singh 4. Nao Nihal Singh

Codes:

A. 2, 4, 1 and 3 B. 2, 1, 4 and 3
C. 1, 3, 2 and 4 D. 1, 4, 3 and 2

15. Which is the correct chronological sequence of the following events

1. Occupation of Shikarpur by the British
2. Occupation of Ferozpur by the British
3. Succession of Dalip Singh as the ruler of Punjab
4. Appointment of British resident at Ludhiana

Codes:

A. 1, 3, 4 and 2 B. 4, 3, 1 and 2
C. 3, 4, 2 and 1 D. 2, 1, 4 and 3

16. Arrange the followng battles of the First Anglo-Sikh War in the chronological order

1. Buddewal 2. Aliwal
3. Ferozpur 4. Sobroan
5. Mudki

Codes:

A. 1, 3, 5, 4 and 2 B. 5, 3, 1, 2 and 4
C. 2, 4, 3, 5 and 1 D. 3, 2, 1, 4 and 5

17. The treaty of Lahore contained:

1. Ceding of the Jallendar Doab to the British and payment of a war indemnity of about 11/2 crore
2. appointment of a British resident at Lahore
3. derecognition of Dalip Singh as the ruler of Punjab
4. reduction of Sikh army to 20,000 infantry and 12,000 cavalary
5. permission to the ruler of Punjab to employ any European without the consent of the British.

Codes:

A. 1, 3 and 2 B. 1, 2 and 4
C. 2, 4 and 5 D. 3, 4 and 5

18. Which of the following were the cause for the second Anglo-Sikh War?

A. Desire of the Sikh army to avenge their humiliation in the First Anglo-Sikh War
B. Discontentment of the Sikh Sardars with the British control over Punjab
C. Mistreatment of Rani Jindan by the British
D. Revolt of the Governor of Multan leading to the outbreak of General rebellion by the Sikhs.

Codes:

A. 1, 2 and 4 B. 1, 3 and 4
C. 2, 3 and 4 D. All of them

19. Two English officers sent to Multan to help Sardar Khan Singh, the newly appointed Governor, in taking over its administration were murdered by the Sikhs in April 1848. Who were they?

1. VansAgnew
2. Herbert Edwards
3. Lt. Nicholson
4. Lt. Anderson
5. Richard Temple

Codes:

A. 1 and 3 B. 2 and 4
C. 1 and 4 D. 3 and 4

20. Who was the founder of the autonomous state of the carnatic?

A. Safdar Ali
B. Dost Ali
C. Sadatullah Khan
D. Anwaruddin

21. Which of the Lists are correctly matched?

List I		*List II*
1. Lal Singh	—	The Prime Minister of Punjab before and during the First Anglo-Sikh War
2. Tej Singh	—	The Commander-in-Chief of Punjab before and during the First war
3. Mulraj	—	The Governor of Multan who resigned and then revolted against the British in 1848
4. Sher Singh	—	The person who was sent by the British to supress the revolt at Multan but who himself joined the revolt.

Codes:

A. 1, 2 and 3 B. 2, 3 and 4
C. 1, 3 and 4 D. All of them

22. Arrange the following battles and events of the Second-Anglo Sikh War in the chronological order:

1. Battle of Gujarat
2. Battle of Ramnagar
3. Surrender of Sher Singh
4. Capture of Multan and Surrender of Mulraj
5. Batte of Chillianwala

Codes:
A. 3, 2, 1, 4 and 5
B. 1, 2, 3, 4 and 5
C. 4, 2, 1, 5 and 3
D. 2, 5, 4, 1 and 3

23. After the annexation of Punjab by the British, a Board of three commissioners was constituted in 1849 to administer Punjab. Who were those three Britishers?
1. Henry Lawrence
2. John Lawrence
3. Walter Gilbert
4. Charles G. Mensel
5. V. Richard Temple

Codes:
A. 1, 3 and 5 B. 1, 2 and 4
C. 2, 3 and 4 D. 2, 4 and 5

24. Which of the following statements about Bahadur Shah are true?
(*a*) He fought a war of succession with his brothers before he became the emperor.
(*b*) After becoming the emperor he assumed the title of Shah Alam-I.
(*c*) His reign lost between 1700 and 1712.
(*d*) His reign witnessed the outbreak of the Maratha Civil war between Shahu and Tara Bai.

Codes:
A. *a* and *b* B. *b*, *c* and *d*
C. *a*, *b* and *d* D. *c* and *d*

25. Bahadur Shah did
1. execute Govind Singh, tenth Guru of the Sikhs.
2. take Chatrasal, the Bundela chief into his service
3. release, Sahu, the son of Shambhaji
4. defeat and kill Churaman, the jat chief

Codes:
A. 1 and 2 B. 2 and 3
C. 3 and 4 D. 2 and 4

26. Arrange the following Mughal emperors in the chronological order.
1. Alamgir II 2. Akbar II
3. Shah Alam II 4. Bahadur Shah II

Codes:
A. 2, 4, 3 and 1 B. 1, 3, 4 and 2
C. 2, 3, 1 and 4 D. 1, 3, 2 and 4

27. Which of the following statement about the Sayyid brothers is correct?
1. They played a decisive role in the succession of Farruksiyar as the emperor
2. They are known in Indian history as king makers
3. Abdullah Khan, the elder of the two brothers, was made the Mir Bakshi by Farruk Siyar
4. They murdered Faruksiyar in 1719 and made two young princes emperors in quick succession.

Codes:
A. 1, 2, 4 and 5 B. 2, 3 and 4
C. 1, 2, 3 and 5 D. 2, 4 and 5

28. Arrange the following Mughal emperors in the correct chronological sequence.
1. Faruk Siyar 2. Jahandar Shah
3. Ahmed Shah 4. Shah Alam I
5. Muhammad Shah

Codes:
A. 4, 2, 1, 5 and 3 B. 2, 1, 4, 3 and 5
C. 1, 4, 3, 2 and 5 D. 5, 4, 1, 3 and 2

29. Hyder Ali did
1. assumed all power by over throwing Nanjaraja
2. conquer and annex several territories such as Coorg, Malabar, Bellary, Gooty etc.
3. Fight the First and Second Anglo-Mysore War against the British
4. Get killed by the British in the second Anglo-Mysore War

Codes:
A. 2 and 3 B. 2 and 4
C. 1, 2 and 4 D. 2, 3 and 4

30. Which of the following statements are not true about Haider Ali?
1. He began his career as a soldier of the Mysore state, ruled by the rulers of Hindu wodeyar dynasty
2. During his term as the faujdar of Dindigul, he established a modern

dockyard

3. Due to his successful defence of Srirangapattanam against the Marathas in 1759 he was given the title of "Fateh Haider Bahadur" by Nanraja the king of Mysore.
4. He was not only a capable military leader and efficient administrator, but also a well read man.

Codes:

A. 2 and 3 B. 2 and 4
C. 1, 2 and 4 D. 2, 3 and 4

31. Who was the governor of Madras who concluded the treaty of Mangalore with Tipu Sultan?

A. Lord Harris
B. Lord Hamilton
C. Lord Macarteney
D. Lord Stephenson

32. Tipu Sultan did

1. attempt to introduce modern industries in Mysore by inviting foreign experts.
2. send embassies to France, Turkey, Iran and Pegu to develop foreign trade.
3. attempt to set-up a state trading company on the European lines
4. introduce a new system of coinage, new scales of weights and measures, and a new calendar
5. establish modern arsenal at Dindigual with French help

Codes:

A. 1, 3, 4 and 5 B. 1, 2, 3 and 4
C. 2, 3, 4 and 5 D. 1, 2, 4 and 5

33. Which of the following statements about Tipu Sultan is/are incorrect?

1. He tried to increase the state income by introducing the practice of revenue farming
2. He reduced the hereditary possessions of the poligars.
3. He checked the collection of illegal cesses from the peasants.
4. He refused to grant remmission of land revenue to the peasantry even in adverse situations.

Codes:

A. 1 only B. 1 and 2
C. 3 and 4 D. 1 and 4

34. Assertion (A): Colonel Clive caused the signature of Admiral Watson to be forged on a duplicate copy of the treaty signed with Mir Jafar and his supporters.

Reason (R): Clive wanted to cause trouble to Admiral Watson.

Codes:

A. A and R are true and R is the correct explanation of A.
B. A and R are true but R is not the correct explanation of A.
C. A is true but R is false.
D. A is false but R is true.

35. Assertion (A): The British won the battle of Plassey without any real fighting.

Reason (R): The Battle of Plassey gave the British a political foothold in Bengal.

Codes:

A. A and R are true and R is the correct explanation of A.
B. A and R are true but R is not the correct explanation of A.
C. A is true but R is false.
D. A is false but R is true.

36. Assertion (A): Mir Qasim abolished all duties on internal trade in 1763 after his unsuccessful attempts, to check the misuse of the 'Dastaks' by the Servants of the company.

Reason (R): He wanted to place the Indian and British traders on the same footing without either group getting an advantage.

Codes:

A. A and R are true and R is the correct explanation of A.
B. A and R are true but R is not the correct explanation of A.
C. A is true but R is false.
D. A is false but R is true.

37. Assertion (A): Within a short period of Mir Qasim accession as the Nawab, serious difference arose between him and the British.

Reason (R): The British got dissatisfied with the inefficient rule of Mir Qasim.

Codes:

A. A and R are true and R is the correct explanation of A.

B. A and R are true but R is not the correct explanation of A.

C. A is true but R is false.

D. A is false but R is true.

38. Assertion (A): From the military point of view, the battle of Buxar was much less important than the Battle of Plassey.

Reason (R): The British won the Battle of Buxar due to their superior military techniques.

Codes:

A. A and R are true and R is the correct explanation of A.

B. A and R are true but R is not the correct explanation of A.

C. A is false but R is true.

D. A is true but R is false.

39. Assertion (A): The British acquired an effective control over the administration of Bengal from February 1765.

Reason (R): In Feb, 1765 the British concluded a treaty with the new Nawab by which he aggreed to leave the entire administration in the hands of a British nominated Dy. Subedar, who could be removed only with their consent.

Codes:

A. A and R are true and R is the correct explanation of A.

B. A and R are true but R is not the correct explanation of A.

C. A is true but R is false.

D. A is false but R is true.

40. Assertion (A): Clive was sent to India in 1765 by the home authorities to serve his second term as the Governor of Calcutta and consolidate the gains made by the British after the Battle of Buxar.

Reason (R): He proved himself to be an honest and sincere officer during his first term as the Governor.

Codes:

A. A and R are true and R is the correct explanation of A.

B. A and R are true but R is not the correct explanation of A.

C. A is true but R is false.

D. A is false but R is true.

41. Assertion (A): The treaty of Allahabad was concluded by the British with the Mughal emperor Shah Alam-II.

Reason (R): The Mughal emperor granted the Diwani of Bengal, Bihar and Orissa to the East India Company in 1765.

Codes:

A. A and R are true and R is the correct explanation of A.

B. A and R are true but R is not the correct explanation of A.

C. A is true but R is false.

D. A is false but R is true.

42. Assertion (A): In the Dual system of government in Bengal, the British had all the power but no responsibility.

Reason (R): In this system of government, the Nawab had neither power nor responsibility.

Codes:

A. A and R are true and R is the correct explanation of A.

B. A and R are true but R is not the correct explanation of A.

C. A is true but R is false.

D. A is false but R is true.

43. Assertion (A): The Dual System of Government was an adorit measure of Clive to mark the real position of the company in Bengal.

Reason (R): The serious defects inherent in the Dual Government caused immense misery to the people of Bengal.

Codes:

A. A and R are true and R is the correct explanation of A.

B. A and R are true but R is not the

correct explanation of A.

C. A is true but R is false.

D. A is false but R is true.

44. Who was the first British Governor of Sind?

A. Sir Charles Napier

B. Sir John Keane

C. Sir Henry Lawrence

D. Robert Montgomery

45. Who was the governor-general of India when Sind was annexed?

A. Lord Auckland

B. Lord Ellenborough

C. Lord Dalhousie

D. Lord Hardinge-I

46. Who confessed "The defeat of many Bailles and Braith waites will not destroy them. I can ruin their resources by land, but, I cannot dry up the sea?

A. Haider Ali B. Tipu Sultan

C. Sher Singh D. Anwaruddin

47. Who was the Governor-General who remarked "what a man is this Lord Macarteny! I yet believe that, in spite of peace, he will effect the loss of the carnatic?

A. Warren Hastings

B. Lord Cornawallis

C. Lord Wellesly

D. Lord Dalhousie

48. Who declared "However contrary it may be to our past views and to our present views, annexation of Punjab is the most advantageous policy for us to pursue.

A. Lord Hugh Gough

B. Sir John Lawrence

C. Lord Ellenborough

D. Lord Dalhousie

49. To which place Murshid Ali Khan transfer his Capital from Dacca?

A. Kasim Bazar B. Monghyer

C. Murshidabad D. Gaur

50. Who captured and executed Siraj-ud-Daula after the battle of Plassey?

A. Miran, the son of Mir Jafar

B. Robert Clive, the new Governor of Fort William

C. Mir Jafar, the new Nawab of Bengal

D. Mir Kasim, the son in law of Mir Jafar

51. After the recovery of Calcutta in January 1757 by the English under Clive, Siraj-ud-Daula signed a treaty with the English conceding almost all their demands. What is the name of this treaty?

A. Treaty of Alinagar

B. Treaty of Calcutta

C. Treaty of Fulta

D. Treaty of Kasimbazar

52. All the information concerning the so-called, "Black Hole episode" is found in a single-sided account of it by an Englishman. What is the name of this Englishman?

A. William Hamilton

B. John Surman

C. Holwell

D. Stephenson

53. Murshid Quli Khan did not

1. Stop paying tribute and homage to the Mughal emperor, though he was practically independent.
2. transfer parts of Jagir lands into Khalsa lands.
3. introduce the system of revenue farming in place of direct revenue collection by Govt. officials.
4. discriminate between Hindus and Muslims in providing employment opportunities?

Codes:

A. 1 and 2 B. 2 and 4

C. 1 and 3 D. 1 and 4

54. Which of the following statements about Aliveradi Khan are true?

1. He paid Rs. 2 crore to the Mughal emperor and received a Farman in 1740, confirming his position as Governor of Bengal, Bihar and Orissa.
2. He refused to pay any tribute to the Mughal emperor when the later demanded it in 1748 through a farman.
3. He favoured and choose Shaukat Jang, one of his sons, as his successors.

4. He prohibited the French and the English from fortifying their factories at Calcutta and Chandranagar.

Codes:

A. 1, 2 and 3 B. 2 and 3
C. 1, 3 and 4 D. 1, 2 and 4

55. Which of the following statements are true about Siraj-ud-Daula?

1. He besieged and captured Calcutta in June, 1756.
2. He returned to Murshidabad, leaving Calcutta in charge of Mir Jafar.
3. He was not responsible for the "Black Hole Tragedy" in which 123 Englishman were supposed to have died.
4. He received whole hearted support from his nobles and soldiers in the Battle of Plassey against the British.

Codes:

A. 1 and 2 B. 2 and 3
C. 1 and 3 D. 3 and 4

56. Mir Qasim did

1. grant the British the Zamindari of Burdwan, Midnapore and Chittagong.
2. transfer his capital from Murshidabad to Dacca.
3. Stop the British from missing the Dastaks.
4. escape alive after his defeat in the Battle of Buxar.

Codes:

A. 1 and 2 B. 2
C. 1 D. 1 and 4

57. Which is the correct chronological sequence of the following events?

1. Reinstatement of Mir Jafar as the Nawab
2. Election of Clive as the Governor of Calcutta
3. Battle of Plassey
4. Grant of the Diwani of Bengal, Bihar and Orissa to the British by the Mughal emperor
5. Return of Clive to India for his second term as Governor of Calcutta

Codes:

A. 3, 2, 1, 5 and 4 B. 3, 1, 2, 4 and 5
C. 2, 3, 1, 5 and 4 D. 1, 3, 2, 4 and 5

58. Only a few of the officials of Siraj-ud-Daula fought for him in the Battle of Plassey. Which of the following are those?

1. Rai Durlabh 2. Mohan Lal
3. Kadim Khan 4. Rajballabh
5. Mir Madan

Codes:

A. 1, 2 and 4 B. 2 and 5
C. 3 and 4 D. 4 and 5

59. Where did the so-called Black Hole Tragedy take place?

A. Murshidabad B. Dacca
C. Monghyr D. Calcutta

60. Who was the author of the following passage?

"Shall I only say that such a sense of anarchy, confusion, bribery, corruption and extortion was never seen or heard of in any country but Bengal, nor such and so many fortunes acquired in so unjust and rapacious manner".

A. Colonel Melleson
B. Colonel Clive
C. Nabin Chandra Sen
D. Admiral Watson

61. Who was the leader of English embassy sent to the Mughal Court in 1715 which succeeded in getting the Farman of 1717 from the Mughal emperor, Farukh Siyar?

A. Thomas Pitt
B. William Hamilton
C. Edward Stephenson
D. John Surman

62. Who was the author of the "Siyar-us-Mutakherim" a contemporary historical account?

A. Gulam Hussain
B. Nasir Hussain
C. Arif Muhammad
D. Shahabuddin

63. Who was the British officer who defeated Mir Quasim in series of battles in 1763?

A. Major Hector Munro

B. Major Adams
C. Colonel Malleson
D. Colonel Holwell

64. In 1773 Warren Hastings signed a treaty with the Nawab of Awadh giving back the later two districts of Kara and Allahabad for a payment of Rs. 50 lakhs. Name of the treaty is
A. Treaty of Allahabad
B. Treaty of Lucknow
C. Treaty of Banaras
D. Treaty of Faizabad

65. **Assertion (A):** The people of the Mughal Empire looked the spirit of the political nationalism.
Reason (R): The Jats, the Marathas, Rajputs etc. rebelled against the Mughals to consolidate their regional and tribal power.
Codes:
A. A and R are true and R is the correct explanation of A.
B. A and R are true but R is not the correct explanation of A.
C. A is true but R is false.
D. A is false but R is true.

66. **Assertion (A):** Some of the religious reformers through their preaching indirectly helped in the disintegration of the Mughal Empire.
Reason (R): In the Deccan, Ramdas insisted on the acquisition of political sovereignty for the defence of the Maharashtra Dharma.
Codes:
A. A and R are true and R is the correct explanation of A.
B. A and R are true but R is not the correct explanation of A.
C. A is true but R is false.
D. A is false but R is true.

67. **Assertion (A):** During the reign of the later Mughals, the practice of "Ijara' became more common in the jagir as well as the Khalsia lands.
Reason (R): The ijaradars caused a great amount of damage to agriculture in general and the agriculturists in particular.
Codes:
A. A and R are true and R is the correct explanation of A.
B. A and R are true but R is not the correct explanation of A.
C. A is true but R is false.
D. A is false but R is true.

68. **Assertion (A):** None of the Indian power that rose on the ruins of the Mughals empire could replace the Mughals.
Reason (R): The British who replaced the Mughals in India as the imperial power had a superior socio-economic system than that of the Indian powers.
Codes:
A. A and R are true and R is the correct explanation of A.
B. A and R are true but R is not the correct explanation of A.
C. A is true but R is false.
D. A is false but R is true.

69. **Assertion (A):** In 1761 Haider Ali became the defacto ruler of Mysore.
Reason (R): Haider Ali continued to recognize Chikka Krishna Raj I as the lawful ruler of Mysore.
Codes:
A. A and R are true and R is the correct explanation of A.
B. A and R are true but R is not the correct explanation of A.
C. A is true but R is false.
D. A is false but R is true.

70. **Assertion (A):** Tipu Sultan established two dockyards and the models of the ships were supplied by himself.
Reason (R): How was one of the few Indian rulers to have realised importance of a modern navy.
Codes:
A. A and R are true and R is the correct explanation of A.
B. A and R are true but R is not the correct explanation of A.

C. A is true but R is false.
D. A is false but R is true.

71. Assertion (A): Tipu Sultan planted a "Tree of Liberty" at Mangalore.
Reason (R): He became a member of Jacolian Club after the French revolution.
Codes:
A. A and R are true and R is the correct explanation of A.
B. A and R are true but R is not the correct explanation of A.
C. A is true but R is false.
D. A is false but R is true.

72. Assertion (A): By the treaty of Lahore, the British troops were permitted to pass through Sikh territories whenever the need arose.
Reason (R): Ranjit Singh permitted the British troops to march through his territory in 1838.
Codes:
A. A and R are true and R is the correct explanation of A.
B. A and R are true but R is not the correct explanation of A.
C. A is true but R is false.
D. A is false but R is true.

73. Assertion (A): The British sold Kashmir to Gulab Singh in return for 1 million in 1846.
Reason (R): The British acquired Kashmir from the ruler of Punjab in lieu of a part of the war indemnity which he could not pay in cash.
Codes:
A. A and R are true and R is the correct explanation of A.
B. A and R are true but R is not the correct explanation of A.
C. A is true but R is false.
D. A is false but R is true.

74. Assertion (A): Dalip Singh, the last ruler of independent Punjab, was deposed and pensioned off by Lord Dalhousie.
Reason (R): Dalip Singh was implicated in a conspiracy and executed by the British.
Codes:
A. A and R are true and R is the correct explanation of A.
B. A and R are true but R is not the correct explanation of A.
C. A is true but R is false.
D. A is false but R is true.

75. Assertion (A): In 1801 Nawab Sadat Ali of Awadh ceded almost half of his territory to the British.
Reason (R): Sadat Ali signed the subsidary treaty with Lord Wellesley.
Codes:
A. A and R are true and R is the correct explanation of A.
B. A and R are true but R is not the correct explanation of A.
C. A is true but R is false.
D. A is false but R is true.

76. Assertion (A): Wazir Ali was the last ruler of Awadh.
Reason (R): Lord Dalhousie annexed Awadh in 1756 on grounds of misgovernment.
Codes:
A. A and R are true and R is the correct explanation of A.
B. A and R are true but R is not the correct explanation of A.
C. A is true but R is false.
D. A is false but R is true.

77. Assertion (A): After 1748, the Nawabs of Awadh came to be called the "Nawab Wazirs".
Reason (R): Since 1748 the Nawabs of Awadh held both the Nawabship of Awadh and the Wazirship of the Mughal empire simultaneously.
Codes:
A. A and R are true and R is the correct explanation of A.
B. A and R are true but R is not the correct explanation of A.
C. A is true but R is false.
D. A is false but R is true.

78. Assertion (A): The rule of Murshid kuli Khan witnessed the rise and growth of a new landed aristocracy in Bengal.

Reason (R): He reorganised the administration and appointed local Hindu Zamindars and Money lenders as revenue farmers.

Codes:

A. A and R are true and R is the correct explanation of A.

B. A and R are true but R is not the correct explanation of A.

C. A is true but R is false.

D. A is false but R is true.

79. Assertion (A): The Mughal farman of 1717 to the British has been described as the "Magna Carta of the Company".

Reason (R): It revoked the priveleges granted to the British by the Farman of 1691.

Codes:

A. A and R are true and R is the correct explanation of A.

B. A and R are true but R is not the correct explanation of A.

C. A is true but R is false.

D. A is false but R is true.

80. Assertion (A): In 1751, Alivardi Khan bought peace with the Marathas by the cessation of the revenues of a part of Orissa and an annual payment of Rs. 12 lakh as the 'Chauth' of Bengal.

Reason (R): The first decade of his regime was spent in an unceasing warfare with the Marathas whose repeated incursions caused untold miseries to the people of Bengal.

Codes:

A. A and R are true and R is the correct explanation of A.

B. A and R are true but R is not the correct explanation of A.

C. A is true but R is false.

D. A is false but R is true.

81. Assertion (A): Shuja-ud Daula seized the English factory at Chandranagore in June 1756.

Reason (R): The British gave protection to the enemies of Siraj-ud-Daula and refused to surrender them to the Nawab.

Codes:

A. A and R are true and R is the correct explanation of A.

B. A and R are true but R is not the correct explanation of A.

C. A is true but R is false.

D. A is false but R is true.

82. Assertion (A): Siraj-ud-Daula defeated and executed Shaukat Jang, who was his step brother.

Reason (R): Shaukat had plans to become the Nawab and even acquired a Farman from the titular Mughal emperor.

Codes:

A. A and R are true and R is the correct explanation of A.

B. A and R are true but R is not the correct explanation of A.

C. A is true but R is false.

D. A is false but R is true.

83. Which of the following statements about Rani Jindan are not true?

1. She was the wife of Ranjit Singh and mother of Dalip Singh
2. She became the Regent of Punjab in 1845.
3. She was removed from the regency by the treaty of Lahore.
4. After Anglo-Sikh war, She was implicated in a conspiracy against the British and transported to Shikarpur first and then to Banaras.
5. She was sentenced to Death by the British after the Second Anglo-Sikh War.

Codes:

A. 1 and 4 B. 3 and 5

C. 2 and 3 D. 4 and 5

84. Which of the following statements about Nizam-ul-Mulk are true?

1. His original name was chinquilich Khan.
2. He served his first term as the Vice-

roy of the Deccan between 1713-15.
3. He was the Wazir of the Mughal empire between 1715-20.
4. He served his second term as the Wazir of the Mughal empire beteen 1720-26.
5. 'Nizam-ul-Mulk' and Khan-i-Dwra' were the titles given to him by emperor Farukh Siyar.

Codes:
A. 2 and 3 B. 2, 3 and 4
C. 2, 3 and 5 D. 1, 2 and 5

85. Nizam-ul-Mulk did
1. give up his Wazirship of the Mughal empire Voluntarily and march to the Deccan without taking the Emperor's permission.
2. found the state of Hyderabad in 1720
3. get the conformation of his Vice-Royality of the Deccan and the title of "Asaf Jah" from emperor Muhammad Shah in 1725.
4. Continued to recognise the Mughal emperor as his sovereign.

Codes:
A. 1, 2 and 3 B. 1, 3 and 4
C. 2, 3 and 4 D. 1, 2 and 4

86. Arrange the following Nizams in the chronological order:
1. Salabat Jang
2. Sikhandar Jang
3. Muzaffar Jang
4. Nasir Jang
5. Nizam Ali

A. 3, 1, 4, 2 and 5 B. 4, 2, 3, 5 and 1
C. 3, 2, 1, 4 and 5 D. 4, 3, 1, 5 and 2

87. Which of the following statements about the Anglo-Nizam relations are true?
1. The British tried to interfere in the affairs of Hyderabad for the first time in 1750.
2. They supported Nasir Jang against Muzafiar Jang in the succession dispute between the two
3. Colonel Forde concluded a friendship treaty with Muzaffar Jang in 1760.
4. The Nizam cooperated with Mysore in the 3rd and 4th Anglo-Mysore Wars.

Codes:
A. 1, 2 and 3 B. 2, 3 and 4
C. 1, 2 and 4 D. 1, 3 and 4

88. Which of the following statements about the Nizam of Hyderabad are not true?
1. Nasir Jang was murdered by Muzaffar Jang with the help of the French
2. Muzaffar Jang was murdered by Salabat Jang with the help of the British
3. Sikandar Jah succeeded Muzaffar Jang
4. Usman Ali Khan was the last Nizam of Hyderabad.

Codes:
A. 1 and 2 B. 1 and 3
C. 2 and 3 D. 2 and 4

89. Which of the following statements about Saadat Khan Burhan-ul-Mulk are true.
1. He founded the state of Avadh
2. He Supressed the rebellions zamindars in Awadh, and established law and order there.
3. He discriminated against Hindus in the matter of the employment.
4. He made Avadh economically and military strong by carrying out revenue and military reforms

Codes:
A. 1, 2 and 3 B. 1, 2 and 4
C. 1, 3 and 4 D. 2, 3 and 4

90. Which of the following statements about Saadat Khan Burhan-ul-Mulk are incorrect?
1. He was appointed as the Governor of Awadh by Muhammad Shah.
2. He became the wazir of Mughal empire in 1735.
3. He was murdered by Nadir Shah in 1739.
4. He committed suicide in 1739.

Codes:
A. 1 and 2 B. 1 and 3
C. 2 and 3 D. 3 and 4

91. Which of the statements about the Safdar Jang are true?
1. He succeeded to the Governorship of

Awadh in 1739.
2. He was given the additional charge of the Wazirship of the Mughal empire in 1748.
3. He extended his territories by successfully waging wars against the Jats, Rohillas etc.
4. He was killed by the Marathas in a Battle.

Codes:

A. 1, 2 and 3 B. 2, 3 and 4
C. 1, 2 and 4 D. 1, 3 and 4

92. Shuja-ud-Daula did
1. Succeed to the Nawabship of Awadh as well as the wazirship of the Mughal empire in 1764.
2. get defeated by the Rohillas in 1774.
3. Signed a subsidiary treaty and paid a huge war indemnity to the British due to his defeat in the Battle of Plassey.
4. purchase Kara and Allahabad from the British in 1773.

Codes:

A. 1, 2 and 3 B. 1, 3 and 4
C. 3 and 2 D. 1 and 4

93. Asaf-ud-Daula did
1. conclude the Treaty of Faizabad with the British
2. transfer his capital from Lucknow to Faizabad in 1775
3. mistreat the Begams of Awadh and extract huge amounts from them by force
4. get removed from the Nawabship of Awadh for mismanagement by the British.

Codes:

A. 1 and 3 B. 2 and 4
C. 1 and 4 D. 2 and 3

94. Which was the capital of the state of carnatic?

A. Trichonoply B. Arcot
C. Srirangam D. Tanjore

95. Which of the following statement are true about the first carnatic war?
1. It began in 1745 and ended in 1748.
2. Anwaruddin, the Nawab of the Carnatic, intervened in the war on behalf of the English.
3. The French refused to obey the Nawab and were defeated by him, at St. Thimes near the Adyar river.
4. Madgao was restored to the English by the French after the war.

Codes:

A. 2, 3 and 4 B. 1, 2 and 3
C. 1, 2 and 4 D. 1, 3 and 4

96. Who was the English General who defeated Count De Lally in the Battle of Wandiwash, fought on 22nd Jan, 1760.

A. General Forde
B. General Hamilton
C. General Hariris
D. General Eyre Coote

97. When and by which Governor General was the carnatic state annexed?

A. 1792 — Lord Cornawallis
B. 1797 — John Shore
C. 1801 — Lord Wellesley
D. 1808 — Lord Minto

98. Which of the following statements are true about the state of Sind?
1. It became independent under the Kaloras after the decline of the Mughal empire.
2. In 1783, the Amirs of the Talpura tribe of Baluchistan overthrew the last of the Kaloras.
3. Under Amirs, Sindh was divided into five units, each under a separate branch of the tribe.
4. The Amirs of Sind owed a nominal allegience to the ruler of Afghanistan.

Codes:

A. 1, 2 and 3 B. 1, 2 and 4
C. 1 and 2 D. 3 and 4

99. When and whom Sir Charles Napier replace as the British resident in Sindh?

A. 1840 — Alexander Burnes
B. 1841 — Sir John Keane
C. 1842 — Major James outram
D. 1843 — Sir Ayre Coote

100. Which of the following were the causes for

the annexation of Sind by the British?

1. Commercial possibilities of the Indus
2. Refusal to the Amirs to allow the British troops to pass through Sind
3. British fear of expansion of the Russian empire towards the east
4. British desire to increase its influence in Persia and Afghanistan through control over sind
5. Refusal of the Amirs to Comply with Auckland's demand for a heavy sum.

Codes:

A. 1, 3 and 4 B. 2, 3 and 4
C. 3, 4 and 5 D. 2. 4 and 5

101. Pick out the two places which witnessed battles between the England and the Amirs before the formal annexation of Sind?

1. Hyderabad 2. Dabo
3. Miani 4. Mirpur

Codes:

A. 1 and 2 B. 2 and 3
C. 3 and 4 D. 1 and 3

ANSWERS

1	2	3	4	5	6	7	8	9	10
A	D	A	B	D	D	C	B	C	A
11	12	13	14	15	16	17	18	19	20
D	B	C	A	D	B	B	D	C	C
21	22	23	24	25	26	27	28	29	30
D	D	B	C	B	D	A	A	C	D
31	32	33	34	35	36	37	38	39	40
C	B	D	C	B	A	C	D	A	C
41	42	43	44	45	46	47	48	49	50
D	C	B	A	B	A	A	D	C	A
51	52	53	54	55	56	57	58	59	60
A	C	D	C	C	D	A	B	D	B
61	62	63	64	65	66	67	68	69	70
D	D	B	C	A	A	B	A	A	A
71	72	73	74	75	76	77	78	79	80
D	C	A	C	A	D	A	A	C	A
81	82	83	84	85	86	87	88	89	90
D	A	B	D	B	D	A	C	B	C
91	92	93	94	95	96	97	98	99	100
A	D	A	B	C	D	C	B	C	A
101									
B									

THE MARATHA KINGDOM

1. Who was the founder of the line of Peshwas?
A. Shivaji
B. Tara Bai
C. Baji Rao I
D. Balaji Vishwanath

2. Which Maratha leader revived the Jagir or Saranjanmi System?
A. Sambhaji B. Sahu
C. Raja Ram D. Baji Rao I

3. Which of the following transferred the capital of the Maratha empire from Satara to Poona?
A. Sambhaji
B. Sahu
C. Baji Rao I
D. Balaji Vishwanath

4. Who was the first Maratha leader to entertain the idea of an all Indian Maratha empire?
A. Sahu
B. Raja Ram
C. Baji Rao I
D. Balaji Vishwanath

5. Which of the following fought a civil war?
A. Raja Ram and Tara Bhai
B. Sahu and Tara Bhai
C. Raja Ram and Sahu
D. Raja Ram and Baji Rao I

6. The conquests of the Marathas outside their original kingdom was made by the
A. Central army under the Maratha King
B. Central army under the Peshwa
C. Private armies of Maratha Sardars
D. None of these

7. When did the Mughal invade Bijapur?
A. 1620 AD B. 1650 AD
C. 1657 AD D. 1660 AD

8. When was Afzal Khan killed by Shivaji?
A. 1650 AD B. 1659 AD
C. 1660 AD D. 1662 AD

9. Who was Dabir in Shivaji's Administration?
A. Master of troops
B. Master of religious ceremonies
C. Master of ceremonies
D. Master of correspondence

10. When did the Peshawa becomes the official head of the Maratha administration?
A. 1740 B. 1745
C. 1746 D. 1749

11. When was Purander beseiged?
A. 1660 AD B. 1662 AD
C. 1665 AD D. 1670 AD

12. Shivaji levied ¼ of land revenue of the neighbouring states which was known as
A. Surdeshmukhi B. Kharaji
C. Jakat D. Chauth

13. Match the following.
(a) Peshawa 1. Nagpur
(b) Bhonsles 2. Gwalior
(c) Gaekwards 3. Baroda
(d) Halkars 4. Poona
(e) Scindhias 5. Indore

Codes:

	(a)	*(b)*	*(c)*	*(d)*	*(e)*
A.	1	2	3	4	5
B.	4	3	1	2	5
C.	4	1	5	2	3
D.	4	1	3	5	2

14. What was Kesaria?
A. Maratha Flag
B. Maratha guerilla warfare units
C. Maratha Fort in Malwa
D. Maratha oath of revenge

15. When was Shambhuji put to death by Aurangzeb?
A. 1686 AD B. 1689 AD
C. 1690 AD D. 1693 AD

16. When was Shivaji born?
A. 1617 AD B. 1627 AD
C. 1637 AD D. 1647 AD

17. State's share in the produce of the land in the Maratha Kingdom was
A. 25% B. 16%
C. 35% D. 40%

18. When was the coronation of Shivaji car-

ried out
A. 1670 AD B. 1672 AD
C. 1674 AD D. 1678 AD

19. When did Shivaji conquer Jauli?
A. 1656 AD B. 1660 AD
C. 1670 AD D. 1676 AD

20. Which of the following helped the Sayyid brother in overthrewing Farrukh Siyar?
A. Baji Rao I
B. Balaji Vishwanath
C. Balaji Baji Rao
D. None of these

21. Which Maratha Senapati was defeated and killed by Baji Rao I?
A. Sambhaji II
B. Trimbak Rao Dhabade
C. Chimnaji Appa
D. Narayan Rao

22. Which statement on the Maratha confederacy is correct.
A. It was a combination of autonomous units presided over by man who were as good as rulers though united for certain common purposes like defence and foreign affairs.
B. The Maratha captains established themselves at Indore, Gwalior, Dhar, Baroda and Nagpur.
C. The central authority as represented by the Peshwa was a nominal one.
D. All the above

23. From whom did Shivaji receive Poona as a jagir?
A. The Mughals
B. The Adil Shahis
C. The Nizam Shahis
D. The Portuguese

24. Match the following.

(a) Shivaji's mother	1. Ahilaya Bai
(b) Shivaji's guardian	2. Jija Bai
(c) Shivaji's guru	3. Dadaji Kondadeo
	4. Ram Das

Codes:

	(a)	(b)	(c)
A.	1	4	3
B.	2	4	3
C.	2	3	4
D.	1	3	4

25. Shivaji was born at the Fort of
A. Jinji B. Shivner
C. Javli D. Champaner

26. Which port on the western coast was attacked and plundered by Shivaji in 1664?
A. Surat B. Chaul
C. Goa D. Bassein

27. Who wrote "We shall hear Shivaji in like the centre of a circle?
A. Raja Jai Singh B. Shiasta Khan
C. Aurangzeb D. None of these

28. Which of the following was not alive at time of Shivaji's coronation in 1674?
A. Gaga Bhatt
B. Tukaram
C. Dadaji Kondadeo
D. Ram Das

29. Shivaji was assisted by a council of 8 ministers called the 'Astha Pradhan'. Match the following 4 ministers with their respective functions.

(a) Peshwa	1. General administration
(b) Amatya	2. Foreign affairs
(c) Nyayadhisha	3. Justice
(d) Samant	4. Finance

Codes:

	(a)	(b)	(c)	(d)
A.	1	2	3	4
B.	1	4	3	2
C.	1	3	2	4
D.	1	4	2	3

30. Shivaji's kingdom was divided into four provinces. Each provice was under the charge of a
A. Subedar or Mamlatdar
B. Subedar or Deshmukh
C. Subedar or Jamladar
D. None of these

31. What were Saranjams?
A. Hereditary nights in land
B. Cash salaries
C. Revenue grants
D. Tax-free lands

32. Match the following.

(a) Deshmukh	1. Loose auxiliaries
(b) Silhadars	2. Zamindars
(c) Mirasdars	3. Hereditary holder of land
	4. Revenue officials

Codes:

	(a)	*(b)*	*(c)*
A.	2	3	4
B.	2	1	3
C.	3	4	1
D.	3	2	1

33. What was Paga?
A. Guerilla warfare tactics
B. Regular army
C. Area adjoining a Maratha fort
D. Military expedition

34. What was Mokasa?
A. Jagirs
B. Religious ceremonies
C. Cavalry
D. None of these

35. In 1680 the Marathas obtained a naval victory over
A. The French B. The Portuguese
C. The Dutch D. The English

36. What was Shivaji's greatest achievement?
A. He welded together the Maratha race
B. He inflicted crushing defeats on the Mughal armies
C. His land revenue and military administrations were followed by other Deccan powers
D. He popularised guerilla warfare

37. Tara Bai was the widow of
A. Shivaji B. Sambhaji
C. Sahu D. Raja Ram

38. Kavi Kulash was the brahmin advisor of
A. Shivaji B. Sahu
C. Shambhaji D. Raja Ram

39. Given below are the 4 Maratha leaders. Arrange them chronologically.
1. Shivaji 2. Shahji
3. Sahu 4. Sambhaji

Codes:
A. 1, 2, 3 and 4 B. 2, 3, 1 and 4
C. 2, 1, 4 and 3 D. 2, 1, 3 and 4

40. Muhammad Quli a Muslim convert was recovered to Hinduism by Shivaji in 1676. What was his real name?
A. Vyankoji
B. Ragunath Pant
C. Netaji Palkar
D. Nischal Puri Goswami

41. Which of the following fort is not connected with Shivaji's life?
A. Raigarh B. Shivner
C. Javli D. Lohgarh

42. Which of the following fort is connected with Shivaji's childhood?
A. Shivner B. Troma
C. Javli D. Panhala

43. Who imprisoned Tara Bai during her struggle against Shahu?
A. Rajas Bai B. Jija Bai
C. Jodha Bai D. Yesu Bai

44. Shivaji II was the son of
A. Tara Bai B. Yesu Bai
C. Jija Bhi D. Jodha Bai

45. Which wife of Shivaji had committed Sati
A. Sai Bai B. Gunwanta Bai
C. Sakwar Bai D. Putli Bai

46. Which of the following stood on the right side of the throne to pour holy water on the king's head
A. Peshwa B. Senapati
C. Sachiv D. Mantri

47. The official incharge of the tarfs under Shivaji was designated as
A. Patel B. Pant
C. Havaldar D. Kulkarni

48. Shivaji introduced a uniform unit of measurement for the purpose of land revenue. This unit was known as
A. Jarib B. Kathi
C. Gaz D. Tanab

49. The highest rank in the Paga or State cavalry was
A. One Jumladar B. Five Havaldar
C. Five Hazari D. Ten Jumladar

50. In the infantry of Shivaji, a Havaldar commanded
A. Five Nayaks B. Ten Nayaks

C. Twelve Nayaks D. Fifteen Nayaks

51. Identify the fort where the Mughals laid seize on Raja Ram for 8 years?
A. Purandhar B. Satara
C. Jinji D. Kolhapur

52. One of the following was in favour of Shahu ascending the throne in place of Shivaji II. Identify him
A. Paras Ram Timbak
B. Dhanji Jadav
C. Ram Chandra Pant
D. Shankarji Narain

53. Who was the Peshwa at the time of the third Battle of Panipat fought between the Marathas and Ahmad Shah Abdali
A. Madhav Rao B. Balaji Baji Rao
C. Baji Rao D. Narayan Rao

54. Who was the ultimate beneficiary of the 3rd Battle of Panipat after the Maratha army had been routed?
A. Ahmad Shah Abdali
B. Shah Alam II, the Mughal Emperor
C. The Marathas
D. The English

55. Which of the following Maratha Chiefs was the cast to join the subsidiary alliance with the British?
A. The Peshwa B. Mokkar
C. Bhonsle D. Scindia

56. Trimbakji was the famous minister of
A. Narayan Rao
B. Baji Rao II
C. Madho Rao Narayan
D. Madhav Rao I

57. Who was the governor general during the Poona Settlement
A. Lord Masting
B. Lord Clive
C. Lord Wellesly
D. Lord Marques of Hastings

58. The Battle of Mukand Dara was fought during the
A. First Anglo – Maratha war
B. Second Anglo – Maratha war
C. Third Anglo – Maratha war
D. Fourth Anglo – Maratha war

59. The Treaty of Rajput was signed in 1806 between the British and
A. Holkar B. Gaekward
C. Scindia D. Bhonsle

60. The name of Mustani a dancing girl is associated with
A. Balaji Vishwanath
B. Baji Rao
C. Balaji Baji Rao
D. Madhav Rao

61. Which Peshwa is associated with the Sangola Agreement
A. Balaji Vishwanath
B. Baji Rao
C. Balaji Baji Rao
D. Madhav Rao I

62. Which Maratha – Peshwa was known as Nana Saheb?
A. Baji Rao B. Balaji Baji Rao
C. Madhav Rao I D. Narayan Rao

63. Which Maratha – Peshwa was murdered by Ragunath Rao?
A. Madhav Rao I
B. Narayan Rao
C. Madho Narayan Rao
D. Baji Rao II

64. Who led the Maratha forces in the 3rd Battle of Panipat in 1761.
A. Vishwanath Rao
B. Sadashiva Rao
C. Madhav Rao
D. Dattaji Scindhia

65. Name one of the following who is regarded as the creator of great Maharashtra and next only to Shivaji in his military acumen?
A. Sahu B. Baji Rao I
C. Nana Pharnavis D. Mahadji Schindia

66. The 2nd Anglo Maratha war (1803-1805) resulted in the victory for the British in 1806 the British made peace with Marathas why?
A. They wanted Maratha support
B. Their finances were getting exhausted
C. They faced renewed danger from the Afghans

D. They were afraid that the Marathas may regroup to take revenge

67. Where did Shahu locate the seat of his kingdom after the kingdom was divided between Shahu and Shivaji III?

A. Kolhapur B. Poona
C. Satara D. Jinji

68. "The Maratha Confideracy was a curious and baffling political puzzle". Whose words are these.

A. V.A. Smith B. Sardesai
C. P.E. Roberts D. Grant Duff

69. What occasion in 1719 prompted Balaji Vishwanath to timely military support to Saiyid Hussain Ali who together with his brother were considered king makers?

A. Joint attack on the ruler of Mysore
B. Supression of a revolt in Hyderabad
C. Overthrowing Farrukhsiyar the Mughal Emperor at Delhi
D. The rebellion of Afghan tribes in the North west

70. In the 3rd Battle of Panipat the Maratha had a contingent of European style infantry and artilery which was commanded by

A. Ibrahim Khan Gardi
B. Timur Shah
C. Najib-ud-daulah
D. Malhar Rao Holkar

71. The Sidis of Janjira were defeated by

A. Balaji Baji Rao
B. Baji Rao I
C. Baji Rao II
D. Balaji Vishwanath

72. Which of the following Maratha leaders captured Delhi?

A. Raghoji B. Sadashiv Rao
C. Narayan Rao D. Raghunath Rao

73. In 1751, the Nawab of Bengal had to cede Orissa to the Maratha Peshwa. Who was he?

A. Baji Rao I
B. Baji Rao II
C. Balaji Baji Rao
D. Balaji Vishwanath

74. Who among the following is called the Maratha Machiavelli?

A. Nana Phadnavis
B. Madhav Rao
C. Balaji Baji Rao
D. Raja Ram

75. Which Maratha Chief is associated with the Karnataka expedition of 1740-41.

A. Raghuji Bhonsle
B. Ranoji Scindia
C. Pilaji Gaekward
D. Malhar Rao Holkar

76. Which Maratha leader was responsible for the outbreak of two civil wars?

A. Raja Ram
B. Tara Bai
C. Madhav Rao
D. Balaji Vishwanath

77. Given below 3 statements about Balaji Rao, which is correct.

1. He abandoned Baji Rao's idea of uniting all Hindu chiefs under one flag.
2. his lieutenants ravage both the Muslims and the Hindus including the Rajputs.
3. He tried to introduce Western method of warfare.

Codes:

A. 1, 2 and 3 B. 1 and 2
C. 2 only D. 2 and 3

78. There were seven Peshwas of the Marathas. The last 4 ruled from 1761-1818. Arrange them chronologically.

1. Narayan Rao 2. Baji Rao II
3. Madhav Rao 4. Madhav Rao II

Codes:

A. 2, 3, 1 and 4 B. 2, 1, 3 and 4
C. 3, 1, 4 and 2 D. 3, 1, 2 and 4

79. The third Battle of Panipat was fought in 1761 AD between

A. The Marathas and Ahmad Shah Abdali
B. Akbar and Hemu
C. The Marathas and the English
D. None of these

80. Within 11 years, that is from 1761-72, which Peshwa restored the lost fortunes of the Maratha Empire?

A. Madhav Rao B. Madhav Rao II

C. Baji Rao II D. Narayan Rao

81. Haidar Ali of Mysore was defeated in 1771 by the Marathas who were led by
A. Nana Fadanvis B. Nana Saheb
C. Baji Rao II D. Madhav Rao

82. The last Maratha Peshwa was worthless. He ruled from 1795-1818. Identify him.
A. Madhav Rao B. Narayan Rao
C. Baji Rao II D. Madhav Rao II

83. The treaty of Rajghat was signed in 1806 between the British and
A. Holkar B. Gaekward
C. Scindia D. Bhonsle

84. Which Peshwa fought the Third Anglo-Maratha war of 1816-19?
A. Narayan Rao B. Baji Rao II
C. Madhav Rao D. Madhav Rao II

85. Which among the following was responsible for the downfall of the Maratha Empire?
A. The feudal system and its fatal results
B. Absence of well-drilled army and modern guns and ammunitions
C. No sound economic policy had to depend on uncertain and precarious sources of income like chauth
D. All of the above

86. Who was the founder of the Scindia dynasty of Gujarat?
A. Raghuji B. Ranaji
C. Mahadaji D. Malhar Rao

87. Which of the following supported the Marathas in the third Battle of Panipat?
A. The Rajput Princes
B. Nawab Shuja-ud-daulah of Awadh
C. The Ruhela Chief
D. None of the above

88. Which one of the following events regarded as a turning point in Maratha-Mughal relations?
A. Shivaji's attack on Shaistakhan, the Mughal Governor of the Deccan.
B. Shivaji's attack on Surat the premier Mughal Fort
C. The treaty of Purandar
D. Shivaji's Agra visit.

89. In 1719 Balaji Vishwanath helped the Sayyid brothers in overthrowing.
A. Farrukhsiyar B. Azam Shah
C. Bahadur Shah D. Jahandar Shah

90. Poona became the headquarters of the Maratha Government during the Peshwaship of
A. Balaji Vishwanath
B. Baji Rao
C. Balaji Baji Rao
D. Madhav Rao

91. Which one of the following Ashtapradhans did not hold a military command besides his civil duties?
A. Peshwa or the Prime Minister
B. Sachiv or Home Secretary incharge of the King's correspondence
C. Amatya or the Finance Minister
D. Pandit Rao or Royal Chaplain

92. At which one of the following forts did Rajaram remain under the siege of the Mughals for 8 years?
A. Satara B. Purandar
C. Jinji D. Kolhapur

93. Which of the following treaty gave Shabhuji the entire region south of river warna?
A. Treaty of Warna
B. Treaty of Nunji Shivgaon
C. Treaty of Durari Sarai
D. Treaty of Surat

94. Which robe did Shivaji adopted for his flag?
A. Ramdas
B. Nischal Puri Goswami
C. Ganga Bhatta
D. Balam Bhatta

95. Which of the following term applied to the independent territories of Maharashtra which formed the independent kingdom of Shivaji?
A. Prant B. Twarf
C. Swarajya D. Mahal

96. Which of the following Ashtrapradhan was also known as Chitnis?
A. Sumant B. Pandit Rao

C. Sachiv D. Amatya

97. Which statement on the Maratha confederacy is correct?

A. It was a combination of autonomous units presided over by men who were as good as rulers though united for certain common purpose like defence and foreign affairs.

B. The Maratha Captains established themselves at Indore, Gwalior, Dhar, Baroda and Nagpur.

C. The central authority as represented by the Peshwa, was a nominal one

D. All the above

98. Which among the following was helpful to Shivaji in his conquer of Karnataka?

A. Mughals B. Golkunda

C. Bijapur State D. Berar State

99. One of the following was not a Maratha Chieftaincy. Identify it

A. Holkar B. Gaekwar

C. Rohilla D. Scindhia

100. Chhatrasal, who revolted against Aurangazeb was a

A. Bundela Prince B. Sikh Chieftain

C. Rohilla Leader D. Jat Prince

101. Which statement is incorrect about the Treaty of Purandar (1665) that was signed between Shivaji and the Mughal general Raja Jai Singh of Amber?

A. Shivaji surrendered

B. A Mansab of 5000 was granted to Shivaji's Son, Sambhaji

C. Teroritory worth 12 lakhs of huns in a year in the Bijapuri Konkan was given to Shivaji.

D. Shivaji promised to join personally in any Mughal Campaign in the Deccan.

102. Sadashiv Rao and Vishvasa Rao defeated Nizam Ali in the Battle of

A. Und B. Udita

C. Udgir D. Uch

103. The Battle of Bhopal resembles in all respects, the battle of

A. Ashti B. Palkhed

C. Khed D. Goregaon

104. Nizam was surrounded by Baji Rao in the waterless waste called

A. Rajasthan B. Malwa

C. Bhopal D. Palkhed

105. Chauth was a tax collected from non-Maratha states and it formed.

A. 1/3 of the revenue

B. 1/6 of the revenue

C. 1/4 of the revenue

D. 1/5 of the revenue

106. One of the following was not a Maratha statesman in the 18th century. Who was he?

A. Ahilya Bai

B. Nana Farnavis

C. Mahadaji Sindhia

D. Mahadev Govind Ranade

107. Shambhuji was succeeded on the Maratha throne-by

A. Shahu B. Shambhuji II

C. Rajaram D. Tara Bai Mohite

108. The last military exploit of Aurangzeb was the capture of

A. Panhala B. Satara

C. Khelna D. Wagiugera

109. One of the movements against Aurangzeb was trial in character. Identify.

A. Afghan B. Maratha

C. Jat D. Sikh

110. Religion played a role in one of the following movements against Aurangzeb. Identify.

A. Maratha Movement

B. Sikh Movement

C. Jat Movement

D. Afghan Movement

111. The Nizam signed a treaty with Baji Rao in 1728 AD at

A. Mungi – Shevgaon

B. Surji – Arjangaon

C. Shevagram

D. Argaon

112. What was the importance of the Treaty of Salbai?

A. It kept peace between the Marathas and the British for two decades.

B. It completed the disintegration of the Mughals.
C. It marked the rise of the Sikhs
D. It ended the aspiration of the Rohillas

113. The Peshwa who had the head to plan and the hand to execute was
A. Balaji Vishwanath
B. Baji Rao II
C. Baji Rao I
D. Balaji Baji Rao

114. In 1713 AD Shahu left the administration of the land in the hands of his
A. Pratinidhi B. Ashtapradhan
C. Peshwa D. Senapati

115. Who was the one who advised Shah Alam I to release Shahu?
A. Asaf Jah B. Zulfikar Khan
C. Shuja-ud-daulah D. Robert Clive

116. Which one of the following was not stipulated by the treaty of Purandhar?
A. Shivaji should surrender 23 forts
B. Shivaji should visit Agra
C. Shivaji must help the Mughals against Bijapur
D. Shivaji's son would be made a Mansabdar.

117. What was the principal reason that caused the discomfiture of Aurangzeb in the fight against the Marathas?
A. Military tactics of the Marathas
B. Desertion of his own generals
C. Mughals being strained to the utmost
D. Fight against a new born nation

118. Shivaji initially expanded at the cost of
A. The Mughals
B. Bijapur
C. Berar
D. Ahmednagar Kingdom

119. Shivaji's visit to Agra proved that Aurangzeb
A. was a clever diplomat
B. was short sighted
C. at the time was not interested in Deccan affairs
D. dislike the Marathas

120. Which one of the following was not a feature of Shivaji's Army?
A. Neither women nor dancing girls were allowed to accompany the army.
B. The Plundar taken by each soldier was strictly accounted for
C. Cash Salaries were given to regular soldiers
D. Deserters were executed on the spot

121. Which one of the following is of no significance regarding the rise of the Marathas?
A. The march of the Marathas to Delhi in 1719.
B. Revival of the jagir system led to the rise of independence principalities under Maratha adventures.
C. The Maratha officers securing the right of collecting chauth and Sardeshmukhi
D. The office of the Peshwa becoming hereditary.

122. Who said : Let us strike at the trunk of the withering tree, the branches will fall of themselves.
A. Balaji Viswanath
B. Baji Rao
C. Balaji Baji Rao
D. Shivaji

123. What did the term 'Hindu-Pad-Padshahi' mean in the early history of the Marathas?
A. Defiance of the Mughal State
B. Hindus should be shown deference but not sufference
C. Establishment of Hindu state
D. Crusade against the Muslims

124. Which of the following was an original contribution of the Maratha Policy?
A. levying of chauth and Sardeshmukhi
B. more reliance on forts
C. reliance on guerilla warfare
D. a department of admirality

125. In theory the office of the "Pratinidhi" was?
A. Senior to that of the Peshwa
B. Equal to that of the Peshwa
C. Junior to that of the Peshwa
D. An office close to the people

126. Which one of the facts in the Post-Shivaji era was the chief cause for transforming the nature of the Maratha state?
A. Feudal tendencies from the time of Sahu
B. Imperialistic ambitious of Balaji Baji Rao regardless of Shivaji's high deals
C. Corrupt and cast ridden administration
D. Favouritism shown to the Brahmans

127. How did Baji Rao I evoke the Sympathy of the Hindu chiefs and secure their support
A. by following Hindu Laws of Succession
B. by preaching Hindu Pad-Padshahi
C. by giving high place to Brahmans
D. by organising the army according to the Hindu Puranas

128. The Maratha Council of Ministers consisted of
A. 4 members B. 6 members
C. 8 members D. 10 members

129. The Maratha Government under the Peshwa was
A. highly centralised
B. democratic in nature
C. highly despotic
D. loose confederacy

130. Who persuaded Shivaji to visit the Mughal court?
A. Raj Singh B. Ram Singh
C. Jai Singh D. Jaswant Singh

131. The Marathas received their first training in guerilla warfare from
A. Shahji B. Shivaji
C. Malik Ambar D. Jaswant Singh

132. Which one of the following was not a cause of the fall of the Mughal Empire
A. declining strength of their army
B. outdated weapons
C. lack of a powerful navy
D. mutual rivalry of their officers

133. Which Jagir was left by Shivji for his senior wife
A. Ranthambhor B. Pune
C. Jamli D. Konkan

134. Who was Mastani?
A. Beloved of Baji Rao
B. Shahji's wife
C. Shivaji's wife
D. Beloved of Shahu

135. Who was responsible for the collection of land revenue?
A. Hirasdar B. Kulkarni
C. Silahdar D. Patel

136. Who was attacked by Shivaji in his harem?
A. Jai Singh B. Shaista Khan
C. Afzal Khan D. Aurangzeb

137. The Peshwaship was abolished by the English at the time of Peshwa
A. Baji Rao II B. Madhav Rao I
C. Narayan Rao D. None of above

138. Identify one of the following Maratha Saints who was a great social reformer patriot?
A. Eknath
B. Tukaram
C. Samarth Ramdas
D. Vaman Pandit

139. On what occasion did Shivaji have a first trial of strength with the Mughals?
A. His raid on the Mughal district of Ahmednagar and Junagarh
B. His encounter with Afzal Khan
C. His encounter with Shaista Khan
D. His attack on Surat

ANSWERS

1	2	3	4	5	6	7	8	9	10
D	C	D	C	B	C	C	B	C	D
11	12	13	14	15	16	17	18	19	20
C	D	D	A	B	B	D	C	A	B

21	22	23	24	25	26	27	28	29	30
B	D	C	C	B	A	A	C	B	A
31	32	33	34	35	36	37	38	39	40
C	B	B	A	D	A	D	C	C	C
41	42	43	44	45	46	47	48	49	50
D	A	A	A	D	C	A	B	C	A
51	52	53	54	55	56	57	58	59	60
C	C	B	D	D	C	A	C	A	B
61	62	63	64	65	66	67	68	69	70
C	A	B	B	B	D	C	C	C	A
71	72	73	74	75	76	77	78	79	80
B	D	C	A	A	B	A	C	A	A
81	82	83	84	85	86	87	88	89	90
D	B	A	B	D	B	D	D	A	B
91	92	93	94	95	96	97	98	99	100
D	C	A	A	C	C	D	B	C	A
101	102	103	104	105	106	107	108	109	110
C	C	B	D	C	D	C	D	A	B
111	112	113	114	115	116	117	118	119	120
A	A	C	C	B	B	D	B	B	D
121	122	123	124	125	126	127	128	129	130
D	A	B	A	A	A	B	C	D	C
131	132	133	134	135	136	137	138	139	
D	C	B	A	D	B	A	C	A	

BEGINNING OF EUROPEAN COMMERCE

1. Which of the following was the Ist proprietory holding of the English in India?
A. Madras B. Surat
C. Masulipatam D. Hariharpur

2. The lease of Madras in 1639 A.D. was obtained by the English from
A. The ruler of Chandragiri
B. The ruler of Bijapur
C. The ruler of Mysore
D. The ruler of Golkunda

3. Which of the following was not one of the three Villages for which the English were granted Zamindari in Bengal in 1698 and where they built Fort William around their Factory?
A. Sutanati B. Burdwan
C. Kalikata D. Govindpur

4. In which year were factories opened for the first time in Orissa.
A. 1613 A.D. B. 1632 A.D.
C. 1639 A.D. D. 1663 A.D.

5. From which Mugal Emperor did John Middenhall tried to obtain a Farman for trade in Gujarat?
A. Akbar B. Jahangir
C. Aurangzeb D. None of these

6. The battle of 'Swally Hole' was fought in the year
A. 1605 A.D. B. 1612 A.D.
C. 1498 A.D. D. 1526 A.D.

7. Where was the first trading station of the Britishers established in the South?
A. Madras B. Bombay
C. Surat D. Masulipatam

8. The Dutch had no trading stations at
A. Masulipatam B. Pulicat
C. Calicut D. Cassimbazar

9. Due to commercial rivalry the Dutch indulged in the massacre of Englishmen-at
A. Malacca B. Amboyna
C. Surat D. Mugli

10. The Dutch company established monopoly of trade with
A. India B. Egypt
C. China D. Indonesia

11. In 1622 the Portuguese lost Ormuz in the Persian Gulf to
A. Britain B. Spain
C. Portugal D. France

12. Goa was acquired by Albuquerque from
A. Ahmadnagar B. Bijapur
C. Golkunda D. Berar

13. Which one of the following was not a portuguese settlement
A. Mugli B. Dutch
C. Bombay D. Chaul

14. Vasco-da-Gama founded a factory during his 2nd visit to India in 1501 at—
A. Bassein B. Salsette
C. Chaul D. Cannanore

15. Vasco-da-Gama established friendly relations with the Zamorin, who was the ruler of—
A. Calicut B. Goa
C. Travancore D. Cochin

16. Vasco-da-Gama who discovered first the direct sea-route from Europe to India reached Calicut in the year—
A. 1946 A.D. B. 1500 A.D.
C. 1498 A.D. D. 1495 A.D.

17. The Cape of Good Hope was discovered by—
A. Vasco-da-Gama
B. De Almeida
C. Albuquerque
D. Bartholomew Diaz

18. Which one of the following powers was the first to establish trade links with India?
A. English B. Dutch
C. Portuguese D. French

19. The Portuguese established their Ist business centre at—
A. Calicut B. Surat

C. Goa D. Cochin

20. Who was the first portuguese viceroy in India?
A. Vasco-da-Gama
B. Albuquerque
C. Da Almeida
D. Duarte Pacheo

21. Who is commonly known as the Navigator?
A. King John II
B. Prince Hery
C. King Emmanuel
D. Pope Alexander VI

22. The Danish establish a factory in 1620 at
A. Pondicherry B. Calicut
C. Tranquebar D. Goa

23. The trade links of the Swedish East India Company which was formed in 1731, was exclusively confined to
A. Indonesia B. China
C. Ceylon D. Malaya

24. Vasco-da-Gama was the native of
A. Portugal B. Germany
C. France D. Russia

25. Who captured Goa in 1510
A. Vasco-da-Gama
B. William Hawkins
C. Franciscode Almeida
D. Albuquerque

26. Who founded the French East India Company?
A. Colbert B. Francois Caron
C. Francis Martin D. Dumas

27. When did East India Company receive a charter from Queen Elizabeth?
A. 1598 A.D. B. 1599 A.D.
C. 1600 A.D. D. 1602 A.D.

28. When did Hawkins reach the court of Jahangir
A. 1606 A.D. B. 1607 A.D.
C. 1608 A.D. D. 1609 A.D.

29. Who was largely responsible for virtual plunder or loot of India in the early stages of British conquest?
A. Clive B. Warsen Hastings
C. Cornwallis D. Dalhousie

30. The British made vigorous attempts to restrict and crush Indian manufacturers by various measures and internal duties
A. during the merchantilist period
B. during the beginning of industrial revolution in England
C. duirng the governor-generalship of Bentinck
D. during the governor-generalship of Dalhousie

31. Who was responsible for the establishment of Portuguese power in India?
A. Vasco-da-Gama
B. Pardo-Carbag
C. Alfonso-d'-Albuquerque
D. Francis Xavier

32. Which European was bigoted in its altitude towards Indian religions?
A. Dutch B. Portuguese
C. French D. English

33. What was the major factor for the British triumph over the French in India?
A. Government support
B. Financial Strength
C. British navy
D. British diplomacy

34. The Dutch shifted their trading centres from Pulicat to—
A. Nagapattinam
B. Tranquebar
C. Salsette
D. None of the above

35. What was the nucleus for French power in India?
A. Chandarnagar B. Pondicherry
C. Cochin D. Tranquebar

36. What was the major centre for French trade in the east?
A. Ceylon B. Java
C. Mauritius D. Pondicherry

37. If Dupleix was responsible for the French weakness India, it was due to his
A. Treachery to local nuclear
B. Incapacity as a general
C. Visionary schemes
D. Over-ambitiousness

38. Who obtained Madras for the East India Company?
A. Francis Drake B. Francis Day
C. Francis D. Lord Francis

39. Which official of the East India company adopted aggressive tactics to further British trading interests?
A. Job Charnock B. Robert Clive
C. Josiah Child D. Thomas Roe

40. Where did the English open their first factories in Eastern India?
A. Bihar B. Orissa
C. Bengal D. Assam

41. From which one of the following Deccan Sultanates did Albuquerque Capture Goa?
A. Berar B. Ahmadnagar
C. Bijapur D. Golkunda

42. In 1602 Dutch Limited East India Company was given an exclusive right
A. 5 year B. 21 year
C. 25 year D. 50 year

43. Who is connected with the 'Blue water' Policy?
A. Albuquerque B. Dupleix
C. De Almeida D. Robert Clive

44. "The discovery of America and the cape route to India were the two greatest and most important events recorded in the history of mankind." Who wrote these words?
A. G.B. Shaw
B. Adam Smith
C. Thomas Stephen
D. J.S. Mill

45. By the Cartage system Indian ships sailing to destinations not reserved by an European power for its own trade had to buy passes if it was to avoid seizure and confiscation of its merchandise while European power followed this system?
A. The Portuguese B. The French
C. The English D. The Swedes

46. The first printing press in India was set up by
A. The Portuguese B. The Dutch
C. The French D. The English

47. Which European power was not organised on Commercial lines?
A. The Portugues B. The Dutch
C. The French D. The English

48. Bengal was well known for the export of
A. Indigo B. Raw Silk
C. Cotton D. Precious Stones

49. What was the name of the man, whom Dupleix supported for the masnad of Arcot?
A. Muhammad Ali
B. Salabat Jung
C. Chanda Sahib
D. Muzaffar Jang

50. What was the name of the French, about whom Dupleix said that "He had signed the ruin of the country and dishonours of the nation"?
A. Bussy B. Godhean
C. Dumas D. Lally

51. During whose government the French started dreaming of establishing an Empire in India?
A. Dupleix B. Francois Martin
C. Tenoir D. Dumas

52. Identify the founder of the French East India Company?
A. Cobert B. Francois Martin
C. Delehaye D. Francois Caron

53. Which of the following causes was not responsible for the success of the English against the French in India?
A. Mughal emperors helped the English
B. Expensive financial resources of the English
C. Superior naval power of the English
D. Better support to the English in India from England

54. The Capital and Centre of French activities in India was
A. Cassim Bazar B. Chandernagar
C. Pondicherry D. Surat

55. Who granted to the French area in Andhra known as Northern Sarkars
A. Anwar-ud-din B. Asaf Jah
C. Muzzafar Jang D. Salabat Jang

56. The Second carnatic war was different from the other two carnatic wars in the sense that
A. It did have its origin in Europe
B. In this war the Britishers were defeated
C. This war gave the French a victory in the seas
D. The Britishers won this war by treachery

57. The First Carnatic war ended with
A. Treaty of Aix-la-Chappale
B. Treaty of Paris
C. Treaty of Ryswick
D. Treaty of Bassein

58. The Battle of Adyar or St. Thomas was fought between
A. The English and the French
B. The English and the Mughals
C. The French and the Dutch
D. The French and Nawab of Arcot

59. Which one of the following European wars in associated with the third carnatic war?
A. The seven years war
B. The war of the Austrian Succession
C. The war of Roses
D. The Austro-Prussian war

60. Which of the following is incorrect about the failure of Dupleix
A. He was short of man power
B. He lacked courage and his strategy was inferior to that of the English
C. He lacked money
D. His generals were timid and insincere

61. Where was the decisive battle of the third carnatic war fought between the French and the English?
A. Pondicherry B. Jinji
C. Arcot D. Wandiwash

62. "I know these people are best treated with the sword in one hand and the Caducean in the other".
A. William Hawking
B. Thomas Roe
C. Alburquerque
D. Joshna Chid

63. The new Company named "The United Company of Merchants of England trading to the East Indies", came into being in
A. 1705 A.D. B. 1796 A.D.
C. 1707 A.D. D. 1708 A.D.

64. What were Calicoes?
A. Indigo exported from India
B. Cotton exported from India
C. Textile exported from India
D. Precious stories exported from India

65. Which of the following British strong holds were fortified?
A. Bombay B. Madras
C. Calcutta D. All the above

66. The first article in which the English started trading was
A. Indigo B. Saltpetre
C. Cotton D. Pepper

67. The Mughals granted trading concessions to the Portuguese because of
A. the handsome returns they got from Portugese trade
B. the Portuguese threat to Mughal shipping
C. the protection they got as a result of Portuguese forces stationed at their parts.
D. previous unprofitable trade with the Arabs

68. The greatest enemy that the British encountered in their ambition to establish an empire in India were the
A. French B. Mughals
C. Marathas D. Dutch

69. One privilege was exploited by the Company's servants to serve the purpose of their private trade. Identify it.
A. Bhatta B. Double Bhatta
C. Dastak D. Dastur

70. Vasco-da-Gama discovered the sea-route to India in
A. 1498 B. 1550
C. 1489 D. 1600

71. European countries established many factories in India which originally meant the

places where
A. goods were manufactured processed
B. the traded materials were sorted out and processed
C. officials of the company worked for the purpose of buying and selling
D. traders and their escorts rested for a while

72. What geographical advantage did the English possess over the Nawabs of Bengal?
A. the passage along the Eastern Ghats
B. access to the sea
C. the fertile deltas of the areas
D. the Brahmaputra river

73. Which officer led the English to victory in the Battle of Buxar?
A. Lally B. Watson
C. Clive D. Hector Munro

74. The English gained the Diwani of Bengal, Bihar and Orissa from the Mughal Emperor.
A. Militarily B. Commercially
C. Legally D. As a gift

75. Which Mughal Emperor granted the Dewani to the English?
A. Farrkhsiyar
B. Shah Alam II
C. Bahadur Shah
D. Shah Alam

76. Who introduced first the quinquennial settlement of the land revenue granting farming leases to the highest bidders for five years?
A. Cornwallis B. Warren Hastings
C. Dalhousie D. Clive

77. Battle of Buxar was fought on
A. 21st January 1764
B. 12th March 1764
C. 22nd October 1764
D. 20th October 1765

78. Which one act of the company during the period of Diwani led to the intervention of British crown?
A. The Nawab was made a mere puppet
B. The servants of the company enriched their own pocket, and after returning to England (The Indian Nawabs) made their way into the English Parliament.
C. Although a severe famine broke out in 1770, the revenue for the year was exacted in full
D. Since the company fell into arrears in making the stipulated payment of 4,00,000 pounds a year, it applied for a loan to the Home Government

79. Robert Clive satisfied himself with only Diwani rights because
1. he had a lot of respect for the Mughal Emperor
2. he has not in a position to oust the Mughal emperor
3. the company lacked in trained personnel to carry out the task of administration
4. the company was afraid of rousing the jealously of other European powers holding possessions in India.
5. the company could not assume direct rule as it would have been contrary to English law of the time.

Codes:
A. 1, 2 and 3 B. 2, 3 and 4
C. 3, 4 and 5 D. 1, 2 and 5

80. The first modern arsenal was established at
A. Dindigul B. Hyderabad
C. Bengal D. Bombay

81. When did the English East-India Company obtain permission to establish a factory at Surat?
A. 1600 B. 1613
C. 1661 D. 1715

82. Which one of the following rulers gave special trading privileges to the English East-India Company?
A. Bahadur Shah B. Jahandar Shah
C. Farukhsiyar D. Rafi-ud-Daula

83. Which factory of Bengal was established by the Dutch?
A. Bandel B. Hooghly
C. Chinsura D. Serampore

84. The grant of Diwani to the East India Company led to
A. the emergence of a free holding peasantry in India
B. fixity in land revenue
C. phenomenal increase in the income of the Nawabs
D. unchecked exploitation of the raiyots.

85. The important cause of India's poverty under the British in 19th Century was
A. over population
B. British polices
C. disastrous famines
D. failure of crops

86. Who benefited most by the land revenue system under the British?
A. the moneylender
B. the zamindar
C. the peasant
D. the merchant

87. The British Government monopolised the manufacture of

1. Salt	2. Opium
3. Sugar	4. Steel

Codes:

A. 1 and 2	B. 2 and 3
C. 1 and 3	D. 1, 2 and 3

88. Arrange the following territories in the chronological order they were occupied or conquered by the British in India—
1. United Provinces
2. Punjab
3. Madras
4. Bengal, Bihar and Orissa
5. Sind
6. Mysore

Codes:
A. 4, 3, 6, 1, 5 and 2
B. 2, 6, 4, 5 1 and 3
C. 3, 4, 6, 1, 5 and 2
D. 3, 2, 4, 1, 5 and 6

89. Which city or territory remained under the British rule for the longest period?
A. Bengal
B. Madras
C. Bihar
D. Bombay

90. Who helped most the British in their trade with India and subsequently in its conquest?
A. Indian merchants and moneylenders
B. Hindu traitors
C. Muslim traitors
D. Indian feudal classes

91. European companies have been matched with the years of their formation. Which pair is incorrect?
A. English East India Company 1600 AD
B. Dutch East India Company 1602 AD
C. Danish Company 1610 AD
D. The French East India Company 1664 AD

92. Which place did not have a Dutch factory?

A. Pulicat	B. Surat
C. Chinsura	D. Franquba

93. Charles II, the king of England, received Bombay in 1661 as a part of dowry of Catherine of Branganza from the

A. Dutch	B. Portuguese
C. Spanish	D. French

94. In 1668 Bombay was transferred to the East India Company by Charles II at an annual rental of

A. £ 10	B. £ 100
C. £ 1000	D. £ 3000

95. Who granted the lease of Madras to the English Company in 1639?
A. the rulers of Golkunda
B. The ruler of Chandragiri, a representative of the ruined Vijayanagar Empire
C. the Nawab of Carnatic
D. The Mughal governor of Deccan

96. The book 'Poverty and Un-British rule in India' was written by
A. M.N. Roy
B. Dadabhai Naoroji
C. C. Rajagopalacharya
D. Gopala Krishna Gokhale

97. What made the British invest their Capital in India?
A. The British rule was characterised by

benevalent despotism. Hence they believed in the welfare of the people.
B. The British wanted India to become an industrial country
C. British capitalism was confronted with the problem of surplus capital
D. The British wanted to improve trade with India

98. Which was not a result of British imperialism?
A. decline of indigenous industries
B. paucity of capital
C. dearth of téchnical education
D. deindustrialisation during the first half of the British Rule

99. What were the main exports of India in the early eighteenth century.
1. Textiles
2. Saltpetre
3. Sugar
4. Slaves
5. Iron ore

Codes:
A. 1, 2 and 3 B. 1, 3 and 4
C. 2, 3 and 4 D. 3, 4 and 5

100. Which two are the most intriguing statements?
1. Those parts of India which had been longest under the British rule are the poorest today, if one consider the conditions of the masses
2. The mass level and standard of living highest in the Punjab
3. Indian merchants supported the British traders
4. The British were able to seek trading concessions from the Mughal rulers and other Indian Nawabs and kings

A. only 1 and 2 B. only 1, 2 and 4
C. all the four D. only 2 and 4

101. Who was the largely responsible for virtual plunder or loot of India in the early stages of British conquest?
A. Clive B. Warren Hastings
C. Cornwallis D. Dalhousie

102. The Chief business of the East India Company in its early period was to
A. close Indian markets for European goods.
B. carry Indian manufactured goods, textiles etc. as well as spices and the like from the East to Europe.
C. develop Indian markets for European goods.
D. open Indian markets to British manufacturers.

103. The British made vigorous attempts to restrict and crush Indian manufacturers by various measures and internal duties
A. During the Mercantilist period
B. After the beginning of industrial Revolution in England
C. During the Governor generalship of Bentinck
D. During the Governor generalship of Dalhousie

104. Who among the Governors-General of India reported that the misery hardly finds a parallel in the history of commerce, the bones of the cotton weavers are bleaching the plains of India?
A. Lord Bentinck
B. Lord Cornwallis
C. Lord Ripon
D. Warren Hastings

105. During which period did the East India Company begin to build up its territorial power in India?
A. In the beginning of 18th Century
B. In the last quarter of 17th Century
C. In the middle of 18th Century
D. In the first quarter of 19th Century

106. Which was the most decisive period of the East India company's domination and exploitation of India?
A. Second half of 18th Century
B. first half of 18th Century
C. middle of 19th Century
D. first half of 19th Century

107. Which was the most crucial problem of the East India company in the initial stages in India?
A. French rivalry

B. Refusal by Indian Nawabs and kings to grant substantial trade concessions and opportunities.
C. Europe had no goods to exchange with Indian cotton, Silk and Spices, hence the need to make payment in precious metal
D. Criticism by the English people at home.

108. With the beginning of Industrial Revolution in England one interest group demanded a change in the mercantile basis of the East Indian Company. Identify it.
A. manufacturing interest
B. mercantile interest
C. finance capitalist interest
D. rising industrial labour

109. After 1829 the East India Company in India was more interested in
A. trade
B. building Indian industries
C. revenue
D. English Capital investments in India.

110. Name the English merchant who attempted to obtain from Akbar a firman for trade in Gujarat?
A. Thomas Stephens
B. Ralph Fitch
C. John Middenhale
D. Sir Thomas Roe

111. The Presidency of Fort William came into existence in
A. 1700 B. 1725
C. 1757 D. 1740

112. In Bengal the chief Agency of English was at
A. Balasore B. Hoogly
C. Kasim Bazar D. Chittagong

113. Match the following.

(a) The First Carnatic War	1. 7 years war in Europe
(b) The 2nd Carnatic War (1748-55)	2. Trade rivalry in India
(c) The 3rd Carnatic War (1756-63)	3. War of Austrian

Codes:

	(a)	*(b)*	*(c)*
A.	1	2	3
B.	3	2	1
C.	2	3	1
D.	1	3	2

114. Match the following.

(a) Bombay	1. 200,000
(b) Madras	2. 300,000
(c) Calcutta	3. 70,000

Codes:

	(a)	*(b)*	*(c)*
A.	1	2	3
B.	2	1	3
C.	3	2	1
D.	3	1	2

115. The East India Company secured Diwani or right to collect revenue, in Bengal, Bihar and Orissa from.
A. Shah Alam I B. Shah Alam II
C. Shuja-ud-Daulah D. None of these

116. The United East India Company of the Netherlands was established in
A. 1598 B. 1600
C. 1602 D. 1605

117. By what means did the East India company acquire Bombay?
A. Captured by force
B. gifted by Chander II
C. acquired it on rent from Chales II
D. Sold to the company by the Emperor

118. Who granted the (Golden Firman) which meant free trade for the company of the English?
A. Ruler of Mysore
B. Ruler of Golconda
C. Mughal Emperor Aurangzeb
D. Ruler of Tanjore

119. How was Madras acquired by the British?
A. Lease B. Occupation
C. Rent D. Gift

120. Who among the Mughal Governors adopted a belligerent attitude towards the 1716 grant of 'firman by Farrukhsiyar'?
A. Siraj-ud-Daulah
B. Mushid Quli Khan
C. Shaista Khan
D. Shuja-ud-Daulah

ANSWERS

1	2	3	4	5	6	7	8	9	10
A	A	B	D	A	B	D	C	B	D
11	**12**	**13**	**14**	**15**	**16**	**17**	**18**	**19**	**20**
A	B	B	D	A	C	D	C	A	C
21	**22**	**23**	**24**	**25**	**26**	**27**	**28**	**29**	**30**
B	C	B	A	B	A	C	D	A	B
31	**32**	**33**	**34**	**35**	**36**	**37**	**38**	**39**	**40**
B	B	C	A	B	C	D	B	C	B
41	**42**	**43**	**44**	**45**	**46**	**47**	**48**	**49**	**50**
C	B	C	B	A	A	A	B	C	B
51	**52**	**53**	**54**	**55**	**56**	**57**	**58**	**59**	**60**
A	A	A	C	B	A	A	D	A	D
61	**62**	**63**	**64**	**65**	**66**	**67**	**68**	**69**	**70**
D	B	D	C	D	A	D	C	C	A
71	**72**	**73**	**74**	**75**	**76**	**77**	**78**	**79**	**80**
C	B	D	A	B	B	C	D	C	A
81	**82**	**83**	**84**	**85**	**86**	**87**	**88**	**89**	**90**
B	C	C	D	B	A	A	C	B	A
91	**92**	**93**	**94**	**95**	**96**	**97**	**98**	**99**	**100**
C	D	B	A	B	B	C	C	A	A
101	**102**	**103**	**104**	**105**	**106**	**107**	**108**	**109**	**110**
A	B	B	A	C	A	C	A	C	C
111	**112**	**113**	**114**	**115**	**116**	**117**	**118**	**119**	**120**
A	B	B	C	B	C	C	B	A	A

BRITISH ECONOMIC IMPACT IN INDIA

1. Who was the President of the Indian Education Commission of 1882?
A. Thomas Releigh B. W.W. Hunter
C. Macualay D. Sadler
2. When did the Indian universities assure teaching functions as well?
A. 1857 B. 1882
C. 1897 D. 1904
3. By which act did education officially came under Indian control for the first time
A. Indian Councils Act of 1892
B. Indian Councils Act of 1909
C. Government of India Act of 1919
D. Government of India Act of 1935
4. When was the "Double Government consisting of the Board of Control and the court of directors created at the Home government level?
A. 1784 B. 1813
C. 1833 D. 1853
5. Which act was responsible for the ultimate death of the presidency system?
A. Regulating Act of 1773
B. Pitt's India Act of 1784
C. Charter Act of 1813
D. Charter Act of 1833
6. Who was the first to attempt decentralisation of Financial administration?
A. Ripon B. Mayo
C. Curzon D. Lytton
7. Who is generally acknowledged as the pioneer of local-self government in modern India?
A. Ripon B. Mayo
C. Lytton D. Curzon
8. Which Act created the official legislature in India?
A. Indian Councils Act, 1861
B. Indian Councils Act, 1892
C. Charter Act 1833
D. Charter Act 1853
9. Who among the following did not belong to the so-called "Indian School" which favoured a limited paternalistic role for the collector as opposed to his limited role of the "English school"?
A. Thomas Munro B. Elphistone
C. Cornawallis D. John Lawrence
10. When did the practice of holding I.C.S. examinations simultaneously in England as well as in India begin?
A. 1912 B. 1922
C. 1932 D. 1935
11. During which period did India properly witness the process of "Deindustrialisation due to British economic policies?
A. 1600 – 1715 B. 1757 – 1813
C. 1813 – 1860 D. 1860 – 1947
12. Warren Hasting's experiment of actioning the right to collect revenue to the higher bidder is almost similar to:
A. poligar system of Vijayanagar empire
B. Iqta system of Delhi Sultans
C. Jagir system of Mughals
D. Ijara system of Mughals
13. The British restarted to the "Downward Filtration Theory" till 1854 to justify one of their colonial policies in India?
A. Social policy
B. Commercial policy
C. Industrial policy
D. Educational policy
14. Who was the president of the Board of Revenue when Lord Cornawallis introduced permanent settlement in Bengal and Bihar?
A. Sir John Shore
B. Sir Metcalfe
C. Sir Charles Napier
D. Sir Denison
15. Who was mainly responsible for the introduction of the Ryotwari-System in Madras?
A. Eliphinstone B. Thomas Munro
C. Macartny D. John Lawrence
16. Which of the following is not one of the

causes responsible for the rise of money-lenders in British India?

A. New Revenue Policy
B. New Legal System
C. New educational System
D. Commercialisation of agriculture

17. The proportion of agriculture labourers to agricultural population was:

A. The highest in Zamindari areas and lowest in the Ryotwari areas.
B. The highest in the Mahalwari areas and lowest in the Zamindari areas.
C. The highest in the Ryotwari areas and lowest in the Zamindari areas
D. The highest in Ryotwari areas and lowest in the Mahalwari areas.

18. Which one of the following is not result of the destruction of Indian handicraft industries by the British?

A. Depopulation and ruins of towns and cities
B. Rise of self-sufficient village economies
C. increase in unemployment
D. overcrowding agriculture

19. Who was the founder of the "Drain Theory" Which, among others, exposed the constant drain of wealth from India to England?

A. Dadabhai Naoroji
B. Gokhle
C. R.C. Dutt
D. S.N. Banerjee

20. Which one of the following was not one of the earliest-machine based modern industries to come into existence in India?

A. Cotton Textile Industry
B. Jute Industry
C. Iron and Steel Industry
D. Coal-Mining Industry

21. Which of the following was not a plantation industry in British India?

A. Indigo B. Tea
C. Coffee D. Salt-petre

22. The first telegraph line introduced by Lord Dalhousie in 1853 ran between?

A. Bombay and Thana
B. Calcutta and Madras
C. Bombay and Agra
D. Calcutta and Agra

23.

List I	List II
(a) Queen Victoria's proclamation	1. Lytton
(b) Statistical survey of India	2. Canning
(c) Strachey Faminine Commission	3. Mayo
(d) Repeal of the Vernacular Press Act	4. Ripon

Which of the above are incorrectly matched?

Codes:

A. All of them
B. 1, 2, 3
C. 2, 3, 4
D. 1, 3, 4

24. Match the following.

A. Scholarship Scheme	*(a)* Dufferin
B. Scheme of statutory civilians	*(b)* John Lawrence
C. Aitchison Commission	*(c)* Reading
D. Lee Commission	*(d)* Lytton

Codes:

	1	2	3	4
A.	*(a)*	*(c)*	*(d)*	*(b)*
B.	*(c)*	*(a)*	*(d)*	*(b)*
C.	*(d)*	*(b)*	*(c)*	*(a)*
D.	*(b)*	*(d)*	*(a)*	*(c)*

25. Assertion (A): In the mercantile stage of British Colonialism in India, large scale export of British goods to India was absent.

Reason (R): In the first stage of Colonialism the British did not introduce any basic change in India's economy society and culture.

Codes:

A. A and R are true and R is the correct explanation of A.
B. A and R are true but R is not the correct explanation of A.
C. A is true but R is false.

D. A is false but R is true.

26. **Assertion (A):** From 1813 onwards the economic as well as non-economic policies of the British in India were determined by the interests of the industrial bourgeoise of England.
Reason (R): In the second stage of British Colonialism, India was made an equal trading partner with England.
Codes:
A. A and R are true and R is the correct explanation of A.
B. A and R are true but R is not the correct explanation of A.
C. A is true but R is false.
D. A is false but R is true.

27. **Assertion (A):** The Court of directors established the East India College at Haileybury to replace the College of Fort William at Calcutta.
Reason (R): The Home government did not want to leave the task of establishing and consolidating British rule in India to the Indians.
Codes:
A. A and R are true and R is the correct explanation of A.
B. A and R are true but R is not the correct explanation of A.
C. A is true but R is false.
D. A is false but R is true.

28. **Assertion (A):** The British introduced a uniform civil code for all Indians irrespective of their different religions.
Reason (R): A law commission headed by lord Macaulay codified all the available Indian laws.
Codes:
A. A and R are true and R is the correct explanation of A.
B. A and R are true but R is not the correct explanation of A.
C. A is true but R is false.
D. A is false but R is true.

29. **Assertion (A):** The British government in India generally followed a policy of only partial transformation and cautions modernisation of Indian society.
Reason (R): All Englishmen, whether they were conservatives or radicals, desired the safety and perpetuation of British rule in India.
Codes:
A. A and R are true and R is the correct explanation of A.
B. A and R are true but R is not the correct explanation of A.
C. A is true but R is false.
D. A is false but R is true.

30. **Assertion (A):** English education made good progress in the three presidencies of Bengal, Bombay and Madras after 1844.
Reason (R): Lord Hardinge decided to give government employment to these Indians who were educated in English schools.
Codes:
A. A and R are true and R is the correct explanation of A.
B. A and R are true but R is not the correct explanation of A.
C. A is true but R is false.
D. A is false but R is true.

31. **Assertion (A):** Mass education hardly made any real progress all through the period of British rule in India.
Reason (R): The British government in India, generally followed a policy of opening a large number of elementary schools instead of a few Colleges.
Codes:
A. A and R are true and R is the correct explanation of A.
B. A and R are true but R is not the correct explanation of A.
C. A is true but R is false.
D. A is false but R is true.

32. **Assertion (A):** Wood's despatch of 1854 is generally known as the "Magna Carta" of English education in India.
Reason (R): It outlined a comprehensive plan for the future development of education system in India.

Codes:

A. A and R are true and R is the correct explanation of A.

B. A and R are true but R is not the correct explanation of A.

C. A is true but R is false.

D. A is false but R is true.

33. Assertion (A): Under the Zamindari system, the revenue collectors and other intermediaries in revenue administration were overnight converted into landlords.

Reason (R): Under this system, the Zamindar could keep for himself only $^1/_{11}$th of the rental that he got from the peasantry, while paying 10/11th of it to the government.

Codes:

A. A and R are true and R is the correct explanation of A.

B. A and R are true but R is not the correct explanation of A.

C. A is true but R is false.

D. A is false but R is true.

34. Assertion (A): The permanent settlement is said to have intially resulted in increased agricultural production.

Reason (R): In this system, the Zamindar could keep for himself any increase in the rental of his estate.

Codes:

A. A and R are true and R is the correct explanation of A.

B. A and R are true but R is not the correct explanation of A.

C. A is true but R is false.

D. A is false but R is true.

35. Assertion (A): In the Ryotwari areas, the peasant had to pay land revenue to the government when his produce was totally or partially destroyed.

Reason (R): Under the Ryotwari system the land-revenue demand of the government was fixed.

Codes:

A. A and R are true and R is the correct explanation of A.

B. A and R are true but R is not the correct explanation of A.

C. A is true but R is false.

D. A is false but R is true.

36. Assertion (A): In the Mahalwari areas each peasant was individualy responsible to the government for the payment of revenue.

Reason (R): In these areas the government resumed the right to revise land revenue demand periodically.

Codes:

A. A and R are true and R is the correct explanation of A.

B. A and R are true but R is not the correct explanation of A.

C. A is true but R is false.

D. A is false but R is true.

37. Assertion (A): Under the new land as well as land revenue systems, the peasant was in constant need of finding ways to get money.

Reason (R): The right of modern industries in England resulted in a growing demand for raw materials from India.

Codes:

A. A and R are true and R is the correct explanation of A.

B. A and R are true but R is not the correct explanation of A.

C. A is true but R is false.

D. A is false but R is true.

38. Who among the following governor generals created the covenated Civil Service of India, which came to be known as Indian Civil Service from 1861 onwards?

A. Bentinck B. Wellesley

C. Cornawallis D. Warren Hastings

39. Who was responsible for the establishment of the college of Fort William at Calcutta to train the young Civil Servants of India?

A. Wellesley B. Dalhousie

C. Bentinck D. Cornawallis

40. During whose viceroyship did the High

Courts came into existence at the three presidential cities of Calcutta, Madras and Bombay?
A. Warren Hastings
B. John Lawrence
C. Dalhousie
D. Canning

41. Who passed the widown remarriage act?
A. Canning B. Dalhousie
C. Auckland D. Bentinck

42. Johnthan Duncan founded the Sanskrit College in 1792 at
A. Calcutta B. Allahabad
C. Bombay D. Varanasi

43. When did the British make English the medium of instruction in India?
A. 1813 B. 1833
C. 1835 D. 1844

44. Who among the following gave official Sanction to the educaiton of girls in India?
A. Dalhousie
B. William Bentinck
C. Hardinge
D. Ellenborough

45. Sir Charles Wood, who drafted the educational dispatch of 1854, was then
A. Secretary of state for India
B. President of the Court of Directors
C. President of the Board of Control
D. Prime Minister of England

46. **Assertion (A):** The commercialisation of Indian agriculture during the British period adversely affected the economic positon of the peasant.
Reason (R): The commercialisation, besides making the peasants heavily dependant on the middleman for the sale of his product, made him subject to all the viscitudes of the erratic Indian as well as world market.
Codes:
A. A and R are true and R is the correct explanation of A.
B. A and R are true but R is not the correct explanation of A.
C. A is true but R is false.
D. A is false but R is true.

47. **Assertion (A):** After the acquisition of the Diwani of Bengal, the Company directly organised the "Drain of wealth".
Reason (R): After 1765, the company began to send to England the revenue of Bengal through what are called investments.
Codes:
A. A and R are true and R is the correct explanation of A.
B. A and R are true but R is not the correct explanation of A.
C. A is true but R is false.
D. A is false but R is true.

48. The Charter Act of 1883 did:
1. complete the process of throwing open the Indian trade to all British subjects.
2. rename the Governor-General of Fort William as the Governer-General of India.
3. allow the different presidencies to make laws for themselves.
4. include a law member to the council of the Governor-General.

Codes:
A. 1 and 4 B. 2, 3 and 4
C. 1, 2 and 4 D. 2 and 3

49. Match the followings.

(a) First Governor General of Fort William	1. Lord Macauly
(b) First Chief Justice of Supreme Court	2. Lord Canning
(c) First law member of the Governor-General's Council	3. Warren Hastings
(d) First Viceroy as well as the Governor-General of India	4. Eligah Impey

Codes:

	(a)	*(b)*	*(c)*	*(d)*
A.	3	1	4	2
B.	3	4	2	1
C.	2	4	1	3
D.	3	4	1	2

50. Match the followings.

List I	*List II*
(a) Appointment of a separate Lt. Governor for Bengal	1. Charter Act of 1813
(b) Provision of an annual sum of one lakh rupees for the spread of education	2. Charter Act of 1853
(c) Abolition of the Board of Control and Court of Directors	3. Government of India Act of 1858
(d) Introduction of the Portfolio system	4. Indian Councils Act-1861.

Codes:

	(a)	*(b)*	*(c)*	*(d)*
A.	3	2	4	1
B.	3	1	2	4
C.	1	2	3	4.
D.	4	1	3	2

51. Which codes gives the correct pairing of the following lists?

(a) Establishment of the imperial Legislative Council and the Provincial Legislative Councils	1. Charter Act of 1853
(b) Introduction of the system of the direct recruitment to ICS through a compitative exam.	2. Government of India Act 1858
(c) Appointment of a Secretary of State for India	3. Indian Councils Act of 1861
(d) Introduction of the Separate Electorates for the Muslims	4. Indian Council Act, 1909

Codes:

	(a)	*(b)*	*(c)*	*(d)*
A.	3	1	2	4
B.	2	1	3	4
C.	2	4	1	3
D.	1	3	2	4

52. Arrange the following in the chronological order

1. appointment of High Commissioner of India at London.
2. Establishment of direct telegraph link between India and England.
3. Establishment of a Federal Court at Delhi.
4. Introduction of an element of direct elections to the legislative councils.

Codes:

A. 2, 3 and 4 B. 4, 2, 1 and 3
C. 2, 4, 1 and 3 D. 4, 2, 3 and 1

53. Assertion (A): William Bentinck was the first one to be called Governor-General of India.

Reason (R): He also had the additional charge of the Governorship of Bengal.

Codes:

A. A and R are true and R is the correct explanation of A.
B. A and R are true but R is not the correct explanation of A.
C. A is true but R is false.
D. A is false but R is true.

54. Assertion (A): The charter Act of 1853 deprived the court of Directors of its right to appoint and recall officials in India.

Reason (R): The charter empowered the Governor-General to appoint and dismiss the high officials in India.

Codes:

A. A and R are true and R is the correct explanation of A.
B. A and R are true but R is not the correct explanation of A.
C. A is true but R is false.
D. A is false but R is true.

55. Assertion (A): Lord Dalhousie was the first real Governor-General of India.

Reason (R): He was the first Governor-General of India without any additional charge.

Codes:

A. A and R are true and R is the correct explanation of A.
B. A and R are true but R is not the correct explanation of A.
C. A is true but R is false.
D. A is false but R is true.

56. Assertion (A): The "India Council" an advisory body to the secretary of the state for India, consisted of 15 members.

Reason (R): Half of its members were Indian.

Codes:

A. A and R are true and R is the correct explanation of A.

B. A and R are true but R is not the correct explanation of A.

C. A is true but R is false.

D. A is false but R is true.

57. Assertion (A): The Indian Councils Act of 1892 allowed the Legislative Council at the centre and the provinces to discuss and vote the Budget.

Reason (R): The Act of 1892 retained officials majority in the legislative councils at both the central and provincial levels.

Codes:

A. A and R are true and R is the correct explanation of A.

B. A and R are true but R is not the correct explanation of A.

C. A is true but R is false.

D. A is false but R is true.

58. Assertion (A): The Morley-Minto reforms removed the official majority in the imperial legislative council.

Reason (R): Even after the Act of 1909 majority of the non-officials in the imperial legislative council were indirectly elected.

Codes:

A. A and R are true and R is the correct explanation of A.

B. A and R are true but R is not the correct explanation of A.

C. A is true but R is false.

D. A is false but R is true.

59. Assertion (A): The central legislative was made more representative by the Mont-Ford reforms.

Reason (R): The Montford reforms increased the non-official elected majority in the central legislature.

Codes:

A. A and R are true and R is the correct explanation of A.

B. A and R are true but R is not the correct explanation of A.

C. A is true but R is false.

D. A is false but R is true.

60. Assertion (A): From 1919, the Secretary of state for India began to draw his salary from the British exchequer.

Reason (R): The High Commissioner of India at London was paid, from the beginning by Indian government.

Codes:

A. A and R are true and R is the correct explanation of A.

B. A and R are true but R is not the correct explanation of A.

C. A is true but R is false.

D. A is false but R is true.

61. Assertion (A): The Montford reforms introduced "Dyarchy" at the both the central and provincial levels.

Reason (R): In 1919, the provinces were given the power of looking after certain subjects of administration by way of delegation from the centre.

Codes:

A. A and R are true and R is the correct explanation of A.

B. A and R are true but R is not the correct explanation of A.

C. A is true but R is false.

D. A is false but R is true.

62. Assertion (A): The Government of India Act, 1935 introduced provincial autonomy.

Reason (R): The Act itself made a clear-cut division of powers between the centre and the provinces.

Codes:

A. A and R are true and R is the correct explanation of A.

B. A and R are true but R is not the correct explanation of A.

C. A is true but R is false.

D. A is false but R is true.

63. "Reserved Subjects" under Dyarchy in the provinces were administered by the Governor and his executive council. Which of the following were included in them?

1. Law and order 2. Land revenue
3. Agriculture 4. Irrigation
5. Industries

Codes:

A. 1, 2 and 3 B. 1, 2 and 4
C. 1, 2 and 5 D. 1, 4 and 5

64. The "Transferred Subjects" were to be looked after by the Governor and his council of ministers. Which of the following was not/were not included in them?

1. Education
2. Forests
3. Local Self-Government
4. Jails
5. Public Health and Sanitation

Codes:

A. 2 B. 2 and 3
C. 4 D. 2 and 4

65. In which of the following provinces was, "Bicameralism" introduced for the first time in 1935?

a. Bengal
b. Punjab
c. Uttar Pradesh
d. Bihar
e. Central provinces
f. Assam

Codes:

A. *a*, *b*, *c* and *e* B. *a*, *c*, *d* and *f*
C. *a*, *b*, *d* and *e* D. *a*, *d*, *e* and *f*

66. In 1935, the principle of separate electorates were extended to

1. Sikhs 2. Untouchables
3. Europeans 4. Indian Christians
5. Anglo-Indians

Codes:

A. 1, 2, 3 and 5 B. 1, 3 and 5
C. 1, 3, 4 and 5 D. 3, 4 and 5

67. During whose period did the European soldiers staged the so called 'white Mutiny' in India?

A. Dalhousie B. Canning
C. Mayo D. Ripon

68. What is the chronological order of the following Governor-generals?

1. Minto 2. John Shore
3. Cornawallis 4. Warren Hastings
5. Lord Hastings 6. Wellesly

Codes:

A. 4, 3, 2, 6 and 4 B. 4, 2, 3, 6, 1 and 5
C. 4, 6, 2, 3, 5 and 1 D. 4, 5, 1, 3, 6 and 2

69. Arrange the following Governor-General in the chronological sequence?

1. Ellenlorough I
2. William Bentinck
3. Canning
4. Auckland
5. Dalhousie
6. Harding I

Codes:

A. 4, 2, 5, 6, 1 and 3
B. 6, 1, 2, 5, 4 and 3
C. 2, 4, 1, 6, 5 and 3
D. 5, 2, 6, 4, 1 and 3

70. What is the historical order of the following Vice-roys.

1. North Brook 2. Dufferin
3. Lytton 4. Mayo
5. Ripon

Codes:

A. 2, 5, 3, 1 and 4 B. 5, 1, 3, 4 and 2
C. 3, 2, 4, 1 and 5 D. 4, 1, 3, 5 and 2

71. Arrange the following events of Warren Hasting's period in the chronological sequence:

1. Begum's of Awadh affair
2. Nandkumar episode
3. Chait Singh affair
4. Rohilla War
5. Foundation of the Asiatic society of Bengal

Codes:

A. 4, 2, 3, 1 and 5 B. 2, 1, 3, 5 and 4
C. 3, 2, 5, 4 and 1 D. 5, 2, 4, 1 and 3

72. Which is the historical order of the following social and humanitarian events of British period?

1. Prohibition of Human Sacrifice
2. Prohibition of Sati
3. Prohibition of Female infantacide
4. Passage of Native marriage Act
5. Passage of widow remarriage Act

Codes:

A. 2, 4, 1, 3 and 5
B. 3, 1, 2, 4 and 5

C. 1, 2, 3, 5 and 4
D. 2, 3, 1, 5 and 4

73. Match the following List I with List II.

List I	*List II*
1. Cornawallis	*a.* Subsidiary alliance System
2. Wellesley	*b.* Doctrine of Lapse
3. William Bentinck	*c.* Separation of Judicial administration
4. Dalhousie	*d.* Abolition of the provincial courts of appeal and circuit

Codes:

	(1)	(2)	(3)	(4)
A.	*a*	*c*	*d*	*b*
B.	*c*	*a*	*d*	*b*
C.	*c*	*a*	*b*	*d*
D.	*a*	*c*	*b*	*d*

74. Match the following List I with List II.

List I	*List II*
1. Bombay Presidency	*a.* William Bentinck
2. Madras Presidency	*b.* Dalhousie
3. Agra province	*c.* Wallesley
4. Public Works Department	*d.* Hastings
	e. Cornawallis

Codes:

	(1)	(2)	(3)	(4)
A.	*a*	*d*	*b*	*e*
B.	*b*	*e*	*c*	*d*
C.	*d*	*c*	*a*	*b*
D.	*c*	*b*	*d*	*a*

75. Match the following List I with ListII.

List I	*List II*
1. Gorkha War	*a.* Metcalfe
2. Supression of Thugi	*b.* Hastings
3. Freedom of Indian Press	*c.* Dalhousie
4. Introduction of Postal System	*d.* Bentinck

Codes:

	(1)	(2)	(3)	(4)
A.	*c*	*b*	*d*	*a*
B.	*b*	*d*	*c*	*a*
C.	*d*	*b*	*a*	*c*
D.	*b*	*d*	*a*	*c*

ANSWERS

1	2	3	4	5	6	7	8	9	10
B	D	C	A	D	B	A	D	C	B
11	**12**	**13**	**14**	**15**	**16**	**17**	**18**	**19**	**20**
C	D	D	A	B	C	D	B	A	C
21	**22**	**23**	**24**	**25**	**26**	**27**	**28**	**29**	**30**
D	D	B	D	A	C	B	D	A	A
31	**32**	**33**	**34**	**35**	**36**	**37**	**38**	**39**	**40**
C	A	B	A	C	D	B	C	A	B
41	**42**	**43**	**44**	**45**	**46**	**47**	**48**	**49**	**50**
D	D	C	A	C	A	A	C	D	B
51	**52**	**53**	**54**	**55**	**56**	**57**	**58**	**59**	**60**
A	C	B	C	A	C	D	D	A	B
61	**62**	**63**	**64**	**65**	**66**	**67**	**68**	**69**	**70**
D	A	B	D	B	C	B	A	C	D
71	**72**	**73**	**74**	**75**					
A	D	B	C	D					

THE REVOLT AGAINST BRITISH RULE

1. When was the new Enfield Rifle with greased cartridges introduced in the British Indian Army?
A. November1856 B. December 1857
C. January 1857 D. February 1857

2. Which of the following events before the Revolt of 1857 gave jolts to the British armed strength?
1. First Afghan War
2. Anglo-Sikh War
3. First Anglo-Burmese War
4. Grivean War
5. Santhal uprising
6. Third Anglo-Maratha War

Codes:
A. 1, 2, 3 and 6 B. 2, 3, 5 and 6
C. 3, 4, 5 and 6 D. 1, 2, 4 and 5

3. Which of the following were the grievances of the sepoys?
1. Discrimination in payment and pensions.
2. Mistreatment of Sepoys by the British officials.
3. Refusal of the British to pay "Bhatta" while fighting in remote regions.
4. British governments order requiring the sepoys to serve overseas when required.
5. Encouragement given to chirstian missionaries by British army officers.

Codes:
A. 1, 2 and 5 B. 1, 3 and 4
C. 2, 3 and 5 D. All of them

4. Which of the following statements about Mangal Pandey are incorrect?
1. He was a sepoy in the 19th Native infantry stationed at Berhampur.
2. In March 1857, he single handely revolted and killed two English officer.
3. He made a futile attempt to commit suicide when he realised the hopelessness of the situation.
4. He was executed by the British.

Codes:
A. 1 and 2 B. 2 and 3
C. 1 and 4 D. 1 and 3

5. The annexation of some Indian states by Dalhousie was cancelled by the court of Directors. Who were they?
1. Sambalpur 2. Baghat
3. Nagpur 4. Udaipur
5. Jhansi

Codes:
A. 2, 3 and 4 B. 2, 3 and 5
C. 1 and 2 D. 2 and 4

6. What is the chronological sequence in which following places witnessed sepoy revolts?
1. Naushera 2. Delhi
3. Meerut 4. Hoti Mardan

Codes:
A. 2, 3, 1 and 4 B. 3, 2, 1 and 4
C. 4, 3, 2 and 1 D. 1, 3, 4 and 2

7. Which of the following Acts were passed by the British Government in 1856?
1. Hindu widow remarriage Act
2. Abolition of Sati
3. Religious Disabilities Act
4. General service enlistment Act

Codes:
A. 1 and 2 B. 2 and 4
C. 1, 3 and 4 D. 1, 2 and 3

8. Which of the following statements about Nana Saheb are true?
(a) Nana Saheb was the adopted son of the last Peshwa
(b) The original name of Nana Saheb was Dhonda Pandit
(c) The last Peshwa Baji Rao-II, was murdered by Nana Saheb
(d) Dalhousie refused to recognise Nana Saheb as his Peshwa and suspended his pension.

A. *(a), (b), (c)* B. *(a), (b), (d)*
C. *(b), (c), (d)* D. *(a), (c), (d)*

9. What was the ratio of the Indian Sepoys to the Europeans in the British Indian army on the eve of the outbreak of the revolt of 1857?

A. 4 : 1 B. 5 : 1
C. 6 : 1 D. 7 : 1

10. At Delhi the Mughal Emperor's wife is said to have sabotaged the work of the rebels by acting as the informer to the British. What is her name?

A. Hazarat Mahal B. Zinnat Mahal
C. Mumtaz Mahal D. Fatima Begum

11. Which of the following statements about Maulavi Ahmedullah are correct?

1. He was a native of Delhi.
2. Just before the outbreak of the revolt of 1857, he led a minor revolt of the people against the Birtish at Faizabad.
3. He was one of the main leaders of the rebels at Lucknow and after its fall at Bareilly during the revolt.
4. He was caught and executed by the British after the revolt.

Codes:

A. 2 and 3 B. 1 and 4
C. 1 and 3 D. 3 and 4

12. Which of the following statements about Kanpur during the revolt of 1857 are true?

1. The besieged British surrendered to the rebels after a few days of resistance.
2. Despite Nana Saheb's promise of safe conduct to Allahabad, all the English men were murdered by the rebel sepoys while the former were leaving Kanpur in Boats.
3. After a brief period of confinement, all the English women and children were put to death by the followers of Nana Saheb.
4. The British after defeating Nana Saheb, reoccupied Kanpur in July 1857.
5. The mutinious Gwalior regiment under Tatia Tope tried to capture it from the British in November 1857 but failed.

Codes:

A. 1, 2, 3 and 4 B. 1, 2, 4 and 5
C. 2, 3, 4 and 5 D. 1, 3, 4 and 5

13. Arrange the following places of revolt in the chronological order:

1. Mathura 2. Jhansi
3. Bareilly 4. Kanpur

Codes:

A. 1, 3, 4 and 2 B. 2, 4, 1 and 3
C. 3, 2, 1 and 4 D. 4, 2, 3 and 1

14. Match the list:

List I	***List II***
(a) Lt. Baugh	1. The officer who blew up the magazine at Delhi so that would not fall into the hands of sepoys
(b) Colonel	2. The officer who murdered Mughal emperor's sons after the re-capture of Delhi
(c) Lt. Willoughby	3. The officer who was severely wounded by Mangal Pandey.
(d) Lt. Hudson	4. The commanding officer of the 11th Native Infantry at Meerut and who was killed by the Sepoys.

Codes:

	(a)	*(b)*	*(c)*	*(d)*
A.	4	1	2	3
B.	1	2	3	4
C.	3	4	1	2
D.	2	3	4	1

15. Which of the following are correctly matched?

List I	List II
1. Nana Saheb	Kanpur
2. Begam Hazarat Mahal	Lucknow
3. Rani Lakshmi Bai	Jhansi
4. Khan Bahadur Khan	Arrah
5. Kunwar Singh	Bareilly

Codes:

A. All of them B. 1, 2 and 3
C. 2, 3 and 4 D. 3, 4 and 5

16. Which of the following statements about Bakht Khan are true?

1. He was an ordinary Subedar in the British Army
2. He led the revolt to the Sepoys at

Meerut and brought them to Delhi

3. He was the defacto leader of the Sepoys at Delhi, the nominal leader being the Mughal Emperor.
4. After the re-capture of Delhi by the British, he went to Awadh and died fighting the British in May, 1859.

Codes:

A. 1 and 2 B. 3 and 4
C. 1, 3 and 4 D. 2, 3 and 4

17. Match the following.

List I	List II
(a) Azimullah Khan	1. A relative of Mughal emperor
(b) Ahmad Ullah	2. Nephew of Nana Saheb
(c) Amar Singh	3. Adviser of Nana Saheb
(d) Firoz Shah	4. Adiviser of the Ex-Nawab of Awadh
(e) Rao Saheb	5. Brother of Kunwar Singh

Codes:

	(a)	*(b)*	*(c)*	*(d)*	*(e)*
A.	3	5	4	2	1
B.	5	4	3	1	2
C.	4	3	5	1	2
D.	3	4	5	1	2

18. Made the following places with the Britishers who recaptured them using the codes given below:

(a) Gwalior	1. Sir Colin Campbell
(b) Bareilly	2. William Taylor
(c) Arrah	3. Brig. General Neil
(d) Banaras	4. Sir Hugh Rose
	5. General Nicholson

Codes:

	(a)	*(b)*	*(c)*	*(d)*
A.	2	4	3	5
B.	1	3	2	4
C.	5	4	1	2
D.	4	1	2	3

19. Which of the following statements about Tantia Tope are true?

1. He was the brother of Nana Saheb
2. After the fall of Kanpur to the British, he joined Rani Lakshmi Bai against the British
3. After losing Gwalior, he escaped to Central India and carried on Guearrilla War for 10 months.
4. He was betrayed and handed over to the British by Man Singh, a feaudotary of Sindhia
5. He was transported for life by British in April 1859.

Codes:

A. 1, 2 and 5 B. 2, 3 and 4
C. 2, 3 and 5 D. 2, 4 and 5

20. Which of the following were causes for the failure of the rebels in 1857-58?

1. Disorganisation
2. Indiscipline
3. Participation of masses
4. Common interests
5. Decentralised leadership
6. Use of traditional weapon

Codes:

A. 1, 2, 3 and 5
B. 2, 3, 4, 5 and 6
C. 2, 3, 5 and 6
D. 2, 3, 4 and 6

21. Which of the following regions/presidencies did not participate in the revolt of 1857?

1. Bengal 2. Madras
3. Bombay 4. Central India
5. Western Punjab 6. Rajputana

Codes:

A. 1, 2, 3, 5 and 6 B. 2, 3, 4, 5 and 6
C. 2, 3, 5 and 6 D. 2, 4, 5 and 6

22. Which of the following Prime Ministers of Native states cooperated with the British in supressing the revolt of 1857?

1. Sir Dinkar Rao
2. Sir Khan Bahadur
3. Sir Salar Jang
4. Sir Tang Bahadur

Codes:

A. 1, 2 and 3 B. 2, 3 and 4
C. 1, 3 and 4 D. 1, 2 and 4

23. Which of the following rulers of Indian States cooperated with the British in supressing the revolt of 1857?

1. Nizam of Hyderabad

2. Sindhia of Gwalior
3. Holkar of Indore
4. Ex-Nawab of Rohilkhand
5. Gulab Singh of Kashmir
6. Raja of Jodhpur

Codes:

A. 1, 2, 4, 5 and 6 B. 1, 2, 3, 4 and 6
C. 1, 3, 4, 5 and 6 D. 2, 3, 4, 5 and 6

24. Which of the following classes did not participate in the Revolt of 1857?

1. Money Lenders
2. Merchants
3. Modern Intelligentsia
4. Agricultural Labourers
5. Urban based absentee landlords

Codes:

A. 1, 2, 3 and 5 B. 2, 3, 4 and 5
C. 1, 3, 4 and 5 D. 1, 2, 3 and 4

25. Which of the following classes participated in the Revolt of 1857?

1. Peasants
2. Capitalists
3. Handicraftsmen
4. Traditional Zamindars
5. Dispossed rulers

Codes:

A. 1, 3 and 5 B. 2, 4 and 5
C. 1, 2, 4 and 5 D. 1, 3, 4 and 5

26. Which of the following British officers lost their lines at Lucknow?

1. General John Nicolson
2. Brig. General Neil
3. Major General Havelock
4. Sir Henry Lawrence

Codes:

A. All of them B. 1, 2 and 3
C. 2, 3 and 4 D. 1, 3 and 4

27. Who among the following British officers lost their lines at Lucknow

1. General John Nicolson
2. Brig. General Neil
3. Major General Havelock
4. Sir Henry Lawrence

Codes:

A. All of them B. 1, 2 and 3
C. 2, 3 and 4 D. 1, 3 and 4

28. **Assertion (A):** The Sikh army rendered valuable service to the British in the suppression of the revolt of 1857.

Reason (R): Sir Henry Lawrence, the chief Commissioner of Punjab during the revolt, failed to maintain peace in Punjab.

Codes:

A. A and R are true and R is the correct explanation of A.
B. A and R are true but R is not the correct explanation of A.
C. A is true but R is false.
D. A is false but R is true.

29. **Assertion (A):** The British remained as perpetual foreigners in India.

Reason (R): Some of the foreign conquerers of India, like Mughals and Delhi Sultans, made India their home.

Codes:

A. A and R are true and R is the correct explanation of A.
B. A and R are true but R is not the correct explanation of A.
C. A is true but R is false.
D. A is false but R is true.

30. **Assertion (A):** The Indian middle and upper classes were totally excluded from high administrative and military post by the British.

Reason (R): Many of the traditional Zamindars lost their Zamindaries to the new class of urban based absent landlords.

Codes:

A. A and R are true and R is the correct explanation of A.
B. A and R are true but R is not the correct explanation of A.
C. A is true but R is false.
D. A is false but R is true.

31. Which of the following were the main factors for the success of the British in supressing the revolt of 1857?

1. Immense resources
2. Superior military weapons and techniques
3. Able leadership
4. Assistance of some of the Indian rulers
5. End of Crimean War which enabled

them to concentrate most of their troops in India.

Codes:

A. 1, 2 and 4 B. 2, 3 and 5
C. 1, 3 and 4 D. All of them

32. **Assertion (A):** The faulty deployment of troops on the eve of the revolt of 1857 may be considered as one of the main causes for the revolt.

Reason (R): Those was only an insignificant number of European soldiers compared to that of the sepoys at important military centres like Delhi and Allahabad on the eve of the revolt.

Codes:

A. A and R are true and R is the correct explanation of A.
B. A and R are true but R is not the correct explanation of A.
C. A is true but R is false.
D. A is false but R is true.

33. **Assertion (A):** The British though introduced a unitary or highly centralised system of Government of India, continued to follow up the policy of divide and rule.

Reason (R): The British refused to pay foreign service allowence to the Indian sepoys while they were fighting in the remote regions like Punjab and Sind.

Codes:

A. A and R are true and R is the correct explanation of A.
B. A and R are true but R is not the correct explanation of A.
C. A is true but R is false.
D. A is false but R is true.

34. Who was the famous Urdu Poet who witnessed the massacare of male civilians of Delhi by the British soldiers after it was recaptured?

A. Firak Gorakhpuri
B. Josh Malihabadi
C. Mirza Ghalib
D. Mir Babar Ali Anis

35. **Assertion (A):** In some places artisans and craftsmen participated in the revolt of 1857.

Reason (R): The British policy of "one way" free trade destroyed village industries and handicrafts in India.

Codes:

A. A and R are true and R is the correct explanation of A.
B. A and R are true but R is not the correct explanation of A.
C. A is true but R is false.
D. A is false but R is true.

36. **Assertion (A):** The British followed a policy of religious prosecution of Hindus and Muslims in the army in order to forcibly convert them into chirstians.

Reason (R): The British Government gave full protection and encouragement to the christian missionaries in India.

Codes:

A. A and R are true and R is the correct explanation of A.
B. A and R are true but R is not the correct explanation of A.
C. A is true but R is false.
D. A is false but R is true.

37. Who was the British General who esteemed Rani "Lakshmi Bai of Jhansi as the best and bravest military leader of the rebels"?

A. Sir Colin Campbell
B. Major General Havelock
C. Sir James Outram
D. Sir Hugh Rose

38. **Assertion (A):** The immediate cause of the revolt of 1857 was the introduction of the New Enfield Rifle in the British Indian Army.

Reason (R): The sepoys were required to before loading the cartridge into the new rifle, bite off its end which was feared to have been greased with the fat of cows and Pigs.

Codes:

A. A and R are true and R is the correct explanation of A.
B. A and R are true but R is not the correct explanation of A.
C. A is true but R is false.
D. A is false but R is true.

39. Who wrote the following passage?

"In no instance it is a friendly glance directed to the white man's carriage ____ oh! that language of the eye; who can doubt, who can misinterpret it"?

A. G.B. Malleson B. J.W. Kaye
C. W.H. Russell D. T.R. Holmes

40. Which of the following statement about Rao Bharmal are not true?

1. He was the ruler of Mandu in central India.
2. He revolted due to the frequent interference of the British in the internal affairs of his state.
3. He was defeated and killed in a battle with the British.
4. The British imposed a subsidiary treaty on his successor.

Codes:

A. 1 and 2 B. 3 and 4
C. 1 and 3 D. 2 and 4

41. Which of the following statements about Velu Thambi are true?

1. He was the Raja of Travancore State.
2. He revolted because of British demand for his removal.
3. Despite the stiff resistance put up by his forces, Trivandrum the Capital of Travancore, fell to the British forces.
4. He was caputured and executed by the British.

Codes:

A. 2 and 3 B. 1 and 3
C. 2 and 4 D. 3 and 4

42. Arrange in correct sequence:

1. Revolt of Rao Bharmal
2. Revolt of Velu Thambi
3. Rebellion of Birabhadra Rauze
4. Rebellion of Kattabomman

Codes:

A. 4, 2, 1 and 3 B. 2, 3 4 and 1
C. 3, 1, 2 and 4 D. 1, 4, 2 and 3

43. Arrange the following revolts in the correct sequence:

1. Satara disturbances
2. Sambalpur outbreak
3. Bundela revolt
4. Gadkhari rebellion

Codes:

A. 2, 3, 4 and 1 B. 4, 2, 1 and 3
C. 1, 3, 2 and 4 D. 2, 1, 3 and 4

44. Which of the following statements about Virapandya Kattaboman are true?

1.. He was the ruler of Panchalakurichi in the Tirrunelvelli district of Tamil Nadu.
2. He revolted because of British attempts to impose their sovereignty over him.
3. In the end he was captured and executed by the British.
4. The territory was restored to one of his minor sons.

Codes:

A. All of them B. 2 and 4
C. 2 and 3 D. 3 and 4

45. Who was the author of the Book, "The Indian War of Independence 1857"?

A. Sir Sayyed Ahmed Khan
B. V.D. Savarkar
C. S.R. Sharma
D. R.C. Majumdar

46. Match the following.

List I	List II
(a) Chittur Singh	1. Leader of Kittur revolt
(b) Channama	2. Leader of Satara outbreak
(c) Dhar Rao Pawar	3. Leader of Bundel rebellion
(d) Madhukar Shah	4. Leader of Ramosi revolt

Codes:

	(a)	(b)	(c)	(d)
A.	4	2	1	3
B.	4	1	2	3
C.	1	2	4	3
D.	2	3	1	4

47. Which of the following statements about the Paiks are true?

1. They were a militia class in Orissa occupying rent free land under the Zamindar
2. After the British occupation of Orrisa, they were also required to pay land revenue to the British

3. They revolted first under the leadership of the Raja of Parlakimedi
4. In their second revolt, they defeated the British forces and occupied Puri for a short period.

Codes:

A. 1, 2 and 3 B. 1, 2 and 4
C. 2, 3 and 4 D. 1, 3 and 4

48. Arrange the following revolts in the chronological order?

1. Kittur Rising 2. Ramosi Revolt
3. Paik Rebellion 4. Satavadi Revolt

Codes:

A. 2, 4, 1 and 3 B. 4, 2, 3 and 1
C. 1, 3, 4 and 2 D. 3, 2, 1 and 4

49. Which of the following statements about Ramosis are true?

1. Under the Peshwa they served in the inferior ranks of police.
2. After the annexation of Peshwa's territory, the British despensed with their service.
3. Their revolt created serious disturbances in Poona and the surrounding areas for quite sometime.
4. All the Ramosis who participated in the revolt were finally captured and executed by the British.

Codes:

A. 1, 2 and 3 B. 2, 3 and 4
C. 1, 2 and 4 D. 1, 3 and 4

50. The British attached the Zamindari and property of a number of Zamindars for non-payment of revenue, resulting in the revolt of those Zamindars against the British. Which of the following Zamindars fall under this category?

1. Zamindar of Palkonda
2. Zamindar of Kurnool
3. Zamindar of Parlakimedi
4. Zamindar of Gumsur

Codes:

A. 1, 2, 3 B. 2, 3, 4
C. 1, 2, 4 D. 1, 3, 4

51. Which of the following statements about the Fazari Movement are true?

1. It was founded in 1804.
2. In the beginning it was mainly a religious reform movement.
3. Its activities were confined to Bihar and Uttar Pradesh.
4. In the later stages, it was amalgmated with the Pagal Panthi movement.

Codes:

A. 1 and 3 B. 2 and 4
C. 1 and 3 D. 3 and 4

52. Arrange the following leaders of the Wahabi Movement in the chronological order?

1. Inayat Ali 2. Vilayat Ali
3. Abdullah 4. Sajid Ahmed
5. Maqsud Ali

Codes:

A. 4, 1, 2, 3 and 5 B. 2, 3, 1, 4 and 5
C. 1, 5, 3, 4 and 2 D. 4, 2, 1, 5 and 3

53. Which of the following statements about Wahabi movements are true?

1. It was founded in India in 1810 as a religo-political movement.
2. In its religious aspect, it was a reform movement to remove abuses from the Islamic Society.
3. In its political aspect, it was a movement to revive and restore muslim power in India.
4. The movement first began in Rohilkhand.

Codes:

A. 1, 2 and 3 B. 2, 3 and 4
C. 1, 2 and 4 D. 1, 3 and 4

54. Which of the following statements about Satara disturbances are incorrect?

1. The Satara disturbances were mainly due to the disposal and banishment of its popular rule by the British.
2. In 1840 the people of Satara revolted against the British.
3. The people of Satara revolted for a second time in 1845 and siezed Badami.
4. Satara was conquered and annexed by the British in 1845.

Codes:

A. 1 and 2 B. 3 and 4
C. 2 only D. 4 only

55. Which of the following is correctly matched?

A. Shivalinga Rudra — 1. The ruler of Satara who was deposed by the British

B. Pratap Singh 2. The ruler of Sambalpur who was deposed by the British
C. Mohan Kumari 3. The Desai of Kittur who died without leaving any male issue.
D. Khen Savant 4. The ruler of Satavandi who was deposed by the British.

56. Which of the following statements are true?
1. Kittur was a small chief-dom in Kathiawar
2. It's chief, known as the Desai, died without having any male issue of his own.
3. The British refused to recognise an adopted by as the Desai of Kittur and assumed the administration.
4. The supporters of the late Desai revolted and murdered some English officers.
5. The British suppressed the revolt, but restored Kittur to a descendant of the late Desai.

Codes:
A. 1, 2 and 4 B. 2, 3 and 4
C. 2, 3 and 5 D. 1, 2 and 5

57. Which of the following areas were affected by the Wahabi movement?
1. Bihar
2. Bengal
3. Assam
4. Punjab
5. Frontier Province North-West
6. Rajasthan
7. Deccan

Codes:
A. 1, 2, 3, 5 and 6 B. 1, 2, 5, 6 and 7
C. 1, 2, 4, 5 and 7 D. 1, 3, 4, 6 and 7

58. Which of the following were the leading personalities of the revolt of Satavandi?
1. Ram Kumar 2. Phond Savant
3. Appa Sahib 4. Anna Sahib
5. Karan Savant

Codes:
A. 1 and 2 B. 2 and 3
C. 2 and 4 D. 3 and 5

59. Which of the following statements about the Wahabis are true?
1. The Wahabis occupied a part of Punjab after the death of Ranjit Singh.
2. After the occupation of Punjab by the British, the Wahabis were defeated and expelled from Punjab by the British.
3. The Wahabis under Inayat Ali were defeated in a major encounter by the British.
4. Inayat Ali was captured and executed by the British.

Codes:
A. 1, 2 and 3 B. 2, 3 and 4
C. 1, 2 and 4 D. 1, 3 and 4

60. Which of the following statements about the Kukas are true?
1. Destruction of idols and shrines and murder of butchers by the Kukas brought them into open conflict with the British.
2. In January 1872, a group of Kukas openly revolted and attacked Malaudh and Kotla Killing some people.
3. 68 rebellions Kukas surrendered to the British unconditionally.
4. All the surrendered Kukas were given a general pardon by Mr. Cowan, Deputy commissioner of Ludhiana.

Codes:
A. 1, 2 and 3 B. 2, 3 and 4
C. 1, 2 and 4 D. 1, 3 and 4

61. Which of the following was included in the religious reforms of the Kukas?
1. Prohibition of all worship
2. Abolition of caste
3. Abstinence from meat, liquor and drugs.
4. Prohibition of free intercourse between the sexes.
5. Prohibition of intermarriage.

Codes:
A. 1, 2 and 3 B. 2, 3 and 4
C. 3, 4 and 5 D. 1, 2 and 4

62. Which of the following tribes lives in the Chota Nagpur area?
1. Hos 2. Garos

3. Kols 4. Mundas
5. Anganis 6. Oraons

Codes:

A. 1, 3, 4 and 5 B. 2, 3, 5 and 6
C. 1, 3, 4 and 6 D. 2, 3, 4 and 6

63. Who were the leaders of revolts of Khasis in 1820-32?

1. Tirut Singh 2. Shambhu Singh
3. Bar Manik 4. Bir Manik

Codes:

A. 1 and 3 B. 3 and 4
C. 1 and 3 D. 2 and 4

64. Arrange the following state trails of the Wahabis in the chronological sequence:

1. Patna Trail 2. Rajmahal Trail
3. Malda Trail 4. Ambala Trail

Codes:

A. 2, 1, 3 and 4 B. 4, 2, 1 and 3
C. 3, 2, 1 and 4 D. 4, 1, 3 and 2

65. Match the followings.

State Trail	**Wahabi Leaders**
(a) Malda trail	1. Yahya Ali
(b) Patna trail	2. Ahmadullah
(c) Rajmahal trail	3. Maulvi Amiruddin
(d) Ambala trail	4. Ibrahim Mandals

Codes:

	(a)	*(b)*	*(c)*	*(d)*
A.	1	4	2	3
B.	4	1	3	2
C.	3	2	4	1
D.	2	3	1	4

66. Which of the following statements about the leaders of the Kukas are incorrect?

1. Sian Sahib was succeeded by Balak Singh
2. Balak Singh was captured and executed by the British
3. Balak Singh was succeeded by Hari Singh
4. Ram Singh was the last leader of the Kukas.
5. Ram Singh was transported to Rangoon by the British.

Codes:

A. 1 and 3 B. 2 and 4
C. 1 and 5 D. 2 and 3

67. Which one of the Sikh Gurus was recognised the only true Guru of the Sikhs by the Kukas?

A. Guru Angad
B. Guru Amar Das
C. Guru Hargovind
D. Guru Govind Singh

68. Ram Singh did:

1. became the leader of Kukas in 1860
2. appoint 'Subas' the 'Naib Subas' to organise the sect in different parts of Punjab.
3. recruit a large number of jats as members of his sect.
4. import military training to his followers
5. died in 1885 at Ludhiana.

Codes:

A. 1, 2 and 4 B. 1, 2 and 5
C. 2, 3 and 4 D. 2, 4 and 5

69. Which of the following persons played a prominent role in the Santhal revolt?

1. Sidhu 2. Shambhu
3. Kahhu 4. Birsa
5. Jagat

Codes:

A. 1 and 2 B. 2 and 4
C. 1 and 3 D. 3 and 5

70. Which of the following were the main cause for the tribal revolts against the British?

1. Resentment of the tribals against extension of British rule to their areas.
2. Resentment against penetration of their areas by out-siders from the plains and against the protection given to these outsiders by the British
3. Resentment against the tightening British control over forest zone.
4. Resentment against British efforts to recruit unpaid labour for manual work.

A. 1, 2 and 3 B. 2, 3 and 4
C. 1, 3 and 4 D. All of them

71. Which tribe revolted due to British efforts to suppress the practice of human sacrifice?

A. Thado kukis B. Khonds
C. Oraons D. Naikdas

72. Which of the following statements about the Bhils of Banswara and Dungarpur in Southern Rajasthan are true?

1. Govind Guru began a purification

movement among them.
2. It soon developed in a political movement against the British.
3. They set up a Bhil Raj with Govind Guru as their head.
4. They British supressed their political movement through quick military action.

Codes:
A. 1, 2 and 3 B. 1, 2 and 4
C. 2, 3 and 4 D. 1, 3 and 4

73. Which of the follwing statements about Bisra Munda are true?
1. He founded a new religious sect with Sing Bonga as the only true God.
2. He was arrested and imprisoned by the British for his preaching among the Mundas.
3. After two years of imprisonment he escaped from the British prison and revived his preachings among the mundas.
4. The mundas under him revolted and attacked Churches and Police stations.

Codes:
A. 1, 2 and 3 B. 2, 3 and 4
C. 1, 2 and 4 D. 3, 4 and 5

74. Who was the leader of the revolt of the Oraons?
A. Jatra Bhagat B. Joria Bhagat
C. Kanhu Bhagat D. Buddh Bhagat

75. Which of the following statements about the Naikdas of Panchmahal are true?
1. They revolted against the British in 1858 under Rup Singh
2. Rup Singh conducted peace with the British in 1859.
3. They revolted again in 1868.
4. They set up one independent kingdom with Rup Singh as the spiritual head and Joria Bhagat as the temporal head
5. The British suppressed the revolted but pardoned Rup Singh and Joria Bhagat.

Codes:
A. 1, 2 and 3 B. 2, 3 and 4
C. 3, 4 and 5 D. 2, 4 and 5

76. Which tribal revolt is example of the reaction of the tribals to the activities of the christian missionaries in their areas?
A. Chenchu revolt B. Koya revolt
C. Munda revolt D. Chuar revolt

ANSWERS

1	**2**	**3**	**4**	**5**	**6**	**7**	**8**	**9**	**10**
C	D	D	A	D	B	C	B	D	B
11	**12**	**13**	**14**	**15**	**16**	**17**	**18**	**19**	**20**
A	A	A	C	B	C	D	D	B	C
21	**22**	**23**	**24**	**25**	**26**	**27**	**28**	**29**	**30**
A	D	B	A	D	C	C	C	B	B
31	**32**	**33**	**34**	**35**	**36**	**37**	**38**	**39**	**40**
D	A	B	C	A	D	D	A	C	C
41	**42**	**43**	**44**	**45**	**46**	**47**	**48**	**49**	**50**
A	C	D	C	B	B	B	D	A	D
51	**52**	**53**	**54**	**55**	**56**	**57**	**58**	**59**	**60**
C	D	B	B	D	B	C	C	A	A
61	**62**	**63**	**64**	**65**	**66**	**67**	**68**	**69**	**70**
A	C	C	D	C	D	D	C	C	D
71	**72**	**73**	**74**	**75**	**76**				
B	B	C	A	A	C				

SOCIAL AND CULTURAL AWAKENING

1. What was the first and fundamental idea with which the Brahma Samaj was started?
A. monotheism
B. widow remarriage
C. removal of purdah for women
D. university education

2. Where was Brahma Samaj first established?
A. Bengal B. The Punjab
C. Bombay D. Madras

3. In which one of the following regions was the Indian family matrilineal?
A. Kerala B. Bengal
C. Assam D. Andhra

4. Where was the purdah system not practised in the 18th Century?
A. South Indian B. Rajasthan
C. The Punjab D. Gujarat

5. Which one of the following was not known to Raja Rammohan Roy?
A. Sanskrit B. Persian
C. Hebrew D. Malayalam

6. In what language did Rammohan write his Gift to Monotheists?
A. Sanskrit B. Bengali
C. Persian D. Hindi

7. Against which of the following social evils did Rammohan organise the historic agitations?
A. Sati
B. Female infanticide
C. Early
D. Untouchability

8. Who founded the Hindu College?
A. David Hare B. William Jones
C. Rammohan Roy D. Dayananda

9. Who among the following was not associated with Rammohan?
A. David Hare
B. Alexander Duff
C. Annie Besant
D. Prasanna Kumar Tagore

10. To which of the following categories of people did Vivian Derozio belong?
A. Irishman B. Anglo-Indian
C. Englishman D. Frenchman

11. Who were discribed by Surendranath Benerji as pioneers of the modern civilisation of Bengal, the conscript fathers of our race?
A. Brahma Samajists
B. Asiatic Society of Bengal
C. Derozians
D. Arya Samajists

12. In which one of the following persons one cannot find a happy blend of Indian and Western culture?
A. Rammohan Roy
B. Ishwar Chandra Vidyasagar
C. Dayananda Saraswati
D. Dwarkanth Tagore

13. Outside Bengal, where did Brahma Samaj take a firm root?
A. Rajasthan B. Andhra
C. Orissa D. Maharashtra

14. Who took the pen-name of Lokahitawadi?
A. G.H. Deshmukh
B. Jotiba Phule
C. Karsondas Mulji
D. Ishwar Chandra Vidyasagar

15. Who founded the Deccan Education Society?
A. R.G. Bhandarkar
B. Kaka Kelkar
C. Jotiba Phule
D. M.G. Ranade

16. Who among the following was the greatest Sanskrit scholar?
A. R.G. Bhandarkar
B. Swami Dayananda
C. Ramakrishna Paramahansa
D. Annie Besant

17. Who was known in early life as Mula Sankara?
A. Dayananda
B. Ramakrishna

C. Vivekanand
D. Rabindranath Tagore

18. Which among the following started a crusade against other religions?
A. Brahma Samaj
B. Prarthana Samaj
C. Theosophical Society
D. Arya Samaj

19. Which of the following is said to have contributed to the growth of communa-lism in India in the 20th Century?
A. Brahma Samaj
B. Arya Samaj
C. Prarthana Samaj
D. Ramakrishna Mission

20. What was the first association founded by Rammohan Roy?
A. Atmiya Sabha
B. Brahma Sabha
C. Tattvabodhini Sabha
D. Young Bengal Movement

21. Which one of the following does occupy an intermediate position between reform and revivalism?
A. Brahma Samaj
B. Arya Samaj
C. Prarthana Samaj
D. Ahmadiya Movement

22. Who was the leader of the young Bengal Movement?
A. G.F. Andrews B. Rammohan Roy
C. H.V. Derozio D. Dayananda

23. Where was Paramahansa Mandali started?
A. Bengal B. Gujarat
C. The Punjab D. Maharashtra

24. Who gave the call 'Back to the Vedas'?
A. Swami Vivekananda
B. Ramakrishna Paramahansa
C. Dayananda
D. Raja Rammohan Roy

25. Who said the different creeds are but different paths to reach the same God (yatmat tata path)?
A. Ramakrishna B. Annie Besant
C. Vivekananda D. Dayananda

26. Who wrote 'Ramakrishna — His life and Sayings'?
A. Swami Vivekananda
B. Max Muller
C. Rasmani
D. Keshab Chandra Sen

27. Who among the following was not a follower of Dayananda?
A. Lala Hansraj B. Pandit Guru Dutt
C. Lala Lajpat Rai D. M.G. Ranade

28. The Gurukul of Hardwar was started as a countermove to
A. Dayananda Anglo-Vedic College of Lahore
B. Muhammedan Anglo-oriental College
C. Sanskrit College
D. Banaras Hindu College

29. When was the parliament of Religions held?
A. 1893 A.D. B. 1902 A.D.
C. 1883 A.D. D. 1913 A.D.

30. Where did the Theosophists establish their headquarters?
A. Calcutta B. Lahore
C. Poona D. Adyar

31. Among the following which one proved to be an important factor in Socio-religious reform movement especially in South India?
A. Arya Samaj
B. Prarthana Samaj
C. Brahma Samaj
D. Theosophical Society

32. Who said the following words? 'So long as the millions live in hunger and Ignorance, I held every man a traitor'
A. Rammohan Roy
B. Ishwar Chandra Vidyasagar
C. M.K. Gandhi
D. Swami Vivekananda

33. Who said the following words? 'liberty in thought and action is the only condition of life, growth and well-being, where it does not exist, the man, the race and the nation must go down'.
A. Swami Vivekananda
B. M.K. Gandhi

C. B.G. Tilak
D. Dadabhai Naoroji

34. Whose followers are said to belong to Aligarh school?
A. Sayyid Ahmad Khan
B. Muhammad Iqbal
C. Maulana Abul Kalam Azad
D. Muhammad Ali Jinnah

35. Who invented the term 'Pakistan'?
A. Muhammad Iqbal
B. Sayyid Ahmad Khan
C. M.A. Jinnah
D. Rahmat Ali

36. Who started the Ahmadiya Movement?
A. Sayyid Ahmad Khan
B. Mirza Ghulam Ahmad
C. Ahmad Ullah
D. Ahmad Shah of Delhi

37. Who founded the Servants of India Society?
A. G.K. Gokhale
B. Surendranath Banerjee
C. B.G. Tilak
D. M.G. Ranade

38. Who started the Indian women's university?
A. D.K. Karve B. M.G. Ranade
C. B.G. Tilak D. G.K. Gokhale

39. Who among the following does not belong to the branch of study in which the other three had specialised?
A. J.G. Bose B. C.V. Raman
C. B.N. Seal D. Meghnad Saha

40. Who founded a Sanskrit College at Banaras?
A. William Jones B. Jonathan Duncan
C. Charles Grant D. Warren Hastings

41. Who among the following did not establish an English school?
A. William Carey B. David Hare
C. Rammohan Roy D. Jonathan Duncan

42. Who made a powerful plea in favour of Western education in his minute of 2nd February, 1835?
A. Alexander Duff
B. T.B. Macaulay
C. William Bentinck
D. Jonathan Duncan

43. Where was the first university established in India?
A. Bombay B. Poona
C. Madras D. Calcutta

44. Who organised the Non-Brahmin Movement in Maharashtra?
A. Jotiba Govind Phule
B. M.G. Ranade
C. B.G. Tilak
D. G.H. Deshmukh

45. When was the Non-Brahmin movement started in Tamil Nadu?
A. 1914 A.D. B. 1916 A.D.
C. 1928 A.D. D. 1939 A.D.

46. What was the political party that grew out of the South Indian people's Association limited?
A. D.M.K.
B. Dravida Kazhagam
C. Justice Party
D. Swarajists

47. Who started the Dravida Kazhagam?
A. E.V. Ramasami (Periyar)
B. C.N. Annadurai
C. T.M. Nair
D. K. Veeramani

48. Who among the following Scheduled caste people launched a spirited depressed classes fight against caste tyranny?
A. B.R. Ambedkar
B. M.C. Rajah
C. Jagjivan Ram
D. Rao Bahadur Srinivasan

49. Who said the following words? "Nobody can remove your grievance as well as you can and you cannot remove these unless you get political power into your hands".
A. B.G. Tilak
B. M.K. Gandhi
C. Jawaharlal Nehru
D. B.R. Ambedkar

50. What was the first labour organisation formed in India?
A. The Bombay Mill hands Association

B. Amalgamated Society of the Railways of India and Burma
C. The Printers Union
D. Bombay Postal Union

51. When did the All-India Trade Union Congress first meet?
A. 1920 A.D. B. 1914 A.D.
C. 1926 A.D. D. 1985 A.D.

52. Whom do you consider as a major curse of the rural people?
A. Zamindars B. Government
C. Money-lenders D. Robbers

53. Who among the following was not among those who came to defend I.N.A. prisoners?
A. Jawaharlal
B. Tej Bahadur Sapru
C. Kailash Nath Katju
D. Vallabhbhai Patel

54. Who said the following words?
"Long years ago we made a tryst with destiny, and now the time comes when we shall redeem our pledge..."
A. M.K. Gandhi
B. Subhas Chandra Bose
C. Jawaharlal Nehru
D. M.A. Jinnah

55. What method did the British follow to deal with the boycott of the Simon Commission?
A. Brutal Suppression
B. Bilateral talks with the Congress
C. Concessions
D. Persuasions

56. Who said the following words?
"The Muslims were fools to ask for Safeguards and the Hindus were greater fools to refuse them".
A. Maulana A.K. Azad
B. Muhammad Iqbal
C. M.A. Jinnah
D. Jawaharlal Nehru

57. How many km did M.K. Gandhi walk to reach Dandi?
A. about 375 km B. about 200 km
C. about 400 km D. about 250 km

58. Who was the first governor-general of Pakistan?
A. Quid-I-Azam M.A. Jinnah
B. Khwaja Nazim-ud-din
C. Ghulam Mohammad
D. Liaquat Ali Khan

59. Who was the first prime minister of Pakistan?
A. Qaid-i-Azam M.A. Jinnah
B. Liaquat Ali Khan
C. Khwaja Nazim-ud-din
D. Z.A. Bhutto

60. Under what Plan/Act was partition of India effected?
A. Wavell's Plan
B. Indian Independence Act of 1947
C. Cabinet Mission Plan
D. Government of India Act of 1935

61. Who formed Khudai Khidmatgars in 1929?
A. M.A. Jinnah
B. Ali brothers
C. Khan Abdul Ghaffar Khan
D. Maulana Abul Kalam Azad

62. Jawahar Lal Nehru wrote in 1937 that a day would come when India would remember and Cherish her. About whom did Nehru write in this way?
A. Rani Gaidilieu B. Rani of Jhansi
C. Capt. Laxmi D. Aruna Asaf Ali

63. Which one of the following princely states did not hesitate to accede to India?
A. Junagadh
B. Jammu & Kashmir
C. Hyderabad
D. Baroda

64. Who is called the 'prophet of Modern India'?
A. Lord William Bentinck
B. Swami Vivekananda
C. Raja Rammohan Roy
D. B.G. Tilak

65. When was an Industrial Exhibition held in connection with National Congress?
A. 1905 A.D. B. 1885 A.D.
C. 1896 A.D. D. 1881 A.D.

66. Who among the following was not an extremist?
A. B.G. Tilak
B. G.K. Gokhale
C. Bipin Chandrapal
D. Lala Lajpat Rai

67. Who organised the Abhinav Bharat?
A. Aurobindo Ghosh
B. Lala Lajpat Rai
C. V.D. Savarkar
D. C.R. Das

68. Who started the Home Rule movement?
A. Motilal Nehru
B. C.R. Das
C. Sir C.P. Ramasami Iyer
D. Mrs. Annie Besant

69. Who had sown the seeds of Muslim Communalism?
A. Maulana Abul Kalam Azad
B. Nawab Salimulla
C. Sayyid Ahmad Khan
D. M.A. Jinnah

70. Chronologically which of the following events took place first?
A. Rowlatt Act
B. August Announcement of Montagu
C. Khilafat agitation
D. Jallianwala Bagh tragedy

71. At which Congress session was it decided that 26th January should be observed as the Poorna Swaraja Day?
A. Surat Session of 1916
B. Lahore Session of 1929
C. Bombay Session of 1942
D. Calcutta Session of 1942

72. Who among the following Congress leaders criticised the quit India policy?
A. Maulana Abul Kalam Azad
B. C. Rajagopalachari
C. Amrit Kaur
D. Jawaharlal Nehru

73. Who among the following was not a member of the India league Delegation sent by India league, London to get first-head information about the situation in India?
A. L.W. Matters
B. Sir Stafford Cripps
C. V.K. Krishna Menon
D. Monica what

74. Which of the following was characterised as 'a post-dated cheque on a crashing bank'?
A. August offer of 1940
B. Cripps' offer
C. Wavell's plan
D. Cabinet Mission's plan

75. Who was the left wing leader who became the congress president in 1938 A.D.?
A. Subhas Chandra Bose
B. Pandit Jawaharlal Nehru
C. Pattabhi Sitaramayya
D. C. Rajagopalachari

76. Which of the following was characterised by M.A. Jinnah as an offer of "Maimed, Mutilated and moth-eaten Pakistan"?
A. Sir Stafford Cripps' offer
B. Wavell Plan
C. Cabinet Mission's offer
D. Rajaji formula

77. Who was the author of June 3rd plan?
A. Lord Mountbatten
B. Lord Wavell
C. A.V. Alexander
D. Sir Stafford Cripps

78. Who among the following was not connected with the Azad Hind Fauj?
A. Netaji
B. Shah Nawaz Khan
C. Captain Laxmi
D. V.D. Savarkar

79. Who was the chairman of the two Boundary Commissions appointed in 1947 A.D.?
A. Cyril Radcliffe
B. Mortimer Durand
C. Mac Mohan
D. A.V. Alexander

80. The Poona Pact of 1932 was the immediate effect of
A. First Round Table Conference
B. Gandhi-Irwin Pact
C. Montford Reforms

D. Communal Award of Ramsay Mac Donald

81. When was provincial autonomy granted?
A. 1909 A.D. B. 1919 A.D.
C. 1935 A.D. D. 1947 A.D.

82. Why did Raja Rammohan Roy publish the Bengali translation of the Vadas and the Upanishads?
A. To show that the principal Hindu scriptures preach monotheism
B. To lend support to the Caste system
C. To popularise Bengali literature
D. To show the hollowness of Hinduism.

83. Why was Derozio removed from the Hindu College?
A. He was a christian
B. He hated Hinduism
C. He was radical in his views
D. He was not a good teacher

84. Vidyasagar was hated most by the Orthodox Hindus because he
A. advocated widow remarriage
B. was interested in the education of women.
C. opened the Sanskrit College to Non-Brahmin students
D. Introduced the Study of Western thought in the Sanskrit College

85. Which of the following statements cannot be attributed to Dayananda?
A. The vedas are infallible
B. The vedas were to be interpreted by Himself and others.
C. The puranas contain true teachings
D. The Hindu religion was perverted by selfish and ignorant priests.

86. Which of the following statements cannot be attributed to Dayananda?
A. He said that every person had the right of direct access to God.
B. He led a revolt against Hindu orthodoxy.
C. He favoured the study of western sciences.
D. He considered the priests as highly learned and selfless.

87. Which of the following statements cannot be regarded as true with regard to the Arya Samajists?
A. They fought untouchability
B. They taught social equality
C. They did not favour conversion to Hinduism
D. They wanted the conditions of woman to be improved.

88. Which one of the following cannot be attributed to Ramakrishna?
A. Service to humanity is service to divinity
B. Woman should be treated with honour
C. Renunciation of worldly life is essential for realisation of God.
D. The worship of images is not incompatible with the highest spiritual development.

89. What was the occassion that was used to convene the parliament of all religions at Chicago?
A. To mark the four hundredth anniversary of the discovery of America by Columbus
B. To mark the birth Centenary of George Washington.
C. To mark the 120th anniversary of the Declaration of Independence of America
D. To mark the Centenary of the Treaty of versailles.

90. What was the aim of the Ahmadiya Movement?
A. To restore the true and unpolluted faith of Islam to the Muslims
B. To bring about Hindu-Muslim unity
C. To fight against the abolition of the Khalifate
D. To fight for India's freedom

91. Which of the following is the correct description of the Servants of India Society?
A. It was a society established to promote education among the Indians.
B. It was a society formed to eradicate

social evils which afflicted India

C. It was a society formed to wipe out poverty in India.

D. It was a group of men who were trained and equipped for some form of service to the motherland.

92. Lady Irwin college was established for the purpose of helping women to

A. acquire proficiency in medicine

B. get training in nursing

C. get training in fine arts

D. qualify themselves as High School teacher of Home Science.

93. Which one of the following was mostly responsible for English education's popularity and rapid progress?

A. Regulation introduced by Lord Harding that preference should be given to people having a knowledge of English while appointing public servants.

B. T.B. Macaulays minute of 1835.

C. Rammohan Roy's pleadings

D. Appointment of Alexander Duff on the Committee of Public Instruction.

94. Which one of the following was not a feature of the new educational System based on Wood's Despatch?

A. English alone should be the medium of instruction

B. Education should be exclusively secular

C. There was to be adequate number of efficient teaching institutes such as primary schools, high schools and colleges each leading to the next higher step.

D. A special department of education was to be created.

95. What was the main objective of the Justice Party?

A. To secure greater and due representation for Non-Brahmins in government services

B. To fight against the Home Rule Movement

C. To carry from within the legislature the struggle for freedom

D. To free the peasants from the tyranny of the Zamindars.

96. What made B.R. Ambedkar lead the Movement of mass conversion of the Depressed classes to Buddhism?

A. No great efforts were taken to abolish caste system.

B. Buddhism was easy to follow

C. Buddhism was against doing harm to others

D. Buddhism was popular in India.

97. What is the most serious of the defects of the Trade Union Movement in India?

A. Predominance of small-sized unions

B. Poor finance

C. Absence of whole time paid officials of the union

D. Leadership is provided by outsiders especially professional politicians.

98. The Santhal rising was not due to

A. appressive exactions of the money-lenders

B. Exactions of the revenue officials

C. Dispossession of their lands by Zamindars.

D. Failure to improve irrigational facilities.

99. Why did M.K. Gandhi go to Champaran?

A. To launch Salt Satyagraha

B. To launch non-cooperation movement

C. To inquire personally into the grievances of the indigo cultivators

D. To fight against the zamindars.

100. Why was Simon Commission sent to India?

A. To suggest ways and means of eradicating India's poverty

B. To study the working of the Indian universities.

C. To solve the communal problem

D. To go into the question of further constitutional reform.

101. What was the important cause of the boycott of Simon Commission?

A. It was sent after the due date

B. It came at a time when famine ravaged the country.
C. All its members were Englishmen.
D. It offered to study further constitutional reform instead of complete independence.

102. Which one of the following features was not included in the Nehru Reports?
A. India should be a federation
B. Executive should be responsible to legislature
C. Elections should be by separate electorates
D. Voting right should be given to all adults.

103. What was the chief aim of Ghadar Party?
A. To free India from British rule through an armed insurrection
B. To give financial assistance to the Indians
C. To persude the British government to give independance to India.
D. To end communal strife in India.

104. Which one of the following statements is wrong?
A. Satyagraha Ashram developed into Sabarmati Ashram
B. Gandhi was prohibited to enter Champaran in 1917 A.D.
C. Michael O'Dwyer was responsible for the brutal firing at Jallianwala Bagh
D. Gandhi presided over the all India Khilafat Conference in 1919 A.D.

105. Why did Gandhi suspend the Civil Disobedience Movement in 1922?
A. C.R. Das never supported the movement.
B. Motilal Nehru started the Swarajya Party.
C. Vithalbhai J. Patel became the president of the Central legislative assembly.
D. Twenty-Two policemen were killed at Chauri Chaura.

106. The Congress Session at Karachi in 1931 authorised Gandhi to act in a certain way. Which of the following in the above context is correct?
A. To meet the viceroy Irwin
B. To open talks with viceroy willingdon.
C. To take part in the Second Round table conference.
D. To participate in the third Round conference.

107. Which one of the following statements is wrong?
A. Lord linlithgow inaugurated the working of the Government of India Act of 1935
B. The Cabinet Mission consisted of Pethick lawrence, S. Cripps and A.V. Alexander
C. Sardar Patel was the first defence Minister of India.
D. The August rebellion took place in 1942 A.D.

108. Which one of the following statements about Rammohan Roy is correct?
A. Raja Rammohan Roy relied blindly on India's own past.
B. Rammohan aped blindly the western system.
C. He wanted that new India should acquire all that was best in the East and the West.
D. He did not want India to learn from the west.

109. In which regions was the evil of dowry widespread in the 18th Century?
1. Bengal
2. Rajputana
3. The Punjab
4. Maharashtra

Select the correct answer from the codes given below:
A. 1 and 4
B. 1 and 2
C. 2 and 3
D. all the four

110. In which regions was widow remarriage quite common among Non-Brahmins?
1. Maharashtra
2. Area occupied by the Jats.
3. Hill regions of the North.
4. Bengal.

Select the correct answer from the codes

given below:

A. 1 and 2 B. 1, 2 and 3

C. 1 and 4 D. 2 and 4

111. Why did the orthodox condemn Rammohan?

1. He criticised idolatry.
2. He admired christianity.
3. he admired Islam.
4. He preached worship of one God.

Select the correct answer from the codes given below:

A. all the four B. 1, 2 and 3

C. 1 and 2 D. 3 and 4

112. Why did the Social reformers of the first half of the 18th Century fail to create a movement?

1. Social conditions were not yet ripe for their ideas.
2. There was no other group or class in Indian society at that time which could support them.
3. They failed to maintain their links with the people.
4. Their radicalism was bookish.

Select the correct answer from the codes given below:

A. 1 and 3 B. 1, 3 and 4

C. 3 only D. all the four

113. Who were contemporaries of Ramakrishna?

1. Saradamani
2. Narendranath Dutta
3. Kesheb Chandra Sen
4. Rasmani

Select the correct answer from the codes given below:

A. 1 only B. 1 and 2

C. 1, 2 and 3 D. all the four

114. Which one of the Sadhana was practised by Ramakrishna?

A. Tantric mode of Sadhana

B. Mode of Sadhana laid down by the Vaishnava Cult

C. Vedantic Sadhana

D. Sadhana according to Christian rite

Select the correct answer from the codes given below:

A. 1 and 2 B. 1, 2 and 3

C. 2, 3 and 4 D. all the four

115. In what respects does the Ramakrishna Mission stand distinguished from the Arya Samaj?

A. It continued to be purely a monastic order.

B. It had no proselytising zeal.

C. It did not develop into a Separte Sect.

D. It derived its basic principles from India's ancient scriptures.

Select the correct answer from the codes given below:

A. 1 only B. 1 and 3

C. 1 and 4 D. 1, 2 and 3

116. What are the reform movements which took their inspirations from India's past?

1. Brahma Samaj
2. Prarthana Samaj
3. Arya Samaj
4. Ramakrishna movement

Select the correct answer from the codes given below:

A. 1 and 2 B. 2 and 3

C. 1 and 4 D. 3 and 4

117. Who started the South Indian people's Association limited in 1916 A.D.?

1. T.M. Nair
2. P Thyagaraja Chetti
3. K.V. Reddy
4. A. Ramaswami Mudaliar

Select the correct answer from the codes given below:

A. 1 and 2 B. 1 and 3

C. 2 and 4 D. 3 and 4

118. Why were the depressed classes displeased with the Harijan Sevak Sangh?

1. It did not have Scheduled Caste members on the Central Board of the Sangh after the retirement of three scheduled caste members.
2. It did not spend much on Harijan uplift
3. It functioned as a wing of the congress.
4. It was not interested in the well-being of the Harijans.

Select the correct answer from codes given below:

A. 1 only B. 1 and 2
C. 1, 2 and 3 D. all the four

119. Why are the early 1930s said to be a period of unfavourable climate to the growth of trade union movement?
1. Failure of the Bombay Textile Strike
2. Economic depression
3. Prosecution of the Communists involved in the Meerut Conspiracy case
4. Fresh outburst of national sentiments caused by the Civil Disobedience Movement.

Select the correct answer from the codes given below:
A. 1 and 2 B. 2, 3 and 4
C. 3 and 4 D. all the four

120. Which of the following provinces did not have congress ministries in 1937 A.D.?
1. Bengal 2. The Punjab
3. Madras 4. Bombay

Select the correct answer from the codes given below:
A. 1 only B. 1 and 2
C. 1, 2 and 3 D. all the four

121. What is the correct chronological order of the following governors-general?
1. Irwin
2. Willingdon
3. Linlithgow
4. Wavell

Select the correct answer from the codes given below:
A. 1, 2, 3 and 4 B. 2, 1, 3 and 4
C. 3, 1, 2 and 4 D. 1, 4, 2 and 3

122. What is the correct chronological sequence of the following events?
1. Khilafat Movement
2. First meeting of Indian National Congress in Bombay
3. Partition of Bengal
4. Morley-Minto Reforms

Select the correct answer from the codes given below:
A. 1, 2, 3 and 4 B. 2, 3, 4 and 1
C. 3, 2, 4 and 1 D. 2, 4, 3 and 1

123. What is the correct chronological order of the events mentioned below?
1. Cripps offer
2. Azad Hind Fauj
3. Simala Conference
4. Cabinet Mission

Select the correct answer from the codes given below:
A. 1, 2, 3 and 4 B. 2, 1, 4 and 3
C. 1, 3, 2 and 4 D. 1, 4, 3 and 2

124. Which one of the following pairs is not correctly matched?
A. Raja Sawai Jai Singh — Widow remarriage
B. Sauda — Urdu Poetry
C. Tayumanavar — Sittar poetry
D. Dayaram — Lyricist of Bengal

125. Which one of the following pairs is not correctly matched?
A. Shah Abdul Latif — Poetry
B. General Parashuram Bhau — Marathi-literature
C. Dayaram — Lyricist of Gujarat
D. Warris Shah — Punjabi epic

126. Which one of the following pairs is not correctly matched?
A. Tattvabodhini Patrika — Debendranath Tagore
B. Satyartha Prakash — Dayananda
C. The Precepts of Jesus, the Guide to place and happiness — Annie Besant
D. Tuhfat-ul-Muwahhidin — Rammohan Roy

127. Which one of the following pairs is correctly matched?
A. Seva Sadan Society — Ramabai Ranade
B. The National Association for supplying Medical Aid by women to the woman of India — Countess of Dufferin
C. Victoria Memorial Scholar Ships fund — Queen Victoria
D. The Bhil Seva Mandal — Gurusaday Dutta

ANSWERS

1	2	3	4	5	6	7	8	9	10
A	A	A	A	D	C	A	A	C	B
11	**12**	**13**	**14**	**15**	**16**	**17**	**18**	**19**	**20**
C	C	D	A	D	A	A	D	B	A
21	**22**	**23**	**24**	**25**	**26**	**27**	**28**	**29**	**30**
B	C	D	C	A	B	D	A	A	D
31	**32**	**33**	**34**	**35**	**36**	**37**	**38**	**39**	**40**
D	D	A	A	D	B	A	A	C	B
41	**42**	**43**	**44**	**45**	**46**	**47**	**48**	**49**	**50**
D	B	D	A	B	C	A	A	D	A
51	**52**	**53**	**54**	**55**	**56**	**57**	**58**	**59**	**60**
A	C	D	C	A	A	A	A	B	B
61	**62**	**63**	**64**	**65**	**66**	**67**	**68**	**69**	**70**
C	A	D	C	C	B	C	D	C	B
71	**72**	**73**	**74**	**75**	**76**	**77**	**78**	**79**	**80**
B	B	B	B	A	D	A	D	A	D
81	**82**	**83**	**84**	**85**	**86**	**87**	**88**	**89**	**90**
C	A	C	A	C	D	C	C	A	A
91	**92**	**93**	**94**	**95**	**96**	**97**	**98**	**99**	**100**
D	D	A	A	A	A	D	D	C	D
101	**102**	**103**	**104**	**105**	**106**	**107**	**108**	**109**	**110**
C	C	A	C	D	C	C	C	B	B
111	**112**	**113**	**114**	**115**	**116**	**117**	**118**	**119**	**120**
B	D	D	D	D	D	A	C	D	B
121	**122**	**123**	**124**	**125**	**126**	**127**			
A	B	A	D	B	C	B			

THE FREEDOM STRUGGLE

1. Who among the following Viceroys became a victim of one of the convicts during his visit to Andamans?

A. Lytton B. Ripon
C. Mayo D. Curzon

2. Who are known as the "Liberators of the Indian Press"?

A. Sir Charles Metcalfe
B. Lord Minto
C. Sir Thomas Munro
D. Lord Macauly
E. Lord Wellesly

3. The Indian press played an important role in spreading the message of patriotism and modern ideas among the people. Which of the following is/are not true about its activities?

1. Criticising the official policies.
2. Urging the people to unite and work for national welfare.
3. Putting toward the views of Indians as well as those of the British Government.
4. Popularising modern ideas of self-governments democracy etc.
5. Enabling nationalist workers to exchange views with one another.

Codes:

A. 3 B. 1
C. 1, 3 D. 4, 5

4. Which of the following are correctly matched?

1. Hindu Patriot (1853) Girish Chandra Ghosh
2. Rast Goftar (1851) Dadabhai Naoroji
3. Akbar-O-Saidagas (1852) Dadabhai Kavasji
4. Indian Mirrior (1862) Devendra Nath Tagore

Codes:

A. 2, 3, 4 B. 1, 2, 3
C. 1, 3, 4 D. 1, 3, 4

5. Which of the following are correctly matched?

1. Statesman (1875)— Devendra Nath Tagore
2. National Paper (1865) — Rober Knight
3. Tribune (1862) — Dayal Singh Majeethia
4. Bengalee (1881) — Girish Chandra Ghosh

Codes:

A. 1, 2 B. 2, 3
C. 3, 4 D. 1, 4

6. Match the following.

List I	List II
(a) National Indian Association (1867)	1. William Adam
(b) Indian Society (1872)	2. Gokhale
(c) Servants of India Society (1905)	3. Mary Carpenter
(d) British India Society (1839)	4. Anand Mohan Bose

Codes:

	(a)	*(b)*	*(c)*	*(d)*
A.	1	3	2	4
B.	3	4	2	1
C.	4	1	2	3
D.	3	1	2	4

7. Which of the following are correctly matched?

(a) Second Session of the Congress	1. Pheroz Shah Mehta
(b) Third Session (Madras)	2. Dadabhai Naoroji
(c) Fourth Session (Allahabad)	3. Sir William Wedderton
(d) Fifth Session (Bombay)	4. Badruddin Taiebji
(e) Sixth Session (Calcutta)	5. George Yule

Codes:

	(a)	*(b)*	*(c)*	*(d)*	*(e)*
A.	2	4	5	3	1
B.	2	1	3	4	5
C.	3	2	1	4	5
D.	1	5	3	2	4

8. Match the following.

List I	List II
(a) Banga-Duta	1. First paper from Bombay
(b) Madras Courier	2. First paper from Madras
(c) Bombay Herald	3. A weekly paper in four language
(d) Bombay Samachar	4. First paper in Gujarat
	5. First paper from Bengal

Codes:

	(a)	*(b)*	*(c)*	*(d)*
A.	5	2	4	1
B.	3	2	1	4
C.	4	3	1	2
D.	3	2	1	5

9. Which is the correct chronological sequence of the following associations?
1. Poona Sarvajanik Sabha
2. Indian Association of Calcutta
3. Bombay Presidency Association
4. Madras Mahajan Sabha

Codes:
A. 1, 2, 4, 3 B. 2, 3, 4, 1
C. 1, 4, 2, 3 D. 3, 2, 1, 4

10. Who is the founder of the Amrit Bazar Patrika?
A. Sisir Kumar Ghosh
B. Girish Chandra Ghosh
C. Harish Chandra Mukherjee
D. S.N. Banerjee

11. Who was the Secretary of States for India at the time of the foundation of Indian National Congress.
A. Lord Morley B. Lord Elgin
C. Lord Hamilton D. Lord Cross

12. Which of the following statements is/are true about the Vernacular Press Act, 1878?
1. It was passed by Lord Mayo.
2. It came to be known as the "Gagging Act".
3. It liberated the Indian Press from restrictions.
4. It was replaced by Lord Ripon in 1882.

Codes:
A. 1, 2 B. 2, 4
C. 1, 3 D. 3, 4

13. The administrative and economic unification of India by the British also paved the way for the rise of Indian National Movement. Which of the following statements is/are incorrect in this regard?
1. The British Unified India administratively by introducing a uniform and modern system of government throughout the country.
2. The destruction of local self sufficient economy had increasingly atomised India's economic life.
3. The introduction of modern trade and industries had inter-linked the economic-fate of the people living in different parts of India.
4. The introduction of the modern means of transport and communication had promoted natural contact.

Codes:
A. 2, 3 B. 2
C. 3 D. 3, 4

14. Which of the following statements is incorrect?
A. Amrit Bazar Patrika work originally a Bengali Paper, but became a fullfledged English paper in 1878 in order to escape from the Vernacular Press Act.
B. Hindu was founded by G.S. Aiyar and Viraraghava Chari.
C. Sanjibani, started in 1883, was a Marathi Paper.
D. The Bombay Times became the Times of India in 1861.

15. Who among the following did not attend the first session of Congress at Bombay?
A. W.C. Banerjee
B. S.N. Banerjee
C. Badruddin Tayebji
D. K.T. Tailong

16. What is the name of Bengali monthly founded and edited by Bankim Chandra

Chatterjee from 1873?

A. Somprakasha B. Bangaduta
C. Bangadarsna D. Bengalee

17. Which of the following statements about the Ilbert Bill is/are not true?

1. The controversy around the Ilbert Bill helped Indian nationalism to take up an organised form.
2. According to the original Bill, Indian Judge could try Europeans also.
3. It was passed without any amendment despite the vehement opposition of the British residents in India.
4. The Indians did not organise any campaign in favour of the Bill.

Codes:

A. 1, 4 B. 2, 3
C. 3, 4 D. 4 only

18. Arrange the following organisations in the chronological order:

1. East India Association in London
2. Land holders Society at Calcutta
3. Madras Native Association
4. Bengal British Indian Society
5. British Indian Association

Codes:

A. 2, 3, 1, 4, 5 B. 1, 4, 3, 5, 2
C. 3, 5, 4, 1, 2 D. 2, 4, 5, 3, 1

19. Match the following.

(a) Digdarsana (1818)	1. First Paper in Urdu
(b) Bengal Gazette (1818)	2. First Bengali Monthly
(c) Mirat-ul-Akbar (1822)	3. First Journal in Persian
(d) Bombay Samachar	4. First Bengali Newspaper

Codes:

	(a)	*(b)*	*(c)*	*(d)*
A.	4	2	1	3
B.	2	4	1	3
C.	4	2	3	1
D.	2	4	3	1

20. **Assertion (A):** The introduction of western system of education and English language was an important cause for the rise and growth of nationalism in India.

Reason (R): The Indian national movement would not have been possible without the English language as a medium.

Codes:

A. A and R are true and R is the correct explanation of A.
B. A and R are true but R is not the correct explanation of A.
C. A is true but R is false.
D. A is false but R is true.

21. **Assertion (A):** Dadabhai Naoroji organised the East India Association in London.

Reason (R): He wanted to influence the British public opinion.

Codes:

A. A and R are true and R is the correct explanation of A.
B. A and R are true but R is not the correct explanation of A.
C. A is true but R is false.
D. A is false but R is true.

22. Who was the first woman president of the Indian National Congress?

A. Sarojini Naidu
B. Sucheta Kripalani
C. Rajkumari Amrit Kaur
D. Annie Besant

23. Who was the first Muslim president of the Indian National Congress?

A. Muhammed Ali Jinnah
B. Badruddin Tayebji
C. Sir Syed Ahmed Khan
D. Abul Kalam Azad

24. The extremist method of "passive resistance" did not include:

1. Refusal to co-operate with the Government.
2. Sending petitions to the Government
3. Boycott of Government service, courts, schools and Colleges
4. Refusal to pay rent to the Zamindars.

Codes:

A. 2 B. 1, 2
C. 4 D. 2, 4

25. Which of the following statements about Gokhale are not true?

1. He was a moderate in politics, but a radical in matters of social reforms.
2. He wanted political progress and social reforms to go simultaneously.
3. He was opposed to "passive resistance" in India as well as in South Africa.
4. He was totally opposed to western civilisation.

Codes:

A. 4 B. 3, 4
C. 2, 4 D. 2, 3, 4

26. Who is the first profounder of the Doctrine of "Passive resistance"?

A. B.G. Tilak B. Arobindo Ghosh
C. G.K. Gokhale D. M.K. Gandhi

27. Who described Tilak, as the "Father of Indian unrest"?

A. Valentine Chiro B. Disraeli
C. Minto II D. Chelmsford

28. Who presided over the Surat session of the Indian National Congress?

A. Dadabhai Naoroji
B. Gopal Krishna Gokhale
C. Rashbehari Ghosh
D. S.N. Banerjee

29. Who exclaimed, "when the Queen desires that none should die, what the Governor declares that all should live ..... will you kill yourself by timidity and starvation"?

A. Bipin Chandra Pal
B. Dadabhai Naoroji
C. Tilak
D. Gokhale

30. Who said "The Congress movement was neither inspired by the people, nor devised or planned by them"?

A. Lala Lajpat Rai B. Sir Syed Ahmed
C. Lord Curzon D. Lord Dufferin

31. Which of the following statements about Tilak are incorrect?

1. Believed that political freedom should precede social reform.
2. Favoured initiative by the Congress in the matter of social reforms.
3. Opposed British Government's initiative in the matter of the social reforms.
4. Did not consider social and political reforms to be interlinked.
5. Separated religions from politics.

Codes:

A. 5 B. 2, 5
C. 2, 4, 5 D. 4

32. When did Tilak declare, "Swaraj is my birthright, and I will have it"?

A. 1905 B. 1909
C. 1914 D. 1916

33. When did the British pass a law it an offence to preach nationalism?

A. 1890 B. 1895
C. 1898 D. 1904

34. **Assertion (A):** Arya Samajists were responsible for the rise of extremism in the Indian National Congress.

Reason (R): Many of them were in the forefront of the national movement.

Codes:

A. A and R are true and R is the correct explanation of A.
B. A and R are true but R is not the correct explanation of A.
C. A is true but R is false.
D. A is false but R is true.

35. **Assertion (A):** British residents in India Vehemently opposed the Ilbert Bill.

Reason (R): The Bill proposed to establish social equality in the administration of Justice.

Codes:

A. A and R are true and R is the correct explanation of A.
B. A and R are true but R is not the correct explanation of A.
C. A is true but R is false.
D. A is false but R is true.

36. **Assertion (A):** Dwarka Nath Tagore was one of the founder members of the

"Landholders Society" of Calcutta.

Reason (R): The society was the first example of an organised constitutional agitation for redress of grievances.

Codes:

A. A and R are true and R is the correct explanation of A.

B. A and R are true but R is not the correct explanation of A.

C. A is true but R is false.

D. A is false but R is true.

37. Assertion (A): Raja Rammohan Roy was one of the first Indian leaders to start an agitation for political reforms.

Reason (R): He founded the Landholders Society at Calcutta in 1838.

Codes:

A. A and R are true and R is the correct explanation of A.

B. A and R are true but R is not the correct explanation of A.

C. A is true but R is false.

D. A is false but R is true.

38. Match List-I with List-II.

List-I	List-II
(a) Hindu Mahasabha	1. 1906
(b) Indian Liberal Foundation	2. 1915
(c) Muslim League	3. 1916
(d) Home Rule League	4. 1918

Codes:

	(a)	(b)	(c)	(d)
A.	2	4	1	3
B.	2	1	4	3
C.	3	2	4	1
D.	4	1	3	2

39. Match the following.

(a) Foundation of Women's University	1. Lord Lands downe
(b) Creation of Governorship for Bengal	2. Lord Curzon
(c) Ancient Movements Preservation Act	3. Lord Hardinge II
(d) Indian Council Act of 1891	4. Lord Chelmsford

Codes:

	(a)	(b)	(c)	(d)
A.	2	1	3	4
B.	4	3	1	2
C.	3	4	2	1
D.	4	3	2	1

40. Assertion (A): In the life of Dadabhai Naoroji, there was a slow transition from liberalism and modertism to some form of radicalims and extremism.

Reason (R): He was gradually disallusioned with British Politicians and their policies.

Codes:

A. A and R are true and R is the correct explanation of A.

B. A and R are true but R is not the correct explanation of A.

C. A is true but R is false.

D. A is false but R is true.

41. Assertion (A): Till the Fag end of the 19th Century, Tilak did not advocate "passive resistance".

Reason (R): Till his death, his idea of self-government meaning to him complete autonomy, did not change.

Codes:

A. A and R are true and R is the correct explanation of A.

B. A and R are true but R is not the correct explanation of A.

C. A is true but R is false.

D. A is false but R is true.

42. Assertion (A): Gokhale claimed self-government not as a matter of right but as a reward by the display of wisdom, experience, moderation etc.

Reason (R): He was greatly influenced by the British ideas of moderation and peaceful evolution.

Codes:

A. A and R are true and R is the correct explanation of A.

B. A and R are true but R is not the correct explanation of A.

C. A is true but R is false.

D. A is false but R is true.

43. Which of the following was/were not contributed by the revolutionary terrorists?

1. Setting a rare example of death-defying heroism in the cause of motherland.
2. Being the first to demand "Dominian States" much before the Congress did
3. Production of a wealth of patriotic songs, and creation of a new interest in regional and local history and folk traditions.
4. Establishment of world-wide contacts.

Codes:

A. 2 B. 4

C. 2, 4 D. 3, 4

44. Which of the following persons was/were not involved with the foundation of the Anushilan Samiti of Calcutta in 1902?

1. Promotha Mitter
2. Abani Mukherji
3. Barindra Kumar Ghosh
4. Jatindra Nath Benerji
5. Pulin Das

Codes:

A. 2, 4 B. 3, 5

C. 2, 5 D. 3, 4

45. Which of the following were the causes for the emergence and growth of revolutionary terrorism in India?

1. Frustration of the youth with the constitutional methods of the moderates and the passive resistance of the extremists
2. Failure of the Swedeshi and anti-partition movements to get the partition of Bengal repeated.
3. Protection and co-operation given by the masses to the terrorists.
4. Growing hatred among the youth for foreign rule due to social arrogance of the British and the represive measures adopted by the Government.
5. Influence of the Irish terrorists and the Russian Nihlists.

Codes:

A. 1, 2, 4 B. 2, 3, 5

C. 1, 2, 4, 5 D. 2, 3, 4, 5

46. Which of the following newspaper/journal was not from Bengal?

A. Yugantar B. Kal

C. Bandi Jivan D. Dhumketu

47. Which of the following statements about revolutionary terrorists are not true?

1. They came mainly from the lower classes.
2. Most of them belonged to the upper classes.
3. Most of them came from the rural areas.
4. They neglected the real demands of the peasants and workers.

Codes:

A. 1, 2, 3 B. 2, 4

C. 2, 3, 4 D. 1, 3

48. Which of the following newspaper/journal was from Maharashtra?

A. Kranti B. Atmasakti

C. Sarathi D. Sandhya

49. Who was the revolutionary terrorist who ended his days as Ramkrishna Mission's Swamiji?

A. Aurobindo Ghosh

B. Hemchandra Kanungo

C. Ajit Singh

D. Jatindranath Bandopadhyay

50. Who was the founder of the secret society, "Abhinava Bharat"?

A. Naren Bhattacharji

B. Jatin Mukherjee

C. Ganesh Saverkar

D. Damodar Chapekar

51. Which of the following are correctly matched?

1. Sandhya — Brahmobandheb Upodhyay
2. Bande Matram — Satish Chandra Mukherjee
3. New Delhi — Bipin Chandra Pal
4. Dawn — Aurobindo Ghosh

Codes:

A. 1, 2 B. 2, 3

C. 3, 4 D. 1, 3

52. Which of the following correctly matched?

A. Punjabee	T. Prakasham & M. Krishna Rao
B. Bharat Mata	Ajit Singh
C. Krishna Patrika	M.G. Ranade
D. Quarterly Journal	Lajpat Rai

53. Which of the following are correctly matched?

(a) Comrade	1. Annie Besant
(b) Al-Hilal	2. Muhammad Ali
(c) Zamindar	3. Abdul Kalam Azad
(d) Commonweal	4. Zafar Ali Khan

Codes:

	(a)	*(b)*	*(c)*	*(d)*
A.	1	2	4	3
B.	3	2	4	1
C.	2	3	4	1
D.	1	3	4	2

54. Match the following.

List-I	List-II
(a) Rabindranath Tagore	1. Nil Darpan
(b) Dadabhai Naoroji	2. Economic History of India
(c) Dinbandhu Mitra	3. Gora
(d) R.C. Dutta	4. Poverty and British rule in India

Codes:

	(a)	*(b)*	*(c)*	*(d)*
A.	3	4	2	1
B.	3	2	4	1
C.	3	2	1	4
D.	3	4	1	2

55. Assertion (A): Aurobindo Ghosh was the most typical representative of the extremist nationalism in its intense metaphysical and religious form.

Reason (R): Nationalism to him, is not a mere political programme, but a religion that has come from God.

Codes:

A. A and R are true and R is the correct explanation of A.

B. A and R are true but R is not the correct explanation of A.

C. A is true but R is false.

D. A is false but R is true.

56. Which of the following novels was/were written by Bankim Chandra Chatterji?

1. Sitaram
2. Devi Chaudharani
3. Anand Math
4. Ghare Baire

Codes:

A. Only 3 B. 1, 2, 3

C. 3, 4 D. 4

57. What is the chronological sequence of the following happenings?

1. August Declaration
2. Lucknow Pact
3. Jalianwala Bagh Massacre
4. Khera Satyagraha

Codes:

A. 4, 2, 3, 1 B. 3, 1, 2, 4

C. 2, 4, 1, 3 D. 2, 1, 4, 3

58. Which of the following statements is/are not true about the Hindustan Republican Association?

1. It was founded by Sachin Sanyal and Jogesh Chandra Chatterji
2. It was the first revolutionary terrorist association at the All India level.
3. It was renamed as "Hindustan Communist Republican Association" by Chandra Shekhar Azad.
4. It was later joined by Bhagat Singh
5. In 1929, some of its members tried to blow Lord Reading train near Delhi.

Codes:

A. Only 3 B. 3, 4

C. Only 5 D. 3, 5

59. Who was the author of "Pather Dabi" a novel which glorified the path of violent revolution and which was banned by the British Government?

A. Prem Chand

B. Sarat Chandra Chatterji

C. Bankim Chandra Chatterji

D. Ajay Ghosh

60. Assertion (A): Bipin Chandra Pal was

moderate till 1904.

Reason (R): Bipin Chandra Pal, along with Ajit Singh, was departed by the British in 1907 for his extremist views.

Codes:

A. A and R are true and R is the correct explanation of A.

B. A and R are true but R is not the correct explanation of A.

C. A is true but R is false.

D. A is false but R is true.

61. Match the following.

List-I	List-II
(a) Yugantar	1. Santokh Singh
(b) Sandhya	2. Barindra Kumar Ghosh
(c) Kirti	3. Sachin Sanyal
(d) Bandi-Jivan	4. Brahmobandh Upodhyay

Codes:

	(a)	*(b)*	*(c)*	*(d)*
A.	2	4	1	3
B.	3	1	2	4
C.	2	1	4	3
D.	4	2	1	3

62. Which one of the following is correctly matched?

A. Chapekar Brothers	1. Rand
B. Mohanlal Dhingra	2. Rand and Lt. Ayerst
C. Gopinath Saha	3. Curzon Wyllie
D. Bhagat Singh	4. Saunders

63. Assertion (A): Rash Behari Bose was captured and executed by the British.

Reason (R): He along with Sachin Sanyal, planned to organise a coordinated revolt in February 1915.

Codes:

A. A and R are true and R is the correct explanation of A.

B. A and R are true but R is not the correct explanation of A.

C. A is true but R is false.

D. A is false but R is true.

64. Assertion (A): Bengal revolutionaries under Jatin Mukherjee planned to organise disruption of rail communication, siezure of fort William etc in Bengal.

Reason (R): Jatin Mukherjee was popularly known as "Bagha Jatin".

Codes:

A. A and R are true and R is the correct explanation of A.

B. A and R are true but R is not the correct explanation of A.

C. A is true but R is false.

D. A is false but R is true.

65. Match the following.

List-I	List-II
(a) Matrydom in jail while doing-hunger strike	1. Chandra ShekharAzad
(b) Arrest and execution by the British	2. Jatin Mukherjee
(c) Death in a shooting encounter with police in the public park	3. Jatin Das
(d) Arrest and Transportation for life	4. Bhagat Singh
(e) Death near Balasore while fighting with the police	5. Sachin Sanyal

Codes:

	(a)	*(b)*	*(c)*	*(d)*	*(e)*
A.	2	5	3	1	4
B.	4	5	1	3	2
C.	3	2	5	1	4
D.	3	5	1	4	2

66. Arrange the following in the chronological order.

1. Throwing of a bomb in the Central Legislative Assembly by Bhagat Singh and B.K. Dutta
2. Attempt on the life of Lt. Governor of East Bengal Mr. Fuller by B.K. Ghosh and Bhupen Datta
3. Attempt to blow up Lord Ervinis train near Delhi

4. Attempt on the life of Lord Hardinge by Rash Bihari Bose and Sachin Sanyal.

Codes:

A. 2, 1, 3, 4 B. 2, 4, 1, 3
C. 1, 3, 4, 2 D. 1, 4, 2, 3

67. **Assertion (A):** The daring plans and desperate deeds of the revolutionary terrorists won them a lasting place in the memory of the nation.

Reason (R): Most of the politically conscious people did not agree with their political approach.

Codes:

A. A and R are true and R is the correct explanation of A.
B. A and R are true but R is not the correct explanation of A.
C. A is true but R is false.
D. A is false but R is true.

68. **Assertion (A):** The Chittagong armoury was seized by Surya Sen and his group.

Reason (R): Surya Sen escaped to Japan along with his followers.

Codes:

A. A and R are true and R is the correct explanation of A.
B. A and R are true but R is not the correct explanation of A.
C. A is true but R is false.
D. A is false but R is true.

69. The masses were attracted to Gandhi due to his certain simple and saintly habits. Which of the following was/were not included in them?

1. Nature – Therapy
2. Experiments in Sexual restraint
3. Use of English in preference to Hindustani
4. Travelling by third class
5. Wearing only a loin cloth from 1921 onwards.

Codes:

A. 2 B. 2, 3
C. 3 D. 1, 3

70. The technique of Satyagraha included various methods. Which of the following was/were not included by Gandhi in those methods?

1. Fasting
2. Hizrat or voluntary migration
3. Scorched earth policy
4. Strikes and Hartals
5. Underground activities

Codes:

A. 3, 5 B. only 3
C. 5 D. 4, 5

71. Who among the following played an important role in signing of the Gandhi-Irwin Pact?

1. Motilal Nehru
2. Tej Bahadur Sapru
3. Madan Mohan Malviya
4. Jayakar
5. Chintamani

Codes:

A. 1, 2 B. 2, 4
C. 2, 3 D. 4, 5

72. All the established political parties and groups, except two, boycotted the Simon Commission. Which were these two?

1. Hindu Mahasabha
2. Justice Party
3. Muslim League
4. Punjab Unionists

Codes:

A. only 2 B. only 3
C. 2, 4 D. 3, 4

73. Which of the following clauses was/were not included in the Gandhi-Irwin Pact?

1. Withdrawing all ordinances and ending prosecutions.
2. Release of all kinds of political prisoners.
3. Restoration of the confiscated property of the Satyagrahis
4. Permitting peaceful picketting of liquor, open and foreign cloth shops.
5. Permitting all the Indians to collect or manufacture salt, free of duty.

Codes:

A. only 2 B. 1. 2
C. 2, 5 D. 1

74. The Civil disobedience movement was an advance over the Non-Cooperation Movement in many respects, except a few, which are those exceptions.
1. Stated objective
2. Methods adopted
3. Participation of woman and teenagers
4. Hindu-Muslim Unity
5. Response from Business Groups
6. Participation of labourers

Codes:

A. 3, 4, 6 B. 4, 6
C. 4, 5 D. 3, 5

75. Which of the following social groups and classes did not participate in the non-cooperation movement?
1. Students and teachers
2. Peasants and labourers
3. Landlords
4. Merchants
5. Big capitalists and industrialists.

Codes:

A. 3, 4, 5 B. 3, 5
C. 2, 3, 5 D. 3, 4

76. The non-cooperation movement was started by Gandhi to pressurise the British to concede certain demands. Which of the following was/were not included in those demands?
1. Remedying the "Punjab Wrong"
2. Remedying the "Khilafat Wrong"
3. Satisfy the nationalists urge for Poorna Swaraj
4. Annullment of the Rowlatt Act.

Codes:

A. 3 B. 3, 4
C. 4 D. 2, 3

77. Gandhi attracted the masses also by his socio-economic programmes. Which of the following was not one of those programmes?
1. Programme of Khadi
2. Programme of Industrialisation
3. Programme of Village re-construction
4. Programme of Hindu-Muslim unity
5. Programme of Harijan Welfare

Codes:

A. 5 B. 4
C. 2 D. 1

78. An Anti-Non-cooperation Association was started in 1920 by a group of industrialists. Which of the following person did not belong to that group?
1. Puroshottam Thakurdas
2. Jamanalal Bajaj
3. Jamunadas Dwarkadas
4. Setalvad
5. G.D. Birla

Codes:

A. 2, 5 B. 1, 2
C. 3, 4 D. 4, 5

79. Which of the following were the causes for the India Movement or the revolt of 1942?
1. The popular mood of August 1942, caused by the rout of the British by an Asian power (Japan) is South-East Asia.
2. The condemnable behaviour of most of the foreign troops stationed in India
3. Shooting up of prices and shortages of certain essential commodities like rice and salt
4. Calculations by the Congress leaders with an allied defeat very much on the cards in mid 1942.
5. British provocation before the passage of the "Quit India" resolution and their policy of wholesale repression after its passage.

Codes:

A. 1, 2 ,3, 5 B. 1, 2, 5
C. 1, 3, 5 D. All of them

80. Who among the following capitalists served as a AICC treasures for many years and went to jail in 1930?

A. G.D. Birla
B. Jamnalal Bajaj
C. J.R.D. Tata
D. Welchand Hirachand

81. Which of the following novels were written by Prem Chand?
1. Premashram 2. Char Adhyay
3. Rangbhoomi 4. Godan

Codes:

A. 1, 2, 4 B. 1, 4

C. 1, 3, 4 D. 2, 3

82. Who made the Deepawali Declaration and when?

A. Lord Irwin in 1929

B. Lord Linlithgow in 1940

C. Gandhi in 1930

D. Subhas Bose in 1941

83. Who said, "The Muslims were fools to ask for safeguards, and the Hindus were greater fools to refuse them.

A. Jawaharlal Nehru

B. Abdul Kalam Azad

C. Muhammad Ali

D. Subhas Bose

84. Who said, "This orderly discipline anarchy should go and if as a result there is complete lawlessness I would risk it"?

A. Nehru B. Gandhi

C. Rajgopala Chari D. Patel

85. Match the following.

List-I	List-II
(a) Appointment of the Simon Commission	1. Lord Reading
(b) Government of India Act 1935	2. Lord Irwin
(c) Repeal of the Rouslatt Act	3. Lord Irwin Wellingdon
(d) Cripps Mission	4. Lord Linlithgow

Codes:

	(a)	*(b)*	*(c)*	*(d)*
A.	2	3	1	1
B.	1	3	2	4
C.	3	1	4	2
D.	2	4	3	1

86. Which of the following is correctly matched?

A. Formation of All India Kisan Sabha — 1935

B. Foundation of the Congress Socialist Party — 1934

C. Foundation of the Forward Block — 1936

D. Foundation of Communist Party of India — 1939

87. When was the Federation of India Chambers of Commerce and Industry founded?

A. 1905 B. 1907

C. 1917 D. 1927

88. What is the name of the newspaper published by the Indian Muslim League?

A. Quam

B. Inqualab

C. State of India

D. Bombay Chronicle

89. Match the following.

List-I	List-II
(a) Formation of the Swaraj Party	1. 1922
(b) First meeting of the All India Youth-Congress	2. 1925
(c) Foundation of the Rashtriya Swayam Sewak Sangh	3. 1927
(d) First Convention of the All India States people Conference	4. 1928

Codes:

	(a)	*(b)*	*(c)*	*(d)*
A.	2	4	3	1
B.	1	2	4	3
C.	1	4	2	3
D.	2	1	3	4

90. Arrange the following in right sequence.

1. Escape of Subhas Chandra Bose from India
2. Celebration of the "Deliverance Day" by the Muslim League
3. Resignation of Congress Ministers
4. Lahore resolution of the league demanding separate state for Muslims
5. "Quit India" resolution by the Congress

Codes:

A. 3, 4, 2, 1, 5

B. 3, 1, 2, 4, 5

C. 3, 2, 4, 1, 5

D. 3, 4, 1, 2, 5

91. Which is the correct chronological order?
1. Simla Conference
2. Formation of the Azad Hind by Subhas Bose
3. Gandhi-Jinnah talks
4. Naval Mutiny
5. INA Trials

Codes:
A. 1, 3, 2, 4, 5
B. 2, 3, 1, 5, 4
C. 2, 1, 4, 3, 5
D. 1, 3, 2, 5, 4

92. Assertion (A): Gandhi's technique of "Satyagraha" was based on the twin concepts of truth and non-violence.

Reason (R): The literal meaning of "Satyagraha" is holding on the truth.

Codes:
A. A and R are true and R is the correct explanation of A.
B. A and R are true but R is not the correct explanation of A.
C. A is true but R is false.
D. A is false but R is true.

93. Assertion (A): The Federation of Indian Chambers of Commerce and Industry (FICCI) opposed the civil disobedience movement.

Reason (R): G.D. Birla donated between one to five lakh rupees to the civil disobedience movement.

Codes:
A. A and R are true and R is the correct explanation of A.
B. A and R are true but R is not the correct explanation of A.
C. A is true but R is false.
D. A is false but R is true.

94. Assertion (A): The second Round Table conference failed to achive anything.

Reason (R): The British refused to commute the death sentence of Bhagat Singh and anyone of his comrades to life imprisonment, and carried on their execution.

Codes:
A. A and R are true and R is the correct explanation of A.
B. A and R are true but R is not the correct explanation of A.
C. A is true but R is false.
D. A is false but R is true.

95. Assertion (A): The Bill which later became the Rowlatt Act was opposed unanimously by all the non-official Indian members in the imperial legislative council.

Reason (R): The bill proposed to give unlimited powers to the Government to arrest and imprison anyone without trial.

Codes:
A. A and R are true and R is the correct explanation of A.
B. A and R are true but R is not the correct explanation of A.
C. A is true but R is false.
D. A is false but R is true.

96. Assertion (A): The Indian Nationalist Movement for the first time in its history acquired a real massbase during the Non-Cooperation Movement.

Reason (R): A large number of peasants and workers participated in the Non-Cooperation Movement.

Codes:
A. A and R are true and R is the correct explanation of A.
B. A and R are true but R is not the correct explanation of A.
C. A is true but R is false.
D. A is false but R is true.

97. Assertion (A): Civil disobedience movement marked a major step forward in the emancipation of Indian Woman.

Reason (R): A large number of women took active participation in the civil disobedience movement.

Codes:
A. A and R are true and R is the correct explanation of A.
B. A and R are true but R is not the cor-

rect explanation of A.
C. A is true but R is false.
D. A is false but R is true.,

98. **Assertion (A):** Subhas Chandra Bose defeated Pattabhi Sitaramayya in his re-election as president of the Congress at the Tripuri Session in 1939.
Reason (R): Sitaramayya's candidature in this election was supported by Gandhi.
Codes:
A. A and R are true and R is the correct explanation of A.
B. A and R are true but R is not the correct explanation of A.
C. A is true but R is false.
D. A is false but R is true.

99. **Assertion (A):** The "August offer" of Linlithgow proposed to give "dominian states" to India immediately.
Reason (R): The Congress rejected the offer and Gandhi started his programme of individual Satyagraha, with Binova Bhave as the first Satyagrahi and Nehru as the second.
Codes:
A. A and R are true and R is the correct explanation of A.
B. A and R are true but R is not the correct explanation of A.
C. A is true but R is false.
D. A is false but R is true.

100. Who presided over the third Congress session at Madras?
A. Badruddin Tayebji
B. Annie Besant
C. Tilak
D. Dadabhai Naoroji

101. When was the Battle of Vandiwash fought?
A. 1760 B. 1770
C. 1780 D. 1758

102. Who led the revolt of 1857 in Bundelkhand?
A. Hazrat Mahal
B. Pir Ali
C. Khan Bahadur Khan
D. Kunwar Singh

103. Who made the statement, "The lover of the cotton weavers are bleaching the planes of India"?
A. Lord Dalhousie
B. William Bentinck
C. Lord Hardinge
D. Warren Hastings

104. Which workers Association was formed in 1884 by the Lokhanday?
A. The Bombay workers Association
B. The Bombay Millhands Association
C. The Indian Workers Congress
D. The Bombay Textile Mill Workers Association

105. What was the Abhinava Bharata set up by V.D. Savarkar?
A. A newspaper
B. A revolutionary association
C. A religious shrine
D. An institution of learning

106. What was the motive behind the improvement in the communications by the British?
A. Military Startegy
B. Economic gains
C. Political penetration
D. Social change

107. Under whose leadership did the Baradoli peasants organise a campaign?
A. Mahatma Gandhi
B. Sardar Patel
C. G.S. Ghorpade
D. Bhulabhai Desai

108. What was the main aim of the "Dandi March" organised by Mahatma Gandhi?
A. Opposition to Simon Commission
B. Protesting against the "divide and rule" policy of the British Government
C. Breaking the Salt laws
D. To protest against press prohibition

109. Dandi, where Gandhi violated the Salt act is situated on the:
A. Orissa Coast
B. Gujarat Coast
C. Andhra Coast

D. Kerala Coast

110. What was the main reason why the peasant once in debt found it difficult to get out of it?
A. False accounting
B. Fake signatures
C. Making the debtors sign for more amounts than he had borrowed
D. High rate of interest

111. What was the attitude of British government in India towards matters of social and religious concern?
A. Neutrality B. Interference
C. Reformation D. Degradation

112. Name the district whose Zamindari rights were given to the East India Company by Mir Zafar?
A. Murshidabad B. 24-parganas
C. Singhbhum D. Hoogly

113. Pitts India act was passed in:
A. 1763 B. 1784
C. 1781 D. 1773

114. The year 1931 is associated with
A. Jallianwallan Bagh Massacre
B. Baradoli Movement
C. Champaran Satyagraha
D. Gandhi Irwin Pact

115. Who founded the Bhill Seva Mandal in 1922?
A. C.F. Andrews
B. Gurusadev Dutta
C. Vithaldas Thakkar
D. Keshav Damle

116. The name of the journal started by the British committee of the Indian National Congress in London was
A. India
B. Bharat
C. The native opinion
D. Independent

117. The Indian National Congress was founded in 1885 with the objective of:
A. achieving independence for India
B. promoting friendly relations among the nationalists in different parts of India
C. Raising a violent revolt against the exploitation by the British
D. For popularising Indian religion in England

118. Bahadur Shah I was succeeded by
A. Jahandar Shah
B. Faruk Siyar
C. Nasiruddin
D. Shah Alam

119. Which one of the following industries was the worst hit due to the economic exploitation of the British?
A. Coir Industry
B. Pottery
C. Cotton textile
D. Jute Industry

120. Who founded the autonomous kingdom of Awadh or Oudh?
A. Safdar Jang B. Sadat Khan
C. Ahmed Shah D. Shah Alam II

121. Where was the first French factory in India established?
A. Surat B. Chandranagar
C. Pondicherry D. Mahe

122. The All India Muslim League was founded in the year
A. 1906 B. 1900
C. 1930 D. 1960

123. The All India Trade Union Congress was formed in
A. 1900 B. 1920
C. 1926 D. 1930

124. In the Surat Congress (1907) the split came sharp on the question of
A. Swarajya
B. Boycott and National Education
C. Legislative election
D. Self-Government, Boycott and National education

125. Who founded the kingdom of Awadh?
A. Sadat Khan B. Safdar Jang
C. Aliwandi Khan D. Zafar Khan

126. After the fourth Anglo-Mysore war (1799) which of the following did not get a share in Tipu's territories?
A. The English
B. The Marathas

C. The Nizam
D. The old Hindu reigning dynasty of Mysore

127. Which nationalist leader is considered the pioneer of western knowledge?
A. Dayanand Saraswati
B. Raja Ram Mohan Roy
C. Rama Krishna Paramhansa
D. Jawaharlal Nehru

128. Who incited the sepoys in Jhansi to defy the British?
A. Rani Laxmi Bai
B. Tantia Tope
C. Lachman Rao
D. Sadashiv Rao

129. Between whom was the Battle of Buxar fought?
A. Mir Kasim and Mir Jafar
B. Mir Jafar and the English
C. Shah Alam II and the French
D. Mir Kasim and his allies on one side and the English on the other

130. With which European war the first Carnatic war associated?
A. The seven year war
B. The war of Austrain succession
C. The war of Roses
D. The war of Yorks

131. Which war has been described as Duplex's private war?
A. The Second Carnatic war
B. The Second Sikh war
C. The Second Anglo-Maratha war
D. The Sind-Campaign

132. What did the "Puna Pact" do about the elections seats of the Depressed classes?
A. Increased
B. Decreased
C. Introduced proper qualifications
D. Abolished

133. The first Round Table Conference could not come to a positive conclusion because of the
A. Unhelpful attitude of the British Government
B. Absence of Gandhiji
C. Minority problem
D. Hindu-Muslim riots

134. Which of the following caused the heaviest drain on the country's resources?
A. Home charges
B. Railways
C. Military Expenditure
D. None-commercial exports

135. Tilak thought that the most potent weapon against the British was
A. Passive resistance
B. Non-cooperation movement
C. Swedeshi movement
D. Boycott

136. Which one of the following newspapers did not bring to light the suffering of the indigo planters in Bengal.
A. Hindu Patriot
B. Amrit Bazar Patrika
C. Indian Mirror
D. Bengal Gazette

137. The state of Hyderabad became a dependency of the East-India Company when the Governor-General of the Company was
A. Hardinge B. Dalhousie
C. Sir John Shore D. Lord Wellesley

138. Who supported the Marathas in the third Battle of Panipat?
A. The Rajput Kings
B. Nawab Siraj-ud-dulah of Bengal
C. The Buhela Chief
D. None of the above

139. The first jute mill was started in Bengal in
A. 1849 B. 1852
C. 1859 D. 1861

140. Who propounded the motto, "Back to the Vedas"
A. Swami Dayanand Saraswati
B. B.G. Tilak
C. Vishnu Shastri Chiplumkar
D. Swami Vivekananda

141. The Communist Party came into existence in
A. 1919 B. 1910

C. 1925 D. 1920

142. Who was the brain behind the attempted assassination of Viceroy Hardinge in December 1912?
A. Bhagat Singh B. Ras Bihari Bose
C. V.D. Savarkar D. Bhikaji Cama

143. Who said,"Freedom is my birthright and I shall have it."
A. Lala Lajpat Rai
B. V.D. Savarkar
C. Subhas Chandra Bose
D. Bal Gangadhar Tilak

144. The Permanent settlement helped the landlords because they
A. had the right to eviet the tenents
B. had the right to confiscate tenants property for non-payment of rent
C. were able to exploit Ryots
D. evade taxes imposed on them

145. The resolution for complete independence was passed by the Congress in the year
A. 1830 B. 1929
C. 1936 D. 1938

146. The Quit India resolution proposed the starting of a non-violent mass-struggle, who gave the mantra 'Do or Die' for this struggle?
A. Mahatma Gandhi
B. Aurobindo Ghosh
C. Jawaharlal Nehru
D. Vallabhbhai Patel

147. Which of the following cannot be regarded as a major cause of the poverty of the India under British rule?
A. Stagnation of agriculture
B. High taxation
C. Famines
D. Industrial decentralisation

148. Which one of the following factors helped the rise of extremism in India?
A. The Russian Revolution of 1905
B. The economic exploitation of India
C. The victory of Japan over Russia
D. All of the above

149. "For once in the annals of modern India, Baji Rao held out great promises, great possibilities for the fallen Hindu race" who said it?
A. J.N. Sarkar B. H.N. Sinha
C. Dr. Tripathi D. Sehadri

150. Who founded the French East India Company?
A. Cobbert B. Francois Caron
C. Duplix D. Monseratii

151. The moderates and the extrimists broke-up in the year 1907. They were reunited in the year
A. 1917 B. 1916
C. 1925 D. 1980

152. Who organised the All India Trade Union Congress in 1920?
A. B.P. Vadia B. Mahatma Gandhi
C. V.V. Giri D. M.N. Joshi

153. The moderates in the Indian National Congress believed in the principle of
A. Co-operation B. Rapid reform
C. Divide and rule D. Violent agitation

154. Which of the following was organised by Dadabhai Naoroji, the Grand old man of India?
A. East Indian Association 1866
B. East India House 1864
C. Land Owners Association
D. The Indian National Congress

155. The machine age in India started in the year
A. 1860 B. 1850
C. 1881 D. 1886

156. Which Bengal Sultan shifted his capital from Dacca to Murshidabad?
A. Murshid Quli Khan
B. Sarafaraj Khan
C. Siraj-ud-dulah
D. Alivardi Khan

157. Gandhi-Irwin pact was signed in London in the year
A. 1919 B. 1930
C. 1936 D. 1920

158. Khudiram Bose and Profulla Chaki were
A. moderators
B. revolutionaries
C. extremists

D. revolutionary terrorists

159. Among the following who had denied to accept the revolt of 1857 as the "first war of independence"?
A. Ashok Mehta B. Vincent Smith
C. S.M. Sen D. R.C. Mazumdar

160. Hyder Ali was defeated by the British at 'Porto nova'. The entry of which one of the following English Army commanders changed the situation of the English Army?
A. Col. Wellesley B. Col. Munro
C. Col. Clive D. Sir Eyre Corte

161. Who wrote "Unhappy India"?
A. B.G. Tilak B. M.K. Gandhi
C. M.A. Jinnah D. Lala Lajpat Rai

162. Who founded the young Bengal Movement?
A. Henry Vivian Deorozio
B. Rabindranath Tagore
C. C.R. Das
D. Sir Sayyed Ahmad Khan

163. Which of the following were the organisers of the Khilafat movement?
A. Mahatma Gandhi and Aurobindo Ghosh
B. Motilal Nehru and C.R. Das
C. Sayed Ahmed Khan and Hakin Ajmal Khan
D. Mohammad Ali and Shaukat Ali

164. In 1905 there was a division between extremists and the moderates in the Congress. The two groups different in
A. the objective
B. the method of achieving the objective
C. heir outlook toward minorities
D. their attitude towards the people

165. Which saint said, "one stone is adored, another is trodden under foot. If one is god the other is also a god.
A. Kabir B. Namdeva
C. Surdas D. Tukaram

166. One of the greatest peasant movement of the 19th century India was the indigo agitation that engullfed Bengal in
A. 1859-60 B. 1862-63
C. 1863-64 D. 1964-65

167. Which newspaper was edited by Aurobindo Ghosh?
A. Kal B. Sandhya
C. Vande Matram D. Maratha

168. Which one was not one of the results of the Dual system of Government of Bengal?
A. Agriculture and Commerce, industry of Bengal suffered
B. Administration broke down in Bengal
C. The servants of the Company grew wealthy
D. The company's trade flourished adundantly

169. Which of the following leaders entered the political scene of India, in 1914 and captured the minds of the Indian people with his personality?
A. B.G. Tilak B. Motilal Nehru
C. Shubhash Bose D. Mahatma Gandhi

170. Who ordered firing on the public meeting in Jaliawallan Bagh in 1919?
A. General Dyer
B. Hardinge
C. Lord Chelmsford
D. Montague

171. In the search for allies, Tipu sent emissaries to many foreign countries. Which of the following was not one of the countries to which he sent emissaries?
A. Arabia B. Kabul
C. Persia D. Constantinopole

172. Which of the following came to constitute the crux of the rising middle class before the battle of Plassey (1757)?
A. Money-changers
B. Revenue officials
C. Dadni merlhants
D. Gomasthas

173. The Congress and the league came together by signing the Congress-League pact known as the Lucknow Pact (1916). Who played an important role in the bringing the two together?
A. Lokmanya Tilak

B. Dadabhai Naoroji
C. M.A. Jinnah
D. Hakin Ajmal Khan

174. What did all the religious reform movements have in common?
A. Most of them got their support from the masses.
B. All of them appealed to faith and laws.
C. Most of them were based on the doctrine of Reason and Hamumism.
D. All of them preached communism

175. From which year did the drain of wealth started in Bengal
A. 1570 B. 1765
C. 1770 D. 1790

176. Quit India resolution was passed by the Indian National Congress in the
A. Lahore session
B. Madras session
C. Calcutta session
D. Bombay session

177. Which social reformer founded the Widow Remarriage Association in 1850?
A. Jotiba Phule
B. Vishnu Shastri Pandit
C. M.G. Ranade
D. Gandhiji

178. Simla Conference of political leaders was summoned by the Viceroy to discuss
A. Lord Wayell report
B. Hunter Commission report
C. Rajaji formula
D. Cabinet mission plan

179. Waht did the Cabinet mission plan of 1946 suggest?
A. An interim national government.
B. A federal union
C. Division of provincial and Federal power
D. All of the above

180. The first split in the A.I.T.U.C. took place in the year
A. 1927 B. 1925
C. 1930 D. 1940

181. The pattern of trade that the British developed was one of
A. Marginal profit
B. Steady returns
C. Spectacular returns
D. Occasional profit

182. Which Nationalist leader wrote, "poverty and British rule in India"?
A. Dadabhai Naoroji
B. Tilak
C. Gandhi
D. Bipin Chandra Pal

183. One of the factors responsible for the awakening of Indian women and their emanicipation was
A. Teaching of religious reforms
B. Impact of western culture
C. Participation in National Movement
D. Government laws

184. Which one of the following measures of social reforms of the British Government did not provide opposition from the Indian people?
A. Prohibition of female infantacide
B. Abolition of Sati
C. Abolition of Slavery
D. Removal of disabilities due to change of religion

185. Safdar Jung had to fight several wars during the course of his rule over Awadh, which of the following were his staunch foes?
A. Satanamis
B. Marathas
C. Bangash Pathans
D. Rohillas

186. The peasants along with the students and workers provided the back bone to the
A. Anti-partition movement
B. Home-rule movement
C. Khilafat agitation
D. Quit-India movement

187. Which of the following revolutionaries was associated with the Indian Independence Leage founded in California in the late 19th Century?
A. Rasha Bihari Bose

B. Lala Hardayal
C. S.C. Bose
D. Madam Cama

188. Which of the following revolutionaries was associated with the Indian Independence founded in California in the late 19th century?
A. Rasha Bihari Bose
B. Lal Hardyal
C. S.C. Bose
D. Madam Cama

189. By the Pitt's India Act of 1784 the powers of the Board of control lowever gradually came to be concentrated in the hands of
A. Board of Directors
B. Governor General in Council
C. President of the Board of Control
D. Finance Minister

190. Who was the Viceroy of the India when the Indian National Congress was founded in 1885?
A. Lord Ripon
B. Lord Handsdowne
C. Lord Dufferin
D. Lord Wavell

191. Who set up the Calcutta madrasah to study the teachings of Muslim law and related studies?
A. Lord Hordinge
B. Lord Minto
C. Lord Dalhousie
D. Warren Hastings

192. Which one of the following educational institutions was not started in the 1920's with the purpose of arousing national statements in the minds of young people in North India?
A. Kashi Vidyapith
B. Bihar Vidyapith
C. Jamia Milia Islamia
D. Benaras Hindus University

193. In 1872-73 there was a peasent struggle in Bengal which was confined to the district of
A. Pabna B. Nadia
C. Murshidabad D. Dacca

194. Madras was raised to the rank of presidency in the year
A. 1652 B. 1680
C. 1706 D. 1725

195. Who said, Not mercy, but service for man must be regarded as God?
A. Aurobindo B. Vivekananda
C. Ramakrishna D. Mahatma Gandhi

196. With which one of the following associations was Lokhitwadi closely connected with?
A. Brahmo Samaj
B. Prathana Samaj
C. Arya Samaj
D. Theoropied movement

197. Who founded the Kirti and communist movement in Punjab?
A. The Swarajist
B. The revolutionary terrorist
C. The Chadarites
D. The Communist Party of India

198. The most important feature of the Political technique of Mahatma Gandhi was
A. enlisting the support of educated man
B. enlisting the support of the Capitalist
C. Hindu-Muslim unity
D. Non-violence

199. Who started the Tatvabodhini Sabha in 1839 to propagate Rammohan Roy's view?
A. Debendra Nath Tagore
B. C.R. Das
C. Vivekananda
D. Shankaracharya

200. Who composed, "Sare Jahan Se Achcha?
A. Rabindranath Tagore
B. Kishna Rao
C. Bankim Chandra Chatterji
D. Mohammad Iqbal

201. The Burden of taxation during the British period was
A. Light
B. Average
C. Heavey and discriminatory
D. Oppressive

202. Which was not one of the taxes which the British rulers imposed or increased in

order to augment its resources in India?
A. Income B. Profession tax
C. Octroi D. Famine Cess

203. The tribal revolts of Kols occurred in
A. 1820 and 1830's B. 1840 and 1850's
C. 1870 D. 1880

204. Who first made the demand for Swarajya or self-government in 1905?
A. Gokhale
B. Mahatma Gandhi
C. Dadabhai Naoroji
D. Nehru

205. Who founded Azad Hind Fauj?
A. V.D. Savarkar
B. Pulin Das
C. Ras Bihari Bose
D. Subhas Chandra Bose

206. Which of the following did not participate in the first Round Table conference?
A. The Hindu Mahasabha
B. The Muslim League
C. The Indian National Congress
D. The British

207. With the arrest of which one of the following rebels in April 1858, revolt ended?
A. Kunwar Singh B. Nava Shed
C. Tantia Tope D. Bahadur Shah

208. Democratisation of local administration was emphasised by
A. Charles Metcalfe
B. Lord Mayo
C. Lord Ripon
D. Lord Dufferin

209. For how many years was the Dutch East India Company given exclusive rights to trade?
A. Ten years
B. Twenty one years
C. Five years
D. Sixty years

210. Which of the following did not form part of the so-called home charge "in the Drain of wealth"?
A. Interest on public debt
B. Charges for civil administration
C. Guranteed interest on the railways
D. payment of dividends to the share-holders.

211. The East India Company was given a royal charter and the exclusive right to trade with by the Queen Elizabeth in the year
A. 1599 B. 1600
C. 1604 D. 1606

212. Who founded the Ramakrishna Mission in 1896?
A. Ramkrishna Paramhansa
B. Narendra Nath Dutta
C. Annie Besant
D. Keshav Chandra Sen

213. The name Assam is derived from the tribe of Ahoms. To which tribe the Ahoms belong to?
A. Bodo B. Shan
C. Bhuiyas D. Kacharis

214. Swadeshi movements refers to the
A. Boycott of British Goods
B. Quit India movement
C. Non-cooperation movement
D. None of the above

215. Who is known as Colonel Clive's Jacke?
A. Amichand B. Manikchand
C. Mir Zafar D. Siraj-ud-daulah

216. Dev Samaj was founded by
A. Vallabhbhai Patel
B. Dadabhai Naoroji
C. Srinarayan Agnihotri
D. Ramkrishna Paramhansa

217. Name the first nationalist poet modern India?
A. Bankim Chandra Chatterjee
B. Subramaniya Iyer
C. Debendranath Tagore
D. Henry Derozio

218. The Company ultimately accepted the principle of limiting the land tax to one third of the gross produce in which of the following regions?
A. Punjab
B. The Gangetic Valley
C. Calcutta
D. The Madras presidency

219. "In my belief Congress is tottering to its fall and one my great ambitions while in India is to assist to a peaceful demise". Who said these words?
A. Lord Dufferin B. Lord Curzon
C. Lord Minto D. Lord Moorby

220. The Congress Khilafat Swaraj Party was formed after the Gaya session in 1922. Who among the following was not associated with this new party?
A. C.R. Das B. Motilal Nehru
C. Vinoba Bhave D. Vithal Bhai Patel

221. Which amongst the following industries was mainly run by Indian Capital during the 19th Century?
A. Cotton textile B. Jute
C. Iron D. Coal

222. Where was the "Depressed class Mission Society started with the object of improving, "the social as well as the spiritual conditions of the depressed classes" in 1906?
A. Poona B. Calcutta
C. Bombay D. Bihar

223. What was the main items of export of the English from Hoogly and Balasore in Orissa?
A. Raw Silk and Sugar
B. Tea and Tobacco
C. Raw Silk and Jute
D. Salt and Muslim

224. Which was faught outside India is associated with the first-carnatic war?
A. War of Austrian succession
B. War of Roses
C. Seven years war
D. Crimean War

225. Tilak was released from jail in 1914 and the formed the Home Rule League in
A. 1911 B. 1914
C. 1916 D. 1919

226. Which of the following was not one of the social reforms measures introduced by William Bentinck in India?
A. Abolition of Sati
B. Abolition of Polygamy
C. Removal of disabilities due to change of religion
D. Supression of Thugs

227. Which was not one of the reforms on which the Congress laid special emphasis during the first phase in the national movement?
A. Spread of Education
B. Abolition of the Indian Council
C. Boycott of Legislature
D. Development of Self-Government

228. Which Governor-General was responsible:
A. Lord Canning
B. Lord Hastings
C. Lord Dalhousie
D. Lord Wavell

229. The extremists came into full swing with:
A. Partition of Bengal in 1905
B. Champaran Satyagrah
C. Non-Cooperation Movement
D. Death of Tilak

230. The famous Hindu College was founded in 1817 in Calcutta by
A. Raja Rammohan Roy
B. David Hare
C. Dayanand Saraswati
D. Dwarka Nath Tagore

231. Who among the following, abolished the Dual system of Government of Bengal?
A. Lord Auckland
B. Spencer
C. Warren Hastings
D. Lord Lytton

232. One of the most terrible famines occured in Bengal in
A. 1768 B. 1770
C. 1772 D. 1790

233. The first census in India during the British period was held during the vice-royality of
A. Lord Ripon B. Lord Curzon
C. Lord Elgin D. Lord Mayo

234. The Tatvabodhini Sabha was founded in the years 1839 by
A. Keshav Chandra Sen

B. Ishwar Chandra Vidya Sagar
C. Devendra Nath Tagore
D. Madan Mohan Malviya

235. Who was popularly known as Deshbandhu?
A. Vivekananda B. Chitranjan Das
C. Motilal Nehru D. C.F. Andrews

236. The motive of the British Government of India to introduce Communal politics in India was
A. Incentive to start Muslim League
B. Partition of Bengal in 1905
C. Introduction of separate electorates for the Muslims
D. Reservation of seat for Muslims

237. The Congress socialist party was set up in the year
A. 1920 B. 1939
C. 1930 D. 1936

238. Name of the odd man out in the following list
A. Kudhi Ram Bose
B. Mahatma Gandhi
C. Chandra Shekhar Azad
D. Sukhdeva

239. A separate representation to Muslims was introduced through
A. The Act of 1791
B. The Indian Council Act 1909
C. The Government of India Act 1919
D. Government of India Act 1935.

ANSWERS

1	2	3	4	5	6	7	8	9	10
C	A	A	A	C	B	A	B	A	A
11	**12**	**13**	**14**	**15**	**16**	**17**	**18**	**19**	**20**
D	B	B	C	B	C	C	D	D	A
21	**22**	**23**	**24**	**25**	**26**	**27**	**28**	**29**	**30**
C	D	B	D	B	B	A	C	C	A
31	**32**	**33**	**34**	**35**	**36**	**37**	**38**	**39**	**40**
B	D	C	A	C	D	C	A	D	A
41	**42**	**43**	**44**	**45**	**46**	**47**	**48**	**49**	**50**
C	A	A	C	C	B	B	A	D	C
51	**52**	**53**	**54**	**55**	**56**	**57**	**58**	**59**	**60**
D	B	C	D	A	B	D	D	B	C
61	**62**	**63**	**64**	**65**	**66**	**67**	**68**	**69**	**70**
A	D	D	B	D	B	B	C	C	A
71	**72**	**73**	**74**	**75**	**76**	**77**	**78**	**79**	**80**
B	D	C	B	B	A	C	A	D	B
81	**82**	**83**	**84**	**85**	**86**	**87**	**88**	**89**	**90**
C	A	B	B	A	B	D	C	C	C
91	**92**	**93**	**94**	**95**	**96**	**97**	**98**	**99**	**100**
B	B	C	B	A	A	A	B	D	A
101	**102**	**103**	**104**	**105**	**106**	**107**	**108**	**109**	**110**
A	C	B	B	B	B	B	C	B	D
111	**112**	**113**	**114**	**115**	**116**	**117**	**118**	**119**	**120**
A	B	B	D	C	A	B	A	C	B
121	**122**	**123**	**124**	**125**	**126**	**127**	**128**	**129**	**130**
A	A	B	D	A	B	B	C	D	A

131	132	133	134	135	136	137	138	139	140
A	A	C	C	D	C	D	D	C	A
141	**142**	**143**	**144**	**145**	**146**	**147**	**148**	**149**	**150**
C	B	B	B	B	A	C	D	B	A
151	**152**	**153**	**154**	**155**	**156**	**157**	**158**	**159**	**160**
B	D	A	A	B	A	B	D	D	D
161	**162**	**163**	**164**	**165**	**166**	**167**	**168**	**169**	**170**
D	A	D	B	A	A	C	D	D	A
171	**172**	**173**	**174**	**175**	**176**	**177**	**178**	**179**	**180**
C	C	A	C	B	D	B	A	D	B
181	**182**	**183**	**184**	**185**	**186**	**187**	**188**	**189**	**190**
B	A	C	C	D	D	D	B	C	C
191	**192**	**193**	**194**	**195**	**196**	**197**	**198**	**199**	**200**
D	D	A	A	C	A	C	D	A	D
201	**202**	**203**	**204**	**205**	**206**	**207**	**208**	**209**	**210**
C	B	A	A	D	C	C	C	B	D
211	**212**	**213**	**214**	**215**	**216**	**217**	**218**	**219**	**220**
B	B	B	A	C	C	D	D	A	C
221	**222**	**223**	**224**	**225**	**226**	**227**	**228**	**229**	**230**
A	C	A	C	C	B	C	A	A	B
231	**232**	**233**	**234**	**235**	**236**	**237**	**238**	**239**	
C	B	D	C	B	B	D	B	B	

WORLD HISTORY

Multiple Choice Questions (MCQ)

1. In which year, Alexander the Great become the king of Macedonia?
A. 336 BC B. 323 BC
C. 350 BC D. 200 BC

2. The European renaissance started from which country?
A. England B. France
C. Italy D. Greece

3. On which island of France, Napoleon was born?
A. Saint Helena B. Corsica
C. Elba D. Oleron

4. The Battle of Waterloo was fought in the year:
A. 1800 B. 1805
C. 1807 D. 1815

5. In which year America got independence?
A. 1760 B. 1776
C. 1780 D. 1782

6. Who is known as the Artist of the world famous painting 'Mona Lisa'?
A. Filippo Brunelleschi
B. Michelangelo
C. Vincent van Gogh
D. Leonardo da Vinci

7. Who was the king during the French revolution?
A. Napoleon B. Louis XV
C. Louis XVI D. Charles IX

8. The Hundred Years' War (from 1337 to 1453) was fought between:
A. England and France
B. Germany and Russia
C. America and Argentina
D. England and Germany

9. Queen Elizabeth I of England belongs to which dynasty?
A. Stuart B. York
C. Tudor D. Normandy

10. 'Boston Tea Party' protest was associated with the revolution of:
A. America B. Italy
C. France D. India

11. Which king of England was forced to signed the 'Magna Carta'?
A. King Richard I B. King Louis
C. Henry III D. King John

12. When the first Ancient Greek Olympic Game was begun?
A. 776 BC B. 552 BC
C. 800 BC D. 235 BC

13. Who was the author of United States Declaration of Independence?
A. Thomas Jefferson
B. George Washington
C. Abraham Lincoln
D. Benjamin Franklin

14. Napoleon was exiled to the Saint Helena after the defeat in the war of:
A. Russia B. Waterloo
C. Peninsular D. Rivoli

15. Who was the President of America during American Civil War?
A. Abraham Lincoln
B. Andrew Jackson
C. George Washington
D. James Madison

16. Industrial Revolution was started from which country?
A. France B. Germany
C. Italy D. England

17. Which city was recaptured at the end of the first war of Crusade?
A. Rome B. Venice
C. Jerusalem D. Vienna

18. First war of Crusade was ended in the year:
A. 1099 B. 1095
C. 1123 D. 1323

19. Who was one of the teachers of Alexander the Great?
A. Plato B. Aristotle
C. Socrates D. None of the above

20. In which year Christopher Columbus discovered America?
A. 1502 B. 1339
C. 1405 D. 1492

21. Which were the two countries that fought during the Falklands War?
A. Britain and France
B. Germany and Austria
C. Argentina and Britain
D. Austria and Russia

22. Who was the Chinese Emperor when Marco Polo visited China?
A. Temur Khan B. Kublai Khan
C. Genghis Khan D. Ogedei Khan

23. Aztec civilization was originated in which country?
A. USA B. Greece
C. Egypt D. Mexico

24. Which famous book was written by Nostradamus?
A. Les Propheties B. Das Kapital
C. The Tempest D. None of the above

25. Who was the Emperor of Russia during Russian Revolution?
A. Alexander III B. Nicholas II
C. Nicholas I D. Alexander II

26. When did the second Russian Revolution start?
A. August, 1905 B. February, 1917
C. October, 1917 D. March, 1921

27. Leonardo da Vinci was born in the city of:
A. Rome B. Milan
C. Florence D. Madrid

28. In which year did the Suez Canal was open for trade?
A. 1869 B. 1880
C. 1774 D. 1620

29. Who was the first Roman Emperor?
A. Caligula B. Claudius
C. Augustus D. Nero

30. Who was the founder of Ottoman Empire?
A. Osman I B. Orhan
C. Mura I D. Bayezid I

31. Crimean War was started in the year:
A. 1853 B. 1857
C. 1862 D. 1870

32. Who is known as the 'Father of History'?
A. Homer B. Thucydides
C. Herodotus D. Archimedes

33. 'Mein Kampf' is the autobiography of which political leader?
A. Joseph Stalin B. Benito Mussolini
C. Winston Churchill D. Adolf Hitler

34. Benito Mussolini was the Prime Minister of which country?
A. French B. Belgium
C. Italy D. Turkey

35. Who was the US President during World War II?
A. Winston Churchill
B. Joseph Stalin
C. Franklin D Roosevelt
D. Harry S Truman

36. In which year Adolf Hitler was appointed as Chancellor of Germany?
A. 1933 B. 1935
C. 1938 D. 1940

37. World renowned philosopher Karl Marx was born in the country:
A. Austria B. Germany
C. Russia D. Italy

38. Who gave the famous quote 'Government of the people, by the people, for the people, shall not perish from the Earth'?
A. Winston Churchill
B. Abraham Lincoln
C. Vladimir Lenin
D. George Washington

39. The organisation 'League of Nations' was founded after the end of:
A. World War I B. World War II
C. Crimean War D. Vietnam War

40. First Sino-Japanese War was fought in the year:
A. 1848 B. 1894
C. 1901 D. 1896

41. Who build the St. Basil's Cathedral in Moscow, Russia?
A. Peter I　B. Vladislav I
C. Ivan the Terrible　D. Feodor I

42. Which dynasty of China began the construction of the Great Wall?
A. Ming Dynasty　B. Qin Dynasty
C. Shun Dynasty　D. None of the above

43. In which year Bastille of Paris stormed by the people which lead to the French Revolution?
A. 1746　B. 1779
C. 1789　D. 1808

44. Which King was executed by guillotine during French Revolution in 1793?
A. Charles X　B. Louis XIII
C. Henry IV　D. Louis XVI

45. Who was the first Christian emperor of the Roman Empire?
A. Julius Caesar　B. Nero
C. Constantine　D. Domitian

46. Who was the last Emperor of Rome?
A. Nero
B. Romulus Augustulus
C. Julius Nepos
D. Julius Caesar

47. When the first communist manifesto was written by Karl Marx and Friedrich Engels?
A. 1848　B. 1859
C. 1872　D. 1890

48. Which country first invented Gunpower in around 270 AD?
A. China　B. India
C. Korea　D. England

49. Which pharaoh build the largest pyramid known as Great Pyramid of Giza?
A. Sneferu　B. Tutankhamun
C. Khufu　D. None of the above

50. During which dynasty Paper was invented in China?
A. Xia Dynasty　B. Tang Dynasty
C. Yuan Dynasty　D. Han Dynasty

51. Who is known as the father of American Constitution?
A. James Madison　B. George Washington
C. John Adams　D. Thomas Jefferson

52. Who is the first crowned Czar (Tsar) of Russia?
A. Peter I
B. Ivan IV (the Terrible)
C. Nicholas I
D. John Adams

53. The famous painting 'Last Supper' is a creation of:
A. Michaelangelo
B. Vincent van Gogh
C. Leonardo Da Vinci
D. Sandro Botticelli

54. Who was the commander of 'Seventh Coalition' army that defeated Napoleon in the Battle of Waterloo?
A. Arthur Wellesley
B. Jean-de-Dieu Soult
C. Robert Clive
D. John Carnac

55. What was the name of the atom bomb dropped in Hiroshima city?
A. Fat Boy　B. Fat Man
C. Little Boy　D. Scorpion

56. What was the name of the atom bomb dropped in Nagasaki city?
A. Fat Boy　B. Fat Man
C. Scorpion　D. Death Kiss

57. American Civil War was started in the year:
A. 1756　B. 1806
C. 1861　D. 1890

58. Who founded the Great Seljuq Empire in 1037?
A. Seljuq Beg　B. Tughril Beg
C. Alp Arslan　D. Malik-Shah I

59. The Parliament of Great Britain was formed in the year:
A. 1707　B. 1729
C. 1774　D. 1823

60. In which European country feudalism process is first started?
A. Italy B. England
C. French D. Russia

61. Who is consider as the first Pope of Christianity?
A. St. Peter B. St. Linus
C. St. Evaristus D. St. Alexander I

62. Who is known as the first pope of Vatican City?
A. Pope Benedict XV B. Clement XIII
C. Pope Pius XI D. Benedict XIII

63. Which Nazi Field Marshal is known as the 'Desert Fox'?
A. Viktor Brack B. Erwin Rommel
C. Hans Frank D. Hermann Goring

64. Communist Revolutionary Che Guevara was born in the city:
A. Havana B. Rosario
C. Matanzas D. San Juan

65. Which Roman Emperor is also known as 'little boot'?
A. Nero B. Julius Caesar
C. Caligula D. Augustus

66. The Greek War of Independence against the Ottoman Empire started in the year:
A. 1805 B. 1821
C. 1852 D. 1895

67. The Franco-Prussian War (1870-1871) was ended with the sign of:
A. Treaty of Vienna B. Treaty of Munich
C. Treaty of Paris D. Treaty of Versailles

68. In European history, which year is known as the year of revolution?
A. 1732 B. 1765
C. 1848 D. 1896

69. Which monarch is known as 'the Sun King' and also the longest of monarchs of major countries in European history?
A. Louis XIV of France
B. Henry III of England
C. Louis XIII of France
D. Edward I of England

70. In which country the revolution of 1848 first begins that lead to a series of revolutions?
A. Italy B. Germany
C. France D. Austria

71. The Renaissance movement is described as the ending of:
A. Pre-historic Era B. Ancient Era
C. Medieval Era D. Modern Era

72. Which city is known as the birthplace of the Renaissance?
A. Florence B. Venice
C. Rome D. London

73. Constantinople, the capital of Roman Empire was captured by Turks in the year:
A. 1385 B. 1415
C. 1453 D. 1469

74. Who was known as the Morning star of Renaissance?
A. Montesquieu B. Dante
C. Shakespeare D. Geoffrey Chaucer

75. Who become the Chancellor of Germany for One Day after the death of Hitler during Second World War?
A. Hermann Goering B. Henerich Himmler
C. Rudolf Hess D. Joseph Goebbels

76. Total number of Theses written by Martin Luther on Power of Indulgences are:
A. 81 B. 87
C. 95 D. 101

77. What was the name of the secret police party of Nazi in Germany?
A. Gestapo B. NKVD
C. OVRA D. Palace Guard

78. Who is known as the founder of the Durrani Empire?
A. Timur Shah Durrani
B. Zaman Shah Durrani
C. Mahmud Shah Durrani
D. Ahmad Shah Durrani

79. Who is regarded as the founder of modern Egypt?
A. Muhammad Ali B. Ibrahim Pasha
C. Abbas I D. Sa'id Pasha

80. In which year British East India Company established in Singapore?
A. 1808 B. 1819
C. 1832 D. 1849

81. In which year Francis II, founded the Empire of Austria?
A. 1804 B. 1809
C. 1820 D. 1822

82. The term 'Cold War' was coined by:
A. Barnard Baruch B. Prof. Lippmann
C. Palmer Perkins D. Roosevelt

83. During the First World War, which country signed the Peace of Treaty (1917) with Germany?
A. England B. USA
C. Russia D. Austria

84. When United Kingdom declared war on Germany which lead to World War II?
A. 4th April 1939
B. 18th August 1939
C. 28th August 1939
D. 3rd September 1939

85. Who was the last Byzantine Emperor during the fall of Constantinople in 1453?
A. Manuel II B. John V
C. John VIII D. Constantine XI

86. The Triple Alliance agreement between Germany, Austria-Hungary, and Italy was formed in the year:
A. 1881 B. 1889
C. 1901 D. 1909

87. In which year, America joined the Second World War?
A. 1939 B. 1940
C. 1941 D. 1942

88. During which US President period, the Cuban Missile Crisis conflict was occurred?
A. Lyndon B. Johnson
B. Richard Nixon
C. Ronald Reagan
D. John F. Kennedy

89. Marco Polo was a traveller from ________:
A. Portugal B. England
C. Italy D. Spain

90. The First Opium War was fought between British and ________:
A. Chinese B. Indian
C. Japanese D. Thai

91. Rivers Tigris and Euphrates are associated with?
A. Mesopotamian Civilization
B. Egyptian Civilization
C. Harappan Civilization
D. Chinese Civilization

92. Which is considered as the oldest civilization of the world?
A. Mesopotamian Civilization
B. Egyptian Civilization
C. Harappan Civilization
D. Chinese Civilization

93. Which among following is called "Gift of the Nile"?
A. China B. India
C. Iraq D. Egypt

94. Marco Polo, Venetian traveller, travelled from Venice to China and Japan in:
A. 1285-90 B. 1288-93
C. 1290-96 D. 1295-1301

95. In which year Bartholomew Diaz reached Cape of Good Hope?
A. 1480 B. 1487
C. 1495 D. 1500

96. Magna Carta or The Great Charter was signed in:
A. 1210 B. 1215
C. 1220 D. 1225

97. Who is known as Man of Blood and Iron?
A. Napoleon
B. Bismarck
C. Ho Chi Minh
D. Sir Walter Scott

98. What is Chivalry?
A. The code Charlemagne implemented
B. The code by which a Christian family lived
C. The code by which knights lived
D. The code by which young men lived

99. Which of the following was the most important 'God' of ancient Egyptians?
A. The Moon
B. Jackal
C. The Sun
D. None of these

100. Which of the following statement is/are correct?
A. The ancient Egyptians firmly believed in life after deaths.
B. The dead body of ancient Egyptians was embalmed in spices and then wrapped in strips of fine linen. Such a preserved body is called 'mummy'.
C. The pyramids were the tombs of great kings.
D. All the above

101. Whose model is based on the Mandate of Heaven?
A. Ban Gu B. Li Ling
C. Qin Shi Huang D. Sima Qian

102. Who is the author of "The History of the World-Conquerer"?
A. Annemarie Schimmel
B. Clifford Edmund Bosworth
C. Gustaf John Ramstedt
D. John Andrew Boyle

103. Who was the first to distinguish between cause and immediate origins of an event?
A. Herodotus B. Pericles
C. Plutarch D. Thucydides

104. The Peloponnesian War was fought between which cities?
A. Athens and Macedonia
B. Carthage and Athens
C. Sparta and Carthage
D. Sparta and Athens

105. When did the rise of Median Empire occur?
A. 745 BC B. 722 BC
C. 750 BC D. 728 BC

106. When was Nineveh destructed?
A. 612 BC B. 600 BC
C. 599 BC D. 563 BC

107. Who founded the Achaemenid Empire?
A. Alexander the Great
B. Cambyses II
C. Cyrus the Great
D. Darius I

108. When did Cambyses II conquer Egypt?
A. 525 BC B. 512 BC
C. 509 BC D. 508 BC

109. Who developed system ranks of binary patterns?
A. Baudhayana B. Aryabhata
C. Mahavira D. Pingala

110. When did King Leonidas die?
A. 480 BC B. 479 BC
C. 475 BC D. 469 BC

111. When was Socrates born?
A. 469 BC B. 465 BC
C. 460 BC D. 449 BC

112. When was Xerxes I murdered?
A. 465 BC B. 460 BC
C. 449 BC D. 447 BC

113. Who founded the philosophy of Stoicism in Athens?
A. Chrysippus B. Cleanthes
C. Epictetus D. Zeno of Citium

114. Who defeated Hannibal at Battle of Zama?
A. Cato the Elder B. Scipio Aemilianus
C. Scipio Africanus D. Hasdrubal

115. Who officially instituted the first system of imperial examinations in China?
A. Han Wu Di B. Huo Qubing
C. Wei Qing D. None

116. How did Saint Boniface help to shape the German church?
A. Preaching against divorce, incest, and polygamy
B. Preaching against the importance of monasteries
C. Writing the epic 'Beowulf
D. Writing 'The Rule of Saint Benedict'

117. Who took control of the kingdoms of Austrasia and Neustria in a coup of 753?
A. Carloman B. Charles Martel
C. Pepin of Herstal D. Pepin the Short

118. Where was the Ottonian dynasty established?
A. Denmark B. Germany
C. Iceland D. Scandinavia

119. "Middle Ages" in Western Europe includes the period ______.
A. AD 300 - AD 1600
B. Beginning of Byzantine through the end of the Roman Empire
C. Beginning of Early Christian through the 13th or 14th centuries
D. End of the Roman Empire through the Byzantine period

120. What does the opening scene of Beowulf describe?
A. The arrival of Scyld Scefing in Denmark
B. The birth of Beowulf
C. The death of Beowulf
D. The defeat of the monster Grendel

121. Tsarist power in Russia collapsed in the year:
A. 1905 B. 1916
C. 1917 D. 1920

122. Jadidists were .... within the Russian empire.
A. Muslim reformers
B. Muslim educationists
C. Parsi reformers
D. German refugees

123. The main occupation of the people of Russia in the beginning of the twentieth century was:
A. manufacturing B. poultry farming
C. fishing D. agriculture

124. A Labour Party in Britain was formed by socialist and:
A. trade unionists B. peasants
C. industrialists D. young students

125. The Central powers during the First World War included countries like Germany, Turkey and:
A. France B. Austria
C. Britain D. Russia

126. The successor of Lenin was:
A. Stalin B. Kerenskii
C. Trotskii D. Louis Blance

127. Which among the following groups was against any kind of political or social change?
A. Nationalists
B. Conservatives
C. Liberals
D. Radicals

128. Which of these statements is/are correct about Europe after the French Revolution?
A. Suddenly it seemed possible to change the aristocratic society of the 18th century.
B. However not everyone wanted a complete transformation of society.
C. Some wanted gradual shift, while others wanted complete change of society.
D. All the above

129. How can you say that the 'liberals' were not 'democrats'?
A. They did not believe in universal adult franchise
B. They felt that only men of property should have a right to vote
C. Women should not have to vote
D. All of the above

130. Who conspired in Italy to bring about a revolution?
A. Bismarck
B. Karl Marx
C. Giuseppe Mazzini
D. None

131. In the World War I, which started in 1914, Russia fought against:
A. Britain and France
B. Germany and Austria
C. America
D. All the above

132. Which of the following statements is/are correct?
A. By 1916, railway lines in Russia began to break down
B. There were labour shortages and small workshops producing essentials were shut down
C. Large supplies of grain were sent to feed the army
D. All the above

133. Which of these demands is/are referred to as Lenin's 'April Theses'?
A. World War I should be brought to an end
B. Land should be transferred to the peasants
C. Banks should be nationalised
D. All the above

134. Socialists took over the government in Russia through the?
A. October Revolution in 1917
B. November Revolution in 1918
C. December Revolution in 1919
D. February Revolution in 1920

135. At the beginning of the 20th century, the majority of Russian people worked in the:
A. Industrial sector
B. Agricultural sector
C. Mining sector
D. Transport sector

136. Which country was defeated after the First World War?
A. France B. Germany
C. Russia D. Britain

137. The Nazi Party had become the largest party by the
A. 1920 B. 1925
C. 1926 D. 1932

138. Hitler became the Chancellor or Germany in the year
A. 1931 B. 1932
C. 1933 D. 1934

139. Who could enter Jungvolk?
A. Ten-year-old boys
B. Twelve-year-old boys
C. Fourteen-year-old boys
D. Eighteen-year-old boys

140. A bronze cross was given to the woman who produced:
A. two children B. four children
C. six children D. eight children

141. The game Hitler glorified was:
A. Wresting B. Kabaddi
C. Hockey D. Boxing

142. Which of the following statements is false about soldiers in the World War I?
A. The soldiers, in reality, led miserable lives in trenches, survived with feeding on the copra's
B. They faced poisonous gas and enemy shelling and loss of comrades
C. All soldiers were ready to die for their country's honour and personal glory
D. Aggressive propaganda glorified war

143. What was Hitler's historic blunder and why?
A. Attack on Soviet Union in 1941 was a historic blunder by Hitler
B. He exposed his western front to British aerial bombing
C. The Soviet Red Army inflicted a crushing and humiliating defeat on Germany at Stalingrad
D. All the above

144. Which of the following bodies was set up to try and prosecute the Nazi war criminals at the end of World War II?
A. International Military Tribunal
B. British Military Tribunal
C. Allied Military Tribunal
D. Allied Judicial Court

145. Why did the Nuremburg Tribunal sentence only 11 Nazis to death for such a massive genocide?
A. Only these 11 Nazis were found guilty
B. The Allies did not want to be harsh on the defeated Germany as they had been after World War
C. Germany promised never to repeat such an act
D. Germany was ready to pay a huge compensation to the Allied countries for these killings

146. War in 1917 led to the strengthening of Allies and the defeat of Germany because of entry of:
A. China B. Japan
C. the USA D. Spain

147. What gave Nazi state its reputation as the most dreaded criminal state?
A. Extra-constitutional powers were given to the newly organised forces like Gestapo, the SS and SD

B. People could be detained in Gestapo torture chambers and sent to concentration camps
C. No legal procedures were there for the arrested people
D. All of the above

148. When and among which countries was the Tripartite Pact signed?
A. 1940, Germany, Italy and Japan
B. 1939, Germany, Austria and USSR
C. 1940, England, France and USA
D. 1938, England, Germany and USSR

149. Which incident persuaded the USA to join the war?
A. Hitler's attack on Eastern Europe
B. Hitler's policy of genocide of the Jews
C. Helplessness of England and France
D. Japan's attack on the US base at Pearl Harbour

150. Identify the French artist who prepared a series of four prints visualising his dream of a world from the following:
A. Kitagewa Utamaro B. Richard M Hoe
C. Voltaire D. Frederic Sorrieu

151. Who was proclaimed King of united Italy in 1861?
A. Victor Emmanuel II
B. Louis Philippe
C. Mazzini
D. Cavour

152. Which of the following artists painted the image of Germania?
A. Philip Veit B. Frederic Sorrieu
C. Ernst Renan D. Richar M Hoe

153. What happened to Poland at the end of 18th century. Which of the following answers is correct?
A. Poland achieved independence at the end of the 18th century.
B. Poland came totally under the control of Russia and became part of Russia.
C. Poland became the part of East Germany.
D. Poland was partitioned at the end of the 18th century by three Great Powers: Russia, Prussia and Austria.

154. Three wars over seven years with Austria, Denmark, Germany and France, ended in:
A. Danish victory B. Prussian victory
C. French victory D. German victory

155. Which one of the following was not the feature of Napoleonic Code?
A. Equality before the law
B. Universal Adult Franchise
C. Right to Property
D. Privileges based on birth

156. The political and constitutional changes brought about by the French Revolution were:
A. it ended the absolute monarchy.
B. It transferred power to a body of the French citizens.
C. It proclaimed that henceforth people would constitute the nation and shape its destiny.
D. All the above

157. The first clear expression of nationalism came with:
A. The American Revolution
B. The French Revolution
C. The Russian Revolution
D. The Industrial Revolution

158. What was the main intention behind 'Treaty of Vienna of 1815'?
A. Restore republics
B. Restore democracies
C. Restore monarchies
D. None of these

159. What did Germania symbolize?
A. French nation B. German nation
C. British nation D. None of the above

160. Name the customs union formed by Prussia to abolish tariff barriers.
A. Elle B. Zollverein
C. Zweibiicken D. La Patrie

161. What did 'Das Volk' stand for?
A. Democracy B. Factory workers
C. Slum dwellers D. Common people

162. Which of the following is true with reference to Romanticism?
A. Concept of government by consent
B. Freedom of markets

C. Cultural movements
D. Freedom of an individual

163. Who were the Junkers?
A. Soldiers B. Large landowners
C. Aristocracy D. Nobility

164. Pearl Harbour, an American Naval and Air Force base was attacked by:
A. Germany B. Japan
C. France D. England

165. Who was popularly known as Africa's Gandhi?
A. Mir Karzai B. Firoz Gandhi
C. Nelson Mandela D. M.K. Gandhi

166. Who made tripartite periodisation standard?
A. Andreas Cellarius B. Christoph Cellarius
C. Flavio Biondo D. Genseric

167. Democracy is a "government in which everyone has a share" was the opinion of:
A. Jeovans B. Seeley
C. Plato D. Abraham Lincoln

168. Marco Polo was a traveller from __________.
A. Portugal B. England
C. Italy D. Spain

169. Whom did Henry Tudor defeat in 1485?
A. Edward IV B. Richard I
C. Richard III D. Edward V

170. When did Henry Tudor seize the crown?
A. 1420 B. 1431
C. 1453 D. 1485

171. In which year Napoleon I crowned himself as Emperor of France:
A. 1799 B. 1804
C. 1807 D. 1812

172. Who united Norway, Denmark and Sweden?
A. Albert, King of Sweden
B. Eric of Pomerania
C. Haakon VI of Norway
D. Margaret I of Denmark

173. The policy of racial discrimination followed in South Africa was called:
A. Non-Aligned
B. Civil Rights Movement
C. Apartheid
D. Suffrage

174. Which of the following group of thinkers influenced Fascism?
A. Plato, Machiavelli and Herbert Spencer
B. Aristotle, St. Augustine and T.H. Green
C. Kant, Fichte, Hegel and Rosenberg
D. Karl Marx, Engels and Lenin

175. Napoleon-I and the Duke of Wellington fought the famous:
A. Battle of Austerlitz
B. Battle of Leipzig
C. Battle of Borodino
D. Battle of Waterloo

176. Who was the king during the french revolution?
A. Napoleon B. Louis XV
C. Louis XVI D. Charles IX

177. Genghis Khan died in the year:
A. 1209 B. 1219
C. 1227 D. 1232

178. Queen Elizabeth I of England belongs to which dynasty?
A. Stuart B. York
C. Tudor D. Normandy

179. When was 'Hammer of the Witches' published?
A. 1414 B. 1471
C. 1484 D. 1487

180. Who was the first to distinguish between cause and immediate origins of an event?
A. Herodotus B. Pericles
C. Plutarch D. Thucydides

181. The famous painting 'Monalisa' was the creation of:
A. Michael Angelo
B. Leonardo-da-Vinci
C. Picasso
D. Van Gogh

182. Who is the oldest British monarch to sit on the Throne?
A. Queen Victoria
B. Queen Elizabeth-II
C. Queen Mary Tudor
D. Queen Anne

183. Who officially instituted the first system of imperial examinations in China?

A. Han Wu Di B. Huo Qubing
C. Wei Qing D. None

184. Which Mountain's volcano buried Pompeii city with ash in 79 AD?

A. Mount Pelee B. Mount Tambora
C. Mount Etna D. Mount Vesuvius

185. Who was a founder member of the Russian Populist Movement "Anarchism"?

A. Mikhail Bakunin B. Gorky
C. Leo Tolstoy D. Turgenev

186. Fascism believes in the application of the principle of:

A. Dictatorship B. Democracy
C. Utilitarianism D. Totalitarianism

187. Who proclaimed the First Crusade?

A. Alexios I Komnenos
B. Peter the Hermit
C. Pope Gregory VII
D. Pope Urban II

188. Which one was the capital city of Byzantine Empire?

A. Venice B. Rome
C. Vienna D. Constantinople

189. In which year, Alexander the Great become the king of Macedonia?

A. 336 BC B. 323 BC
C. 350 BC D. 200 BC

190. The world's first drainage system was build by the people of:

A. Egyptian civilization
B. Indus Valley civilization
C. Chinese civilization
D. Mesopotamian civilization

191. From which language, has the term 'democracy' been derived?

A. Greek B. Hebrew
C. English D. Latin

192. Who made the famous statement "Man is born free, but everywhere he is in chains."

A. John Locke
B. Mirabeau
C. Voltaire
D. Jean Jacques Rousseau

193. When was the All Red Line inaugurated?

A. 1901 B. 1902
C. 1922 D. 1872

194. When was ancient Rome founded?

A. 776 BC B. 753 BC
C. 752 BC D. 742 BC

195. When was Bulgaria founded?

A. 681 B. 864
C. 917 D. 923

196. When was NATO signed?

A. 1949 B. 1990
C. 1948 D. 1950

197. When was Socrates born?

A. 469 BC B. 465 BC
C. 460 BC D. 449 BC

198. When was Sputnik 1 launched?

A. 1970 B. 1957
C. 1980 D. 1990

199. Who advanced Russia's boundary to the Black Sea?

A. Catherine the Great
B. Elizabeth of Russia
C. Peter the Great
D. Peter III of Russia

200. Whose model is based on the Mandate of Heaven?

A. Ban Gu B. Li Ling
C. Qin Shi Huang D. Sima Qian

201. Aztec civilization was originated in which country?

A. USA B. Greece
C. Egypt D. Mexico

202. When did Congress pass the Sherman Antitrust Act?

A. 1890 B. 1911
C. 1900 D. 1872

203. Which civilization is known as the birthplace of democracy?

A. Romans B. Indian
C. Greeks D. Persians

204. Who is regarded as the founder of modern Egypt?
A. Muhammad Ali B. Ibrahim Pasha
C. Abbas I D. Sa'id Pasha

205. Who is generally consider as the first pharaoh of Egypt?
A. Menes B. Semerkhet
C. Takelot I D. Tutankhamun

206. Sir William Wallace is known as the independence fighter of:
A. Denmark B. Scotland
C. Ireland D. Italy

207. When was the Tripartite Pact signed?
A. 1939 B. 1940
C. 1941 D. 1945

208. The Battle of Waterloo was fought in the year:
A. 1800 B. 1805
C. 1807 D. 1815

209. In U.S.A. the President is elected by:
A. The Senate
B. Universal Adult Franchise
C. The House of Representatives
D. The Congress

210. Who is known as the father of American Constitution?
A. James Madison
B. George Washington
C. John Adams
D. Thomas Jefferson

211. Who was the second Great Khagan of the Mongol Empire?
A. Guyuk Khan B. Ogedei Khan
C. Kublai Khan D. Temur Khan

212. When did the Battle of Nicopolis take place?
A. 1396 B. 1453
C. 1305 D. 1378

213. What did the ninth-century Scandinavian invasions do in England?
A. Promoted various small kingdoms to merge into a large kingdom
B. Led to disintegration of a large kingdom into smaller kingdoms
C. Gave way to colonization by the Vikings
D. Brought down Anglo-Saxon alliance

214. Which of the following is a wonder of the ancient world?
A. The statue of Jupiter Zeus at Olympia
B. The colosseum of Rome
C. The Leaning Tower of Pisa
D. The Mosque at St. Sophia (Constantinople)

215. Bangladesh was created in:
A. 1970 B. 1972
C. 1973 D. 1971

216. When did Battle of Marathon take place?
A. 490 BC B. 480 BC
C. 479 BC D. 475 BC

217. When did the Third Battle of Panipat take place?
A. 1707 B. 1761
C. 1751 D. 1765

218. When did the Battle of Plassey take place?
A. 1707 B. 1751
C. 1757 D. 1765

219. Napoleon got finally over thrown in the Battle of Waterloo in the year:
A. 1814 B. 1813
C. 1815 D. 1816

220. Who said "Liberty consists in obedience to the general will"?
A. Hobbes B. Rousseau
C. Green D. Laski

221. Who declared that Bolshevism must be "strangled in its cradle"?
A. Adolf Hitler
B. Benito Mussolini
C. Franklin D. Roosevelt
D. Winston Churchill

222. When did the British establish colonies in New Zealand?
A. 1814 B. 1840
C. 1872 D. 1830

223. What was the name of the atom bomb dropped in Hiroshima city?
A. Fat Boy
B. Fat Man
C. Little Boy
D. Scorpion

224. What was the name of the atom bomb dropped in Nagasaki city?
A. Fat Boy B. Fat Man
C. Scorpion D. Death Kiss

225. When was Hong Kong leased to Britain for 99 years by China?
A. 1898 B. 1900
C. 1901 D. 1903

226. The Parliament of Great Britain was formed in the year:
A. 1707 B. 1729
C. 1774 D. 1823

227. Which city is known as the birthplace of the Renaissance?
A. Florence B. Venice
C. Rome D. London

228. During 18th century who among the following philosophers said these famous words? "Man is born free but is every where in chains."
A. Voltaire
B. Jack Dareda
C. Jean Jacques Rousseau
D. Montesqueue

229. The Battle of the Hydaspes was fought by Alexander the Great against:
A. King Darius III B. Bessus
C. King Porus D. Spitamenes

230. Like Vedic Aryans, the custom of Sacrificial fire was also followed by:
A. Romans B. Greeks
C. Iranians D. All of the above

231. Constantinople, the capital of Roman Empire was captured by Turks in the year:
A. 1385 B. 1415
C. 1453 D. 1469

232. Pablo Picasso, the famous painter was:
A. French B. Italian
C. Flemish D. Spanish

233. The Law of Twelve Tables was concerned with which civilization:
A. Egypt B. Greece
C. Rome D. China

234. Of the following, in which did Napoleonic France suffer final defeat?
A. Battle of Trafalgar
B. Battle of Wagram
C. Battle of Pyramids
D. Battle of Austerlitz

235. The chief advocate of Fascism was:
A. Mussolini B. Adolf Hitler
C. St. Simon D. Robert Owen

236. Indonesia was a colony of which of the following countries?
A. Dutch B. Portugal
C. Spain D. Belgium

237. When was Seville incorporated into the Christian Kingdom of Castile?
A. 1200 B. 1248
C. 1203 D. 1261

238. The Industrial Revolution in England represented the climax of the transition from:
A. Slavery to feudalism
B. Feudalism to capitalism
C. Capitalism to socialism
D. Socialism to market socialism

239. Which one of the following is included in the rights of serfs?
A. The right to work on certain land and pass the lands to their heirs
B. The right to move from one manor to another
C. The right to marry whomever they wanted to marry
D. All the above

240. When was "The Communist Manifesto" written?
A. 1848 B. 1872
C. 1890 D. 1882

241. In which year British East India Company established Singapore?
A. 1808 B. 1819
C. 1832 D. 1849

242. Which dynasty of China began the construction of the Great Wall?
A. Ming Dynasty B. Qin Dynasty
C. Shun Dynasty D. None of the above

243. The world's oldest continuously inhabited city is:
A. Jerusalem B. Baghdad
C. Istanbul D. Damascus

244. Who was the first Roman emperor who converted to Christianity?
A. Augustus
B. Caligula
C. Constantine the Great
D. Cicero

245. Hernan Cortes was a Conquistador from:
A. England B. Holland
C. Portugal D. Spain

246. Which monarch is known as 'the Sun King' and also the longest of monarchs of major countries in European history?
A. Louis XIV of France
B. Henry III of England
C. Louis XIII of France
D. Edward I of England

247. Who is the first crowned Czar (Tsar) of Russia?
A. Peter I
B. Ivan IV (the Terrible)
C. Nicholas I
D. John Adams

248. The capital city of Umayyad Caliphate was:
A. Baghdad B. Madina
C. Kahira D. Damascus

249. Slash and burn agriculture is known as 'Milpa' in:
A. Venezuela
B. Brazil
C. Central Africa
D. Mexico and Central America

250. When did Otto I secure recognition of his title?
A. 936 B. 972
C. 973 D. 967

251. D-Day is the day when:
A. Germany declared war on Britain
B. US dropped the atom bomb on Hiroshima
C. Allied Troops landed in Normandy
D. Germany surrendered to the allies

252. How many years did Elizabeth I reign England?
A. 32 Years B. 36 Years
C. 40 Years D. 44 Years

253. Which Goddess was worshipped as the "Goddess of Wisdom" by the Greeks?
A. Athena B. Apollo
C. Zeus D. Diana

254. When did Europe capture Jerusalem?
A. 1081 B. 1088
C. 1095 D. 1099

255. When did Saladin capture Jerusalem?
A. 1118 B. 1187
C. 1193 D 1203

256. When did the Sasanian Empire rise?
A. 226 B. 238
C. 280 D.. 285

257. When did the Soviet Union collapse?
A. 1970 B. 1980
C. 1990 D. 1991

258. When did William I conquer England?
A. 1066 B. 1084
C. 1105 D. 1111

259. When Alexander invaded India, Taxila was ruled by:
A. Ambhi B. Porus
C. Ashoka D. Bimbisara

260. Who was the first president of the Republic of China?
A. Chiang Kai-shek
B. Mao Zedong
C. Sun Yat-sen
D. Yuan Shikai

261. When was the last Bulgarian noble surrendered to the Byzantine Empire?
A. 924 B. 927
C. 1014 D. 1018

262. Who is known as the founder of the Rome city in 753 BC?
A. Julius Caesar
B. Augustus
C. Romulus and Remus
D. Camillus

263. Who was the founder of the Satavahana dynasty?
A. Gautamiputra Satakarni
B. Deimachus
C. Nahapana
D. Simuka

264. In which year the Act of Union passed which joined England and Scotland into a single United Kingdom?
A. 1702 B. 1707
C. 1715 D. 1756

265. On which island of France, Napoleon was born?
A. Saint Halena B. Corsica
C. Elba D. Oleron

266. Cortez discovered Mexico in the year:
A. 1506 B. 1519
C. 1532 D. 1560

267. The Triple Alliance agreement between Germany, Austria-Hungary, and Italy was formed in the year:
A. 1882 B. 1889
C. 1901 D. 1909

268. When did the King Ferdinand VII die?
A. 1808 B. 1829
C. 1833 D. 1898

269. When did the Nanking Massacre start?
A. 1935 B. 1936
C. 1937 D. 1939

270. When did the Indian Rebellion begin?
A. 1818 B. 1857
C. 1858 D. 1819

271. From which port of England, Titanic started its journey?
A. Liverpool B. Southampton
C. Manchester D. Sunderland

272. Pearl Harbour, where the American Pacific Fleet was stationed, was attacked by Japanese in:
A. 1935 B. 1939
C. 1941 D. 1944

273. Who was one of the teachers of Alexander the Great?
A. Plato B. Aristotle
C. Socrates D. None of the above

274. In which country the revolution of 1848 first begins that lead to a series of revolutions?
A. Italy B. Germany
C. French D. Austria

275. In which year Russian Revolution happened?
A. 1912 B. 1915
C. 1917 D. 1921

276. Which one of the following is not a salient features of the renaissance age?
A. Humanism
B. Feudalism
C. Rationalism
D. Scientific Temperament

277. The Great Wall of China was built by:
A. Li-tai-pu B. Shih Huang-ti
C. Lao-tze D. Confucius

278. When did the Battle of France take place?
A. 1940 B. 1941
C. 1945 D. 1942

279. When did the Battle of Kosovo take place?
A. 1261 B. 1366
C. 1389 D. 1396

280. When were concave spectacles invented?
A. 1286 B. 1320
C. 1360 D. 1000

281. When did the second Russian revolution start?
A. August, 1905 B. February, 1917
C. October, 1917 D. March, 1921

282. During which US President period, the Cuban Missile Crisis conflict was occurred:
A. Lyndon B. Johnson
B. Richard Nixon
C. Ronald Reagan
D. John F. Kennedy

283. Who defeated Hannibal at Battle of Zama?
A. Cato the Elder
B. Scipio Aemilianus
C. Scipio Africanus
D. Hasdrubal

284. When did the Soviet Union disintegrated into Independent Republics?
A. 1990 B. 1991
C. 1992 D. 1993

285. Which king of England was forced to signed the 'Magna Carta'?
A. King Richard I B. King Louis
C. Henry III D. King John

286. Communist Revolutionary Che Guevara was born in the city:
A. Havana B. Rosario
C. Matanzas D. San Juan

287. When was the Fourth Crusade diverted from the Holy Land to Constantinople?
A. 1203 B. 1204
C. 1261 D. 1291

288. Independence movement of Vietnam was headed by:
A. Ngo Dinh Diem B. Zhou Enlai
C. Pol Pot D. Ho Chi Minh

289. 'Anti Semitism' to Adolf Hitler meant:
A. Anti Black policy
B. Anti Jewish policy
C. Anti Protestant policy
D. Anti German policy

290. Which country emerged as the biggest colonial power at the end of the nineteenth century?
A. France B. Spain
C. Britain D. Germany

291. John F. Kennedy is the __________th President of United State of America.
A. 25 B. 29
C. 32 D. 35

292. When were ancient Olympic games held first?
A. 776 BC B. 780 BC
C. 790 BC D. 800 BC

293. When did Japanese invasion of Manchuria begin?
A. 1931 B. 1935
C. 1936 D. 1939

294. Where did the practice of Shadow Cabinet originate?
A. United States of America
B. Great Britain
C. Italy
D. France

295. When was the building of the Parthenon at Athens started?
A. 447 BC B. 424 BC
C. 404 BC D. 399 BC

296. When was the Ottonian dynasty replaced by the Salian dynasty?
A. 1024 B. 1084
C. 1105 D. 1111

297. Marxian materialism came from the idea of:
A. Hegel B. Feuerbach
C. Darwin D. Engels

298. Porus was defeated by Alexander at the battle of ________.
A. Herat B. Kabul
C. Hydaspes D. Arbela

299. In which year Christopher Columbus discovered America?
A. 1502 B. 1339
C. 1405 D. 1492

300. Who among the following played a prominent role during the "Reign of Terror" in France?
A. Voltaire B. Marat
C. Robespierre D. Montesquieu

301. Who is known as the founder of the 'Republic of Turkey'?
A. Ismet Inonu
B. Fevzi Cakmak
C. Mustafa Kemal Ataturk
D. None of the above

302. Who is known as the founder of Tudor dynasty in England?
A. Elizabeth I
B. Richard III
C. Henry VII
D. None of the above

303. Total number of theses written by Martin Luther on Power of Indulgences are:
A. 81 B. 87
C. 95 D. 101

304. Who has called the Prime Minister Primus inter pares (first among equlas)?
A. Morely B. Harcourt
C. Laski D. Lowell

305. Who was the author of United States Declaration of Independence?
A. Thomas Jefferson
B. George Washington
C. Abraham Lincoln
D. Benjamin Franklin

306. Zend-Avesta is the sacred book of the:
A. Parsis B. Jains
C. Jews D. Buddhists

307. Hitler became the Chancellor of Germany in:
A. 1930 B. 1929
C. 1936 D. 1933

308. Who was the chairperson of the Chinese Communist Party at the time of liberation of China?
A. Zhou Enlai B. Deng Xiaoping
C. Mao Zedong D. Liu Shaoqi

309. When was the Treaty of Versailles signed?
A. 1918 B. 1919
C. 1920 D. 1923

310. Who is the first European to reach New Zealand?
A. Abel Tasman
B. James Cook
C. Willem Janszoon
D. Anthony van Diemen

311. When did the USS 'Panay' incident happen?
A. 1935 B. 1936
C. 1937 D. 1939

312. 1911 Revolution of China resulted in:
A. Establishment of a Republic
B. Federalism
C. Democracy
D. Increased problems of people

313. Who said, "The State exists because crime exists in society, otherwise there would be no need of a State"?
A. Herbert Spencer B. J.S. Mill
C. John Locke D. Tocqueville

314. Who was the last Byzantine Emperor during the fall of Constantinople in 1453?
A. Manuel II B. John V
C. John VIII D. Constantine XI

315. Where did the February Revolution take place?
A. Moscow B. Petrograd
C. Paris D. London

316. When was the construction of Great Wall of China started?
A. 294 BC B. 252 BC
C. 249 BC D. 221 BC

317. "The word impossible is found, in the dictionary of fools" was the famous quote of:
A. Hitler
B. Alexander the Great
C. Julius Caesar
D. Napoleon

318. Who wrote the book Ninety-Five Theses, which is regarded as initial catalyst for the Protestant Reformation?
A. Michelangelo B. Martin Luther
C. John Calvin D. Huldrych Zwingli

319. Which one was the last city founded in the Russian Empire?
A. Arkhangelsk B. Vologda
C. Veliky Novgorod D. Murmansk

320. Who founded the city of Singapore?
A. Francis Light
B. Herman Willem Daendels
C. Lee Kuan Yew
D. Stamford Raffles

321. In which year Francis II, founded the Empire of Austria?
A. 1804 B. 1809
C. 1820 D. 1822

322. Who is known as the founder of the Durrani Empire?
A. Timur Shah Durrani
B. Zaman Shah Durrani
C. Mahmud Shah Durrani
D. Ahmad Shah Durrani

323. Which one is the first dynasty that ruled China?
A. Shang dynasty B. Xia dynasty
C. Qin dynasty D. Ming dynasty

324. Who was the first Tudor monarch of England?
A. Elizabeth I B. Mary I
C. Henry VII D. Edward VI

325. In which year, the RMS Titanic sank in the North Atlantic Ocean after colliding with an iceberg?
A. 1905 B. 1910
C. 1911 D. 1912

326. Who was the first chairman of Central Committee of the Communist Party of China?
A. Mao Zedong B. Liu Shaoqi
C. Hua Guofeng D. Hu Yaobang

327. Absolute sovereign power of the Monarch was advocated by:
A. Thomas Hobbes B. Rousseau
C. John Locke D. Karl Marx

328. Which one is the last of the ruling Chinese dynasties?
A. Zhou Dynasty B. Shang Dynasty
C. Han Dynasty D. Qing Dynasty

329. Taoism, is an ancient tradition of Philosophy and religious belief deeply rooted in:
A. Taiwanese custom and world view
B. Chinese custom and world view
C. Japanese custom and world view
D. Vietnamese custom and world view

330. With the fall of which among the following the French Revolution began?
A. Bastille B. Communes
C. Jacobin Club D. Pillnitz

331. When did the Space Age bring the first human spaceflight?
A. 1961 B. 1970
C. 1975 D. 1980

332. Synagogue is the place of worship of:
A. Zoroastrianism B. Taoism
C. Judaism D. Shintoism

333. From which European country did Belgium gain independence in 1830?
A. Italy B. England
C. Portugal D. Netherlands

334. Who speaks of Cabinet system as "the steering wheel of the ship of state"?
A. Lowell B. Muin
C. Marriot D. Bagehot

335. In Greek mythology, Apollo is the god of what?
A. Prophecy B. Medicine
C. Love D. Peace

336. What is the name of the World's smallest republic which has an area of 21 sq. km only?
A. Nauru B. Palermo
C. Vatican City D. Namur

337. When did the Battle of Crecy take place?
A. 1327 B. 1337
C. 1346 D. 1376

338. When did the Nawabs of Bengal surrender to the British East India Company?
A. 1707 B. 1751
C. 1757 D. 1765

339. What according to Communism is the chief enemy of the society?
A. Private property B. Religion
C. Surplus value D. Capitalist class

340. When did China start the Civil Services Examination?
A. 605 B. 1905
C. 1920 D. 1949

341. Who was the first Chancellor of Germany?
A. Leo von Caprivi B. Adolf Hitler
C. Otto von Bismarck D. Hans Luther

342. Who was the first to distill petroleum?
A. Benjamin Silliman
B. Cathryn J. Prince
C. Edward Hitchcock
D. James Dwight Dana

343. Who founded the Great Seljuk Empire in 1037?
A. Seljuk Beg B. Tughril Beg
C. Alp Arslan D. Malik-Shah I

344. Which of the following countries is regarded as the home of 'Fabian Socialism'?
A. Russia B. England
C. France D. Italy

345. Who defined the "Long Nineteenth Century"?
A. Benedict Anderson
B. Ernest Gellner
C. Eric Hobsbawm
D. Karl Marx

346. Who brought the education available in the monasteries of Northumbria?
A. Alcuin B. Bede
C. Einhard D. Rabanus Maurus

347. Who was known as the Morning star of Renaissance?
A. Montesquieu B. Dante
C. Shakespeare D. Geoffrey Chaucer

348. The National Emblem of Italy is:
A. Eagle B. White Eagle
C. White Lily D. Lily

349. When did Abyssinian crisis end?
A. 1935 B. 1936
C. 1937 D. 1939

350. When was Byzantines recaptured?
A. 1204 B. 1261
C. 1291 D. 1225

351. Which philosopher said about the Holy Roman Empire that "it is neither Holy nor Roman nor Empire"?
A. Voltaire B. Montesquieu
C. Diderot D. Rousseau

352. Who was the second President of America?
A. Thomas Jefferson
B. Andrew Jackson
C. Abraham Lincoln
D. John Adams

353. The Wailing wall is situated in:
A. Berlin B. Beijing
C. Jerusalem D. Tel Aviv

354. When was the kingdom between the Rhine and Rhone rivers created?
A. 843 B. 864
C. 876 D. 877

355. Ho Chi Minh was a leader of:
A. North Vietnam B. South Vietnam
C. North Korea D. South Korea

356. Who is the Duchess of Cornwall?
A. Diana B. Camilla
C. Anne D. Margaret

357. Who was the first Roman Emperor?
A. Caligula B. Claudius
C. Augustus D. Nero

358. When did the atomic bombings of Hiroshima and Nagasaki happen?
A. 1941 B. 1942
C. 1945 D. 1940

359. In which year the Battle of the Hydaspes was fought between Alexander and Porus?
A. 302 BC B. 310 BC
C. 312 BC D. 326 BC

360. Japan's Parliament is known as:
A. Diet B. Dail
C. Yuan D. Shora

361. John Locke profounded:
A. Social Contract Theory
B. Theory of Divine Rights
C. Patriarchal Theory
D. Theory of Force

362. 'Mein Kampf' is the autobiography of:
A. Maxim Gorky B. Adolf Hitler
C. Oscar Wilde D. Winston Churchill

363. When was the first communist manifesto written by Karl Marx and Friedrich Engels?
A. 1848 B. 1859
C. 1872 D. 1890

364. Which pharaoh build the largest pyramid known as Great Pyramid of Giza?
A. Sneferu B. Tutankhamun
C. Khufu D. None of the above

365. Russian communist leader Vladimir Lenin died in the year:
A. 1924 B. 1922
C. 1920 D. 1921

366. East Timor, in Indonesian, Archipelago, was the former colony of:
A. Dutch B. English
C. French D. Portuguese

367. Who was the last Emperor (Tsar) of Russia?
A. Alexander III B. Nicholas II
C. Alexander II D. Nicholas I

368. The famous painting 'Last Supper' is a creation of:
A. Michelangelo
B. Vincent van Gogh
C. Leonardo Da Vinci
D. Sandro Botticelli

369. In which country the Head of the State gets his office by the law of hereditary succession?
A. China
B. Sri Lanka
C. France
D. Japan

370. Who said "Spanish ulcer was the cause of my ruin"?
A. Metternich
B. Napoleon
C. Marshal Foch
D. Chamberlain

371. Who is known as the Artist of the world famous painting 'Mona Lisa'?
A. Filippo Brunelleschi
B. Michelangelo
C. Vincent van Gogh
D. Leonardo da Vinci

372. In which year Bastille of Paris stormed by the people which lead to the French Revolution?
A. 1746
B. 1779
C. 1789
D. 1808

373. "The Three Emperors League" 1873 was also known as:
A. Dreikaiserbund Treaty
B. Triple Alliance
C. Reinsurance Treaty
D. The Dual Alliance

374. When was the League of Nations established?
A. In 1918
B. In 1920
C. In 1939
D. In 1914

375. The declaration that Democracy is a Government 'of the people, by the people' was made by:
A. George Washington
B. Winston Churchill
C. Abraham Lincoln
D. Theodore Roosevelt

376. Who was the commander of 'Seventh Coalition' army that defeated Napoleon in the Battle of Waterloo?
A. Arthur Wellesley
B. Jean-de-Dieu Soult
C. Robert Clive
D. John Carnac

377. The city of Alexandria was founded by Alexander the Great in the year:
A. 331 BC
B. 325 BC
C. 322 BC
D. 365 BC

378. World renowned philosopher Karl Marx was born in the country:
A. Austria
B. Germany
C. Russia
D. Italy

379. Who was the original inventor of roller spinning?
A. John Kay
B. Lewis Paul
C. Richard Arkwright
D. Samuel Crompton

380. Which one was the slogan during French Revolution?
A. Liberty, Authority, Fraternity
B. Liberty, Equality, Fraternity
C. Liberty, Equality, Freedom
D. Liberty, Law, Fraternity

381. When was the commercial colonization of India commenced?
A. 1707
B. 1751
C. 1765
D. 1757

382. Who founded the philosophy of Stoicism in Athens?
A. Chrysippus
B. Cleanthes
C. Epictetus
D. Zeno of Citium

383. How did Saint Boniface help to shape the German church?
A. Preaching against divorce, incest and polygamy
B. Preaching against the importance of monasteries
C. Writing the epic 'Beowulf'
D. Writing 'The Rule of Saint Benedict'

384. Who was the American leader who led a non-violent movement to obtain full civil rights for American Negroes?
A. Abraham Lincoln
B. John F. Kennedy
C. Martin Luther King Junior
D. George Washington

385. In which year Vatican City was established as an independent state?
A. 1756
B. 1782
C. 1835
D. 1929

386. Which Nazi Field Marshal is known as the 'Desert Fox'?
A. Viktor Brack B. Erwin Rommel
C. Hans Frank D. Hermann Goring

387. In the world history, who is also known as "Little Corporal"?
A. Bismark
B. Adolf Hitler
C. Lord Curzon
D. Napoleon Bonaparte

388. Karl Marx lived in exile and wrote from:
A. Moscow B. London
C. Paris D. Stockholm

389. Marcopolo is known for:
A. Discovering Greenland
B. Travelling to China, India and Asia
C. Travelling round the Cape of Good Hope
D. Discovering Canada

390. Marx belonged to:
A. Germany B. Holland
C. France D. Britain

391. Michelangelo was a __________.
A. Painter B. Sculptor
C. Astronomer D. Poet

392. Where can the finest examples of medieval architecture be seen?
A. Cathedrals
B. Castles
C. Homes of townspeople
D. Universities

393. Who was the first Prime Minister of Great Britain?
A. Oliver Cromwell B. Benjamin Disraeli
C. Robert Walpole D. Gladstone

394. The United Kingdom is a classic example of a/an:
A. Aristocracy
B. Absolute monarchy
C. Constitutional monarchy
D. Polity

395. When was the Communist Party of China founded?
A. 1918 B. 1920
C. 1919 D. 1923

396. When were Jewish communities expelled from France?
A. 1306 B. 1453
C. 1492 D. 1376

397. In which battle did the defeat of Muslims stop their invasions?
A. Battle of Fontenoy
B. Battle of Lechfeld
C. Battle of Verdun
D. Battle of Vouille

398. Which of the following is not a religion developed in ancient time (*i.e.* In B.C.)?
A. Shintoism B. Zoroastrianism
C. Islam D. Taoism

399. When did Nanda dynasty come into power?
A. 424 BC B. 404 BC
C. 399 BC D. 385 BC

400. When was Archduke Franz Ferdinand of Austria assassinated?
A. 1906 B. 1907
C. 1910 D. 1914

401. Who is known as the "Lady with the Lamp"?
A. Joan of Arc
B. Helen Keller
C. Florence Nightingale
D. Sarojini Naidu

402. United Nations was formed in the year:
A. 1944 B. 1945
C. 1947 D. 1948

403. Who said that "Man by nature is a political animal"?
A. Plato B. Aristotle
C. Hobbes D. Rousseau

404. The European renaissance started from which country?
A. England B. France
C. Italy D. Greece

405. The Declaration of American Independence was based on the theory of:
A. Civil Rights
B. Moral Rights
C. Legal Rights
D. Natural Rights

406. "What is the Third Estate?" pamphlet associated with the French Revolution, was written by:
A. Marquis - Lafayette
B. Edmund Burke
C. Joseph Foulon
D. Abbe Sieyes

407. "Middle Ages" in Western Europe includes the period __________.
A. AD 300 - AD 1600
B. Beginning of Byzantine through the end of the Roman Empire
C. Beginning of Early Christian through the 13th or 14th centuries
D. End of the Roman Empire through the Byzantine period

408. When did Alexander the Great die?
A. 399 BC B. 385 BC
C. 335 BC D. 323 BC

409. When did Xinhai Revolution occur?
A. 1872 B. 1900
C. 1911 D. 1912

410. When did the Three Kingdoms period begin in China?
A. 220 B. 226
C. 238 D. 280

411. What does the opening scene of Beowulf describe?
A. The arrival of Scyld Scefing in Denmark
B. The birth of Beowulf
C. The death of Beowulf
D. The defeat of the monster Grendel

412. Which Roman Emperor had banned the ancient Olympic games?
A. Julius Caesar B. Arcadius
C. Theodosius D. Tacitus

413. How did Abu al-Abbas become well known in the court of Charlemagne?
A. Beloved pet from an Indian king
B. Distinguished diplomat from the Islamic world
C. Gift from the Abbasid court
D. Muslim enemy of the king

414. The slogan of the French Revolution was:
A. One nation, one leader and one flag
B. Government of the people, by the people and for the people
C. Liberty, equality and fraternity
D. None of these

415. The painting "Virgin of the rocks" was a work of:
A. Raphael B. Michelangelo
C. Leonardo da Vinci D. Vincent van Gogh

416. Who said "Where there is no law, there is no freedom"?
A. Bentham B. Lenin
C. Marx D. Locke

417. In European history, which year is known as the year of revolution?
A. 1732 B. 1765
C. 1848 D. 1896

418. What were the collective farms under Stalin's Collectivization Programme in Russia known as?
A. Kolkhoz B. Ferma
C. Lider D. Kollektsiya

419. Whose teachings inspired the French Revolution?
A. Locke B. Rousseau
C. Hegel D. Plato

420. How did Europeans use the term 'middle ages'?
A. The crisis of Western Europe
B. The medieval era of European history
C. The fact that Europe became mature from 500 to 1500
D. The time between the fall of Rome and the emergence of Christianity

421. In which year Adolf Hitler was appointed as Chancellor of Germany?
A. 1933 B. 1935
C. 1938 D. 1940

422. Which country first invented Gunpowder in around 270 AD?
A. China B. India
C. Korea D. England

423. When was the first Ancient Greek Olympic Game begun?
A. 776 BC B. 552 BC
C. 800 BC D. 235 BC

424. Who defeated Darius III in the Battle of Gaugamela?
A. Alexander the Great
B. Aristotle
C. Julius Caesar
D. Napoleon Bonaparte

425. Who led prussia in the unification of Germany?
A. Moltke
B. Wilhelm II
C. Otto von Bismarck
D. Friedrich Ebert

426. When was Constantinople captured by Ottomans?
A. 1305 B. 1378
C. 1453 D. 1414

427. Benito Mussolini was a leader of:
A. Germany B. Italy
C. France D. Portugal

428. When was Han Dynasty established?
A. 220 BC B. 209 BC
C. 208 BC D. 206 BC

429. When was Jin Dynasty established?
A. 238 B. 280
C. 285 D. 313

430. Who advocated Nazism in Germany?
A. Frederick William-IV
B. Adolf Hitler
C. Bismarck
D. William-III

431. 'Boston Tea Party' protest was associated with the revolution of:
A. America B. Italy
C. France D. India

432. Who established the Edo society?
A. Akechi Mitsuhide
B. Kuroda Yoshitaka
C. Oda Nobunaga
D. Toyotomi Hideyoshi

433. When did the Constitution of Australia come into force?
A. 1901 B. 1906
C. 1909 D. 1910

434. The island of Corsica is associated with:
A. Mussolini
B. Hitler
C. Napoleon Bonaparte
D. Winston Churchill

435. What was the significance of the Battle of Tours in 732?
A. Charlemagne converted many Muslims to Christianity
B. Charles Martel became King of France
C. It stopped the Muslim advance into Europe
D. Muslims gained control of Spain

436. From which country, the tradition of written Constitution began:
A. Japan B. India
C. Britain D. America

437. 'Mein Kampf' is the autobiography which political leader?
A. Joseph Stalin
B. Benito Mussolini
C. Winston Churchill
D. Adolf Hitler

438. What was the name of the secret police party of Nazi in Germany?
A. Gestapo B. NKVD
C. OVRA D. Palace Guard

439. Who quoted "The problems of day cannot be solved by motions, resolutions and can be solved only by blood and iron."?
A. Hitler
B. Bismarck
C. Kaiser William IV
D. King Frederick William IV

440. According to Marx, the source of value is:
A. Capital B. Land
C. Labour D. None of the above

441. Who is the author of "From the Founding of the City"?
A. Cicero B. Livy
C. Polybius D. Sallust

442. Who wrote, "On the Geneology of Morals"?
A. Friedrich Nietzsche
B. Immanual Kant
C. Karl Marx
D. Sigmund Freud

443. The Inca civilization was raised in which country:
A. Bolivia B. Colombia
C. Peru D. Chile

444. In which year did Chicago and some other cities of USA witness protest by the labour unions which culminated in police firing which lead to the decision to observe May 01 as Labour Day:
A. 1863 B. 1866
C. 1868 D. 1886

445. Which famous book was written by Nostradamus?
A. Les Propheties B. Das Kapital
C. The Tempest D. None of the above

446. 'He, who does not live in a state may either be a saint or an animal'- Who said this?
A. Montesqieu B. Angles
C. Sophists D. Aristotle

447. What was the original name of Santa Claus?
A. St. Christopher B. St. Peter
C. St. John D. St. Nicolas

448. When was the Molotov - Ribbentrop Pact signed?
A. 1939 B. 1940
C. 1941 D. 1945

449. Where was the Ottonian dynasty established?
A. Denmark B. Germany
C. Iceland D. Scandinavia

450. Who is the creator of the world famous statue 'David' in Florence?
A. Leonardo da Vinci
B. Raphael
C. Filippo Brunelleschi
D. Michelangelo

451. When was Government of India Act passed?
A. 1818 B. 1819
C. 1858 D. 1800

452. Who was the last Emperor of Rome?
A. Nero
B. Romulus Augustulus
C. Julius Nepos
D. Julius Caesar

453. Who is known as the 'Father of History'?
A. Homer B. Thucydides
C. Herodotus D. Archimedes

454. Who wrote the book 'Oliver Twist'?
A. William Shakespeare
B. Mark Twain
C. Charles Dickens
D. Christopher Marlowe

455. The "Last Supper" a famous Renaissance Painting was a master piece of:
A. Michael Angelo
B. Titian
C. Leonardo da Vinci
D. Raphael

456. Peking is the sacred place of:
A. Taoism B. Shintoism
C. Confucianism D. Judaism

457. When was Operation 'Condor' implemented?
A. 1970 B. 1975
C. 1980 D. 1990

458. On which theatre house, Abraham Lincoln was assassinated?
A. Senator Theatre B. Ford's Theatre
C. Oscar Theatre D. Gold Theatre

459. Alexander sent back home a portion of his army under an admiral called __________.
A. Ptolemy B. Nearchos
C. Menander D. Porus

460. What was the reason for Franks rapid rise in western Europe?
A. Clovis's conversion to Roman Christianity
B. Clovis's conversion to Arian Christianity
C. Clovis's alliance with the Islamic world
D. Clovis's defeat of the Muslims at the Battle of Tours

461. Frederick the Great was the king of:
A. France B. Italy
C. Britain D. Prussia

462. Who is the second Great Khan of the Mongol Empire?
A. Guyuk Khan B. Ogedei Khan
C. Kublai Khan D. Mongke Khan

463. The Treaty of Versailles humiliated:
A. Austria B. Germany
C. England D. France

464. Which Ottoman Sultan defeat Byzantine Empire and capture Constantinople city in 1453?
A. Mehmed II B. Bayezid II
C. Murad II D. Mehmed IV

465. Who discovered Cape of Good Hope in 1488?
A. Magellan B. Columbus
C. Bartholomew Dias D. Vasco da Gama

466. Who is renowned for his redefinition of sexual desire?
A. Carl Jung B. Friedrich Nietzsche
C. Jacques Lacan D. Sigmund Freud

467. When was the Carolingian dynasty replaced in the western lands?
A. 911 B. 918
C. 987 D. 996

468. The Great Depression in the 1930s refers to:
A. A tropical storm that raged for weeks
B. An ailment afflicting millions overhung to a new vector borne disease
C. An economic hollowing out leading to widespread unemployment and collapse of stock values
D. A prolonged seasonal influence of unpredictable weather owing to earthquakes and tsunamis

469. The declaration of the Rights of Man is related with:
A. The Russian Revolution
B. The French Revolution
C. The American War of Independence
D. The Glorious Revolution of England

470. National Socialist German Workers Party was also known as:
A. Nazi Party
B. The Left
C. National Fascist Party
D. None of Above

471. When did Charlemagne conquer the Lombards?
A. 752 B. 753
C. 757 D. 774

472. Which U.S. President announced the "New Deal" for economic recovery in the aftermath of the Great Depression?
A. Abraham Lincoln B. Benjamin Franklin
C. Roosevelt D. J.F. Kennedy

473. Benito Mussolini was the Prime Minister of which country?
A. France B. Belgium
C. Italy D. Turkey

474. When did the Turkish army defeat the Byzantine army?
A. 1040 B. 1060
C. 1070 D. 1071

475. Which King was executed by guillotine during French Revolution in 1793?
A. Charles X B. Louis XIII
C. Henry IV D. Louis XVI

476. When was the modern petroleum industry started?
A. 1808 B. 1829
C. 1846 D. 1898

477. In which year Genghis Khan was proclaimed as Emperor or Khagan?
A. 1192 B. 1998
C. 1200 D. 1206

478. What was the economic activity of Western Europe in the early middle ages?
A. Commercial and urban
B. Long-distance trade
C. Agriculture
D. All the above

479. Who said, "Adolf Hitler is Germany and Germany is Adolf Hitler. He who pledges himself to Hitler pledges himself to Germany"?
A. R. Hess
B. Mussolini
C. Hitler
D. Communist International

480. Japanese folk tradition and ritual, with no founder or single sacred scripture, is popularly known as:
A. Taoism B. Zoroastrianism
C. Shintoism D. Paganism

481. Who pioneered Christian cenobitic monasticism?
A. Anthony the Great
B. Athanasius of Alexandria
C. Basil of Caesarea
D. Pachomius the Great

482. Who wrote the article "The Gospel of Wealth"?
A. Andrew Carnegie
B. Cornelius Vanderbilt
C. Dale Carnegie
D. Napoleon Hill

483. Who were the three eminent statesmen who started the Non-aligned Movement?
A. Jawaharlal Nehru, Anwar Sadat, Soekarno
B. Jawaharlal Nehru, Chou Enlai, Kwame Nkrumah
C. Jawaharlal Nehru, Fidel Castro, Marshal Tito
D. Jawaharlal Nehru, Gamal Abdul Nasser, Marshal Tito

484. Alexander the Great died at _________.
A. Susa B. Babylon
C. Macedonia D. Kabul

485. According to Gregory of Tours, which of the following was true about Clovis's conversion?
A. He was forced to convert by the bishops
B. He began to consider conversion when his army was defeated by the Christian Alamanni
C. He forced his army to be baptized after he was
D. At the behest of his wife, the queen Clotilde

486. Who said "Man is a social animal"?
A. Aristotle B. Rousseau
C. Laski D. Plato

487. Who is also known as 'Bard of Avon'?
A. William Wordsworth
B. Karl Marx
C. William Shakespeare
D. John Milton

488. Which Roman Emperor is also known as 'little boot'?
A. Nero B. Julius Caesar
C. Caligula D. Augustus

489. 'St. Petersburg' city was founded by the:
A. Peter the Great B. Feodor III
C. Catherine I D. Peter II

490. When did Julius Caesar first invaded Britain?
A. 33 BC B. 44 BC
C. 55 BC D. 66 BC

491. Who build the St. Basil's Cathedral in Moscow, Russia?
A. Peter I B. Vladislav I
C. Ivan the Terrible D. Feodor I

492. Herodotus is considered as the father of:
A. History B. Geography
C. Political Science D. Philosophy

493. Who was the principal author of the United States Declaration of Independence?
A. Benjamin Franklin
B. George Washington
C. Thomas Edison
D. Thomas Jefferson

494. The Renaissance movement is described as the ending of:
A. Pre Historic Era B. Ancient Era
C. Medieval Era D. Modern Era

495. When did the Germans establish colonies in Samoa?
A. 1898 B. 1899
C. 1900 D. 1901

496. Who coined the phrase "survival of the fittest"?
A. Auguste Comte B. Charles Darwin
C. Emile Durkheim D. Herbert Spencer

497. Who are the earliest migrants from Europe to South America?
A. Britishers B. French
C. Portuguese D. Spaniards

498. First meeting of the United Nations General Assembly was held in:
A. Paris B. New York
C. Moscow D. London

499. The policy of 'imperial preferences' adopted by Britain in its colonies in 1932 is also known as the:
A. Hong Kong Agreement
B. London Agreement
C. Ottawa Agreement
D. Paris Agreement

500. When was the Russian Provisional Government established?
A. 1917 B. 1918
C. 1920 D. 1923

501. Who was the 1st President of South Africa after apartheid?
A. Zuma
B. Nelson Mandela
C. Kofi Annan
D. Booker T. Washington

502. Who among the following is referred to as 'Desert Fox'?
A. Lord Wavell
B. Gen. Eisenhover
C. Gen. Rommel
D. Gen. McArthur

503. From which city, the Russian revolution of 1917 begin:
A. Petrograd B. Moscow
C. Warsaw D. Ukraine

504. What was the name of the assassinator of John F. Kennedy?
A. Lee Harvey Oswald
B. John Wilkes Booth
C. John Surratt
D. None of the above

505. When was the Trans-Siberian Railway completed?
A. 1872 B. 1882
C. 1890 D. 1916

506. Which one country is still governed by a monarch?
A. Afghanistan B. Iran
C. Iraq D. Saudi Arabia

507. The first atomic bomb was thrown over:
A. Nagasaki B. Hiroshima
C. Tokyo D. Hong Kong

508. Who developed system ranks of binary patterns?
A. Baudhayana
B. Aryabhata
C. Mahavira
D. Pingala

509. Which decade is called as the "Era of Decolonisation"?
A. 1950's B. 1980's
C. 1990's D. 1970's

510. Which of the following is the name of US Parliament?
A. Diet
B. Senate
C. Congress
D. House of commons

511. Which one is the oldest existing University in the World?
A. University of Oxford
B. University of al-Karaouine
C. Al-Azhar University
D. University of Bologna

512. Who is called the "Greatest Investigator of Antiquity"?
A. Aristotle B. Darwin
C. Cuvier D. Socrates

513. Which one of the following U.S. President visited China in 1972 for strengthening diplomatic ties?
A. Richard Nixon
B. George Bush (Senior)
C. D. Eisenhower
D. J.F. Kennedy

514. Who started the construction of Colosseum in Rome?
A. Nero B. Vespasian
C. Titus D. Domitian

515. In which year did the Suez Canal was open for trade?
A. 1869 B. 1880
C. 1774 D. 1620

516. Where was the Sumerian civilization located?
A. China B. Iran
C. Pakistan D. Iraq

517. The historical monument Al-Khazneh or The Treasury is located in the city of:
A. Baghdad B. Tehran
C. Giza D. Petra

518. When did the British East India Company establish a capital in Calcutta?
A. 1772 B. 1818
C. 1858 D. 1857

519. When did the British establish colonies in Australia?
A. 1788 B. 1840
C. 1872 D. 1814

520. The capital of Pakistan till 1959 was:
A. Islamabad B. Karachi
C. Lahore D. Hyderabad

521. The capital of the Abbasid Caliphs was:
A. Bagdad B. Damascus
C. Constantinople D. Madina

522. When did the Battle of Lechfeld happen?
A. 918 B. 955
C. 987 D. 996

523. Who won the Battle of Poitiers in 732?
A. Carloman B. Charles Martel
C. Pepin of Herstal D. Pepin the Short

524. When was the Bill of Rights sanctioned?
A. 1775 B. 1776
C. 1783 D. 1791

525. The currency of Thailand is:
A. Baht B. Rupiah
C. Yuan D. Yen

526. Who among the following supported the Doctrine of Predestination?
A. John Calvin B. Zwingli
C. Martin Luther D. John Knox

527. Who issued the Emancipation Proclamation?
A. Abraham Lincoln
B. George Washington
C. John F. Kennedy
D. William Wallace Lincoln

528. Who is known as 'The Father of English History'?
A. Jerome B. Alfred the Great
C. John Chrysostom D. Bede

529. Who is known as the father of Modern Medicine?
A. Eratosthenes B. Euclid
C. Hippocrates D. Pythagoras

530. Who was the founder of Ottoman Empire?
A. Osman I B. Orhan
C. Mura I D. Bayezid I

531. Who is consider as the first Pope of christianity?
A. St Peter B. St Linus
C. St Evaristus D. St Alexander I

532. Who is known as the first pope of Vatican City?
A. Pope Benedict XV
B. Clement XIII
C. Pope Pius XI
D. Benedict XIII

533. Alexander the Great died in 323 B.C. in:
A. Persia B. Babylon
C. Macedonia D. Taxila

534. Unification of Germany took place under the leadership of which state?
A. Wuttemberg B. Saxony
C. Prussia D. Hanover

535. When did the invasion of Poland begin?
A. 1935 B. 1936
C. 1937 D. 1939

536. When did the October Revolution occur?
A. 1917 B. 1918
C. 1920 D. 1923

537. The previous name of Zaire was:
A. Benin B. Liberia
C. Congo D. Sierra Leone

538. The battle of Thermopylae was fought between:
A. Sparta and Athens
B. Athens and Rome
C. Greece City States and Persia
D. Rome and Carthage

539. That all appointments made by the President and treaties signed by him must be ratified by the Senate in U.S.A. indicates:
A. Theory of separation of powers

B. Theory of checks and balances
C. Due process of law
D. Rule of law

540. Who was the successor of Charlemagne?
A. Charles the Bald
B. Lothair I
C. Louis the German
D. Louis the Pious

541. Which of the following revolutions is related to the thirteen English colonies?
A. Russian Revolution
B. Industrial Revolution
C. French Revolution
D. American Revolution

542. Who received the title of 'shogun' in 1603?
A. Ishida Mitsunari
B. Kuroda Yoshitaka
C. Oda Nobunaga
D. Tokugawa Leyasu

543. Who secured papal recognition of his kingship in 1328?
A. Edward Bruce
B. Edward I of England
C. Edward II of England
D. Robert the Bruce

544. Who composed 'The History of the Kings of Britain'?
A. Ambrosius Aurelianus
B. Geoffrey of Monmouth
C. Thomas Malory
D. Vortigern

545. Who is the author of "The History of the World-Conquerer"?
A. Annemarie Schimmel
B. Clifford Edmund Bosworth
C. Gustaf John Ramstedt
D. John Andrew Boyle

546. Potato was introduced to Europe by:
A. Portuguese B. Germans
C. Spanish D. Dutch

547. The Chinese Nationalist Party Kuomintang was found by:
A. Pu-yi B. Mao-Tse-tung
C. Chiang-Kai-shek D. Sun-Yat-sen

548. From which country did the USA purchase Alaska to make it the 49th federating state?
A. Canada B. Britain
C. Russia D. France

549. When did the Battle of Sekigahara take place?
A. 1600 B. 1603
C. 1707 D. 1761

550. The sculpture "David" was a creation of:
A. Michelangelo
B. Leonardo da Vinci
C. Raphael
D. Donatello

551. Two Party System is found in:
A. Russia B. U.S.A
C. India D. France

552. The city of "Tashkent" is located in:
A. Uzbekistan B. Kazakhstan
C. Russia D. Kyrgyzstan

553. During which dynasty Paper was invented in China:
A. Xia Dynasty B. Tang Dynasty
C. Yuan Dynasty D. Han Dynasty

554. Who was elected as First Consul of the Consulate of France?
A. Adolf Hitler
B. Napoleon Bonaparte
C. Napoleon III
D. Maximilien Robespierre

555. Who is the founder of Greek historiography?
A. Aristotle B. Herodotus
C. Hippocrates D. Thucydides

556. Who is known as the founder of Yuan Dynasty in China?
A. Kublai Khan B. Genghis Khan
C. Batu Khan D. Berke Khan

557. When were Jewish communities expelled from England?
A. 1290 B. 1306
C. 1492 D. 1453

558. The theory of "natural rights" was propounded by:
A. Hobbes B. Locke
C. Bentham D. Marx

559. Who was the first historian to use tripartite periodisation?
A. Bernardo Rossellino
B. Coluccio Salutati
C. Leonardo Bruni
D. Lorenzo Valla

560. Who was the Emperor of Russia during Russian Revolution?
A. Alexander III B. Nicholas II
C. Nicholas I D. Alexander II

561. When was Russia proclaimed as an Empire?
A. 1682 B. 1721
C. 1725 D. 1762

562. Economic dimensions of justice have been emphasised by:
A. Idealists B. Capitalists
C. Socialists D. Fascists

563. Who has given a call "Go back to nature"?
A. Plato B. Aristotle
C. Rousseau D. Hobbes

564. The British Conservative Party was earlier known as:
A. Whigs B. Fabians
C. Levellers D. Tories

565. In which year 'University of Oxford' was founded?
A. 1096 B. 1562
C. 1117 D. 1342

566. The Greek viewed 'politics' as the basis of:
A. Both ethical and legalistic terms
B. Ethical terms
C. Terms of power
D. Legalistic terms

567. Leonardo da Vinci was born in the city of:
A. Rome B. Milan
C. Florence D. Madrid

568. Where was Christopher Columbus from:
A. Venice B. Genoa
C. Spain D. Portugal

569. The organisation 'League of Nations' was founded after the end of:
A. World War I B. World War II
C. Crimean War D. Vietnam War

570. Alexander the great, was obliged to go back because:
A. he fell ill
B. he suffered defeat in India
C. his forces refused to go further
D. he did not like India

571. Industrial Revolution was started from which country?
A. France B. Germany
C. Italy D. England

572. Alexander the Great was the king of which kingdom?
A. Rome B. Macedonia
C. Epirus D. Cyprus

573. 'Bucephalus' was the name of the horse of:
A. Napoleon B. Alexander
C. Julius Caesar D. Mark Antony

574. Waterloo is located in:
A. England B. France
C. Spain D. Belgium

575. When were Jews expelled from Spain?
A. 1376 B. 1453
C. 1492 D. 1327

576. What is Chivalry?
A. The code Charlemagne implemented
B. The code by which a Christian family lived
C. The code by which knights lived
D. The code by which young men lived

577. What is 'Reformation'?
A. Rise of absolute monarchy
B. Revival of classical learning
C. The revolt against authority of pope
D. Change in attitude of man

578. What was Amphora?
A. A great ruler of Roman Empire
B. A musical instrument of ancient Greece
C. A special pottery to keep liquid in ancient Rome
D. A weapon used in ancient Greece

579. Which explorer discovered Cuba?
A. Christopher Columbus
B. Amerigo Vespucci
C. Vasco da Gama
D. Marco Polo

580. When did Able Archer 83 start?
A. 1959 B. 1975
C. 1962 D. 1983

581. When did July Crisis happen?
A. 1906 B. 1907
C. 1910 D. 1914

582. When did King Leonidas die?
A. 480 BC B. 479 BC
C. 475 BC D. 469 BC

583. When did Louis the Child die?
A. 911 B. 918
C. 987 D. 996

584. When did Louis the Pious die?
A. 813 B. 814
C. 864 D. 840

585. Who was the Chinese Emperor when Marco Polo visited China?
A. Temur Khan B. Kublai Khan
C. Genghis Khan D. Ogedei Khan

586. When was America discovered?
A. 1491 B. 1492
C. 1493 D. 1494

587. When was Xerxes I murdered?
A. 465 BC B. 460 BC
C. 449 BC D. 447 BC

588. Where was St. Paul beheaded?
A. Rome B. Ephesus
C. Kusadasi D. Jerusalem

589. Who captured Beijing in 1644?
A. Chongzhen Emperor
B. Li Zicheng
C. Wu Sangui
D. Yao Xueyin

590. Who discovered America?
A. Vasco Da Gama
B. Columbus
C. Captain Cook
D. Amundsen

591. Who discovered Troy?
A. Arthur Evans
B. Frank Calvert
C. Heinrich Schliemann
D. Homer

592. Who founded Saint Petersburg?
A. Alexis of Russia
B. Ivan the Terrible
C. Peter the Great
D. Peter III of Russia

593. Who murdered Julius Caesar?
A. Augustus B. Marcus Brutus
C. Mark Antony D. Pompey

594. Who invented kerosene?
A. Abraham Pineo Gesner
B. Benjamin Silliman
C. Edwin Drake
D. John William Dawson

595. Who said' 'I am the State'?
A. James-II of England
B. Napoleon-I of France
C. Louis-XIV of France
D. Hitler of Germany

596. Who said "Knowledge is Power"?
A. Shakespeare
B. Milton
C. Francis Bacon
D. Jawaharlal Nehru

597. Who was "The First American"?
A. Benjamin Franklin
B. James Madison
C. John Adams
D. George Washington

598. Who was the first Caliph?
A. Suleiman, the Great
B. Abu Bakr
C. Imam Hussain
D. Constantine

599. Who wrote "Summa Theologica"?
A. Albertus Magnus
B. Aristotle
C. Augustine of Hippo
D. Thomas Aquinas

600. Who was the Chief Architect of the World Trade Centre, New York?
A. Le Corbusier
B. Minoru Yamasaki
C. Edwin Lutyens
D. Charles Correa

ANSWERS

1	**2**	**3**	**4**	**5**	**6**	**7**	**8**	**9**	**10**
A	C	B	D	B	D	C	A	C	A
11	**12**	**13**	**14**	**15**	**16**	**17**	**18**	**19**	**20**
D	A	A	B	A	D	C	A	B	D
21	**22**	**23**	**24**	**25**	**26**	**27**	**28**	**29**	**30**
C	B	D	A	B	C	C	A	C	A
31	**32**	**33**	**34**	**35**	**36**	**37**	**38**	**39**	**40**
A	C	D	C	C	A	B	B	A	B
41	**42**	**43**	**44**	**45**	**46**	**47**	**48**	**49**	**50**
C	B	C	D	C	B	A	A	C	D
51	**52**	**53**	**54**	**55**	**56**	**57**	**58**	**59**	**60**
A	B	C	A	C	B	C	B	A	C
61	**62**	**63**	**64**	**65**	**66**	**67**	**68**	**69**	**70**
A	C	B	B	C	B	D	C	A	A
71	**72**	**73**	**74**	**75**	**76**	**77**	**78**	**79**	**80**
C	A	C	D	D	C	A	D	A	B
81	**82**	**83**	**84**	**85**	**86**	**87**	**88**	**89**	**90**
A	A	C	D	D	A	C	D	C	A
91	**92**	**93**	**94**	**95**	**96**	**97**	**98**	**99**	**100**
A	A	D	B	B	B	B	D	C	D
101	**102**	**103**	**104**	**105**	**106**	**107**	**108**	**109**	**110**
D	D	D	D	D	A	C	A	D	A
111	**112**	**113**	**114**	**115**	**116**	**117**	**118**	**119**	**120**
A	A	D	C	A	C	D	B	C	A
121	**122**	**123**	**124**	**125**	**126**	**127**	**128**	**129**	**130**
C	A	D	A	B	A	B	D	D	C
131	**132**	**133**	**134**	**135**	**136**	**137**	**138**	**139**	**140**
B	D	D	A	B	B	D	C	A	B
141	**142**	**143**	**144**	**145**	**146**	**147**	**148**	**149**	**150**
D	C	D	A	B	C	D	A	D	D
151	**152**	**153**	**154**	**155**	**156**	**157**	**158**	**159**	**160**
A	A	D	B	D	D	B	C	B	B
161	**162**	**163**	**164**	**165**	**166**	**167**	**168**	**169**	**170**
D	C	B	B	C	B	D	C	C	D
171	**172**	**173**	**174**	**175**	**176**	**177**	**178**	**179**	**180**
B	D	C	C	D	C	C	C	D	D
181	**182**	**183**	**184**	**185**	**186**	**187**	**188**	**189**	**190**
B	B	A	D	A	D	D	D	A	B
191	**192**	**193**	**194**	**195**	**196**	**197**	**198**	**199**	**200**
A	D	B	B	A	A	A	B	A	D

201	202	203	204	205	206	207	208	209	210
D	A	C	A	A	B	B	D	B	A
211	**212**	**213**	**214**	**215**	**216**	**217**	**218**	**219**	**220**
B	A	A	A	D	A	B	C	C	B
221	**222**	**223**	**224**	**225**	**226**	**227**	**228**	**229**	**230**
D	B	C	B	A	A	A	C	C	D
231	**232**	**233**	**234**	**235**	**236**	**237**	**238**	**239**	**240**
C	D	C	A	A	A	B	B	A	A
241	**242**	**243**	**244**	**245**	**246**	**247**	**248**	**249**	**250**
B	B	D	C	D	A	B	D	D	B
251	**252**	**253**	**254**	**255**	**256**	**257**	**258**	**259**	**260**
C	D	A	D	B	A	D	A	A	C
261	**262**	**263**	**264**	**265**	**266**	**267**	**268**	**269**	**270**
D	C	D	B	B	B	A	C	C	B
271	**272**	**273**	**274**	**275**	**276**	**277**	**278**	**279**	**280**
B	C	B	A	C	B	B	A	C	A
281	**282**	**283**	**284**	**285**	**286**	**287**	**288**	**289**	**290**
C	D	C	B	D	B	A	D	B	C
291	**292**	**293**	**294**	**295**	**296**	**297**	**298**	**299**	**300**
D	A	A	B	A	A	B	C	D	C
301	**302**	**303**	**304**	**305**	**306**	**307**	**308**	**309**	**310**
C	C	C	A	A	A	D	C	B	A
311	**312**	**313**	**314**	**315**	**316**	**317**	**318**	**319**	**320**
C	A	A	D	B	D	D	B	D	D
321	**322**	**323**	**324**	**325**	**326**	**327**	**328**	**329**	**330**
A	D	B	C	D	A	A	D	B	A
331	**332**	**333**	**334**	**335**	**336**	**337**	**338**	**339**	**340**
A	C	D	B	A	A	C	C	D	A
341	**342**	**343**	**344**	**345**	**346**	**347**	**348**	**349**	**350**
C	A	B	B	C	A	D	C	C	B
351	**352**	**353**	**354**	**355**	**356**	**357**	**358**	**359**	**360**
A	D	C	A	A	B	C	C	D	A
361	**362**	**363**	**364**	**365**	**366**	**367**	**368**	**369**	**370**
A	B	A	C	A	D	B	C	D	B
371	**372**	**373**	**374**	**375**	**376**	**377**	**378**	**379**	**380**
D	C	A	B	C	A	A	B	B	B
381	**382**	**383**	**384**	**385**	**386**	**387**	**388**	**389**	**390**
D	D	A	C	D	B	D	B	B	A
391	**392**	**393**	**394**	**395**	**396**	**397**	**398**	**399**	**400**
B	A	C	C	C	A	C	C	A	D
401	**402**	**403**	**404**	**405**	**406**	**407**	**408**	**409**	**410**
C	B	B	C	D	D	C	D	C	A

411	412	413	414	415	416	417	418	419	420
A	C	C	C	C	D	C	A	B	B
421	422	423	424	425	426	427	428	429	430
A	A	A	A	C	C	B	D	B	B
431	432	433	434	435	436	437	438	439	440
A	D	A	C	C	D	D	A	B	C
441	442	443	444	445	446	447	448	449	450
B	A	C	D	A	D	D	A	B	D
451	452	453	454	455	456	457	458	459	460
C	B	C	C	C	C	B	B	B	A
461	462	463	464	465	466	467	468	469	470
D	B	B	A	C	D	C	C	B	A
471	472	473	474	475	476	477	478	479	480
D	C	C	D	D	C	D	C	A	C
481	482	483	484	485	486	487	488	489	490
D	A	D	B	D	A	C	C	A	C
491	492	493	494	495	496	497	498	499	500
C	A	D	C	C	D	D	D	C	A
501	502	503	504	505	506	507	508	509	510
B	C	A	A	D	D	B	D	A	C
511	512	513	514	515	516	517	518	519	520
B	B	A	B	A	D	D	A	A	B
521	522	523	524	525	526	527	528	529	530
A	B	B	D	A	A	A	D	C	A
531	532	533	534	535	536	537	538	539	540
A	C	B	C	D	A	C	C	B	D
541	542	543	544	545	546	547	548	549	550
D	D	D	B	D	C	D	C	A	A
551	552	553	554	555	556	557	558	559	560
B	A	D	B	B	A	A	B	C	B
561	562	563	564	565	566	567	568	569	570
B	C	C	D	A	B	C	B	A	C
571	572	573	574	575	576	577	578	579	580
D	B	B	D	C	C	C	C	A	D
581	582	583	584	585	586	587	588	589	590
D	A	A	D	B	B	A	A	B	B
591	592	593	594	595	596	597	598	599	600
C	C	B	A	C	C	A	B	D	B